THE FOLK MUSIC
REVIVAL IN SCOTLAND

To Sandra and Robin

.7.50

The Folk Music Revival in Scotland
by Ailie Munro

Including *The Folk Revival in Gaelic Song*
by Morag MacLeod

KAHN & AVERILL
London

/

First published in 1984 by Kahn & Averill

British Library Cataloguing in Publication Data

Munro, Ailie
    The folk music revival in Scotland.
    1. Folk music — Scotland — History and
    criticism
    I. Title
    781.7411   ML3655.5

ISBN 0–900707–78–X

The Publisher acknowledges subsidy from the Scottish Arts Council
towards the publication of this volume

784·4941

M UN

Typeset by Alan Sutton Publishing Ltd, Gloucester in 10/11 Plantin

Printed in Great Britain by
Biddles Ltd, Guildford, Surrey

Contents

Acknowledgments

Grateful thanks to Angus Russell, Sheila Douglas, Andrew Douglas, Hilary Cusker, Patrick Shuldham-Shaw, Jean Redpath, John Watt, Dr Andrew Hunter, Dr Peter Shepheard, Adam MacNaughton, Jane Turriff, Ian MacDonald, Lizzie Higgins, Peter Hall, Josh MacRae, Dr Hamish Henderson, Morris Blythman and Norman Buchan, who allowed me to record them talking about the Revival in Scotland. (Listed in chronological order).

To Betsy and Bryce Whyte, Jane Turriff and Danny Stewart, Belle Stewart, Sheila MacGregor, Ian MacGregor, and Bella and Willie MacPhee, for their hospitality and talk.

To Duncan and Linda Williamson for having me to stay in their tent, and for recording songs, stories and talk.

For permission to print their songs: to Sheila Douglas ("Oh Mither, Mither"); to Archie Fisher and Bobby Campbell ("The Fairfield apprentice"); to Ewan MacColl ("The moving on song"); to Mrs. Janette MacGinn, for Matt MacGinn ("A miner's lulluby" and "If it wasnae for the Union"); and to Belle Stewart ("The berryfields o' Blair").

To the singers and recorders of the songs transcribed in Chapters 3, 4 and 5; and to Professor John MacQueen, Director of the School of Scottish Studies, for permission to use tapes from the School's archives.

To Professor John Blacking of Belfast, Derek Bowman, Dr Alan Bruford, Morag Bruford, Dr Ian Campbell, Eric Cregeen, Owen Dudley Edwards, Jan Fairley, Hugh Gentleman, Daphne Hamilton, Dr Hamish Henderson, Dr Rhodri Jeffreys-Jones, Dr Emily Lyle, Hugh MacDonald, Charles K Maisels, Jack Rutherford, Professor Anne Dhu Shapiro of Harvard, Dr Peter Shepheard, Dr J A C Stevenson, and Ronald Stevenson, who read sections of the book and made comments. To Dr Colin G G Aitken for advice on the tables in Chapter 7. Morag MacLeod thanks Donald A MacDonald who read and commented on her chapter. Especial thanks to Dr Campbell and Dr Lyle for help with the book as a whole. Mistakes are the sole responsibility of the two authors.

To Professor Angus McIntosh and Dr Margaret MacKay for material on the beginnings of the School of Scottish Studies.

To Allan Palmer for copies of twelve tapes recorded by him.

To Barry Ould for printing all the music examples.

To the BBC for information on broadcast programmes.

To Morris Blythman for permission to transcribe songs from the *Ding Dong Dollar* disc, and for general help and encouragement. By his death in 1981 the folk movement lost one of its best-loved and most influential pioneers.

To the Music Coporation of America, London Office, for permission to print "Joe Hill", by Alfred Hayes and Earl Robinson.

To Harmony Music Limited, London, and Stormking Music Inc., New York, for permission to print "The moving on song", by Ewan MacColl.

To all those who sent written contributions. These are acknowledged where quoted, with the exception of replies to questionaires in Appendix II where the writer's name was generally not stated. For brevity's sake the name of the institution is usually omitted.

To Sheila Somerville for her cheerfulness and skill in typing the bulk of the manuscript.

Finally, a special thank-you to Hamish Henderson for his unfailing helpfulness and wit in answering queries.

Preface

This book is a collection of facts and opinions, of thoughts and memories, of story and song.

The first step in collecting was to record a number of representative people talking about the Revival in Scotland. The next step involved listening to, and selecting from, many existing music recordings on tape and disc, with particular reference to those more directly connected with the Revival process. Collecting extended to the written word and the written note: ephemera of various kinds, newspapers, folk journals, books, song-books, scrap-books, and replies to questionaires from singer and from teachers. Objectivity became progressively more difficult and indeed less desirable as an aim . . . in the end I became my own informant, as it were.

I hope that the results may suggest lines for further research to students in related disciplines. The subject is vast and would require a whole battery of books to do it justice: history, sociology, folklore, politics, literature . . . the musical aspects alone cover a wide area. Here I have chosen to focus attention on the songs, but have tried to keep the instrumental side in the picture.

I am grateful to my colleague Morag MacLeod, a native Gaelic speaker, for her contribution of Chapter 5.

It is impossible to mention all the fine singers, players, writers, organisers, and even pioneers in the Scottish field, but fortunately folk enthusiasts pay more than lip-service to the concept of anonymity. The friendly and patient co-operation of all those whom I pestered for information is deeply appreciated.

August 1982   Ailie A Edmunds Munro

Alison McMorland
Photograph courtesy John Harrison

Norman Buchan

Hamish Henderson
Photograph courtesy Alec Hawkes

Morris Blythman

I Setting the Scene

Ann an dùbhlachd gharbh a' gheamhraidh
Cha b'e àm bu ghainn' ar spòrs:
Greis air sùgradh, greis air dannsadh,
Greis air canntaireachd is cèol.

The rough dark days of Winter were not the most scarce in joy: a while in
love's company, then in the dance, then at canntaireachd and music.

Neil MacLeod[1]

The musical renaissance in Scotland since 1945 is usually taken to
mean certain major developments in the world of art music. These
include the establishment of the annual Edinburgh International
Festival; the growing reputation of the Scottish National Orchestra;
the birth of Scottish Opera and its rise to such excellence that
audiences are drawn from London and even farther afield; and the
increasing number of composers who have chosen to live and work
here, and whose compositions are documented in the Scottish
Music Archive in Glasgow.

But there is another equally far-reaching phenomenon in this
musical renaissance, part of a movement embracing the whole
world, yet with deeper native associations than any of the four
mentioned above. This is the folk music revival.

"Traditional" is in some ways a better word for this music than
"folk". Although neither is completely satisfactory, and both will be
used here *faute de mieux*, the latter is still the most widely known
term; it was also used by the predominantly English revivalists
of some fifty years earlier, and by all those who supported
their work.

The fore-runner of today's revival was the folk song collecting of
S. Baring-Gould, Cecil Sharp, the Broadwoods, and others during
the late nineteenth century and the early twentieth. Although Lucy
Broadwood made a fine contribution to Scottish Gaelic song,[2]
Sharp and his associates were concerned with collecting English
folk songs from rural districts; but their influence was felt through-

1. See footnotes page 21.

out Britain. Hundreds of these songs were published, the music consisting of the basic shape of the verse tune. The melodies were to have an enormous influence on the new English school of art music composition led by Vaughan Williams (himself a collector), Gustav Holst and later Alan Bush.

Cecil Sharp wrote down the bulk of the tunes and words from acutal performances, seldom using the phonograph.[3] Although he described verbally some features of this singing,[4] he left no musical notation of the vocal decorations, and of the variations of tune in different verses. Such "details" were left to Percy Grainger, who followed up his own phonograph recordings of folk songs by transcribing them in astonishing detail. He published these transcriptions together with a strong plea in defence of his methods.[5] But the basic-shape tunes produced by Sharp and others were more acceptable at that time, and after publication were sung largely by singers trained for art music techniques and expression, and performed in concert-halls and drawingrooms.[6] They were also sung (by school children) in massed unison, as one result of the campaign for carrying the songs into school curricula. Sharp's other great interest and contribution was in folk dance, which goes far towards explaining his lack of interest in preserving the authentic styles of traditional singing. He also had too narrow and arbitrary a view, in his field work, of what constituted "folk song".[7] Then there was the aesthetic, moralistic outlook of this group of collectors: the mental climate of the time led them to bowdlerise many of the down-to-earth verbal texts,rooted as they were in the life and rhythms of nature. All these factors contributed, by the thirties, to the movement's declining hold on public imagination.

In Scotland Gavin Greig and James Duncan, contemporaries of Sharp, collected over three thousand song versions in Aberdeenshire and the surrounding counties. A warmly congratulatory letter from Greig in 1907 addressed Sharp as "the greatest dynamic in the folk-song world.[8] Most of the Greig-Duncan songs were not published, but those that did appear[9] were among the chief printed sources for enthusiasts several decades later. With the basic shifts in opinion which occurred after the 1939 war, and with the advent of the tape-recorder, the time was ripe for a major revival of this music.

The idea of folk music as a separate category, distinct from other kinds of music, does not exist in many parts of the world: it is a concept found chiefly in Europe and America.[10] And whether we call it folk or traditional it's a very difficult kind of music to define. The last attempt at a definition by the I.F.M.C.[11] was made in 1954:

Folk music is the product of a musical tradition that has been evolved through the process of oral transmission. The factors that shape the tradition are: (i) continuity which links the present with the past; (ii) variation which springs from the creative impulse of the individual or the group; and (iii) selection by the community, which determines the form or forms in which the music survives.

The terms can be applied to music that has been evolved from rudimentary beginnings by a community uninfluenced by popular and art music and it can likewise be applied to music which has originated with an individual composer and has subsequently been absorbed into the unwritten living tradition of a community.

The term does not cover composed popular music that has been taken over ready-made by a community and remains unchanged, for it is the re-fashioning and re-creation of the music by the community that gives it its folk character.

This definition concentrates on oral transmission but does not consider transmission by means of print, whether of words or music. It also leaves out of account transmission by disc or tape, a significant factor since the start of the revival circa 1950. But the print factor is more important in the present context, because traditional music in Scotland has been assiduously collected and printed for over three hundred years. (Lists of these collections have been made by Henry G. Farmer, George S. Emmerson and others.) This exceptional richness of collection and publication is connected with the sense of loss of nationhood experienced by many Scots after the unions with England. It was felt that preserving their native traditional music in this way would also help to preserve their national identity.[12] This applied more to literate, urban-dwelling Scots, who were cut off from the living tradition still continuing in the countryside. How important were all these printed collections in keeping alive traditional music? And was this music *heard* by the people who studied the collections? The second question is particularly difficult and only partial answers are given here: more research is needed in this area. As Farmer says, "It may be true that the pen is mightier than the sword, but in the arts the deed is more potent than the pen".[13]

There is some evidence that nobles of the seventeenth century included grass-roots as well as courtly musicians in their country house music-making. "The *Mar Account Book*, to take only one of several such, records within a few months gifts to 'a blind singer at dinner', 'a Highland singing woman', 'Blind Wat the piper', and 'ane woman harper' ".[14] In the eighteenth century, when public concerts first started in Edinburgh, Glasgow and Aberdeen, traditional Scots songs and fiddle music were often included alongside Italian and German art music. As regards fiddle music, a supreme exponent, Niel Gow, was often asked to play at these events, and the craze for dancing ensured its continued hearing. But the songs were sung by singers with trained voices, so that, in the towns at any rate, traditional singing styles were seldom heard. As for drawingroom music-making, folk enthusiasts, such as Sir Walter Scott's daughter Sophia[15] in the early nineteenth century, although singing in a simpler manner, would still be far from traditional in style; they probably sang in a style midway between traditional and art. And the folk-based songs of Robert Burns were, and still are, adapted in style when performed in the drawing-room or concert situation. Bagpipe music, played by the town piper or pipers, was heard at ceremonial occasions of various kinds.

The nineteenth century saw a veritable explosion of amateur music societies, at first mainly choral but soon extending to orchestras and chamber music groups; these practised and performed church music, glees and madrigals, and classics by Handel, Beethoven, Mozart, Spohr, J. C. Bach and others. Members of these societies, and those who attended the growing number of public concerts following on the breakdown of the old system of aristocratic patronage, were not only the middle classes: "the masses also became largely the inheritors of what had hitherto been the possession of the privileged few".[16] After the Industrial Revolution these masses were mainly in urban areas. Some of them would still sing "the auld sangs" in their homes, and in the rural parts these songs still flourished, especially in the Gaelic North West and in the rich ballad and bothy-song areas of the North East. Even as early as 1826 this difference between the industrialised South West and the North East had been remarked on by the ballad collector and editor, William Motherwell, writing from Paisley to Peter Buchan in Aberdeenshire:

> I sincerely rejoice in your good luck in being so fortunate as every other day to meet with venerable sybils who can and are willing to impart to your thirsting soul the metrical riches of "the days of other years". I wish I were at your elbow to assist in the task of transcription. I cannot boast the like good fortune. This part of the country if it ever did abound in this *Song of the people* is now to all intents utterly ruined by every 3 miles of it either having some large town or public work or manufactory within its bounds which absorbs the rustic population and attracts strangers — corrupts ancient manners — and introduces habits of thinking and of living altogether hostile to the preservation and cultivation of traditionary song.[17]

The members of amateur societies in towns did not meet to sing traditional songs or to play traditional music: the desire to better themselves culturally led quite naturally to music of the upper sections of society, to "music of learned origin". [18] Traditional song and the style of singing it came to be despised as uncouth as well as lower-class.

For several hundred years the grass-roots tradition-bearers, the singers and players who had inherited this music orally from generations of their forebears, were rarely heard in those centres where one kind of music flourished. Although a great and a highly developed form, this music of concert-hall, salon and conservatoire is but one of the many kinds of world music. Only in the twentieth century, as the value and beauty of these other musics come to be recognised, are "educated folk" realising that on their very doorstep they have their own other kind: unvarnished rather than rough, unfamiliar (to ears used to learned music) rather than unsophisticated, stoical rather than harsh, with different assumptions of form and of timing, and with melody far more important than harmony. Music of a different genre, yet within Western tradition.

Where can this different genre, traditional or folk music, be heard? You can hear varying forms of it in any large concert hall: the Corries, so successful in presenting it in "popular" guise; Martin Carthy, alone or with the Watersons; the now dispersed Incredible String Band, originally Scottish in origin; Jean Redpath, Dick Gaughan, Alison McMorland; folk-based entertainers like Billy Connolly; the Reel and Strathspey Societies — these and many more can fill such a hall. But the best places to hear it are smaller, more intimate: the folk clubs, the folk pubs, and, in some ways best of all, gatherings of friends in each others' houses, where you will find something nearer the original ceilidh situation.

The Gaelic word "ceilidh" means literally "a visiting", a group of friends in a room. Originally such gatherings do not include music, but gradually the new kind develop at certain houses or occasions. No-one is a star, although some can sing or play better and some can tell stories well, while others may be gifted conversationalists or simply agreeable companions whose presence enlarges and helps to knit the pattern of the evening together. For these were essentially evening, and winter, events, often extending into the small hours of the morning. Originating in rural parts of the country, after the day's darg was over the housewife, the shepherd, fisherman, ploughman, laird, factor, village teacher, and sometimes the local minister or priest, foregathered for company and for an extension of this fellowship. The old songs and ballads, with their images and archetypes of human behaviour and their melodies shaped by generations of singers long since dead; the wordlessness of instrumental music, as the fiddler played a slow air or march and then broke into a strathspey and reel which set feet tapping and often started an impromptu dance session; the symbolism of the stories too, the age-old art of suspension of disbelief . . . all these would inform the unconscious by stretching tentacles far back into the past and bringing it forward, making it relevant to the fleeting and ever-stressful present. These fed mind and spirit, refreshed them anew from the well-springs of human existence with its joy and its pain, brought order out of chaos and beauty out of ugliness.

A. E. Housman once said that if, when he was shaving, he thought of certain lines of poetry, he could feel the bristles stiffen. Then there is Sydney Carter's criterion for recognising the traditional: "What alerts me is a sort of shiver".[19] You could say that both these psycho-physical reactions describe human response to all great art, and I would agree; but with folk poetry, music and story one's reaction seems somehow more immediate, almost more . . . atavistic. This is chiefly due to the content of what one hears, but it is also due to the more intimate and unified nature of a situation where the singer, player and story-teller *are* the audience, and vice versa.

A similar kind of social evening has been gradually spreading into urban areas of present-day life. This is partly a reaction against the passiveness of TV, radio and discs — the same reaction which has driven many people to return to playing an instrument, to join amateur orchestras, choirs, dramatic societies etc., to *do* instead of merely watch or listen — and partly an extension of good fellowship by adding an extra dimension to the evening. This kind of music-making can also be experienced at the folk clubs which have appeared over the last twenty years or so. There are close on forty of these in Scotland now, meeting usually once a week (eight years ago, when petrol was vastly cheaper, there were double this number). There are also pubs which have folk nights ranging from once a week to every night, with occasional lunch-time sessions. Clubs tend to be in the cities and large towns, with only a few in small country towns or villages. Predictably there is much diversity in the content and styles encouraged by different clubs, ranging from those with a strong bias towards the genuinely traditional, to those which present a kind of cabaret folk-pop.

Let us visit a folk club in the capital city, the only one now which combines regular functioning, on a 52-week basis, with open membership. The Edinburgh Folk Club was founded in 1973 by a journalist, a policeman, a technician and a physicist. People sit facing a part of the room where the soloist or group will be performing. This modification of the true ceilidh situation is dictated by the pressure of numbers (between 60 and 100) and by the need for good acoustics.

So what is different here from the ordinary concert, with its "them" and "us" separation of performers and audience? First, the audience always contains a considerable proportion of performers, called "floor" singers or players. These are club members who, regularly or occasionally, contribute to the evening's music-making, more particularly when there is no guest singer or group, (usually professional or semi-professional artists, professionalism being bound to appear within this mainly amateur movement). Second, when guest performers are present they invariably mingle with the rest of the company, not only during the interval and at the close of the evening, but often during breaks between their own items, to chat and to listen to the other singers or players. Last, and most basic, is the music itself. Let us return to our folk club and describe an evening's entertainment, typical of many others in Scotland and elsewhere.

Members of a recently established folk club in a country town are the guests tonight (non-professional). The compère welcomes the company, and announces the artists as they appear. Irish jigs, on fiddle and guitar, are followed by two American songs: in the second of these, Tom Rush's "Honey I'm a jazz-man, tryin' a trick or two", the fiddler weaves a beautiful obbligato round the voice line. An expatriate Highlander gives a spirited unaccompanied version of "The Muskerry Sportsmen", but his second, Gaelic, song about Lochleven, with its tender lyricism and delicate orna-mentation, show where his true roots are. Next comes concertina music, and more songs: an Ulster march, "O'Neill," followed by two jigs; a haunting ancestral folk-version of "Down by the Sally Gardens"; and two mining songs, "The old miner" ("me hair's turnin' grey") and an account of a mine closure. Two young women give us some superb two-part unaccompanied singing, with lots of lovely bare fourths and fifths, and with every word audible: two songs on a similar theme — a girl follows her sailor to "the watery main" — with a modern song, plus guitar accompaniment, sandwiched between.

Then appears the most consistently traditional singer as yet, again with guitar. His songs include "Corachree",[20] as learned from the Aberdeenshire itinerant singer Jimmy MacBeath, and Jeannie Robertson's "The twa recruitin' serjeants" with a chorus which everyone joins in. The last of his group of songs is on a familiar theme in Western folk tradition: that of the deserted woman. A

Shetland woman sings an exquisitely sad song to an Irish tune, explaining first that it enshrines the belief "if you mourn too long for the dead, they can't lie easy", and concludes with a version of the much-loved "She moved through the fair".

During the interval, over drinks, people meet and talk — no formal introductions are needed — and you find visitors from England, Ireland, the Continent and farther afield.

The second half of the programme presents more instrumental music, with a tin-whistler from Somerset plus a famous Border fiddler, the winner of the Kinross Festival's men's singing class in a group of songs with guitar, and two more Border singers to end with, one giving a particularly fine version of "The rigs of rye".

An evening well-spent, you feel as you go home or on to a friend's house for more company or music. There are always some bits, both words and music, which give you that "sort of shiver", which go on singing in your head and seem to illumine the next day.

An even more informal setting for traditional music of different kinds can be found in the folk pubs. It would be difficult to assess how many exist throughout Scotland; Edinburgh alone is reputed to have around twenty, the uncrowned king among them being Sandy Bell's Bar (official name, the Forrest Hill Bar — Bell was the name of a former licensee). It is situated little more than a stone's throw from the Royal Infirmary and from various centres of the city's two universities, from Moray House College of Education, the College of Art, and the Dental Hospital and School. Twenty years ago, before many old tenement blocks were knocked down to make way for new academic buildings, this was still a residential area with a largely working-class community. Members of this community still return to Sandy Bell's, and you find a fair cross-section of society there.

According to several authorities with long memories of the Scottish revival, Sandy's was "where it all started" 'way back in the late forties; through singing, discussion and the making of plans, it became in one sense the first unofficial folk club of Scotland. It is still a centre for information and for meeting other enthusiasts, whether from Edinburgh, from outlying districts, or simply passing through.

The term "uncrowned king" of folk bars was chosen advisedly, to indicate its still predominantly male clientèle. Scottish pubs in the past have notoriously been places where men go, chiefly in order to get drunk, and until recently some of them had "Men Only" signs for part or the whole of the bar rooms. By contrast, in other parts of the U.K. pubs have tended to be places where men and women could foregather socially, with drinking considered as a social factor and therefore more relaxed, more civilised. The abandonment of the rule, whether explicit or implicit, forbidding the admission of women unless accompanied by a man, is a relatively new development, and there are still a few Canute-type establishments where the ban operates "by repute". But it must be a long time since Sandy Bell's had this rule, otherwise it could hardly have become the folk centre it has been since the war.

What is it that draws people like a magnet to Sandy's, to crowd into the single room with its Edwardian décor and its awkward shape, long and narrow? The friendly atmosphere, of course, and the social drinking, but one of the chief attractions over the last thirty years has been the hope of hearing some music, spasmodic and extempore though it may be: the exciting possibility that a good music session may erupt, like a volcano from the seething, molten flow of that "submerged world".[21] You may be having an engrossing conversation (and these four old walls seem to encourage, to draw out good talk) with a miner, a tapestry weaver from an old-town studio, a doctor from the nearby Infirmary, a university lecturer escaping from academia, a mother relegating for a while the awesome responsibility of young children, a labourer, an unemployed teacher, a visiting world-famous authority on some esoteric subject, or a well-known alcoholic on whom the management keeps a watchful eye . . . when suddenly, right beside your ear or at the farthest corner of the room, you hear it. At first only just audible in the hubbub: a jig, hornpipe or reel on the fiddle or penny-whistle, or from a group of players; a voice raised in an old familiar ballad or a song written last week; a rollicking, ranting ditty belted out by a trio of young men; the dancing irresistible lilt of an accordion, or the moan of the older concertina now enjoying renewed popularity. But what happens after those first strains percolate depends on two things: the quality of the music, both content and performance, and the kind of people who happen to be present, for without the right vibrations nothing worthwhile will happen.

If both these factors are right then you're in luck. The babble of talk will gradually or with miraculous speed die down, movement will be stilled, the next drink ignored or unordered, and while the music lasts the varied company will be united in its thrall. Unplanned, unsolicited, a bonus from the gods. . . . "There'd have to be some luck in it, there'd have to be slightly quite a lot of *ac*cident in it".[22]

On the other hand if you're not lucky, if voices rise in pitch and volume to compete with the music, the result can be cacophony;

deafened and exhausted, you remember thankfully that you've a home to go to. Emerging into the street, you find the noise of traffic quite soothing and peaceful.

At a festival you can find a sort of distillation of the folk clubs and the folk pubs scenes, with several added ingredients. Usually a week-end event, lasting from Friday evening to Sunday evening (with the quieter Monday aftermath if you have sufficient stamina and don't have to be at work), there is more time to enjoy the familiar and to absorb the new. Impromptu ceilidhs spring up everywhere — in hotel lounges and bedrooms, in the streets, on the steps of a hall, in pubs, in fields, in tents and caravans — from morning to midnight and long past. There is also the drama of competition classes on the Saturday. Classes are in such sections as: women's singing and men's singing, usually unaccompanied, and at some festivals combined in one class; solo folk instruments such as fiddle, accordion, melodeon, tin whistle, concertina, jew's or jaw's harp, and mouth-organ; ceilidh bands, i.e. combinations of three or more instruments — sometimes including piano, guitar or pipes — playing traditional music for dancing; oral whistling; diddling, i.e. singing to nonsense syllables, which has connections with canntaireachd;[23] and lastly, a recent development at several festivals, story-telling. An even later addition, pioneered by Keith Festival in 1982, is a class for the Highland bagpipes. Although folk festivals often start off with a march, strathspey or reel from a piper, both solo pipers and pipe-bands have their own festivals and competitions, and pipe music has tended to flourish separately from folk events.[24] Accordion and Fiddle Clubs also run separate competitions.[25]

The competitive element in folk festivals, though much debated, is generally liked by the contestants, not just because there is a chance of winning but because they say it brings out that extra ounce of involvement. There is an opening concert on the Friday, a prize-winners' concert on Saturday, and several more official ceilidhs with a compère and invited artists. Many local residents take part in events.

There are around twenty of these festivals in Scotland, most of them held annually, with locales ranging from Thurso and Wick in the far north to Newcastleton near the English Border. Emphasis and organisation vary from place to place, but those affiliated to the T.M.S.A. (Traditional Music & Song Association) lay special emphasis on the traditional; until recently the only guests invited to these were grass-roots or "source" singers and players, as distinct from "revival",[26] although the latter have always done most of the organising. But since 1978 some revival performers have been invited. Several longer festivals now include those at Edinburgh (ten days) and at Glasgow (a week).

The supreme value of festivals is that enthusiasts from widely distant parts can meet, listen to each other and exchange news and views. The atmosphere is one of relaxed celebration.

Footnotes to Chapter I

1. Neil MacLeod, "An gleann 'san robh mi òg" ("My bonnie native glen") in *Clarsach an Doire*, (translation by Dr. John MacInnes). Celtic Press, Glasgow 1893. For "canntaireachd", see note 23.
2. *Journal of the Folk Song Society*, no. 35, 1931; *Journal of the English Folk Dance and Song Society*, vol. 1, nos. 1, 2 and 3, 1932. See also Ethel Bassin, *The old songs of Skye: Francis Tolmie and her circle*.
3. Maud Karpeles, *Cecil Sharp: his life and work*, p. 41.
4. Cecil J. Sharp, *English Folk Song: Some Conclusions*, Chapter 9.
5. *Journal of the Folk-Song Society* 3 (1908–9), 147–242.
6. Cecil J. Sharp, p. 138.
7. Fred Woods, *Folk Revival*, pp. 15–6.
8. Maud Karpeles, pp. 66–7. Greig's letter followed the publication of Sharp's *English Folk Song: Some Conclusions*.
9. Gavin Greig, *Folk-Song of the North-East*, 2 vols, 1909, 1914 (the 1963 reprint incorporates "Folk-Song in Buchan" which contains the only ten tunes in the volume); and *Last Leaves of the Traditional Ballads and Ballad Airs*, ed. Alexander Keith, 1925 (contains many tunes). *The Greig-Duncan Folk Song Collection* (words and tunes), Vol. 1, edited by Patrick Shuldham-Shaw and Emily B. Lyle, was published in 1981 and seven more volumes are planned. The work of editing, under the auspices of the School of Scottish Studies, is being continued by Emily Lyle. Pat Shuldham-Shaw's death in 1977 has been greatly mourned by the folk movement.
10. Klaus P. Wachsman, "Folk music", *The New Grove Dictionary of Music and Musicians*, 6.693.
11. In 1981 the International Folk Music Council changed its name to the International Council for Traditional Music.
12. Scotland is still a country with two languages (and hence two main cultures). Although recent years have seen a resurgence of interest in Gaelic, it is now spoken only in a few areas of the North-West mainland and in the Western Isles, while English is the standard language of the whole of Scotland. Lowland Scots, ultimately of the same origin as English, survives only in dialect, chiefly in rural areas, and in literature and folk song. See *The Languages of Scotland*, ed. Aitken and McArthur, for a helpful account of the development of the linguistic situation.
13. Henry G. Farmer, *A History of Music in Scotland*, p.104.
14. K.N. Colvile, "Scottish Culture in the 17th century (1603–1660)", University of Edinburgh Ph.D. thesis, 1932, p. 28. (I am obliged to Pat Jackson, of the Australian National University, for this reference.)
15. See Ailie Munro, "'Abbotsford Collection of Border Ballads': Sophia Scott's Manuscript Book with Airs", *Scottish Studies* 20 (1976), 155–88
16. Henry G. Farmer, p. 456–8.

17. Letter of 5 September 1826, Glasgow University Library, Robertson MS. 9. Despite Motherwell's despondency, he and his colleagues did manage to make substantial collections in South-West Scotland; see Motherwell's *Minstrelsy: Ancient and Modern* (1827), and *Andrew Crawfurd's Collection of Ballads and Songs* edited by E. B. Lyle.

18. A. L. Lloyd in *Folk Song in England*, p. 15, refers to Bartok's researches in the Balkans, and continues, "He discovered there a submerged world of vigorous music essentially different in many respects from music of learned origin . . ."

19. "Where you find it" by Sydney Carter, *Folk Review*, August 1973, p. 9.

20. See Chapter 4 for a version of this song.

21. See note 18.

22. J. D. Salinger, *Seymour: An Introduction*. Penguin, Harmondsworth, 1964. (From the child Seymour's advice on how to play street-marbles.)

23. Canntaireachd: chanting. In Scottish Gaelic now used to denote the vocal method used in teaching bagpipes. See Christine K. Chambers, "Non-lexical vocables in Scottish traditional music", University of Edinburgh Ph.D. thesis, 1980.

24. See *International Piper* and *The Piping Times*.

25. See *Box and Fiddle* published by the National Association of Accordion and Fiddle Clubs.

26. See the opening section of Chapter 4 concerning this distinction.

Jeannie Robertson

II   The Story of the Revival
Beginnings in the USA

Let me be known as the man who told you something you already know.
Woody Guthrie[1]

It is in the topical songs of the U.S.A. from the early years of this century, in the events and movements which sparked them off and in the social response which they evoked, that we find the beginnings of this revival, and of present-day songs within its context. They form as it were the chief wellspring of the most significant recent tributary to the North American mainstream of traditional music, and in particular traditional song. The springs from which this mainstream flows lie far distant, hidden in the mists of centuries of traditions, from different countries and different classes. The old ballads found in the eastern States by Cecil Sharp, Maud Karpeles, Phillips Barry and many others during these early years, were to come into their own much later: it needed the impetus provided by the topical song movement, and the social consciousness which it both reflected and further aroused, before these traditional songs could be de-submerged and become meaningful to a wider public.

The sense of "topical", as used here to describe a certain genre of songs, has come to include "dealing with especially current or local topics". The fact that these songs are sometimes — though not always — ephemeral does not detract from their importance: they record the reactions of people to what happens at a certain time or in a certain place (and they are sometimes protest songs). Many topical songs must therefore be included under the umbrella term of folk song (see also p. 26). "The mass of the colonists were poor country folk, carriers of traditional melodies. Many were rebels, fleeing from political persecution and longing to express

1.   See footnotes page 37.

their feelings openly. Thus a note of social protest rang through native American balladry, and the lives and problems of the common people became its main concern".[2]

There were other, more distant wellsprings from which contributory influences flowed towards the post-world-war II revival in the States. These include: black music, representing the largest oppressed group in the country;[3] hymns, and perhaps especially revivalist hymns — religion was a powerful influence among the settlers and their descendants; Civil War songs, from both sides and still within living memory by the turn of the last century; hobo songs, from the vast army of migrant workers spawned by the American expansion; and Robin-Hood-type ballads, songs of the Western highwayman. Signs of these influences will also become apparent during the course of this brief survey.

The Industrial Workers of the World (I.W.W., or "Wobblies"), founded in 1905 with the aim of forming One Big Union, free from hierarchical craft divisions and with branches all over the world, provided inspiration for many topical and political songs. The words were usually written to already existing tunes, of popular song-hits, of hymns or of migrant workers' songs. Members of the I.W.W. had learned many of the hymns from the Salvation Army, the organisation with which they frequently found themselves in competition on street corners and which sometimes tried to break up I.W.W. meetings "with blare of trumpet and banging of drum".[4] Since these melodies were often very appealing, both spirited and moving, the Wobbly song-maker would simply pick a suitable one for his own words.[5] Alternatively he would re-write or parody the existing words, in the satiric vein so often employed with devastating effect to expose shallow and misleading sentiments. For example, in "Onward Christian Soldiers", an unsigned parody of the hymn, the chorus is:

> Onward, Christian Soldiers,
> March into the War,
> Slay your Christian Brothers,
> As you've done before.

And the closing lines —

> Onward Christian Soldiers,
> Shoot your brothers through,
> While your chaplain's praying,
> They do the same to you.[6]

The borrowing of tunes reminds one of a remark ascribed to Rowland Hill but quoted by General Booth himself, "Why should the Devil have all the good tunes?". At first it might appear that ironically the wheel had come full circle here — but second thoughts suggest rather that it was the same process at work, with the Wobblies representing true religion as defined in the New Testament parable of the sheep and the goats: ". . . I was hungry and you gave me meat . . . naked and you clothed me . . . in prison and you came to me". The Salvation Army *et al* got the immediate message of this parable but were on the whole blind to its deeper implications, for instance that charity, like patriotism, is not enough, and that finding jobs and organising the Labour movement was an essential way, ultimately, of feeding the hungry, clothing the naked etc. In this context it's worth quoting from an I.W.W. poem entitled "Blasphemy", by Covington Ami:

As brothers work and live. All things in common hold.
Remember this: Love's spirit is not bought nor sold:
He who is without sin let him first cast the stone:
Not by your words but by your works shall you be known.

And this was "blasphemy", so they who heard him said,
And forth to Pilate they, the "rebel Wobbly" led;
And he was hanged. The charges? Oh, the same: "Intent
To dethrone God and overthrow the government".[7]

In many ways the Wobblies were half a century ahead of their times. They could be seen as foreshadowing in the U.S.A. — ". . . the land *par excellence* of revivalism . . ." — the nineteen-sixties protest movements which Ahlstrom has portrayed as examples of secular revivalism.[8] The word "revival" has a common denominator in whatever context it may appear: in particular, the rediscovery of old truths and arts, including the restatement and reshaping of these in modern terms plus commitment to the new movement.

Not all the I.W.W. songs were parodies, and not all used existing tunes. One of the most popular was Ralph Chaplin's "Solidarity Forever"; the words are in a vigorous, rallying vein, with a chorus consisting of the title words repeated thrice and ending 'For the Union makes us strong'. This calls to mind — though it hardly measures up to — William Morris's "The March of the Workers" ("What is this the sound and rumour? What is this that all men hear?"), which was also written to the much-used yet ever-powerful and faintly menacing tune of "John Brown's Body", a Civil War song. And the Swedish immigrant Joe Hill or Hillstrom, the best-known and most prolific of these songwriters, created the tune as well as the words of "The Rebel Girl", inspired by the great Wobbly orator Elizabeth Gurley Flynn. She herself wrote, "Joe writes songs that sing, that lilt and laugh and sparkle, that kindle the fires of revolt in the most crushed spirit and quicken the desire for fuller life in the most humble slave. . . . He has crystallised the organisation's spirit into imperishable forms, songs of the people — *folk songs.* . . ."[9] (My italics).

But the laughter and the sparkle are most evident in the brilliantly hard-hitting parodies and re-writings, many of which appeared in the I.W.W.'s "little red songbook",[10]including a dozen or so by Joe Hill. (This combination of humour and biting satire seems to point prophetically forward, to Scotland's anti-Polaris songs of fifty years later). In place of the hero of the original song, we find "Casey Jones, the Union Scab" (union scabs were skilled or craft workers who broke the strikes of unskilled workers and thereby broke the solidarity of the O.B.U./I.W.W.). "Nearer my God to thee" is transformed into "Nearer my job to thee". The religious song "In the sweet bye and bye" becomes "You will eat bye and bye", from "Pie in the Sky" or "the Preacher and the Slave"; the crunch line from this song, "You'll get pie in the sky when you die",[11] has since entered English-speaking usage — just as a later remark of Joe's, "I don't want to be found dead in Utah", has become an American catch-phrase. The Salvation Army becomes "the starvation army": this is spelt out further in verse 3 of "The Tramp", to the tune "Tramp, tramp, tramp the boys are marching":

Cross the road a sign he read —
"Work for Jesus" so it said,
And he said "Here is my chance; I'll surely try";
So he kneeled upon the floor
Till his knees got rather sore,
But at eating-time he heard the preacher cry:

(*Chorus*)
Tramp, tramp, tramp, keep on a-tramping,
Nothing doing here for you;
If I catch you 'round again
You will wear the ball and chain,
Keep on tramping, that's the best thing you can do.

The bias of the Salvation Army, in the North American Rockies district early this century, is shown up here. In Britain this organisation has consistently worked to feed, clothe and shelter down-and-outs; but in the situation in question the Salvation Army was envisaged as having sold out to the mine-owners.[12]

That the life of Joe Hill showed the most selfless dedication to this cause there can be little doubt. At first a rather marginal figure in the I.W.W. struggles, he was known chiefly for his songs which came to be sung across the world and were linked with working-class agitation as far afield as Australia. In 1914 he was arrested in Salt Lake City, Utah, on a murder charge, convicted on highly circumstantial evidence, and executed after 22 months in prison — despite an international defence movement, and petitions which included two pleas from President Wilson and one from the Swedish minister for further consideration of his case. The grim story of his trial by a hostile court, and the outcome, can be read in Barry Stavis's *The Man Who Never Died*; written after five years of research into the facts, it fully endorses Joe's claim that he was framed as an anti-union, anti-I.W.W. move. This claim is also supported by the Labour historian Foner.[13]

Joe's last message to his friends was "Don't mourn for me — organise". And his last will, written in the death-cell the night before he was shot, has a timeless nobility:

My will is easy to decide,
For there is nothing to divide.
My kin don't need to fuss and moan —
"Moss does not cling to rolling stone".

My body? — Oh! — if I could choose,
I would to ashes it reduce,
And let the merry breezes blow
My dust to where some flowers grow.

Perhaps some fading flower then
Would come to life and bloom again.
This is my last and final will.
Good luck to all of you,
                                        Joe Hill

Joe's body *was* reduced to ashes, which were placed in many small envelopes: "These were sent to I.W.W. . . . sympathisers in all forty-eight states of the U.S. except . . . Utah",[14] and to many other countries throughout the world, to be scattered over the earth on May 1, 1916. But the Harvard-educated revolutionary John Reed wrote, "I have met men carrying next their hearts, in the pockets of their working clothes, little bottles with some of Joe Hill's ashes in them".[15] His funeral in Chicago was attended by an estimated 30,000 sympathisers, who marched through the streets to the cemetery.[16]

Some twenty years later, Alfred Hayes and Earl Robinson wrote this song:

Joe Hill

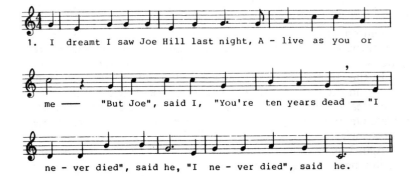

1. I dreamt I saw Joe Hill last night, A - live as you or me — "But Joe", said I, "You're ten years dead — "I ne - ver died", said he, "I ne - ver died", said he.

(*Note*: tunes of the three songs in this chapter, plus the six political songs in the next, are given in skeletal form only — but they are sung generally with rhythmic freedom, lengths of notes being adapted to fit speech rhythms and individual interpretations. "Joe Hill", for instance, is often sung in a free declamatory style.)

1. I dreamt I saw Joe Hill last night,
    Alive as you or me —
    "But Joe", said I,
    "You're ten years dead —
    "I never died", said he,
    "I never died", said he.

2. "The copper bosses shot you, Joe,
    They filled you full of lead."
    "Takes more than guns to kill a man",
    Says Joe, "But I ain't dead,"
    Says Joe, "But I ain't dead."

3. And standing there as large as life,
    And smiling with his eyes,
    Says Joe, "What they forgot to kill
    Went on to organise,
    Went on to organise".

4. "From San Diego up to Maine,
    In every mine and mill,
    Where working men defend their rights,

It's there you'll find Joe Hill,
It's there you'll find Joe Hill."

5. I dreamt I saw Joe Hill last night,
    Alive as you or me —
    "But Joe", said I, "You're ten years dead" —
    "I never died", said he,
    "I never died", said he.[17]

Robinson's fine tune[18] is in the hymn-like style already mentioned which was popular among Labour songs up till the forties and the fifties.

In the sixties, the English composer Alan Bush based his fourth opera on the life and death of Joe Hill as told by Barry Stavis. *Joe Hill: the Man Who Never Died* was first performed at the German State Opera House, East Berlin, in September 1970 and ran for the whole winter season.

Alan Lomax must have the last word: "Surely, if some heavenly visitor had decided to intervene in the troubled life of America in this period, he would have behaved like Joe Hill, would have been misunderstood like him, and would have died like him".[19]

Contrary to popular assumption, the I.W.W. were against violence, although they were prepared to respond with force if it was first used against them. At the 1913 convention a resolution was adopted which described their programme as offering "the only possible solution of the wage question whereby violence can be avoided, or, at the very worst, reduced to a minimum".[20] Many of their leaders were arrested for opposing World War I, and their anti-war songs pioneered a new genre, for few songs carrying this direct message had appeared in the U.S.A. before the early years of the twentieth century. Even after 1924, which marked the end of the I.W.W. as a substantially influential organisation, the songs continued to be sung by ex-Wobblies and others during industrial struggles of the twenties and thirties. (And there are still I.W.W. offices in Detroit and Chicago.)

The Almanacs was the best-known group of singers who followed on in this tradition during the thirties and who supported the Congress of Industrial Organisations (C.I.O.).[21] This group included the outstanding singer and banjo player Pete Seeger, and the Lomaxes, Alan and Bess — their roots were as much in academia as in the Labour movement, and their families were among the early collectors and publishers of folk song; Woody Guthrie, once described by Alan Lomax as "America's greatest living balladwriter"; Huddie Ledbetter ("Leadbelly"), the black "King of the Twelve-stringed Guitar" and a singer of powerful emotional appeal;

Lee Hayes from the Southern Labour-college tradition, with a religious background; Sis Cunningham from Oklahoma, who had taught at Commonwealth Labour College, Arkansas; Burl Ives, actor, singer, song-writer and host of the influential C.B.S. radio show "The Wayfaring Stranger"; their musical director Earl Robinson, a trained composer; the writer Millard Lampell; Cisco Huston, itinerant actor; and the black singers Sonny Terry and Brownie McGhee, close friends of Leadbelly.

The Almanacs sang union songs but also anti-war and anti-fascist songs. When they broke up in 1942, their very considerable influence continued to be felt; they were an integral part of what has been called the proletarian renaissance, circa 1935–9, which included artists, dramatists, novelists and some musicians. "Not only the Almanacs, but many traditional singers in those years identified themselves, intellectually as well as musically, with the broad Left movements. . . . The hard-won victories of the union drives of the 1930s and the anti-fascist crusades of that decade and the 1940s had a great and moving influence on the thinking and action of topical song writers after the war".[22]

Song-collections published regularly included the *Bulletin* of the organisation People's Songs (this had articles as well as traditional and topical songs), its continuation *Sing Out!* — at first a monthly periodical which started in 1950 — and later *Broadside*, 1962. *Sing Out!* published a widely varied collection which included traditional songs from America and elsewhere, popular songs, union songs, soldiers' songs, anti-war songs and children's songs. Amongst these were new songs (and some re-writings) by Guthrie, Ewan MacColl, Pete Seeger, Hamish Henderson, Earl Robinson and many others, and there were more than 800 songs during its first decade.[23] This periodical was supported by People's Artists (the inheritors of People's Songs). The Hootenannies, originally a nickname for concerts sponsored by People's Songs, included good traditional singing, both solo and in groups, theatre turns, Southern protest songs, and songs from many foreign countries. Paul Robeson, of the unique, magnificent bass voice, supported the broad movement for people's songs and possessed a large and varied repertoire, which included spiritual songs such as "I got a home in dat rock" and "Ma soul is a witness".

Reverting to the question whether songs such as those sung by the I.W.W., and those sung by The Almanacs, can be described as folk songs: Elizabeth Gurley Flynn certainly considered that I.W.W. songs, as exemplified by Joe Hill, came into this category (see p. 26), and one of the Almanac Singers declared: "We think this is the *first time* there has ever been an organised attempt of this kind actually to sing the folk songs of America. . . . We are trying to give back to the people the songs of the workers".[24] Denisoff, on the same page as that on which this quotation is given, states that "The I.W.W. evidently disclaimed folk music and rarely used it in their organisational efforts". He explains this apparent contradiction by suggesting that after the First World War the American Left rejected "popular" music, and incorporated "folk music" style as a propaganda vehicle to create Folk Consciousness. Be that as it may, the answer would seem to depend on whether the songs were accepted by the rest of that section of society by whom (Joe Hill, Woody Guthrie, etc.) and for whom they were written, and on whether they were absorbed — partially or wholly, but at least temporarily — into oral tradition. If these two conditions are satisfied, they can be described as folk songs. (Acceptance is after all implied in "selection by the community", one of the three factors in the definition of folk music given in chapter 1; and absorption into tradition implies both "continuity" and "variation"). Periods of conflict and social change produce songs which reflect struggle, and which reflect different points of view in that struggle. For example, 134 songs by Southern U.S. writers have been discovered, which were favourable to the Ku Klux Klan during the period 1922–1927.[25] Conversely, during times of comparative stability, or times when issues are less clear-cut, people will tend to sing about more personal matters and also to be more introverted in their thoughts and hence in their songs: Bob Dylan's career exemplifies this process.[26]

The most influential figure of the thirties and forties period, which led directly into the revival of more traditional music and cast long shadows over the next two decades, was the singer-song-writer Woodrow Wilson Guthrie, known as Woody Guthrie.[27] Born in Oklahoma State in 1912, by the time he reached adolescence he had to fend for himself and was forced to wander all over the country in search of work. His autobiography *Bound for Glory* gives an intensely vivid account of life in an Okie oil-boom town, the subsequent Depression, the terrible dust-storms, and the grinding struggle for existence which he shared with so many others of his time.

Most of Woody's best songs were forged out of his own experience; those mentioned here may be found in his collection of nearly two hundred songs,[28] and he has recorded severeal on his disc *Dust Bowl Ballads*.[29]

"The Great Dust Storm" starts in the time-honoured style of disaster songs — "On the fourteenth day of April of Nineteen Thirty Five" — and describes the devastation of a huge area of countryside by a flood, not of water but of dust.

"Talking Dust Blues" is one of his most famous and dryly humorous ditties: the title indicates the sort of *parlando* tone he uses.[30] "Dust Pneumonia Blues", based on the twelve-bar blues musical structure, ends on a note of stoically ironic laughter:

> Down in Texas my gal fainted in the rain,
> Down in Texas my gal fainted in the rain,
> I throwed a bucket o' dirt in her face just to bring her back again.

"Pretty Boy Floyd" is a Robin Hood-type ballad based on the story of a real-life Oklahoma outlaw of Guthrie's own time; the highwayman-with-the-heart-of-gold is a familiar figure in balladry on both sides of the Atlantic. (The late nineteenth century "Jesse James", also drawn from life, is another American song in this genre.)

> So long, it's been good to know ya [thrice]
> What a long time since I've been home,
> And I gotta be driftin' along

is the chorus of one of his best-known wanderers' songs, and as with many good choruses it follows on the meaning of each succeeding verse. "Tom Joad" is a long heroic ballad which tells the story from John Steinbeck's famous novel of the dustbowl, *The Grapes of Wrath*, and which Woody wrote after seeing the film version.

> Dear Mrs. Roosevelt, don't hang your head to cry
> His mortal clay is laid away but his good work fills the sky.
> *(Refrain)*
> This world was lucky to see him born

is the first verse of a long elegiac ballad which tells the story of Theodore Roosevelt's life and achievements. "Woman at Home" is another twelve-bar blues. "The Union Maid" and "Union Feeling" are very different, in words and melody, from the older type of labour songs. His "Joe Hillstrom", to a fine tune in the Dorian mode, is a tribute paid in a fitting style. Lastly, he wrote some delightful songs for children which have been translated into many different languages.

Most of the airs for these songs were borrowed from other sources; he chose good tunes, and often added excellent refrains, using elements of the tune in a musianly fashion. The main source for these tunes was Country and Western songs, which are related to the "white blues", (the tunes of many hobo songs also come from Country and Western). The blues are a central part of the jazz tradition and are almost certainly of Negro, and ultimately African, derivation.[31] Guthrie and other whites used blues forms, but their expressive style is very different from the black blues style in which the voice is allowed expressive freedom. By contrast, the white blues tend to sound laconic, "flat", especially when couched in the Oklahoma and mid-Western speech style, and part of Woody's genius lay in translating this speech style into song. Blue notes — which became part and parcel of the whole Southern/Southwestern singing style — are those which have been flattened by approximately a semitone at some point or points in the music: the most common are the third and the seventh of the scale,[32] but other notes of the scale are sometimes flattened, by white as well as by black musicians.

Woody sang of topical events, sometimes tragic, sometimes humorous, and of the country he loved. He used the language of the 'little people", of his brothers and sisters and of the vast majority of Americans — "Singing Democrats", to borrow a phrase of Alan Lomax.[33] High Art is very fine but it is not enough in the twentieth century — it was never enough.

"Guthrie rarely strays far from the Anglo-Saxon word-hoard, but the curious associations which he finds in simple terms lead him into fantastic flights of imagery".[34] For example, the last verse of "Dust Bowl Refugee":

> Yes we wander and we work
> In your crops and in your fruit.
> Like the whirlwind on the desert
> That's the Dust Bowl refugee.

He had a strong sense of right and wrong, and most of his work contains a moral tucked away in it, implicit but seldom overt.

Of at least equal importance to the verbal and musical content of these songs was Woody's performance of them. I would go further and say that his recorded singing is the finest and the most memorable of all his legacies to us. The first impression of his singing is that of vitality and a kind of simple magic. But the careful listener will notice that his voice combines a certain edge, or bite, with a liquid, warm, rounded quality; there is also a very exact pitching of notes, and some sliding, with leaning notes or *appoggiature* which provide the only ornamentation in his style. There is no break between different ranges of his voice, and an astonishingly complete absence of vibrato. He bends and varies the tune with great skill to fit the words, pausing on this word or that. His verbal articulation is outstanding, with good vowel sounds and clear though not over-emphasized consonants. Occasional unexpected rests serve to highlight the word or words at that point. Even where the words depict hardship or cruelty, there is no passion, no anger, in his delivery: it is matter-of-fact, but with an occasional chuckle — and not always at the obviously humorous bits. His "Talking Blues" are among his best known and most frequently imitated numbers.

Guthrie's instrumental accompaniment to his singing is very effective. Self-taught, he invariably used the guitar and between verses he often added a mouth-organ, fixed around his neck — no mean feat. His guitar-playing is unobtrusive though skilful, when used as accompaniment, with a good bass line and much rhythmic interest: when played alone, as in the introduction or ending of a song, or in occasional playing of the verse tune without words, it introduces more blue notes and more ornamentation of the melodic line. In his harmonica interludes, again as introduction, conclusion or playing of the tune between sung verses — but always with the guitar continuing — he allows an emotional intensity to appear which is carefully barred from his singing. The wailing, windy sound of this often under-estimated little instrument, with its chirpy melodic ornamentation and with the harmonic concentration — which often sounds like overlapping chords and which thus includes not only sevenths but ninths, elevenths and thirteenths — can be quite heart-rending in its effect. It's as if Woody allows his instruments, especially the mouth-organ, to express the overt poignancy which he denies himself in his singing style.

To hammer home his desire to be down-to-earth, realistic, he himself said he didn't want to sound "like dew dripping off the petals of the morning violet", but "rather . . . like the ashcans of the early morning, like the cab-drivers cursing at one another, like the long-shore men yelling, like the cowhands whooping, and like the lone wolf barking".[35] Of some folks in a New York street who joined in singing his "Normandie" song, he said ". . . their voices sounded good, like coal being dumped down into a cellar".[36] My favourite comment comes from a Paisley schoolboy of fourteen, in an essay on various kinds of music he had heard in my music class: "Woody Guthrie, a folk singer, was very good — although his voice was terrible the noise he made was good, and it was the rotten voice which held your interest in the music. Some singers with excellent voices very well trained were outshone by Woody's voice".[37]

This last quotation sums up beautifully the initial impact of good traditional singing on the open-minded listener who has been conditioned to think that the only "good singing" can come from a voice developed and trained for art-song. . . ."although his voice was terrible the noise he made was good". The reaction of the listener with a closed mind is exemplified by the comment I overheard from a distinguished Scottish art-musician and scholar after first hearing Jeannie Robertson: "Of course that's not really singing at all". The western art-musician, particularly in Britain, is slow to learn the first lesson of every respectable anthropologist, that his own culture and his own value judgments are not the only valid ones, and that he must try to approach the artistic as well as the social mores of a different community from the standpoint of a member of such a community. While he has come some way from Sir Thomas Beecham's notorious remark, "I suppose in my lifetime I've conducted all the world's great music",[38] and would be prepared to admit for instance Indian or Balinese art music into that category, yet he still tends to view with contempt the notion that folk music — of his own or any country — might be "great". Nowhere is this more apparent than in his limited concept of what constitutes good singing. (See chapter 7 for further discussion of this point.)

On the cover of one of Woody Guthrie's early records were the words "Folk song builds up man", and on his guitar case was written "This machine kills fascists".[39] Was this empty rhetoric? How far, in particular, did Woody and his inheritors influence the young folk of the post-war decades, the mature people and leaders of today and tomorrow? Dunson again: ". . . so far as I can see, no poet, no novelist, no speaker, no academic spokesman, has moved so many young people as has the topical songwriter in the North and the Freedom singer in the South"[40] — and Guthrie was the daddy of them all.

Woody Guthrie has been compared with Robert Burns, and has been described as America's Homer; his songs became enormously popular and many were absorbed into oral tradition. Dunson declares that if there was any one man whose work was responsible for the high quality of the new songs, in the fifties and sixties, it was Guthrie.[41] Most of his songs are deceptively simple — as Pete Seeger said, "Any damn fool can get complicated, but it takes genius to attain simplicity".[42]

Mention of damn-foolery calls to mind the practice, indulged in by certain literary pundits, of passing judgment on the words of songs while ignoring the music. In a recent review of *The Penguin Book of Oral Poetry*,[43] Robert Nye referred to "drivel from Woody Guthrie"[44] — an expression of artistic chauvinism. For he quotes the editor's definition of oral poetry as ' "unwritten' — that is, peotry that often takes the form of a song . . . 'or of verse in some way musically accompanied' " — yet he assesses the words on their own, as written or spoken but not sung (no melodies are given in the book). He should consider Prof. Bertrand Bronson's famous question and answer: "When is a ballad not a ballad? When it has no tune"[45] — a stricture applicable not only to ballads and other orally transmitted songs but to all song. The two halves of an artistic whole cannot be considered separately in this arbitrary fashion. The words of some of our greatest Western European lieder emerge rather poorly when cut off from their musical settings. And what about the metrical psalms?[46] Read or spoken, they are in large part so contrived as to be almost parodies of the Old Testament prose psalms, and this is because they attempt a literal faithfulness to the originals; but sung, as they were intended, to the fine old tunes — "Coleshill", "Stroudwater", "Martyrs", etc — they acquire a totally new dimension. Countless people of different persuasions, especially Scots, have taken these noble songs to their hearts over hundreds of years, and continue to do so.

In 1966 Guthrie was awarded the Department of the Interior's Conservation Award, and in his letter announcing this award Stewart L. Udall, the Secretary of the Interior, wrote: ". . . we are also naming a Bonneville Power Administration substation in your honor . . . known hereafter as the Woody Guthrie substation in recognition of the fine work you have done to make our people aware of their heritage and the land. . . . Yours was not a passing comment on the beauties of nature, but a living, breathing, singing force in our struggle to use our land and save it too. The greatness of this land is that people such as you, with creative talent, worked on it and that you told about that work . . . about the power of the Bonneville Dam and the men who harnessed it, about the length of the Lincoln Highway and the men who laid it out. You have summarized the struggles and the deeply held convictions of all those who love our land and fight to protect it".[47] The Guthrie Trust fund for Children was also set up in his memory, with its headquarters in New York city.

Woody's close friend, travelling companion and singing partner for many years was Cisco Huston; in 1943 they both joined the Merchant Marines, and after the war they made many fine recordings together. Cisco died in 1961, and it was chiefly Pete Seeger and Jack Elliott who continued Guthrie's tradition and made his songs known to the new generation in America and far beyond.

Little mention has as yet been made of jazz. Since this kind of music, with all the varied forms it has developed, originated among black people in the United States and has had an increasingly worldwide impact during the twentieth century, it is clearly of paramount importance in any consideration of music of the people. One possible point of contact between jazz and the folk music revival is found in the hypothesis advanced by Drs. Esman and Margolis — quoted in chapter 24 of Marshall Stearns's *The Story of Jazz* — that "Jazz is essentially a protest music".[48] Stearns provides an excellent discussion and modification of this statement. As we shall see, jazz and folk music in Britain were to overlap briefly in the skiffle period, during the mid-fifties.

By 1950, the American Left was under heavy fire from the McCarthyite inquisition, and with the Korean war these attacks grew sharper and more frenzied. In this connection, Gordon Friesen, journalist and critic, noted a curious example of what might be seen as good coming out of evil — good, that is, in the sense of freedom to diversify, to experiment: "The Almanacs, obviously, had committed themselves irrevocably to certain causes. The Weavers," — the group, with Seeger, which took over from the Almanacs after the war — "on the other hand, could branch out. They went down the road of traditional folk music where they enjoyed their greatest success. (By traditional I mean the old classics like "Old Smokey", the old songs, without, at least, an immediate message)".[49]

The last two sentences parallel so closely what later happened in Scotland, as well as in other European countries, that it is time to return to this side of the Atlantic and consider the developments here.

Footnotes to Chapter II

1. Quoted by Peter J. Welding on the disc-sleeve of Woody Guthrie's *Dust Bowl Ballads*, R.C.A. Victor Series, RD 7642.
2. Alan Lomax, *The Folk Songs of North America*, p. xvi.
3. The American Indians were even more oppressed, but because they were isolated their music had little opportunity to influence the mainstream.
4. R. Serge Denisoff and Richard A. Peterson, *The Sounds of Social Change*, p. 62.
5. Philip S. Foner, *History of the Labor Movement in the United States*, vol. 4, *The Industrial Workers of the World 1905–1917*, p. 153.
6. Joyce L. Kornbluh, *Rebel Voices*, p. 327.
7. Joyce L. Kornbluh, p. 326. A satirical Wobbly poster, circa 1917, showed a picture of "Jesus" with the caption: "Wanted dead or alive, dangerous anarchist"; in the Labadie Collection, University of Michigan.

8. Sydney E. Ahlstrom, *A Religious History of the American People*, Chapter 63, "The Turbulent Sixties"; the quotation is from page 1090.
9. Philip S. Foner, p. 154.
10. *Songs of the Workers, to fan the flames of discontent . . . Songs of the Miseries That Are. Songs of the Happiness To Be.* Over thirty editions were published between 1909 and the seventies.
11. Eric Partridge, in his *Dictionary of the Underworld*, quotes "pie in the sky" as in common usage up till around 1910, but quotes the whole line as part of this song parody, whose author he apparently does not know.
12. Melvyn Dubofsky, *We shall be all, a history of the I.W.W.*, pp. 177, 197.
13. Philip S. Foner, *The Case of Joe Hill.*
14. Barry Stavis, *The Man Who Never Died*, p. 115.
15. *Rebel Songs*, ed. Edgar Waters and S. Murray-Smith, p. 46.
16. Philip S. Foner, p. 155.
17. Words by Alfred Hayes. *Rebel Songs*, p. 46; vv. 2, 3 and 4 conflated with other versions from memory.
18. Music by Earl Robinson. *Pocket Song Book*, p. 96.
19. Alan Lomax, p. 412.
20. Fred Thompson, *The I.W.W.: Its First Fifty Years*, p. 85; also pp. 80–89 on the problem of violence. See also Kornbluh, p. 352, for the later I.W.W. leader Paul Seidler's instructions to strikers, 1927: "You are not to strike anyone . . . no rough stuff. . . . If anyone is going to be killed let it be one of our men first".
21. The American Federation of Labor, the A.F.L., represented the skilled workers, and was started in 1886. The C.I.O. was founded during the nineteen-thirties.
22. Josh Dunson, *Freedom in the air*, pp. 17–8.
23. Four volumes of *Reprints from Sing Out!* (1960–2) have been published by Oak Publications, New York. *Sing Out!* still continues, with several issues each year.
24. Don Russell, "Meet the Almanac Singers: They Sing Hard-Hitting Songs That Belong to the People", *Daily Worker*, 14/8/41, p. 7, quoted by Denisoff and Peterson, p. 106.
25. Dennisoff and Peterson, p. 85.
26. Much has been written about this brilliant and charismatic singer/poet, e.g. full length interviews in *Playboy*, March 1966 and March 1978. The second of these is reprinted in *Folk News*, May 1978.
27. See Richard A. Reuss, "Woody Guthrie and his Folk Tradition", *Journal of American Folklore* 83 (1970), 273–303, and Joe Klein, *Woody Guthrie: A Life* (1981).
28. *Woody Guthrie Folk Songs*, ed. Pete Seeger.
29. *Dust Bowl Ballads*, Woody Guthrie (RCA Victor RD 7642).
30. For notes on this style see Alan Lomax, pp. 432–3.
31. Marshall W. Stearns, *The Story of Jazz*; see especially pp. 8, 99, 105.
32. In the study of African scales these notes have been identified more broadly as the "neutral third" and the "neutral second"; see Stearns pp. 277–80.
33. Alan Lomax, p. xvi.
34. John Greenway, *American Folk-songs of Protest*, quoted by Peter Welding in notes on *Dust Bowl Ballads* disc.
35. From a memorial concert script of Guthrie's writings, *California to New York Island*, by Millard Lampell.
36. Woody Guthrie, *Bound for Glory*, p. 299.
37. Also quoted in *Folk Music in School*, ed. Robert Leach and Roy Palmer, p. 70.
38. Quoted by A. L. Lloyd in *Folk Song in England*, p. 37.
39. Cf. two variants of this: Josh MacRae, in an interview with the author, 11/2/77,

said that during his visit to Moscow as a delegate to the World Disarmament Conference of 1962, he felt like paraphrasing Guthrie and writing a sign on his guitar-box, "This machine disarms people"; and in *Folk News*, April 1978, p. 2, a letter about Pete Seeger's concert, in the Albert Hall a few weeks before, states that Pete's banjo carries the warning, "This machine surrounds hate and forces it to surrender".

40. Josh Dunson, p. 114.
41. Josh Dunson, p. 45.
42. Pete Seeger in the introduction to *Woody Guthrie Folk Songs*, p. 6.
43. *The Penguin Book of Oral Poetry*, ed. Ruth Finnegan.
44. Review by Robert Nye in *The Scotsman*, 4/2/78.
45. Bertrand H. Bronson in the introduction to *The Traditional Tunes of the Child Ballads*, l.ix.
46. I am indebted to Professor John MacQueen for the Psalms illustration of this point.
47. Woody Guthrie, *Bound for Glory*, pp. 11–2.
48. Marshall W. Stearns, p. 297.
49. Quoted by Josh Dunson, p. 50.

Matt McGinn

Josh Macrae

III The Story of the Revival
Development in Scotland

The opinion that art should have nothing to do with politics is itself a political attitude.

George Orwell

For over 300 years the demotic vocal music of Scotland consisted of two principal strands, the sacred and the secular. After the Reformation of 1560 the metrical Psalms of David were sung in church services by the whole congregation; so powerful was the appeal of these ancient meditations and prayers, set to their dignified, soul-stirring tunes, that for many Scots psalmody took the place of secular song for recreational purposes. This tendency was greatly strengthened by the censorious attitude of the reformed church towards secular, and especially dance, music. A parallel, alternative tradition thus arose which continued up to the close of the nineteenth century and even after (it can be traced in the writings of James Hogg and George MacDonald, for instance). But both words and tunes of the Psalms were written down; even though not everyone could read them they were fixed, unchangeable. We are concerned here with song which has been for the most part orally transmitted and subject to variation – that is, secular traditional song, or folk song.

We must be concerned with art music as well, in examining the background to the folk revival. (As suggested in chapter 1, this revival was part of the broader mid-twentieth century flowering of the arts.) "Musick fyne", both secular and sacred, was also regarded with hostility by the reformed national church of the sixteenth century, and a further blow fell when the court, the chief patron of the arts, moved to London in 1603. While it could be argued that the political union of a century later opened up fresh cultural vistas, composers of the later eighteenth century art music

1. See footnotes page 80.

renaissance in Scotland were not nourished by that sense of identity which seems vital to the creative artist; certainly this renaissance was short-lived.[2]

A similar under-nourishment was endemic to the composers of the "Scottish National Group" of the late nineteenth–early twentieth century. Inspired by the work of Alexander Mackenzie, this group included William Wallace, Hamish MacCunn, Learmont Drysdale and John B. McEwen, all born in the 1860s. Their search for a national music was part of a wider movement which swept through Europe and which took root latest in the more peripheral countries. Since there was as yet no music conservatoire in Scotland, all five of these gifted composers had to go to London or to the Continent for their higher musical education, and all lived for most of their working lives in London. In spite of their ". . . valiant attempt . . . to demonstrate wholehearted allegiance to their country of origin",[3] and in spite of considerable and deserved acclaim at the time, their music had no continuing appeal and is very rarely performed today.[4] Three possible reasons for this may be suggested: first, that Scotland was not yet ready to sustain such native talent; second, that this music was only superficially Scottish, was still shaped more by German or Italian influences and not based on concentrated study of the native music idiom; third, that it was just not good enough for international recognition. Certainly none of these, perforce emigré, composers appears to have devoted any time to collecting or listening to his own traditional music *in the field*, as for instance Bartók and Vaughan Williams did with theirs. Rather similar comments – with the exception of the word "emigré" – apply to three composers several decades later: F.G. Scott, Ian Whyte and Erik Chisholm. But Scott has left some marvellous songs, an outstanding feature of these being the composer's dedicated attention to speech-rhythms of the Scots language in the poems he set.

This bird's-eye view is given here in an attempt to unearth reasons for the comparative failure of any national art music movement in Scotland, as contrasted with many other European countries. It is given here also because I suspect this failure was at least a marginal factor in the subsequent development of the folk music revival, in view of the unmistakably national/nationalist offshoot which eventually grew within this revival. "Every whit as important and indicative as the composer's relation to the past is his attitude to folk music",[5] and there is a possible clue in this statement. The Scottish composer's relation to his country's chequered past, artistic and political, could hardly fail to be ambivalent and confused, and this may have engendered a similar attitude to his country's folk music.

A more obvious and a more recent factor, in the musical background to the folk revival, has been a reaction against what has been known as Scottish popular music. In this context the word "popular" covers a wide range (and at least a whiff of the sense of "commercial" now attaches to it). Fifty years ago there was the commedian Will Fyffe, whose act included a few music-hall songs. There was also the pawky-Scotsman image-fosterer Harry Lauder whose songs are almost never performed today, though some are remembered. Jimmy Shand after some four or five decades is still regarded as the chief exponent of the enormously well-liked country dance band repertoire, which has traditional roots, and records of this music are bought for listening as well as for dancing to. Robert Wilson was an example of the trained singer whose range covers Burns songs sung in a polished, drawingroom style with piano accompaniment, and "ballads" such as "The northern lights of old Aberdeen" and "Scotland the brave", (his best-known successors include Kenneth MacKellar, Moira Anderson and Peter Morrison). Calum Kennedy is perhaps the best known of a number of singers who specialise in popular Gaelic song. Andy Stewart and the Alexander brothers also became known around the late fifties/early sixties and have had a large following over many years. Pipe bands, and 78 rpm transfers of Orpheus Choir recordings, form two more ingredients of this mixture, which has many devotees at home but is also aimed at the tourist and expatriate market, and which now forms the basis for considerable broadcasting time in Scotland. In most record shops this mixture is still mainly what you find under the label "Scottish". Much of it is good and enjoyable. But even music lovers whose attitude is relatively non-purist and anti-elitist (letting a hundred flowers blossom, etc.) can hardly ignore the mawkish, kitsch element in it . . . what has been described as "cultural sub-nationalism',[6] and as "the persistent curse of Scottish music at the international cultural level"[7] (not to mention the national cultural level). The folk revival movement reacted against this, and is still reacting.

After 1707, the shrinking and the gradual desuetude of the Scots language, first in writing and then in speech (and it's arguable that, historically, Scots is more a language than a dialect) had a numbing, debilitating effect on Scottish literature. This was exacerbated by emigration, by the creaming off of much of the nation's talents in every field, which was in full flood by the mid-nineteenth century. A hundred years later statistics showed that ". . . whereas at the Union, Scotland had about one-fifth the population of England and Wales, she now has about one-ninth;".[8] Walter

Scott's novels had been soaked in Scottish tradition, including song, and in some ways he portrayed well the life and speech of the common people; but he wrote about the past, and chiefly from the point of view of an antiquarian rather than a student of and participator in contemporary events. And nostalgia was a significant element in the work of R.L. Stevenson, for personal as well as historical reasons. Later emigré writers (no less than emigré engineers, farmers, labourers, surgeons, etc.) also became a prey to nostalgia: this affected their own creative work and provided a market for home-based Scottish literature which allowed it to develop into the so-called "kail-yard" school. In defence of this group of writers, which included S.R. Crockett, James Barrie and Ian MacLaren, it should be said that their work preserved some seeds of a languishing Scottish culture and helped to prepare the ground for more fruitful later developments. One could go further and predict that this much-maligned trio are ripe for rehabilitation.[9] As so often happens, the lesser writers of this group may have allowed sentiment to degenerate into sentimentality, while lacking the virtues of the three major writers. With these reservations, one can hardly dismiss the view that ". . . Scotland was figured to the world at the turn of last century through *Punch*'s jokes about golf-caddies, ministers and gawky housemaids, the soft-headed ruralising fiction of the Barrie-MacLaren school, and the century-old genius of Burns. . . ."[10]

Into this backward-looking, nostalgic, almost never-never land, came the precursors of the Scottish literary renaissance: novelists like J. MacDougall Hay, and George Douglas Brown with his now over-harsh realism, and poets such as Violet Jacob with her authentic humanism. Lewis Grassic Gibbon developed a musically idiomatic style, with dialect words an essential part of that idiom. In his trilogy *A Scots Quair*, set in Kincardineshire and Aberdeenshire in the first third of this century, he introduces both traditional song (the wedding, in *Sunset Song*) and protest song (events of Armistice Day, in *Cloud Howe*). But the greatest and most wide-ranging of all the Renaissance literary figures was Hugh MacDiarmid, the nationalist with a world outlook.

Most first-class minds possess a certain humility, a sympathy with the whole human condition, and although MacDiarmid was not without this quality he was also, paradoxically, an uncompromising élitist, and his attitude to folk-song embodies in true Marxist fashion these two diametrically opposed extremes, the unity of opposites. But it was not Marx who first gave utterance to the ever-new cliché that truths can only be expressed in paradoxes. The New Testament is full of this, as are many other religious writings.

Walt Whitman said, "Do I contradict myself? Very well then I contradict myself, (I am large, I contain multitudes)". [11]

In 1964 MacDiarmid referred to traditional folk song as "the simple outpourings of illiterates and backward peasants", [12] and so on . . . but if we look back at the series of articles which he contributed to the *Scottish Educational Journal* fifty years ago, we find these remarks: ". . . so far as music is concerned there has never been any carrying over from purely folk-expression into an art-product – i.e. expressing as art – the process which has built up the musical traditions of every other country. . . . Magnificent opportunities await any Scotsman who has the fortune to be free, or can free himself, of the common inhibitions, and pierce with intuitive genius to the core of this tangle. We hear a great deal about the Scots being a musical people. . . . If [this] has any reality it would make it all the more inexplicable . . . that a people possessed of *a Folk-Song that has probably no equal in the world* . . . should have become so completely disorientated and precluded from the natural exploitation of it" [13] (my italics). The last phrase reveals one possible aspect of his apparently inconsistent position here: this folk song with no equal in the world should be exploited as material for art-music, but has it would seem no value in itself. (And yet, as we shall see, MacDiarmid attended the Edinburgh Peoples' Festival Ceilidhs of 1951–2 and was moved and impressed by what he heard there. In addition to this musical experience, he must surely have realised by then that the submerged world of folk song, and especially the ballads, had been one of the most powerful influences in keeping the Scots language alive.)

By the 1930s the literary scene was a kind of matrix in which new structures and elements, as well as evocative old Scots words, struggled to be born – or to be reborn, for it is often hard to distinguish between birth and rebirth. It is possible that the first vague stirrings of a dual need were felt at that time, throughout the Western world but perhaps more especially in smaller countries which needed to regain their sense of identity: stirrings which were to become stronger, more conscious and more articulate after the second war. On the one hand, people were groping towards a more "democratic" and realistic art, towards a people's art, towards their cultural roots. On the other hand (and the two are not unrelated) many people yearned for melody in music, rather than harmony or complex polyphony. (Certainly there is little melody – in any sense in which this word has been understood since the beginnings of Western music – in this century's atonal music, especially in the dodecaphonic variety.) [14] One answer to both these needs could be found in folk song, in the synthesis of traditional words with traditional melodies, which is largely sung unaccompanied.

In the mid-thirties the young Alistair Cooke's series of broadcasts, "I heard America Singing", which used many of the John A. Lomax recordings from the Library of Congress, made a powerful impact. Cooke drew, not on the Cecil Sharp, Appalachian, Child Ballad tradition, but rather on songs about what was actually happening . . .work songs of all kinds, from those about lumberjacks and rail-road construction workers to chain-gang and prison songs . . . the face of contemporary America. Hamish Henderson recalls how thrilled people here were who listened to them: "It was absolutely the first time that a lot of people had heard this kind of things".[15] And owing to the great prestige already attaching to popular culture in the U.S.A., this present-day folk material had an added kudos in that it came from the States. There were about twelve programmes altogether during the late thirties.

As well as records from across the Atlantic, five series of broadcasts during the next three decades helped to build up interest in this "other" kind of music. Donald MacCullough, of the Ministry of Agriculture, started a series on country music, to project the role of the farmer and the war-time "grow your own food" campaign: "Country Magazine" ran intermittently from 1942 to 1954. The Scottish composer and conductor Francis Collinson joined the search, led by Peter Kennedy, for folk tunes and songs from various regions. There were thirty-five Scottish programmes in all, mostly arranged and performed in art music style: Francis Collinson explained, "Many of the powers-that-be were strongly opposed to the idea of folk songs and so we had to dress them up to fit in with these ideas".[16] By the end of this series it was presenting much more traditional styles of performance.

In 1955 traditional music from different parts of the British Isles was heard in "As I Roved Out", twelve programmes presented by Peter Kennedy and Seamus Ennis which included songs from Galloway, Skye and Barra. Two years later came eight broadcasts entitled "A Ballad Hunter looks at Britain", only two of which were heard in Scotland, and in these Alan Lomax and Hamish Henderson introduced Scots and Gaelic music, including recordings from the School of Scottish Studies. In 1960 a series of six on folk-collectors, "As They Roved Out", was transmitted on the London Home Service only.

The fifth and most impressive series was "Radio Ballads", devised and presented nation-wide by Ewan MacColl and Charles Parker (for a full account see the *Folk Review* articles referred to below). These broke entirely new ground. They presented both traditional and new songs, they dealt mainly with industrial rather than rural subjects, and they introduced the singers and the workers – miners, road builders, fishermen, lorry-drivers etc. – as commentators, so that vernacular and local speech was heard for probably the first time in such broadcasts. Of these, "Singing the Fishing", 1960, which won the Press Association's Documentary award of the Italia prize, and "The Travelling People", 1964, each had about a third of the material drawn from Scotland.

An important new name has just been mentioned. In the hungry years of the depression, maturing amid the unemployment, strikes and hunger-marches of North England, there had appeared a young man who was to become a leading figure in the Revival: the actor-singer-songwriter Jimmy Miller, better known as Ewan MacColl. Born of Scottish parents, and absorbing from them a vast amount of Scottish traditional culture, he grew up in Salford, and by the age of fourteen he had inherited his father's militancy and become active politically. A detailed account of MacColl's career can be found in four issues of *Folk Review*, May to September 1973; these include contributions from his wife, Peggy Seeger (sister of Pete Seeger), the brilliant American singer, instrumentalist and song-writer who has worked with him for some twenty-five years, based in London. MacColl's relationship to the Scottish revival has of necessity been different from that of people living and working in Scotland, but he has made frequent visits to Scotland, including a period from 1948 when Theatre Workshop, the company originally set up by Joan Littlewood and himself in Manchester, performed in Glasgow and Edinburgh. His pioneer work in unearthing Scots songs and ballads, together with his fine voice and unashamedly dramatic as well as authentic style of singing them; his field-work in Scotland at various times;[17] and the many industrial and lyrical songs from his own pen – all these have had a powerful and seminal influence on the whole Scottish scene.

But what of Scotland's Labour and Trade Union songs? – for we have noted the importance of such songs in the American experience. I have found little specifically Scottish from the period between the two world wars;[18] in fact, few protest songs have survived in Scotland from the two and a half centuries which followed 1707.[19] Nationalism within the Scottish Labour movement was probably stronger in the days of John MacLean and Jimmy Maxton than it is today, yet until 1950 music seems to have played a smaller part in the nationalist movement here (in sharp contrast to that of Ireland) than might have been expected. In songs of the Labour movement the enemy was not England but capitalism, and the same songs ("The Red Flag", Blake's "Jerusalem", etc.) were sung both north and south of the Border. A Socialist Sunday

School song-book of 1925, printed in Glasgow, includes in its Preface a note that in the case of a certain song, "the word 'England' is to be broadly interpreted". But, "There was quite a lot of borrowing from America in Clydeside in the twenties and thirties. American tunes and Wobbly songs were sung at climbing clubs, cycling clubs and such".[20]

There were several Socialist choirs, including, between the wars, The Scottish Socialist Choristers, whose conductor Tom Kerr became Lord Provost of Glasgow. But perhaps the best known became the Glasgow Socialist Singers and the Glasgow Young Communist League Choir; under their conductors James Callan and James Service they won many prizes in Music Festivals, and in the early sixties, under guest conductor Alan Bush, they made a recording of "The Red Flag" to the tune for which James Connell actually wrote the words – "The White Cockade". (WMA 101).

The Red Flag

(V.1)The peo-ples' flag is dee-pest red: It shrou-ded oft our

mar-tyred dead. And ere their limbs grew stiff and cold, Their

hearts' blood dyed its e - v'ry fold.(Refr.)Then raise the scarlet

stan-dard high! Wi-thin its shade we'll live or die! Tho'

co-wards flinch and trai-tors sneer, We'll keep the red flag

fly - ing here!

This Scottish dance tune provides a more fitting drive and impetus than the hymnlike, triple-time "Maryland" – the same tune as the German "Der Tannenbaum" – to which the words are usually sung.[21] The change of tune is reported to have taken place after the song had crossed to America. Since a band which was to play it there did not have the parts for the right tune, they substituted "Maryland" . . . and it stuck. It is also said that Jim Connell was angered by this change of tune, saying he had written a song to storm the barricades and not to bring bourgeois Protestant Germans and Dutch Catholics to their knees in prayer.

The Glasgow Orpheus Choir during the first half of this century became internationally famous under the conductorship of Sir Hugh Roberton. It is less widely know that it was cold-shouldered by the BBC for a time, almost certainly because of Roberton's personal political convictions. Although he never allowed politics to touch his choir, he himself was known to have supported the I.L.P. leader James Maxton, and the Republicans in the Spanish Civil War. He was also a pacifist during the First World War. Superb as was the performance standard of this choir, it must be said that some of the arrangements which Roberton made of Scottish songs cannot be justified: the modal character of a tune is destroyed by the introduction of notes which are foreign to its scale.

In 1947 *Ballads of World War II* appeared, collected by Hamish Henderson. Although all these songs were presented anonymously, three are from Henderson's own pen, and in his foreword he pinpoints the difference between these and the more official "straight" patriotic songs put out by radio in war-time: "For the Army balladeer comes of a rebellious house. His characteristic tone is one of cynicism . . . Shakespeare . . . knew him well and called him Thersites".

In November 1948 an event was organised in Glasgow to commemorate the twenty-fifth anniversary of John MacLean's death. A teacher and communist propagandist of courage and integrity whose death was hastened by years of imprisonment, MacLean had commanded wide support and affection throughout Scotland, particularly in the West. The speech by pioneer suffragette Helen Crawfurd Anderson was one of the best of this MacLean Memorial meeting. Then came the poems, two of which demand special mention: Sorley MacLean read his marvellously succinct eight-line "Clan MacLean", first in Gaelic and then in his own English translation; and Morris Blythman read his moving "Til the Citie o John MacLean", which contains this:

They've rieved the live rose frae the leaf
An bluidit aa hir snawy bosom;
Bit rose-buds laved wi rievers' bluid
Wull lowe wi loe, come simmer seasoun.

The lines just before –

An rowed aside that muckle rock
Thit stappit the mou o her makars

– express in a single image the ineluctable connection between politics in its widest sense and the arts. (Blythman's pen-name was Thurso Berwick, the names of the most northerly town and, formerly, the most southerly in Scotland.) William Noble gave the first performance of Hamish Henderson's "The John MacLean March"; written for the occasion, it has been described as the first (new) song in the Revival.[22] A special issue of the magazine *Conflict*, edited then by Norman Buchan, printed the poems read at the concert.

Two years later Alan Lomax came from the U.S.A. to collect material for the disc series *World Library of Folk and Primitive Music*. As editor of these albums he used some of his father John Lomax's material, which Alistair Cooke had drawn on some fifteen years earlier. He met Ewan MacColl and Hamish Henderson, and with the latter made two collecting tours the following summer. "Marvellous", commented Hamish; "it enabled me to watch this world-famous collector at work. . . . I did an exploratory tour first for him. . . ."[23] From this material Lomax produced "I heard Scotland sing", one of his broadcast series of music from many countries. Henderson also introduced Lomax to Gaelic poet Sorley MacLean, to master-piper John Burgess, to singer and piper Calum Johnston and to Gaelic singer Flora MacNeil. In order to get contemporary as well as traditional songs, Lomax recorded Morris Blythman singing three *Sangs o' the Stane*. In the best tradition of Scots satire, these appeared soon after the Stone of Destiny had been taken, or retrieved, from Westminster by four young Scots.

The ancient Scottish Coronation Stone was alleged to have been brought from Ireland not later than the ninth century. It found a home in Scone, near Perth, and the central act in the inauguration ceremony was the placing or seating of the new king on the Stone.[24] It had been removed (or, to use Dunbar's word in *The Flyting of Dunbar and Kennedy*, "spulyeit") to Westminster in 1296 by

Edward I, the Hammer of the Scots. Its cleverly executed "theft" on Christmas Day 1950 and its speedy return to Scottish soil (in the abbey of Arbroath eventually), was regarded by many Scots as the righting of an ancient wrong, as a symbol of their re-emerging national identity. This bold act inspired a spate of poems and songs, most of them written to Scottish tunes; the best known of all became John McEvoy's "The Wee Magic Stane",[25] to the tune of "The Ould Orange Flute" (also known as "Villikens and his Dinah"). This clever and attractive song is in Scots dialect but the second half of verse 5 is sung with a pukka English accent,

> "Now its no use you sending your statues down heah,"
> Said the Dean, "but you've given me a jolly good ideah".

Reference is made later in the song to strong rumours that replicas of the Stone of Destiny had been made, and to the morale-raising idea that possibly the wrong stone was returned to Westminster.[26] In 1951 there occurred several demonstrations at Glasgow's Central Station, and the idea of demonstration songs was then renewed.

The Queen's accession to the throne in 1952 inspired a new flow of songs. "Coronation Coronach", to the Orange tune "The Sash", is in some ways the archetype of the folk-rebel song: it is both Republican and Nationalist, springing from the not unreasonable reaction of many Scots to the Queen's title of Elizabeth II. Elizabeth· I was queen only of England, not of Scotland –

> For ye cannae hae the second Liz
> When the first yin's never been.

This seems to have been the first time a similar objection had been raised since the Union of the Crowns (though some murmurings were heard at the time of Edward VII)[27] – an indication no doubt of raised national consciousness. Another Republican song from this period is "N.A.B. for Royalty", to the tune "The De'il's awa' wi' the Exciseman". (Both these songs were later included in the *Ding Dong Dollar* disc.) Many Scots were finding song a powerful outlet in expressing their feelings and thoughts.

Sandwiched between the Stane and the Coronation there occurred two other events which were important in the story of the Revival: the first Edinburgh People's Festival,[28] and the founding of the School of Scottish Studies.

Since the start of the Edinburgh Festival in 1947 various people had felt that traditional Scottish culture should be represented in it, and many informal ceilidhs had sprouted in private houses and flats. These were very different from the more official "folk" events which took place under the Festival umbrella. The official attitude can be assessed by the notes on a play performed in 1947 which included "folksong *arrangements* of great felicity . . . and sung with natural charm by *an octet of fine voices*"[29] (my italics). Such well-meaning attempts were soon shown to be travesties of the genuine article as revealed by the late-night ceilidhs, especially those occurring after Joan Littlewood and Ewan MacColl's Theatre Workshop performances (1948–53). Many citizens welcomed to their homes not only local enthusiasts but also visiting folk musicians, singers, actors, poets, artists and – a constant ingredient of this mixture – those who were predominantly listeners, all hungrily absorbing this "new" musical experience.

In 1951 the Edinburgh Labour Festival Committee was set up, with representatives from the Labour Party, the Edinburgh Trades Council, various Trade Unions (especially the Musicians' Union), the Co-operative Movement, and a few Scottish members of the Workers' Music Association including Janey Buchan. They had two main specific ends in view: firstly to try and modify the élitist nature of the Festival, which meant arguing about the high prices of tickets, and secondly to include working-class culture as well as high art under the same Festival aegis. Norman Buchan recalls how he went round Trade Union branches talking on the importance of cultural activities, and spoke to dockers from the back of a horse-drawn lorry in Leith Docks as well as to workers on a building site. He found an enthusiastic response from all labour organisations.[30]

It was decided to hold a People's Festival Ceilidh and Hamish Henderson was asked to arrange this. Martin Milligan was the organiser, assisted by Mary Black, wife of the Rev. Calum Black from Iona. They booked Theatre Workshop to return, this time with the famous peace play *Uranium 235* which dealt with the atom-bomb question.

The first People's Festival Ceilidh took place in the Oddfellows Hall, on August 31st, 1951. Alan Lomax was there and recorded nearly all the evening's items. The Ceilidh "had the explicit aim of entering the lists, as far as the official Festival was concerned, by saying, 'Look, we have here in Scotland – and up to now it hasn't received any attention from the big Festival – this fantastic tradition of popular culture, both Gaelic and Scots . . . and here it is!' "[31] There were Gaelic singers Flora MacNeil and Calum Johnston from Barra, Jimmy MacBeath from the North East, piper John Burgess, and prosperous Fyvie farmer John Strachan who knew some of the big ballads, the muckle sangs.

Norman Buchan was one of those for whom this was an entirely new experience, a revelation: "I was indeed 'bowled over',[32] in fact that's an understatement". His most memorable impression was of Jessie Murray from Buckie: ". . . a little old lady dressed in black, sang a song I've never forgotten . . . it was the most fragile and delicate and beautiful tune I'd ever heard . . . 'Skippin' barfit through the heather' . . . it seemed to dissolve, to vaporise in the air with an indescribable effect . . . marvellous".

Jessie Murray: *Skippin Barfit through the Heather*
1st People's Festival, Edinburgh 1951; rec. H.H.   SA/1951/20

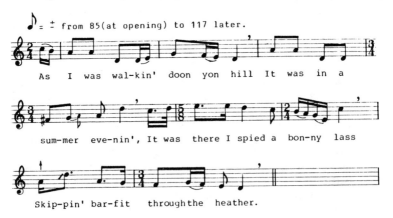

As I was wal-kin' doon yon hill It was in a

sum-mer eve-nin', It was there I spied a bon-ny lass

Skip-pin' bar-fit through the heather.

Note: bars 1, 3 & 7 are always 2-beat; bar 6 is very slightly
longer(though not in V.1 or 2); bar 5 is always 2½ beats,
and the remaining even numbers, 2, 4 & 8 are lengthened
to from 2½ to 3½ beats - it is common to find a pause at
the end of a line of verse.

(1) As I was walkin' doon yon hill
     It was in a summer evenin',
     It was there I spied a bonny lass
     Skippin' barfit through* the heather.

(2) Eh but she was neatly dressed,
     She neither needed hat nor feather;
     She was the queen among them a',
     Skippin' barfit through the heather.

(3)   "Will ye come wi' me, my bonny lass,
      Will ye come wi' me and leave the heather?
      It's silks an' satins ye will wear
      If ye come wi' me and leave the heather."

(4)   She wore a goon o' bonnie blue,
      Her petticoats were a pheasant colour,
      And in between the stripes were seen
      Shinin' bells o' bloomin' heather.

(5)   "Oh young man your offer's good,
      But sae weel I ken ye will deceive me:
      But gin ye tak my hert awa'
      Better if I had never seen ye."

(6)   Oh but she was neatly dressed,
      She neither needed hat nor feather;
      She was the queen among them a',
      Skippin' barfit through the heather. [33]

      *"Through" here rhymes with "bough".

But the People's Festivals did not present only popular culture and topical drama. The 1952 Guide to Events announces concerts of piano and violin music by Beethoven, with an introductory lecture; also poetry readings, art exhibitions and film shows.

The establishment of a centre for the study of native traditional culture had concerned many people within and without Scotland, and in 1949 an advisory board on postgraduate Scottish Studies was set up within Edinburgh University. Amongst press material then appearing was a seminal article in *The Scots Review*, February 1950, by Angus MacIntosh, Professor of English Language. He was a prime mover both in launching the university's Linguistic Survey of Gaelic and Scots dialects and in setting up the proposed traditional studies institute. Two other leading Edinburgh figures should be mentioned in the *fons et origo* of the School of Scottish Studies: the late Professor Sidney Newman, art-musician and folk-music-lover, and Stuart Piggott, Professor of Archaeology, who stressed the importance of Material Culture (methods of agricultural work, implements, buildings, etc.). A powerful influence was also exerted by the late Professor J.H. Delargy, Director of the Irish Folklore Commission; an Antrim man with a personal knowledge of Scottish traditional life, he eloquently advocated the establishment of a national archive of folk culture in Scotland, and wrote and spoke often on this theme.

The late Calum MacLean, brother of Sorley and at that time

working with the Irish Folklore Commission, was "despatched" from Dublin to Edinburgh and in January 1951 became the first Research Fellow in Celtic. Directed by a University Court committee which included heads of principal departments concerned, the School received its official name in October 1951. Other early research appointments included Francis Collinson in Music and Hamish Henderson in Scots Folk Song, and in 1952 Stewart Sanderson became the first Secretary-Archivist. In May of that year a conference on Scottish Studies was attended by those in related disciplines such as Scottish History, Scottish Literature, Social Anthropology and Archaeology.

The School's first office consisted of converted cubicles in an old warehouse, where the early researchers transcribed and annotated the tapes they had recorded. Fieldwork then was mainly in the Gaelic-speaking north-west and in the rich ballad areas around Aberdeenshire. In Spring 1954 the School moved to George Square, eventually occupying three of the few remaining eighteenth-century houses there. Fieldwork and research covered traditional Scots and Gaelic music, Material Culture, Social History and Organisation, Social Anthropology, Archaeology, a Folk-tale Archive, and a Place Names Survey separately housed nearby. An up-to-date laboratory dealt with the work of copying tapes, for preservation, and making example tapes for lectures, and the academic journal *Scottish Studies* started in 1957. At first dealing directly with Edinburgh University Court, in October 1965 the School became a department in the Faculty of Arts.

More will be heard later of the School's development and activities, but a brief statement of its beginnings is necessary in any chronological account of events, because this institution played an important part in the Revival. A two-way process was at work here. For the very first time the actual sound of Scottish folk music was made available not only to posterity but to present-day research workers, to visiting scholars and to folk singers and players themselves. Later this was extended to undergraduate as well as postgraduate students, and to the general public by way of discs and cassettes. The School will always be deeply grateful to its "informants" – that rather clinical name for those kind people who have freely given time to record music, stories, reminiscences and other oral information, now in the huge archive of tapes and still being added to. But the other side of the coin should also be looked at. The work of recording has been a source of encouragement to many tradition-bearers (who in not a few cases – at any rate in the Scots sector – have been unaware of the value of what they had to give) as well as to revival musicians; both could listen to themselves and to each other, and so draw mutual inspiration from the many strands interweaving to form the whole.

A good example of this encouraging influence may be found in the story of the first folk song club in Scotland. This was at Allan Glen's secondary school for boys, in Glasgow, and was started in 1953 by Morris Blythman, who taught French and German there and who felt that more emphasis on the Arts side was needed. He hit on the idea of doing folk song with a rather turbulent form-class (he had already tried this out on a German class which included Robin Hall). He told them, "Turn up at four if you're interested", expecting perhaps three or four – but the whole class came. Supplied with notebooks, they took down the words of songs Morris sang to them. He had complete freedom of scope since the music teacher was not interested in this venture. In contrast to later pioneer clubs, they began straight away with Scottish songs.

"The kids picked up song after song . . . I used to take them to all sorts of places: the Gas Board, Ladies' Guilds, Co-op. organisations . . . anyone who would listen. It was always best at a women's organisation, because they were nice boys and the women took a motherly interest in them." They found that starting with Glasgow songs, e.g. "My Maw's a millionaire", broke the ice and made other Scots songs more acceptable. At a Medical Association meeting, after a "just politely nodding" reception for "The barnyards o' Delgaty" and "Johnnie lad", the boys pitched in with local songs – ". . . and the audience accepted this because they . . . had come to know Glasgow people in their work as doctors. It made us realise the Glasgow patois was a weapon to be used".[34]

Now Morris Blythman stressed how "the thing picked up tremendously" when Hamish Henderson started visiting and recording them. As well as school concerts there were evening ceilidhs at the Blythmans' home; the bothy song "McGinty's meal and ale when the pig gaed on the spree" was once performed by a boy "with no sense of rhythm or tempo, but he was the hit that evening" – notwithstanding Lonnie Donegan's presence. A school pipe-band was formed, and the first guitar-teacher to be appointed by Glasgow Corporation appeared in the person of Josh MacRae,[35] an art student with a remarkable flair for American songs and blues.

Christened Ian, his nickname resulted from a partiality for Josh White's songs. "I lived on diets of Western and Cowboy music . . . I never think of myself as an ethnic Scottish singer, yet oddly enough I can sing in Gaelic and I feel my Gaelic heritage", (his parents came from Skye and Lewis). ". . . *I was much more of a cowboy than a ploughboy.* . . . The relationship between North-

Western Gaelic music and Country and Western is very close, with common themes . . . there's more in common between a Celt and a cowboy than between a Celt and an Englishman".[36] The "tartan cowboys" (a term often used pejoratively, and sometimes so with reason) represent an important stage in the Scottish story. Another Scottish singer who started off as a "cowboy" is the versatile and influential Alex Campbell, who lived for many years on the Continent.

Glasgow folk concerts in the mid-fifties also brought in jazz, e.g. Jim MacHarg and his band, and piping.

By 1955 Morris Blythman and Josh MacRae had started bringing guests to the school concerts: Moyna Flanigan, Enoch Kent, Jimmy MacGregor, Rena Swankey . . . with Jeannie Robertson as the brightest star of all. An Aberdeenshire traveller described by Alan Lomax as "a monumental figure of the world's folk song", she had been discovered by Hamish Henderson in 1953. "Jeannie . . . was tremendously popular with the boys", said Morris. "She would tell stories as well. The headmaster, an Aberdonian, treated Jeannie with the utmost courtesy. . . . She had a sort of duchess nobility but at the same time a popular warmth, that got the boys both ways, and got everybody else". And an impression from the painter Josh: "Jeannie, when she was singing . . . she would sort of de-focus her eyes – which gives everyone in the hall the impression that she's looking right at them . . . it was like a painting . . . she had this trick . . . it was utterly professional".[37]

Jeannie Robertson had already appeared at the third Edinburgh Festival People's Ceilidh in 1953, only a few months after her discovery. She was at the top of her form then and her extensive repertoire included many classical ballads, lyric songs, riddles, bairn-sangs . . . and a wealth of stories.[38] Jeannie's spell-binding gift for story telling would have to be heard and seen to be believed. Although her magnetic physical presence can no longer be experienced, it is possible that a recorded example of one of her best stories may be made available to the public.[39] Many recordings are available of Jeannie's singing and these provide an ever-new source of delight: her magnificent voice, her shaping of phrases so that words and music become an inseparable whole, her versatility of style matching her wide-ranging repertoire, her subtly expressive use of rubato and ornamentation, above all the paradox of a traditional timeless objectivity combined with dramatic, consciously histrionic power. A.L. Lloyd has summed it up best: "A singer sweet and heroic."

Jeannie Robertson: *For Ma Name is Jock Stewart*
School of Scottish Studies, Edinburgh, 1955; rec. H.H.
SA 1955/154

For ma name is Jock Stewart, I'm a can - ny - gaun man, But a ro - ving young fel-low I have been; So be ea - sy an' free when you're cour-tin' wi' me, For I'm a man youse don't meet ev' — ry ,day.

1. For ma name is Jock Stewart, I'm a canny-gaun man,
    But a roving young fellow I have been;
    So be easy an' free when you're courtin' wi' me,
    For I'm a man youse don't meet every day.

2. For I took out my gun, and my dog I did show't
    All down by the river Clare;
    So be easy an' free when you're drinkin' wi' me,
    For I'm a man youse don't meet every day.

3. I have acres of land, I have men at command,
    I have always a shilling to spare;
    So be easy an' free when you're drinkin' wi' me,
    For I'm a man youse don't meet every day.

"Jock Stewart" is a common name among Scottish travellers, and two of
Jeannie's grandparents were Stewarts. The river Clare is in western Ireland,
which lends weight to the theory that this was originally an Irish popular
song. Jeannie had another verse which she often sang:

> So come fill up your glasses of brandy and wine,
> Whatever it cost(s) I will pay.

So be easy an' free when you're drinkin' wi' me,
For I'm a man youse don't meet every day.

Jock Stewart's generosity goes further than helping out with cash or buying
drinks all round: it's a generosity of spirit, which will accept anyone
regardless of class or condition. Belted earl or tramp, he is at home with
either, and his self-respect includes the awareness that this is not a common
attitude. Here is an essential ingredient of the travellers' outlook – echoes
of Walt Whitman's *Inscriptions*:–

One's-self I sing, a simple separate person,
Yet utter the word Democratic, the word En-Masse.

In 1952 the second Edinburgh People's festival had been the only
organisation to honour Hugh MacDiarmid's sixtieth birthday.
MacDiarmid was again present at the ceilidh, as he had been the
year before, and some of his poems were again read at the ceilidh
social, as the late-night sessions following the official events came to
be called.

The same year saw the first production of Ewan MacColl's play
"The Travellers", a political thriller which was baldly – in both the
English and the Scots sense of the word – anti-U.S. imperialism.
But McCarthyism was then at its height and reverberations were
heard across the Atlantic. This might explain possible over-
simplifications within the play, but it would also explain the scared
over-reaction which it produced from sections of the Labour movement including the Edinburgh Trades Council. The Scottish Trades
Union Congress proceeded to ban the People's Festival and called
on Trade Unions to cease giving it financial support. This proscrip-
tion did not stop it from continuing, although on a decreasing
scale, but debts accumulated and 1955 saw the last of these festivals
as such.

But the music which some four years earlier had been heard for
the first time on a city concert platform – and which came with all
the force of a revelation to audiences of questing intellectuals,
industrial workers, students, douce city folk and cosmopolitan
culture-seekers – could not be re-submerged, and Edinburgh
Festival would never be the same again. For these people the bones
of the copious collections of traditional music had at last been given
flesh and blood by actual sound, by the authentic style of performance. Before long the folk music of Scotland and beyond, put on
chiefly by the gradually appearing folk clubs, became an integral
part of the Edinburgh Festival Fringe.[40]

So far this authentic sound had been heard by relatively few
people. The broadcast programmes have already been mentioned; a
few records had percolated across the Atlantic, plus pioneering

discs from the Workers' Music Association (W.M.A.). But a mass audience had not yet been reached. The jazz revival, starting pre-war, was now well established, and jazz enthusiasts were also seeking an "alternative music", something different from art music or the dance band music of that period. Like folk music, jazz was also more anti-Establishment, an important element in most revivals, (the jazz revival was particularly strong in Scotland).[41] It was not surprising therefore that folk and jazz should come together. The surprise was that this should happen so suddenly, that what resulted should spring up almost overnight like Jack's beanstalk. This phenomenon became known as skiffle.

Skiffle has been described as "a virtually universal musical vogue among young Britons . . . a modification of revivalist jazz to suit an even more completely unqualified and lay public".[42] And although Francis Newton on the same page describes the term itself as "dug up from the obscurer recesses of American jazz history, and virtually without meaning for anyone in the U.S.A.",[43] there is no doubt that skiffle was based on American music[44] – from different work-fronts . . . steel workers . . . chain-gang songs . . . and perhaps especially songs about trains. The catalytic agent of this new movement was a record by Lonnie Donegan of Glasgow called "Rock Island Line": riveting in its powerful, on-going drive, it is totally American, delivered in a rich Southern States accent quite amazing to hear from a Glaswegian. The instruments are double bass (Barber), guitar (Donegan) and wash board (Deryl Bryden). Donegan sang with Chris Barber's jazz band, and their album "New Orleans Joy" (1954) included two skiffle songs – "Rock Island Line" and "John Henry" – which were later put out by Decca as a single, the first British record to get into the American top ten. The accompaniment of "Rock Island Line" consists of regular tonic chords during the spoken parts and during all of the singing except the chorus, where it expands into three chords: tonic, dominant and subdominant.

This harmonic and instrumental simplicity, plus the jazzy syncopation and rhythmic drive, formed the basis of skiffle. Its success was part of the rejection of canned music – which was nearing the end of the smooth, cheaply romantic "moon and June" period – and part of people wanting to make their own music. There were usually several singers as well as instrumentalists, and group singing gave confidence to early efforts. The necessary equipment was cheap: galvanised zinc washing-boards gave forth a kind of rattle which took the place of drums, ply-wood tea-chests made rudimentary double basses with a pole and stout string, and a uke, banjo or guitar could be bought for thirty bob. The thing

caught on like wild-fire. Norman Buchan recalls speaking to
Ewan MacColl in London – "he said with eyes aglow, 'There are
about 300 different skiffle groups going now, all within a few
months' ". This was to double by mid-1956 in Greater London
alone.[45]

Remember that this was the first time in Britain that teenagers
had money to spend and were recognised as a section of the public
with their own needs and even their own *mores*. This arose from the
improved job and pay situation for them in the fifties, and the fact
that students could supplement their grants by holiday jobs.
Without this market record companies would hardly have taken the
calculated risk of making "Rock Island Line" and other discs in
the skiffle genre. The net result was that a particular kind of folk
music was for the first time available to a truly mass audience,
extending into millions, and this music stemmed from America.
Here we have yet another facet of the American connection,
immensely influential because of its mass appeal.

I have not found any estimate of how many skiffle groups arose
in Scotland, but people I have recorded who were in that age-group
at that time testified to the widespread influence of skiffle during its
short but exciting life. In Rutherglen Academy alone there were six
groups . . . we have here another concrete example of the way the
Revival worked at this stage.

In the mid-fifties Norman Buchan was teaching English at
Rutherglen Academy, a mixed senior secondary school[46] near
Glasgow. (Morris Blythman left Allan Glen's in 1957 for a period
abroad, and in his absence the school club gradually folded up.)
Norman had been collecting records: some by H.M.V. featuring
Ewan MacColl, and some by W.M.A. which later became Topic,
the first British company to issue folk music discs. Burl Ives was
another influence from across the Atlantic: "I realised there was a
lot of relationship between these American songs and the Scottish
songs – we could learn from these, they were still being sung, you
still had an indigenous thriving folk musical culture in the form of
jazz, negro song and negro worksongs, on a much more overt level
than was our own traditional song which was still being excluded
into the countryside by and large. . . ." During these years he
arranged various folk events in Glasgow, including a Ballads and
Blues concert in 1958 in aid of the Christian Action fund for political prisoners in South Africa.[47] The Weavers, now revived after
some years in limbo during the McCarthy era, were a strong
influence at that time. When Norman Buchan was approached by
Scottish TV for a programme, he christened the group which he
then worked with, "The Reivers":[48] "It sounded like the Weavers,

and had the right idea of raiding for Scotland". Around this time the talented Fisher family, who have Gaelic connections, appeared on the scene: Archie, Ray, and later Cilla, Cindy and Joyce.

When skiffle came, Norman Buchan saw it as a means of getting Scottish material through to his pupils, but it was 1958 before he finally took the plunge. "I took my nerve in both hands – I'm a nervous singer and tend to go off pitch – and sang "The Dowie Dens of Yarrow" to an English class. One kid said 'That sounds like an Arab . . .' – I said, "Well you're not far wrong' – I knew it was pentatonic or modal or whatever. . . ." He pinned on to the school notive-board, "Do you want to learn about skiffle and other songs?" The Ballads Club quickly proliferated, and skiffle groups plus solo singers were soon giving regular concerts attended by several hundred parents, pupils, and other interested people. They also performed to outside bodies, including Old Age Pensioners Associations. A number of boys from Allan Glen's helped at the beginning. A third-year Rutherglen boy taught guitar, and two ceildih bands started, which included fiddlers. Some excellent singers emerged from this school club, notably Gordeanna McCulloch who later became a leading member of the Clutha group, Allan Morris (see Chapter 4 for further mention of these two singers), Fraser and Ian Bruce, John Craig, Alan Knox, Mary Stewart, Ian Young, and Anne Neilson whose singing of "The Baron of Brackley" (Child 103) is a superb example of the art of balladry.[49] "The interesting thing was that starting thus, within months they were wanting to sing the big ballads . . . they began to like them, partly because they found other people were thrilled by them".

But this was late in the day for skiffle: it soon died, killed ironically by its own success . . . for although it had begun as a spontaneous, grass-roots – city rather than rural – answer to Tin Pan Alley, its very popularity caused its take-over by commercial recording companies. In this process it split into Folk on the one hand and Rock on the other.[50] Rock'n'roll had come to Britain in 1956, heralded by Bill Haley's singing of "Rock Around the Clock", the title first of a song and then of the film.[51] Rock, with the varied offshoots which sprang from it, was to become in some ways an even more anti-Establishment voice, acclaimed in particular by young working-class people, and especially by the male sector.[52] Young folk enthusiasts felt that there was no point in doing themselves what they could hear professionals doing much better. But getting to know music which was rooted in the indigenous culture of another country – America – made people aware that they had their own tradition, just as rich and exciting, and on their very doorstep. (This pattern was later repeated else-where – in Denmark and other Continental countries, including Germany where folk music was suspect after the war because of its Hitler movement connections – with the difference that it was often Scottish traditional material which gave the impetus and turned people towards the search for their own roots).[53] The Revival was thus left at a very much higher and more creative level than before.

In support of this statement one need only look at the number of clubs which started to snowball, chiefly in cities and towns at first. 1958 saw the start of Edinburgh University Folk Song Society,[54] with Stuart MacGregor and Hamish Henderson as leading spirits. In the next year a similar club opened at Glasgow University. Amongst its leaders were Adam MacNaughton, then a student and noted later for his collections of Glasgow children's street songs as well as for his own songs, and Ian Davison, another teacher who came to Rutherglen Academy. (Adam later joined this staff when Norman Buchan became an M.P.). In Aberdeen the New Left movement had become active around 1958 and 1959, with influence also from Arnold Wesker's Centre 42; concerts were held with poetry, jazz, and traditional and revival singers (see also p. 79), and Arthur Argo started the Aberdeen Folk Club.

In 1959 a club called the Sporranslitters took over premises in Edinburgh's High Street and expanded into a folk club, the Howff. During the three weeks of the Edinburgh Festival they put on a late show every night and this attracted many visitors, especially those going to and from The Tattoo at Edinburgh Castle, just up the road.

It was around '59 that Jean Redpath, then a student, met Hamish Henderson who helped to foster her shining talent and who directed her towards the University Folk Song Society. St. Andrews started a general folk club in 1960–61, led by an English student, Pete Shepheard, who identified himself both as singer and collector with the folk revival in Scotland and in Ireland. (Pete Shepheard and Jim Craig were instrumental in organising the first Traditional Music and Song festival at Blairgowrie, in 1966: later that year the T.M.S. Association of Scotland was formed.) St. Andrews also had a jazz club. In Dunfermline a folk club was started in a cellar (1961) by John Watt, another pioneering singer, song-writer and lecturer; it also was called the Howff.

In 1961 a successful club was launched in Perth by a group which included John Young, George Craigie and John Thomson, and they were joined in the mid-sixties by Sheila Douglas, a tireless organiser, fine singer and song-writer. Sheila and her husband Andrew have made their home in Scone one of the most hospitable ceilidh-houses in Scotland. Andrew Douglas, though not a singer, has become known as a witty versifier whose more serious ballads are extraordinarily traditional in style.

Ross Paterson was a founder member of Dundee folk club, 1962, and Kirkcaldy folk club was started the same year by a group of teachers from Templehall junior secondary school. Jack Stewart, president of the club, was then headmaster of Templehall School. As a weekly event he started inviting visiting singers and players to visit the school on the morning after a ceildih-concert: to sing, to play, to talk and answer questions, as part of the day's teaching. This was for pupils to listen and discuss rather than to sing, and to show traditional music as part of their Scottish heritage. Concerts were held in schools in different parts of Fife, at which both visiting artistes and school pupils performed. Stewart also initiated the part-time appointment of Archie Fisher and Josh MacRae as guitar (and song) teachers in Fife schools. A concert was held after Jack Stewart's death in 1972, to inaugurate a memorial fund with the aim of helping young people in Fife.

In Glasgow, the first folk club open to the public appeared in 1960; this later became known as the Glasgow Folk Centre when Andrew Moyes took over. Workshops were held in the Iona Community cellar. For its size and population, Glasgow seems never to have had a proportionate number of clubs, but quality has helped to compensate for quantity. The famed Grand Hotel club at Charing Cross (the building was demolished in 1970) ran weekly from 1965 to 1968; Geordie McIntyre writes, "In this relatively short time it mirrored and passed on the best in vocal and instrumental music, with emphasis on the former, (the instrumental 'explosion' was just beginning). . . . It was a friendly and fruitful place where the guests, at most two per month, were invited and responded as friends-of-the-family. . . . The club had a large number of residents, and performed mummers' plays, with other 'feature evenings' e.g. 'Burns as Folklorist', 'The Ballad', 'Songs of the Sea', etc. One regular feature – highly popular, and of considerable value – consisted of Celtic nights with Scots/Irish musicians. . . . An outstanding resident was the late 'old' Davie Stewart, street-singer, whistle- and box-player extraordinary – we mustn't forget his story-telling either! Davie lived in Possilpark, Glasgow, by this time". (Further reference to Davie in the next chapter). The club was organised by a quartet of singers, song-writers and collectors: Ron Clark, Carl McDougall, Geordie McIntyre and Ian Philip.

The following includes a few names of other singers and players invited to Scottish clubs during the sixties. *From Scotland*: Arthur Argo; Norman Kennedy; Donald Higgins (piper and singer, husband of Jeannie Robertson); the Stewarts of Blairgowrie; Pat McNulty (Uileann or Irish pipes); the noted Shetland collector, composer and player Tom Anderson, his pupil Aly Bain, and Simpson Pirie (fiddlers); and the influential guitarist Davey Graham. Gaelic singers: Flora MacNeil; Joan Mackenzie; Willie Matheson (later Reader in Celtic, Edinburgh University); and Norman MacLean (piper and singer). *From England*: Bert (A.L.) Lloyd; Cyril Tawney; Frankie Armstrong; Sandra Kerr; John Faulkner; Jack Warshaw; Martin Carthy; the Watersons; and Colin Ross (Northumbrian pipes). *From Ireland:* the popular Clancy brothers; Joe Heaney; Paddy Tunney; the Furey brothers; and Festy Conlin.

Folk clubs continued to sprout in other centres, including Inverness in 1965.

Matt McGinn, 1928–75, singer and song-writer, was a Glaswegian in whose work all the varied strands of the revival were interwoven. The eighth child in a family whose home was a small room and kitchen, his harsh childhood experiences turned him into a rebel; but this rebellion was channelled into political commitment, partly by his father's socialism and partly by the influence of the socialist "University" near the Trongate, where Sunday afternoon crowds gathered to hear speakers. Matt followed in the footsteps of Woody Guthrie, Pete Seeger and the Almanacs, and wrote many hard-hitting and often very funny topical songs. His humour was irreverent and he lampooned anyone he saw as a *poseur*, even among his own ilk. A thumb-print of his style, especially when putting over his own songs or verses, was to point any irony by affecting a "posh", quasi-genteel – i.e. English upper-class – accent. He could move his listeners deeply, by his delivery no less than by the content of his songs; his voice had an edge to it, effective whether he was shouting out a chorus or almost whispering as at the end of his "Miner's lullaby".

Matt McGinn: *A Miner's Lullaby*
Glasgow Weekend School, 1962; rec. H.H.   SA 1962/13

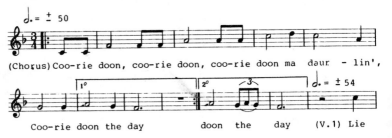

doon ma dear and in yer ear, tae help ye close your eye,

I'll sing a song, a slum-ber song, a mi-ner's lu - la -

- by. Yer dad-dy's doon the mine, ma daurlin', doon in the

Cur -[ə]l-by Main, Your dad-dy's how-kin' coal, ma

daur-lin', for his ain wee wean.

(Chorus) Coorie doon, coorie doon, coorie doon ma daurlin',
Coorie doon the day. (repeat these two lines)

(1) Lie doon ma dear and in your ear, tae help ye close your eye,
I'll sing a song, a slumber song, a miner's lullaby.
Yer daddy's doon the mine, ma daurlin', doon in the Curlby Main:
Your daddy's howkin' coal, ma daurlin', for his ain wee wean.

(2) There's daurkness doon the mine, ma daurlin', daurkness, dust and
damp,
But we must hae oor heat, oor light, oor fire and oor lamp.
Your daddy coories doon, ma daurlin', doon in a three-fit seam,
So you can coorie doon, ma daurlin', coorie doon and dream.

In addition to the words, Matt McGinn created this deceptively simple
tune, which hugs the tonic closely at every cadence and has a dream-like,
near-hypnotic quality. "Coorie doon" means "snuggle down" as well as
"crouch down", and so applies to both the child in bed and the miner in
the pit.

One of his finest songs is "Just a magic shadow-show", with its over-tones of Omar Khayyám. Like Woody Guthrie, Matt also wrote children's songs: two of the best known are "The Kirkcudbright centipede" and "Stop the world, I've lost my yo-yo" (or, "The wee red yo-yo").[55]

Here is another song recorded during this period.

Jean Redpath: (*Rare*) *Willie's Drooned in Yarrow*
Clifton Ceilidh, Edinburgh, 1960; rec. H.H.   SA 1960/205

(1)   Willie's rare and Willie's fair
      And Willie's wondrous bonny,
      And Willie's hecht tae marry me
      Gin e'er he marries ony.

(2)   Yestreen I made my bed fu' braid,
      The nicht I'll mak' it narrow,
      And a' the lee-lang winter's nicht
      I lie twined o' my marrow.

(3)   Oh cam' ye by yon water-side,
      Pu'ed ye the rose or lily?
      Or cam' ye by yon meadow green
      And saw ye my sweet Willie?

(4)   Ye gentle wind that bloweth south
      From where my love repaireth,
      Convey a kiss from his dear mouth
      And tell me how he fareth.

(5)   She socht him high, she socht him lae,
      She socht him braid an' narrow,
      Syne in the cleftin' o' a craig
      She's found him drooned in Yarrow.
      [She's found him drooned in Yarrow.]

The change of tune for the fourth line, and for the last verse only, is striking: it suggests that the lift of a sixth from G to E, (for the first syllable of "marries" in v. 1), is no longer appropriate for the word "drooned", when hope is finally abandoned. The version shown above ends with one statement of this fourth line. The repetition following it, in brackets, with the one note altered by singing "drooned" an octave higher, is given because Jean Redpath has since added it to her version of the ballad: it is intensely dramatic, as if the speaker could not take in the first statement of death and had to repeat it to bring it home, with the only upward octave leap in the whole melody coming on the death-word. Jean has also made a change in the words since 1960 and has dropped v. 4, which is clearly from "a more modern hand" (Palgrave's *Golden Treasury* notes. See Chapter 4 of the present book for Annie Bell's version.) The tune was learned by ear from a recording of Rory and Alex McEwen.

The brevity of the song forms part of its appeal for Jean: in 16 lines it encapsulates the sense of loss which the big ballads express at greater length. Also, the special quality of misfortune resulting from accident, for she herself once arrived just in time to avert tragedy by pulling a child out of water, so that a strong visual image recurs whenever she sings this ballad.

Jean Redpath thinks that all Scots songs, especially the tragic songs, provide an outlet for feelings which Scottish people can't always articulate in a direct way. In fact this touches on one of her reasons for returning to Scotland, after fifteen years of living and working in the U.S.A.: ". . . you can't hawl a roomful of people into the fourth dimension when the words may not mean the same to everyone in the room. We're all bred the same way here . . . it needs the inhibitions we're all brought up with, to channel powerful feelings into songs."

In 1961 an event occurred which induced an immediate reaction and which spawned some of the best protest songs of this century: the American submarine depot ship Proteus, along with smaller ships, sailed into the Holy Loch near Dunoon. "Polaris" was the name of the submarine-launched ballistic missile (A-2) which it carried. Public hostility came from a wide cross-section of thought: the Peace Movement, spear-headed by the C.N.D. (Campaign for Nuclear Disarmament), the Committee for Non-Violent Disarmament, church people and Quakers, the Committee of 100, and members of at least three political parties – Labour, Communist and Scottish Nationalist.

The Scotsman, 22/5/61, reported fully on the first of the larger demonstrations. About a thousand people marched from Dunoon to the Holy Loch where they split into two groups, one to take part in the seaborne attack on the Proteus and the other to demonstrate on shore. A bonfire was lit on the beach and Scottish C.N.D.-ers stayed for an all-night vigil. (Those arrested were later released, but many were fined.)

Songs had already been pouring forth from anti-Polaris pens, and the theme song of the sit-downers, as well as of the commandos of the Holy Loch, was "I shall not be moved". (The following six songs are taken from the disc, *Ding Dong Dollar,* and its accompanying booklet.)[56]

I shall not be moved

1.   I shall not, I shall not be moved,
     I shall not, I shall not be moved,
     Just like a tree that's standing by the Holy Loch
     I shall not be moved.

2.   We dinnae want Polaris, I shall not be moved. (2ce)
     Just like a tree that's standing by the Holy Loch
     I shall not be moved.

3.   It's time tae redd the Clyde, boys, I shall not be moved. (2ce)
     Just like a tree that's standing by the Holy Loch
     I shall not be moved.

4. Hiroshima, I shall not be moved,
    Nagasaki, I shall not be moved,
    Just like a tree that's standig by the Holy Loch
    I shall not be moved.

5. C.N.D. for ever; I shall not be moved. (2ce)
    Just like a tree that's standing by the Holy Loch
    I shall not be moved.

This is based on an American trade unionist song which was connected with the Shellback Fundamentalists, a religious sect whose name has obvious "not to be moved" connotations. A kind of rebel-anthem, it was sung on the marches, in the train from Glasgow and on the boats, by demonstrators and holiday-makers alike.

Other demonstrations were met with slightly more tolerance and the attitude of the police seems to have been a curious and understandable mixture. "The polis are fascinated by every reference to themselves. . . . They don't know whether they're folk-friends, folk-villains, folk-comedians or folk-crowd scenes. But they do know that they're accepted as folk-somethings and relax. They're quite photogenic as they tap out time to the old banjo, and join in the chorus singing. . . ."[57] Morris Blythman, one of the chief anti-Polaris organisers and song-writers, also commented, "The police received a bad press for their handling of demonstrators . . . they reassessed the situation and next time they sent Glasgow policeman Det. Inspector Runcie, famous for his expertise in crowd control. We made up a special song for Runcie . . . when the police heard it, they tried to look serious!"

Ye'll no sit here

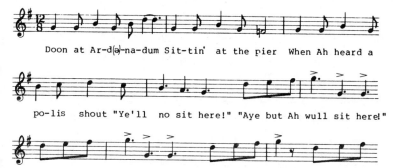

Doon at Ar-d(ə)-na-dum Sit-tin' at the pier   When Ah heard a

po-lis   shout "Ye'll   no sit here!"   "Aye but Ah wull sit here!"

"Naw but ye'll   no sit here!"   "Aye but Ah wull!"   "Naw but ye'll

no!"   "Aye but Ah wull sit here!"

1. Doon at Ardnadam, sitting at the pier
    When Ah heard a polis shout, "Ye'll no sit here!"

    (Chorus)
    "Aye but Ah wull sit here!"
    "Naw, but ye'll no sit here!"
    "Aye, but Ah wull!" "Naw but ye'll no!"
    "Aye, but Ah wull sit here!"

2. 'Twas Chief Inspector Runcie, enhancing his career,
    Prancing up an' doon the road like Yogi Bear.

3. He caa'd for help tae Glesca, they nearly chowed his ear:
    We've got the G'ers an' Celtic demonstrators here.

4. He telephoned the sodgers, but didnae mak it clear,
    The sodgers sent doon Andy Stewart tae volunteer.

5. He radioed the White Hoose, but a' that he could hear,
    Wis . . . *two . . . one . . . zero* – an' the set went queer.

6. For Jack had drapt an H-bomb an' gied his-sel a shroud,
    An' he met wi' Billy Graham on a wee white cloud.

The tune derives from "Hey Jock, ma Cuddy", but was more appreciated popularly as "Ye'll no shite here"; a variant has been collected in Arkansas. This song is hilariously funny and is of the rebel-burlesque genre. Runcie it seems was flattered at thus being immortalised in song.

After the first year or so the Trade Unions joined in. On at least one occasion, the demonstrators walked through Dunoon belting out "The Coonçil o' Dunoon, they went their hauf-a-croon":–

We dinna want Polaris

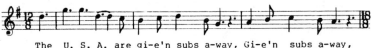

The   U. S. A. are gi-e'n subs a-way,   Gi-e'n   subs a-way,

Gi-e'n subs a - way - hay - hay   The   U.   S.   A.   are

gi-e'n subs a-way But we din-na want Po - la- ris.

1. The U.S.A. are gie'n subs away,
   Gie'n subs away,
   Gie'n subs away – hay – hay
   The U.S.A. are gie'n subs away
   But we dinna want Polaris.

2. Tell the Yanks tae drap them doon the stanks,
   Drap them doon the stanks, etc.

3. The Cooncil o Dunoon, they want their hauf-a-croon,
   Want their hauf-a-croon, etc.

4. The hairies o' the toon are sailin' tae Dunoon,
   Sailin' tae Dunoon, etc.

5. It's suicide tae hae them on the Clyde,
   Hae them on the Clyde, etc.

6. Tak the haill dam show up the River Alamo,
   River Alamo, etc.

7. Anchors aweigh for Poppa Kennedy,
   Poppa Kennedy, Poppa Kennedy, hay-hay,
   Anchors aweigh for Poppa Kennedy,
   An' ta-ta tae Polaris.

The tune is "Three craws sat upon a wa'", and the words are by Jim MacLean who wrote many other uncompromising and sometimes witty songs. (See Chapter 4 for a very different version of "Three Craws".)

"There was extreme opposition to us from some of the people of Dunoon because they knew we were getting at them, but they could see we were fanatical at them betraying Scotland . . . that's what we considered it . . . a type of betrayal . . . 'the traitor toon' . . . they were making a lot from the trade, the girls had Yanks, etc. . . . But this was international . . . there were hundreds of English demonstrators, very troubled people."[58]

Several *Ding Dong Dollar* collections of songs had been printed and sold widely at the modest price of 6d. They were also translated by the Russian Sam Marschak, well known for his children's stories as well as for his translations of Shakespeare and Burns. The title song, with words by John Mack, was one of the most humorous as well as hard hitting and the tune was taken from a Glagow children's street song, "Oh ye canny shove yer Granny aff a bus". It is also the tune of "She'll be coming round the mountain when she comes".

Ding Dong Dollar

(Chorus)
O ye canny spend a dollar when ye're deid,
O ye canny spend a dollar when ye're deid:
Singin' Ding . . . Dong . . . Dollar; Everybody holler
Ye canny spend a dollar when ye're deid.

1. O the Yanks have juist drapt anchor in Dunoon
   An' they've had their civic welcome fae the toon,
   As they cam' up the measured mile
   Bonnie Mary o' Argyll
   Wis wearin' spangled drawers ablow her goun.

2. An' the publicans will a' be daein swell,
   For it's juist the thing that's sure tae ring the bell,
   O the dollars they will jingle,
   There'll be no a lassie single,
   Even though they maybe blaw us a' tae hell.

3. But the Glesca Moderator disnae mind;
   In fact, he thinks the Yanks are awfy kind,
   For if it's heaven that ye're going'
   It's a quicker way than rowin',
   An' there's sure tae be naebody left behind.

(Final Chorus)
O ye canny spend a dollar when ye're deid
Sae tell Kennedy he's got tae keep the heid,
Singin' Ding . . . Dong . . . Dollar; Everybody holler,
Ye canny spend a dollar when ye're deid.

Other children's song tunes were also borrwed, e.g. "Bee Baw Babbity", which became "K-K-Kennedy".
A big Labour Party open-air rally at Ayr was the occasion for

what was probably the sharpest confrontation of all. The Anti-Polaris Singers group had been invited to come and lead the singing and Josh MacRae had the crowd enthralled listening to "Joe Hill". It was a rainy day, and about two hundred yards from the platform were some open shelters. "When the singers were on, the crowd came out from the shelters . . . as soon as the speakers got up to speak, they all went back to their shelters. We had the same sort of experience at all the demos . . . people were getting something from the songs that none of the speakers could give them," – Morris Blythman. Since it is unlikely that many of the words would be audible to the crowd in open-air demo situations, this influence exerted by the songs is important evidence of the power of non-verbal communication.

"10,000 peaceful demonstrators at this critical time would have sorted the Americans out", said Morris Blythman. "They were just on the verge of deciding whether to stay or not . . . they would have got the sense that they'd be under constant pressure. . . ." Josh MacRae: "Only numbers would have made the peaceful demo thing work . . . *if the army had been called in there would have been world coverage.* . . . There was a very good spirit abroad at that time . . . an enthusiasm, an instant sort of comradeship I haven't come across in such large numbers since . . . it was a vital force . . . the important thing was a strong togetherness and a political certainty about things. If we'd had the numbers, we could have done it then."[59]

Whatever argument there may be about this attitude, there can be no doubt that most of the songs were brilliantly on-the-ball, even though not all were equally good. They proved a nice change too from the Aldermaston "Ban-the-Bomb" type of songs, hymns like "Stand to Ban the Bomb", and the apocalyptic "Little man, where're you going to run to?", which though sincere and moving lacked the humour and edge of the anti-Polaris lyrics, including the Republican ones. Pete Seeger took the songs to America where they were enormously successful. At Berkeley, California, he started with "The U.S.A. are gie'n subs away", and one can hear on the tape made of it that the whole student audience rose to it, they got the idea right away at that first line. Moe Asch of the American Folkways company eventually produced the *Ding Dong Dollar* disc; it proved so successful that it was re-issued several times. It's well worth while to beg, borrow or steal this album from anywhere you can find it, along with its scintillating booklet.

Several more of these rebel songs should be mentioned. "The Gleska Eskimos" title stems from Captain Lanin's gaffe in dismissing the Holy Loch demonstrators as "Eskimos", not realising that this race had long been immortalised by the Glasgow children's street song,

Sitting amang the Eskimos
Playing a gemme o' dominoes,
My Maw's a millionaire.

The tune is another American one, "Marching through Georgia" – but is was already popular in Glasgow as "The Brigton Billy Boys", an Orange song! So the Glasgow sectarian songs were drawn into the mêlée.

The tune of "Yankee Doodle" could hardly be missed out of all this, so "Paper hankies" was written for it,

(*Chorus*) Chase the Yankees oot the Clyde
Away wi' Uncle Sammy,
Chase the Yankees oot the Clyde
An' send them hame tae mammy.

and the moving "John Brown's Body" tune, mentioned in Chapter 2, appears again as "Ban Polaris – Hallelujah".

The most beautiful and the most famous of all these songs was written a year before Polaris: "For the Glasgow Peace Marchers, May 1960". This is Hamish Henderson's "Freedom Come-all-ye", which starts "Roch the wind in the clear day's dawin'", written to the poet's own adaptation of the pipe tune "The Bloody Fields of Flanders". It is still sung frequently all over Scotland and beyond. The language is richer, yet so graphically used that the meaning is substantially clear before any glossary is consulted. It rightly took its place among the anti-Polaris songs, although – or perhaps because – its theme is broader, and the "roch wind" is depicted as sweeping away opression and war over the whole world. Both words and music have been widely printed and can be found in *The Scottish Folksinger*. It is on Claddagh's recent record of Henderson's poems and songs (CC A7).

Freedom Come-all-ye

Roch the wind in the clear day's dawin'
Blaws the cloods heelster-gowdie ow'r the bay,
But there's mair nor a roch wind blawin'
Through the great glen o' the warld the day.
It's a thocht that will gar oor rottans
– A' they rogues that gang gallus, fresh and gay –
Tak' the road, and seek ither loanin's
For their ill ploys, tae sport and play.

Nae mair will the bonnie callants
Mairch tae war when oor braggarts crousely craw,
Nor wee weans frae pit-heid and clachan
Mourn the ships sailin' doon the Broomielaw.
Broken faimlies in lands we've herriet
Will curse Scotland the Brave nae mair, nae mair;
Black and white, ane til ither mairriet
Mak' the vile barracks o' their maisters bare.

O come all ye at hame wi' Freedom,
Never heed whit the hoodies croak for doom.
In your hoose a' the bairns o' Adam
Can find breid, barley-bree and painted room.
When MacLean meets wi's frien's in Springburn,
A' the roses and geans will turn tae bloom,
And a black boy frae yont Nyanga
Dings the fell gallows o' the burghers doon.

Finally, one more *Ding Dong Dollar* song, this time in the direct line of the irrepressible Glasgow music-hall tradition – a kind of take-off of the popular "tragic ballad", with overtones of earlier American commercial popular songs – which never failed to make a hit right through the decade following its creation. This is "The misguided missile and the misguided Miss".

The Misguided Missile

He turned his key—then whoosh!   Oh Law-dy Lawd! He

said, "I'm so em-bar-rassed, We'll no be goin'to Paris,For I've

launched the first Po-la-ris Through bein' a drun-ken clod!"

Last line of V.5:   (Finis)

For he's the first Yank on the moon ——————

(1)   Oh the maid was young and pretty
       And she came down from the city
       And maybe 'twas a pity
       That she left old Glesca Toon.
       She met a son of Uncle Sammy
       From the heart of Alabamy,
       He had never left his mammy
       Till he came ower tae Dunoon.

       (Chorus)
       So while you wet your whistle, whistle
       I'll sing you this,
       O' the misguided missile
       and the misguided Miss.

(2)   In his wee bit sailor suitie – och!
       He looked so brave and smart,
       At the Battle o' the Holy Loch
       He won a Purple Heart,
       And noo that he's been overseas
       Six medals and five stars;
       For drinking Johnnie Walker
       He's collecting extra bars.

       So while you wet, etc.

(3)   He said he'd like to thank her
       For those moments by the shore,
       Said his daddy was a banker
       So she loved him more and more:
       You could see he was a ranker

By the rings upon his sleeve,
She wanted rings upon her fingers
But he was just on leave.

So while you wet, etc.

(4) He had some Scotch and scoosh
Then he went back aboard;
He turned his key – then whoosh!
(And) Oh Lawdy Lawd!
He said, "I'm so embarrassed,
We'll be no goin' to Paris,
For I've launched the first Polaris
Through bein' a drunken clod." (or, sod)

So while you wet, etc.

(5) Now there's an awfu' fuss
Aboard the Proteus,
And the maid is on the shore
By the point o' Lazarus,
And she's singing "Hush a baba,
You will see your daddy soon,
When the clouds all roll away
For he's the first Yank on the moon."

Lines 4 to 8 of the second last verse are sung in a hoarse, Blues style.

A curious paradox is embodied within this corpus of songs. Although the American connection was still extremely influential in the Revival, nearly all the anti-Polaris content was *ipso facto* anti-American (and with conscious irony made use of many American tunes). It is hardly necessary to add that this was not anti the American nation but anti their top brass and anti NATO, in particular for the grossly disproportionate number of nuclear bases inflicted on a small country. Of course this enraged some Americans.[60] But many Americans, especially those who supported the anti-nuclear-arms movement, welcomed these songs and even sang them with relish. In Scotland itself, ". . . the anti-Polaris singers . . . were accepted with pride and affection by demonstrators and organisers as their own establishment singers. No one told them what to sing, where to sing, or how to sing it. They kept to the main theme of anti-Polaris, writing and binding the many disparate organisations into one body. And to this body they gave heart, voice and laughter. They were B.B.C.'d, S.T.V.'d, televised, N.C.B.'d,[61] broadcast, telecast, freelanced and pirated,

A.F.N.'d,[62] Radio Moscowed, translated, interpreted and given in evidence in court". (From disc booklet.)

With the exception of "Freedom Come-all-ye", the songs are very seldom heard now (though the subs are still in the loch). One obvious reason is the twenty-years-old topicality of the words. But another reason which has been put forward is that some, in common with many other songs written in the sixties, embody male-sexist attitudes which are no longer acceptable. It could be claimed that such attitudes can be traced in "Coronation Coronach" and in "The Misguided Missile" (if the Miss was misguided, so was the Mister, or Corporal or whatever). Insofar as this is so, these two are simply in the mainstream tradition of folksong over hundreds of years, right up to the beginning of the nineteen-seventies. It took the women's movement to make people aware of these attitudes. Yet plenty of older traditional sexist-type songs are still being sung. The anti-Polaris songs served their turn, they were part of the Revival at that time and they left a lasting influence on the Scottish scene. After all they were without exception couched in the present-day Scots vernacular, more than half of the tunes were Scottish, and this strengthened the trend towards the native traditional which was one result of the demise of skiffle. Many singers were far more interested in this than in the political or protest songs.

Two singer-songwriter individualists spring to mind here, representative of many more. Adam MacNaughton from Glasgow found the strong influence of socialist politics came as "rather a shock . . . with my good Church of Scotland non-political upbringing . . . so being a thrawn kin' o' character, some of the early stuff I wrote was on the other side, e.g. 'Ye canny ban Polaris when it's raining' and other ditties. I've a bit of the rebel in me . . . the establishment in folk song clubs was the Left, and if anything that turned me the other way!"[63] Andy Hunter, from near Clydebank, also had similar reservations. A pupil at Allan Glen's school, and later a devoted disciple of Jeannie Robertson in Aberdeen, he found that when C.N.D. started, a dramatic choice had to be made by young people. ". . . I decided not to opt for it, I'd not much to do with that kind of movement . . . my commitment was to folk song, humanism and the regeneration of ideals . . . I feel it's not good for everyone to be in the same basket. . . ." But he also said, speaking of the struggle to find an "alternative music", "Everything was against us, but everything was for us because it was against us".[64]

(Postscript: Adam MacNaughton later wrote "Blood on the Sands", about Chile, and also a song against the Argentine regime. And Andy Hunter has written several songs in the realm of local politics rather than national or international.)

The annual festivals started with the first Aberdeen one in 1963. This is not held every year now, and it has always been one of the non-competitive variety. The Aberdeen story provides a good example of what happened by around the mid-sixties. People like Tom Paxton and the Corries used to come to the clubs, then when they became commercial successes – though still based on tradition – Peter Hall notes ". . . there was a split, and people who came to the club to hear Paxton, went to Paxton *concerts*. Those who came to hear Jeannie Robertson or [folk] revivalists . . . stayed at the folk song club. This split was to some extent because of the commercial situation – the clubs could no longer afford Paxton . . . there were records, and he sang at concerts".[65] As well as being one of the leading folk musicians and scholars in the North East, Peter Hall was the first to introduce Lizzie Higgins, daughter of Jeannie Robertson, to an Aberdeen club in the late sixties, thus launching her on a distinguished career. (See Chapter 4).

The chief Scottish folk-magazine before the seventies was *Chapbook*, launched by Arthur Argo[66] in 1964; volume 1 was the magazine of Aberdeen Folk Club. Successive volumes, aimed at national coverage, were sponsored by the Scottish Federation of Folk Song Clubs, and continued till the end of the decade: 6 issues per volume, then 3 issues for the fifth and last volume. These are now collectors' pieces, containing songs with music, articles, letters and reviews. Arthur Argo as principal editor was assisted by Carl McDougall and Ian Philip, with a production team based chiefly in Aberdeen.

In addition to writing songs himself, Norman Buchan contributed between 70 and 80 traditional songs, with music, to *The Weekly Scotsman's* column on Bothy Ballads, 1959–60; many of these appeared later in *101 Scottish Songs*.

The songs sung in the first decade or so of the folk clubs were a mixture of American, then Irish, Scottish and English. Occasionally one in another language, notably Scottish Gaelic, would appear, and the emphasis on Scots song increased as the seventies were approached. Here are a few of the titles which were heard:– Blowin' in the wind, Where have all the flowers gone, Spanish boots of Spanish leather, I was born in East Virginia, The last thing on my mind, I can't help but wonder where I'm bound, This land is your land. The wild rover, The craw on the cradle (anti-war song), Fourpence a day (MacColl), The north country maid, Hawl away Joe (a shanty), Woman sweeter than man, Baby lie easy (Cyril Tawney), The jug of punch, The Irish rover, Me husband's got no courage in him (probably introduced by A.L. Lloyd), The Silkie of

Sule Skerry, One morning fair I took the air, Plaisir d'amour, The seeds of love, The wraggle taggle gypsies, The copper kettle, Mary Hamilton, The trees they do grow high, The cruel mither and The bonny hoose o' Airlie (see Chapter 4 for versions of the last three), The gardener, The Highland widow's lament, Lord Gregory, The ballad of the speaking heart, Sally free and easy, To the weavers gin ye go, Rigs o' rye and The water is wide.

Amongst song-writers not as yet mentioned were Peter Ross and actor Roddy MacMillan, both of Glasgow; Bob Bertram of Edinburgh; and Dave Goulder, who lived for some years at a Youth Hostel in Glen Torridon which became a meeting place for singers as well as for climbers. Archie Fisher has been a potent influence for over twenty years, as singer and guitarist as well as song-writer. He has an understated yet compelling vocal style, with exceptionally clear diction.

For the words of songs supporting the Scottish Nationalist Party see Morris Blythman's article in *Chapbook* (vol. 4 no. 6), and Jack Brand's book *The National Movement in Scotland*.

Towards the end of the sixties the increasing popularity of instrumental music was already evident, and groups such as the Corries, and the Chieftains from Ireland, were using a wide variety of folk instruments: stringed, wind and percussion. Many young people began learning to play the pipes and traditional fiddle. Instrumental music has continued in the home and in pubs, perhaps more than in clubs or festivals. (Only within the last decade, for instance, has the enchanting whistle-playing of such a Alex Green been heard at festivals; and in 1976 John Watt declared, "There are some twelve box-players in Milnathort, not one of whom has ever been in a folk club or is ever likely to be".[67]) The Reel and Accordion Clubs and the Reel and Strathspey Societies attracted a large membership – the latter's massed strings still produce an enormously popular sound and regularly fill the largest concert-halls in Scotland.

By 1970 native traditional music was increasingly being heard at folk events throughout Scotland.

Footnotes to Chapter III

1. From "Why I Write" in *Decline of the English Murder and other essays*, p. 184.
2. For the interesting suggestion that Scotland was among the nations where historical events resulted in an "immobilisation" that "preserved them as national and cultural identities", see Gershon Legman, *The Horn Book*, p. 365. It could be argued that a petrification such as he describes was one of the factors that made possible the cultural resurgence in the twentieth century, but it appears to have had an adverse effect at an earlier period.

3.   *A History of Scottish Music* by Kenneth Elliott and Frederick Rimmer, p. 69.

4.   A fine extract from MacCunn's overture *The Land of the Mountain and the Flood* was recently used as the theme music for the TV series *The Sutherlanders*.

5.   Bence Szabolcsi, *A History of Melody*, p. 186.

6.   Tom Nairn, *The Red Paper on Scotland*, ed. Gordon Brown, p. 25.

7.   Kenneth Elliott, "Scotland. I. Art music". *The New Grove Dictionary of Music and Musicians*, 17.70.

8.   David Craig, *Scottish Literature and the Scottish People*, p. 273; statistics refer to the year 1954. This book includes a detailed examination of the gradual anglicisation of the Scots tongue and its effects on Scottish literature.

9.   A spirited defence of the kailyard trio, by Islay M. Donaldson, appeared in the correspondence columns of *The Scotsman*, 2/8/78. See also "The Kailyard Revisited" by Eric Anderson in *Nineteenth Century Scottish Fiction*, ed. Ian Campbell, and Ian Campbell, *Kailyard: A New Assessment*.

10. David Craig, p. 269.

11. Walt Whitman, "Song of Myself", *Leaves of Grass*.

12. *The Scotsman*, 10/4/64, correspondence columns.

13. Essay on Francis George Scott published in the *Scottish Educational Journal*, 11/9/25, and reprinted in Hugh MacDiarmid, *Contemporary Scottish Studies*, p. 33.

14. In contradicting this point of view, Hans Keller once sang a "melody" from a 12-tone work, in a broadcast programme of around 1960. While to some extent agreeing with the definition of melody which he thus implied – i.e. that element of music which the listener, after so many hearings, can himself sing or whistle – one must remember that Hans Keller is a very highly trained musician. The professional, and especially the creative, artist tends always to be at least a jump ahead, but it would seem that many Western composers of the last half-century have moved so far ahead that they have virtually lost touch with their listeners.

15. Hamish Henderson: interview, 10/12/76, Edinburgh.

16. Francis Collinson: conversations, Spring 1978, Edinburgh.

17. Some examples of this can be found in *Travellers' Songs from England and Scotland*, by Ewan MacColl and Peggy Seeger. (A further study of the Stewarts of Blairgowrie is in progress.) See also Chapter 6 below, for reference to the broadcast TV programme on the Stewarts of Blair, 24/9/80.

18. And the Scottish Farm Servants Union had not been founded until 1912; see *Essays in Scottish Labour History*, ed. Ian MacDougall, p. 90. Bothy songs contain some bitter complaints against bad employers and hard conditions of work, but give no hint of organised resistance.

19. See articles by Kenneth Logue and Norman Buchan in *The People's Past*, ed. Edward J. Cowan.

20. Geordie McIntyre: interview with Hamish Henderson in "Resurgimento", *New Edinburgh Review*, August 1973, p. 12.

21. In 1977 the song appeared in the *Big Red Songbook* compiled by Mal Collins, Dave Harker and Geoff White, with the tune wrongly labelled, p. 76; headed "Music: 'The White Cockade'", the tune given is none other than "Maryland".

22. *Homage to John MacLean*, ed. T.S. Law and Thurso Berwick, contains the words of this song and also the two poems referred to here.

23. Hamish Henderson: interview, 6/2/77, Edinburgh.

24. Gordon Donaldson, *Scotland: The Shaping of a Nation*, p. 22.

25. In *101 Scottish Songs*, ed. Norman Buchan. This and its successor, *The Scottish Folksinger*, ed. Buchan and Peter Hall, are invaluable collections. They also contain versions of other songs referred to here.

26. The Stone of Destiny – officially at least – was in time returned to Westminster.

27. Without adverting to William and Mary, or to the later William.
28. This also became part of the Festival "Fringe", which has many more events – often late night – than the official programme. See note 40.
29. Quoted in "Folk at the festival" by David Hamilton, in *New Edinburgh Review*, August–September 1971, pp. 34–7.
30. Norman Buchan: interview, 20/8/77. All the quotations from Norman Buchan in this chapter are from this interview.
31. Hamish Henderson: interview, 6/2/77, Edinburgh.
32. "Bowled over" refers to Hamish Henderson's comment in "Resurgimento"; see note 20.
33. See Chapter 4 for a comparison between this version and Alison McMorland's. Regarding the music transcription in this and the following three songs, see the opening pages of Chapter 4. For notes on scales and song headings, see pp. 91–2.
34. Interview, 11/2/77, Edinburgh, with Morris Blythman and Josh MacRae. The other quotations from Morris Blythman in this chapter are also from this interview.
35. Josh MacRae's death in 1977 was a great loss to the folk movement.
36. Josh MacRae: interview, 10/11/76, Strathmiglo, Fife.
37. Josh MacRae: interview 11/2/77, Edinburgh.
38. See the series of articles in issues of *Scottish Studies*: Herschel Gower, "Jeannie Robertson: Portrait of a Traditional Singer", 12 (1968), 113–26; Herschel Gower and James Porter, "Jeannie Robertson: The Child Ballads", "Jeannie Robertson: The 'Other' Ballads'", and "Jeannie Robertson: The Lyric Songs", 14 (1970), 35–58, 16 (1972), 139–59, 21 (1977), 55–103. Jeannie Robertson died in March 1975. The large crowd assembled for her funeral bore eloquent testimony to the affection and respect that she inspired. In 1968 she had been awarded the M.B.E.
39. In the *Scottish Tradition* series.
40. See Alistair Moffat's book *The Edinburgh Fringe*. On p. 20, the life span of the Edinburgh People's Festival is given as "two years" – in fact there were five of these yearly events, the first in 1951 and the last in 1955; ". . . but", continues Moffat, "its aims to popularise the Edinburgh Festival have been realised in the seventies with the enormous local response to the Fringe from all sections of the community."
41. "Why the Scots have taken to jazz so much more readily than any other part of Britain is obscure, but the fact is not in dispute: ever since the early and middle thirties they have provided by far the largest single contingent of good jazz musicians in these islands". Francis Newton, *The Jazz Scene*, p. 244.
42. Francis Newton, pp. 245–6.
43. It is possible that skiffle may have had a tenuous connection with the American "spasm" band tradition described by Marshall Stearns, *The Story of Jazz*, p. 171–2: ". . . rough-and-ready music on improved instruments . . . a sort of amateur tradition in which anyone who could hum a tune could and did participate".
44. "Skiffle is folk song with a jazz beat. In other words, it is the kind of music which has infiltrated American popular song". Oscar Brand, *The Ballad Mongers*, p. 55.
45. R. Denselow in *The Electric Muse*, by Dave Laing and others, p. 141.
46. A senior secondary school would be called a grammar school, south of the Border, and junior secondary would be secondary modern.
47. Twelve years later another concert was held in Glasgow's City Hall, for exactly the same cause. (This time, it was also the Buchans' typically large-hearted way of celebrating their Silver Wedding.)
48. Moyna Flanigan, Enoch Kent, Josh MacRae and Rena Swankey.

49. A recording of Ann Neilson singing "The Baron of Brackley" (with guitar accompaniment), made by Hamish Henderson in 1964, is one of 43 in *A Collection of Scots Songs*, in booklet form with music transcriptions, made for the School of Scottish Studies' Oral Literature and Popular Tradition I undergraduate course. This booklet and the corresponding *A Collection of Scottish Gaelic Songs* are not as yet available to the public. Tapes of all the songs, as sung by the informants quoted, are available to the students for listening and for study.

50. Robin Denselow, in *The Electric Muse*, p. 142.

51. See Vulliamy and Lee, *Pop Music in School*, pp. 5–6.

52. See Denisoff and Peterson, pp. 173–7.

53. Ewan MacColl's insistence, for a time, that singers should only sing material from their own country, also had an effect in this direction.

54. A note on this appears in *Scottish Studies* 2 (1958).

55. The long queue of mourners at Matt's funeral in Glasgow provided a tribute even more impressive than Norman Buchan's moving oration.

56. *Ding Dong Dollar* (Folkways FD 5444).

57. From disc booklet.

58. Morris Blythman; see note 34.

59. Josh MacRae: interview, 11/2/77, Edinburgh.

60. Perhaps especially some from the Southern States. Although the term "Yankee" originally referred to North Americans in the civil war, by popular usage it has become almost a synonym for the whole U.S. nation, especially in the realm of British-American polemics.

61. National Columbia Broadcasting.

62. American Forces Network.

63. Adam MacNaughton: interview, 6/11/76, Edinburgh.

64. Dr. Andrew Hunter: interview, 26/10/76, Edinburgh.

65. Peter Hall: interview, 9/11/76, Aberdeen.

66. Arthur Argo died in April 1981; his substantial contribution to folk music and the Revival has been widely recognised. He was the great-grandson of Gavin Greig.

67. John Watt: interview, 25/10/76, Milnathort, Fife.

Note on the booklet for *The Muckle Sangs* double album, Scottish Tradition series (TNGM 119/D):
The original booklet contained certain misleading features. A second edition, revised and enlarged, was therefore prepared by the School of Scottish Studies, published in 1979, and accompanied all albums subsequently sold. Copies of the revised booklet can be obtained from Topic Records Ltd., 50 Stroud Green Road, London N4 3EF.

IV   The Story of the Revival
Songs heard in the seventies

Bright is the ring of words
When the right man rings them,
Fair the fall of songs
When the singer sings them.
Still they are carolled and said –
On wings they are carried –
After the singer is dead
And the maker buried.

Robert Louis Stevenson.[1]

Dictionaries provide many different meanings of the word "story": the two which have seemed most apposite so far are "Facts or experiences which deserve narration", and "Past course of person's or institution's life". [2] The latter definition covers the previous two chapters of our story.

The end of the sixties showed an increasing number of discs – and also of TV and radio performances, although these still tended to be more of the smooth, "white heather" type than genuinely traditional in style. The steady consolidation of the trend towards Scottish material was most apparent in the festivals run by the T.M.S.A., which have been described as the quintessence of the best in the Scottish folk scene, but it also showed in the other festivals, in the ceilidh-concerts and to a lesser degree in the folk clubs. The main "facts and experiences" of our former definition consist now of the actual music heard; this chapter gives transcriptions of selected songs, with some commentary.

CHOICE OF SONGS
In choosing the songs to be presented, I listened to over fifty tapes. These had been recorded, in quantitive order, at the annual Blairgowrie/Kinross Festivals, 1970–78, at two big ceilidh-concerts in Edinburgh (the *Stampede* ceilidh at the Heriot Watt University, and the Sir Walter Scott bicentenary ceilidh in Edinburgh, both in 1971), at two of the annual Keith festivals which started in 1976, and at the Inverkeithing T.M.S.A. ceilidh, 1970. A few were recorded in the singers' homes. These tapes contained 680 items,

---

1.   See footnotes page 189.

mostly songs but including some 74 instrumental items and 10 of whistling and diddling. Of the songs, the words of 195 were transcribed wholly and another 50 partly, and the tunes of 268. The final choice of the 46 presented below, plus the 5 in the Appendix, total 51, was made firstly because certain songs are popular and frequently sung – 30 fall into this category, as classified by consultation with four regular festival attenders and also by my own experience in attending, recording and adjudicating at festivals – and secondly because the others are interesting and significant for reasons which will emerge. Of these 21, 10 are heard moderately often, 9 appear to have been sung in each case only, or mainly, by the one person or family (including 4 by the Stewarts of Blairgowrie), and the remaining 2 are heard occasionally.

THE SONGS

These have been divided into groups according to themes, or verbal content. The subject matter is often wide enough for the song to be included in more than one of the categories chosen, so the final classification was made according to what seemed to be the main theme of the song. Some of these are in post-war and earlier collections, usually with skeletal tunes only, and with many differences in both words and tune. The categories are:
1. *Love;* 2. *Rejected love;* 3. *Comedy and music-hall;* 4. *Feuds and war;* 5. *Sexual violence and seduction;* 6. *The pregnant woman in trouble;* 7. *Family pressure regarding marriage;* 8. *Political, social comment and work;* 9. *Sexual symbolism;* 10. *Night-visiting;* 11. *Elegiac;* 12. *Exile and emigration;* 13. *Wanderer's songs;* 14. *The supernatural;* 15. *Philosophical or survival.*

Bothy songs or ballads are not included here as a separate category. Bothy was the name given to the out-houses in which the unmarried male labours were quartered – particularly in the East, northwards from Kincardineshire – in farms before and after the turn of this century. Isolated as they were in country districts, these men had to rely on themselves for entertainment in the evenings after the long day's labour was over: hence the name for the songs with which they lightened these brief times of leisure, along with stories and general social intercourse. Many of these songs recount work and life in the farms, and in the feeing fairs where the men would agree to work for a spell of time with a farmer; examples of these songs are "The Barnyards of Delgaty" (once immensely popular in the Revival but less often heard now), "The hairst o' Rettie", "The hash o' Benegoak", "Sleepy toon", "The muckin' o' Geordie's byre", "The weddin' o' MacGuiness and his cross-eyed pet", "McGinty's meal and ale when the pig gaed on the spree" and "He widna wint his gruel". Versions of the last seven of these appeared on the tapes listened to but the last named is the only one transcribed on these pages (see Appendix I). Interested readers are referred to the definitive disc on *Bothy Ballads*, with its booklet by Hamish Henderson on the songs (with their printed words) and on the background to this way of life. [3]

But this applies only to the stricter definition of bothy songs. John Ord, in the preface to his collection *Bothy Songs and Ballads*, states roundly that "Bothy-song is just another name for folk-song", and not a few of the songs given below, or versions of them, appear in his book.

THE SONGS: Assessment of popularity

Popular

★ The echo mocks the corncrake
I'll lay ye doon, love
The band o' shearers

O gin I were a baron's heir
Johnnie lad
★ Johnnie, my man
Barbara Allan
I once loved a lad
Hannah, loving Hannah
★ He widna wint his gruel
★ Willie Macintosh
The bonny hoose o' Airlie
The laird o' the Dainty doon-bye
★ The banks o' red roses

The cruel mither
Bogie's bonny Belle
Corachree
The Magdalen Green
The dowie dens o' Yarrow
Sic a parcel o' rogues
If it wasnae for the unions
The Fairfield apprentice
The Berryfields o' Blair
I must away, love
The laird o' Udny's wa's
The college boy
The trees they do grow high
Rare Willie's drooned in Yarrow
Jamie Raeburn
Tramps and hawkers

Moderately Popular

Huntingtower
Willie's lyke-wake
Eppie Morrie
'Twas in the month o' January
Andrew Lammie

What can a young lassie dae wi'
   an auld man?
The sprig o' thyme
She was a rum one
The moving on song
Willie's fatal visit

Heard occasionally

The beggar laddie
Skippin' barfit through the heather

★   These five songs are in Appendix I

Sung mainly by one person or family

Betsy Bell
Here's a health to all true lovers } Belle Stewart

My bold chailin donn
When Micky comes home } Sheila MacGregor

Ma laddie's bedside: Duncan Williamson
The belt wi' colours three: Alison McMorland

The 3 Craws, with added verses
If ye only wait a wee } Adam Young

Oh Mither, Mither: Sheila Douglas (now being sung by others see n. 8)

From the above 51, 5 are *new songs, i.e. written within the last 50 years:*

The berryfields o' Blair, by Belle Stewart; The moving on song, by Ewan MacColl; If it wasnae for the Union, by Matt McGinn; The Fairfield apprentice, by Archie Fisher and Bobby Campbell; Oh Mither, Mither, by Sheila Douglas.

These categories are not hard and fast, for the popularity of most songs may wax or wane over a period of much less than ten years. The list gives an approximate assessment of popularity of the songs chosen and refers to a period of at least several years *during* the seventies, not necessarily at the time of writing.

In his chapter on "The Theme of Fertility", in *The Everlasting Circle,* James Reeves points out that folk song has its roots in a form of society, now archaic, in which natural fertility was of paramount importance. "A society which lives by manufacture and commerce is apt to forget its roots in the activities of the soil; the fertility of crops and herds is of no pressing concern. Human fertility alone becomes important. A city community, a town-dwelling and largely middle-class society . . . takes human fertility for granted, and may even regard it as an inconvenience. . . . To read the conditions of today into the past, then, is to miss the point and purpose of folk song: to say many folk songs have to do with sex is only a half-truth". This is pertinent to a large proportion of songs transcribed here. Although "the conditions of today" cannot influence the content of traditional songs, they do however influence the kind of songs that people choose to sing.

"REVIVAL" OR "SOURCE" SINGERS: (Singers appearing in the Appendix are included)

It seemed worthwhile, in the present context, to attempt a classification along these lines. The late Jimmy MacBeath was clearly a source singer (he is included in the Appendix because his version of "He widna wint his gruel", recorded in 1960, was the model for the other three given.) Yet the distinction is becoming less meaningful with each decade. Out of the total of 46, 12 are source singers: of these, 7 are of traveller stock, 4 are aged between 58 and 83 years, and Jimmy MacBeath died in 1972. Stanley Robertson's son Anthony, aged 18, learned most of his songs from his father and grandfather, and from his great-aunt Jeannie Robertson: the travellers still have a close-knit family circle and pass on their lore orally. But after close on thirty years of the revival, one can now see the time approaching when all singers in this genre will just be singers, of folk or traditional songs in the widest sense. All the 45 living singers represented here were asked, "Do you think you are a 'revival' singer or a 'source' singer, and why?": the two terms were deliberately left undefined in order that "why?" might elicit the singers' own definitions. These definitions were fairly clear-cut.

Singers were "revival" if they had learned most of their songs from recorded or printed sources, from other revival singers or from source singers (several stressed the latter), and "source" if the songs had been handed down in the oral tradition, or learned in childhood. But the categories are not clear-cut. Not a few revival singers have source elements in their backgrounds, while many source singers make use of the written word – both in giving copies to other singers, and in obtaining copies of words to add to their own repertoires. Within these reservations, it can be said that 19 of the 46 singers are self-defined "revival", 12 are "probably revival" (including 5 who said "neither – (just) a singer", or words to that effect, but who had told me enough about themselves to justify this modified pigeon-holing), 12 are "source" singers, and 3 are "both". As a confirmed non-purist, I found the "(just) a singer" answers strangely cheering, (1) as pointing the way ahead to post-revival times which we can only begin to envisage, and (2) as helping to kill the last traces of any kind of élitism, inverted or otherwise. Of these 5 answers, Maddy Taylor's was perhaps the most thought-provoking: "*I don't think about it at all. These categories divide us, don't you think? Can't we just be 'singers' and enjoy the music?*" (My italics).

Contradictions abound. One of the most curious concerns literacy: with very few exceptions all singers now consult books and use pen and paper, and I have not come across a single verbally illiterate singer in Scotland, at least amongst those involved in the revival scene. Yet although verbal literacy is now accepted, musical literacy is very rare and is often eschewed by choice. If Jean Redpath wants to learn a new tune she plays and re-plays a recording of it – she says she gets the feel of it better than if she had read the tune from notation.

The singers were also asked why they liked the song in question, what they felt was its theme or "message" (deep waters, here), and any connection between its words and their own experiences in life. (The importance of the singers' own views, especially as regards the meaning of any song they choose to sing, cannot be too strongly emphasized: not nearly enough attention and humble enquiry has been directed towards this). Few of the singers found any connection with their own experience and most gave thoughtful answers to the other two questions; two replies (to single questions) were humorous, one possibly tongue-in-cheek, two "no message", one "don't know", and four had no answer. Many comments by singers will be found in the notes on the songs.

NOTES ON THE MUSIC TRANSCRIPTIONS

These transcriptions are descriptive, not prescriptive[4], and are, with a single exception in this chapter, of one verse of one singer's performance on one occasion. It must be emphasized not only that another singer's version of the song would be likely to differ in various respects, but also that the same singer might possibly sing the same song differently on another occasion. It was decided, with a very few exceptions, not to include variants of the tune in other verses of the same song, although occasionally small notes, in alignment where possible with the larger notes, and distinguishable from ornament notes, show the shape of the tune in other verses. Instead, a transcription of one song, "The belt wi' colours three", has been given in full for all 6 verses. Few singers vary the tune for different verses quite so freely and with such fluidity as Alison McMorland does here, but this example shows how the tune is adapted to fit different words and moods, and how such variants can and often do work out.

There are broadly three kinds of transcriptions of tunes. First, the skeletal type, exemplified by the majority of Bronson's *Traditional Tunes of the Child Ballads*, vols. 1–3[5], and by most collections of folk songs. These are the bare bones which the traditional singer knows how to cover with the flesh and blood of his or her own singing style. Second, at the other extreme, are exact transcriptions which show every nuance of grace-notes, plosives, sung consonants, detailed time-values, etc. These are inordinately time-consuming to make and are also very hard to read, even for an experienced musician, so they are of value only for purposes of comparison. Examples of this kind can be found in *Scottish Studies* and in the *Journal of the Folk Song Society*.[6] Third, there is the compromise type, which we have below: most of the ornaments are given, and the main changes in time structures.

Occasionally, as in "The belt wi' colours three", there is no time signature – this song is unusually free both rythmically and metrically – but in general a time signature is given, if only as the basic pulse-and-accent structure from which the singer may depart. Some structure of this kind is usually connected with the metrical nature of the words.

These transcriptions represent an attempt, aided by some verbal description, to give an idea of the singer's style: very necessary, especially for those readers who are unfamiliar with traditional singing.

There is no single "correct" version of a song – as was said of the legendary Mrs. Harris, there's no sich a person. But there may be a single model. There are to begin with versions which are more traditional, usually because they are older and have stood the test of time, have satisfied countless people through the ages, while other versions have been thrown on the scrap heap of experience. Then there are versions which one 'ikes better, for personal reasons; one would choose such versions to sing oneself. This is an unavoidably subjective area.

Any fears that what is given here may be copied exactly by singers and so "mummified" are groundless: tradition is far too robust a creature to be threatened by this. Realistic transcriptions in print may even reach, and awaken interest in, some people hitherto unexposed to this music, and so provide an impetus for them to listen to the thing. This is what should and must be urged (for transcriptions are at best *faute de mieux*, bound by the limitations of a book). The reader should try to hear the songs, either in disc form (which has its limitations, for every re-play gives exactly the same performance) or – much, much better – should hear them live, at ceilidhs, festivals, folk concerts or clubs.

But some imitation, whether from the printed page or from recorded or live singing, is inevitable, and there is nothing wrong with this in its place. Not only is emulation the sincerest form of flattery, but all creative artists and performers learn something by copying others until they eventually find their own style. This obtains also in art music. In the seventeenth and eighteenth centuries it was the convention for art-singers and instrumentalists to insert their own ornaments, since they were already familiar with these in the Baroque and Classical period styles, and this practice has been revived within the last twenty years or so (e.g. in the works of Bach and Mozart, to name only two.) But the drawback to so many past collections of folk music is that people who studied them did not know the style or styles in which they should be performed, *because they had never actually heard this music*. And such ornaments as were included in print were often misleading, because placed there by persons who for varying reasons were not faithful to the traditional style.

As to the modes, I decided not to attempt classification of the tunes in this way – "attempt", because this whole subject has been much debated in recent years and there is now too much shifting ground to step with any surety.[7] For one thing, we often find that different parts of the same tune may be in different modes, so there is little point in ascribing the tune as a whole to one mode, or a choice of modes. But the scales are given, showing notes which occur in the the tune: first in the same key as the transcription, and then – for purposes of comparison – transposed so that the tonic or home note is on C. Small notes in the scales are those which appear only as grace-notes.

The sharps or flats in key signatures are given only for those notes which occur in the melody concerned. An "inflected" note can best be explained by exemplifying: in "Skippin' barfit through the heather", both chapter 3 and chapter 4 versions, the F more often than not is an F natural as indicated by the key signature, which in this case is: no sharps or flats. But at a certain part of the tune an F sharp appears in every verse, therefore F is described as an inflected note. Inflexion can also occur by the note concerned being flattened, instead of sharpened, by a semitone. *Transcriptions made from recordings by male singers appear an octave higher than the actual sound would be.*

Uncertain intonation sometimes appears and this is indicated by a downward or upward arrow above the note, which means that the sound is slightly flatter or sharper that the note given, but is nearer to it than to the note a semitone below or above. A line drawn slantingly before or after a note indicates a slide. Other signs are confined to those in common musical usage: the stress mark, a short horizontal line above or below a note, implying slight lingering, and the stronger accent mark > , are shown. The marks < and >, denoting variation in dynamics, are not given: they are usually omitted except in the very detailed type of transcription. This does not mean that there is no variation in volume, for some singers make considerable use of this, others less. But such variation is subtly different from that of the art singer, and is generally smaller and less frequent. The pitch of each performance is also omitted – it seems hardly important enough: the key chosen is for simplicity in reading, and in order to avoid leger lines where possible. The old convention, of separating the stalks of quavers and semi-quavers which go with different syllables, has not been adhered to. It is easier to follow the shape and the rhythm of the tune when these are left joined, and slur

marks show the notes which are "set" to a single syllable. The sign
(ǝ) denotes an extra syllable which is produced in the singing if
certain words, e.g. chai-r (ǝ) m-box instead of chairm-box. A cross
for a note-head indicates partial speaking or shouting instead of
singing, with pitch only roughly approximate.

The more complex transcriptions are followed by a skeleton
melody. Unless otherwise stated, when there is a chorus it is sung
after each verse and to the same tune; if at the beginning of the
song as well, it is placed before v.1.

In the song headings, the name preceding the song title is that of
the singer; underneath is the place, the year, the recorder's initials
and the tape number. The recordings were made by Peter Cooke,
Hamish Henderson, Fred Kent, Ailie Munro, Allan Palmer, Ian
Paterson, James Porter, Stephanie Smith, and Linda Williamson.
SA tapes are from the archives of the School of Scottish Studies and
AM tapes are those recorded by Allan Palmer.

Group 1: LOVE

Allan Morris: *The Beggar laddie* (Child 280)
Kinross 1973; rec. P.C.   SA 1973/109.

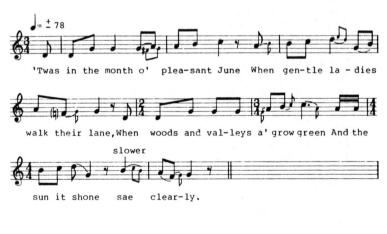

'Twas in the month o' plea-sant June   When gen-tle la - dies
walk their lane, When woods and val-leys a' grow green And the
sun it shone   sae   clear-ly.

(1) 'Twas in the month o' pleasant June
     When gentle ladies walk their lane,
     When woods and valleys a' grow green
     And the sun it shone sae clearly.

(2) Doon in yon grove I spied a swain
     A shepherd('s) sheep-club in his hand,
     He was driving yowes oot owre the knowes
     And he was a weel-faur'd laddie.

(3) "Come tell tae me what is yer trade
     Or by what airt ye win yer breid,
     Or by what airt ye win yer breid
     When herding ye give owre?"

(4) "Makin' spindles is ma trade
     And finding sticks in time o' need,
     For I'm a beggar tae ma trade
     So lassie could ye lo'e me?"

(5) "I could lo'e ye as manifold
     As Rachel loved Jacob of old,
     As Jesse lo'ed his cups o' gold,
     Ma laddie if ye'll believe me."

(6) And when they cam' tae yonder toon
     They bocht a loaf and they both sat doon,
     They bocht a loaf and both sat doon
     And the lassie ate wi' her laddie.

(7) But the lassie's courage began to fail,
     Her rosy cheeks grew wan an' pale
     And the tears came trinklin' doon like hail
     Or a heavy shooer in summer.

(8) "Oh gin I were on yon high hill
     Whaur ma faither's flocks do feed their fill,
     I wad sit me doon and greet a while
     For the followin' o' ma laddie."

(9) And when they came tae yon marble gate
     Sae boldly as he knocked there at;
     He rappit lood and he rappit late
     An he rappit there sae rudely.

(10) Then fower an' twenty gentlemen
     Cam oot tae welcome the beggar hame,
     And just as mony ladies gay
     Tae welcome the young knicht's lady.

(11)   His brother John stood next the wa'
           And he laughed till he was like tae fa';
           "Oh brother I wish'd we had beggit(s) a'
           For sic a bonny lassie."

(12)   "Yestreen I was the beggar's bride,
           This nicht I lie doon by his side.
           I've come to gweed by my misguide
           For noo I'm the young knicht's lady."

In introducing this at Kinross, Allan Morris outlined the theme: " . . .a lassie goes away with a laddie, and at the time she thinks he's a poor pauper and he turns out at the end to be a lord or a knicht . . .". He also gave the alternative title "The Beggar's Dawtie" as in John Ord's collection, and his version is closer to Ord than to any of those in Child. This version is in a Ewan MacColl disc, Riverside RLP 12 – 626 (A5): see Bronson, who adds, "MacColl has filled out his text, transmitted in fragmentary form by his mother, with lines from Greig and Keith, *Last Leaves*, 1925". Greig and Keith's last tune is similar to this but the two halves of the tune end differently and omit the flat seventh. Allan learned this version from the MacColl recording, in the late sixties or early seventies.

Allan Morris, a former pupil of Norman Buchan at Rutherglen Academy, considers himself more of a revival than a source singer. "Most of the songs I know have been learned from books, records, etc., not via the oral tradition as I understand it. I have only learned from recognised 'source' singers *on record*, e.g. Jane Turriff: 'Tifty's Annie'," ("Andrew Lammie", see later in this chapter.) "The message: be faithful to your real feelings and it will often 'pay off' in more than just emotional terms!"

Jimmy Hutchison: *I'll lay ye doon*
Kinross 1972; rec. A.M.   SA 1972/183.

(v.3) Though I've nae gowd nor gear tae of-fer, Nae sil-ver rings fer yer bon-ny hands, Oh my hairt is true and my airms are strang, love,

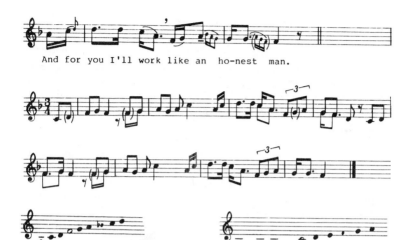

And for you I'll work like an ho-nest man.

(1) As I roved out one summer's evenin'
Doon by the banks o' the pleasant Don,
And as I gaed walkin' I could hear them talkin'
Saying, "Bollel he is a sorried man".

(Chorus)
Oh I'll lay ye doon, love, I'll treat you dacent
Oh I'll lay ye doon, love, I'll fill yer can,
Oh I'll lay ye doon, love, I'll treat ye dacent
For Bollel he is a sorried man.

(2) I'm bound away, my love tae leave ye
For tae cross the hills and the bonny sands,
But when I return then we'll get mairried
And tae you I'll prove an honest man.

(3) Though I've nae gowd nor gear tae offer,
Nae silver rings fer yer bonny hands,
Oh my hairt is true and my airms are strang, love,
And for you I'll work like an honest man.

In 1972, Jimmy Hutchison said in introducing it, " . . .this song's in danger of becoming the most over-sung song in the festival . . .". It is still immensely popular, but Jimmy's singing of it is always something special. Born in South Uist, he lived there until the age of eleven, so that Gaelic was one of his two mother-tongues and he heard Gaelic song from his earliest infancy. Although he has not lived in Gaelic-speaking parts since then, and does not sing Gaelic songs, it needs no stretch of aural imagination to perceive that something of this style of singing has percolated into his own, and remains there still. It is lighter than the Scots, although no less deeply inbued with feeling: less earth-bound, almost floating, with very delicate, fleeting ornamentation, and with an added something which one can only describe as a kind of tenderness. This is only one element of his style, for he is probably more Scots than Gaelic now, but it's an important element.

The story behind this song, as far as it has been possible to unravel the skeins, illustrates both the problems and the fascination of oral transmission. Jimmy Hutchison first heard it in London in the mid-sixties, sung by Enoch Kent who said that he had it as one verse and a chorus from Jeannie Robertson. Enoch added two more verses of his own and these are in *The Scottish Folksinger* version, the tune of which is basically the same but which Jimmy has rounded out beautifully.

But the first verse and the chorus, also attributed there to Jeannie Robertson who it seems was the first to make the song known in the Revival, are different from Jeannie's original verse and chorus, (which she changed herself as time when on.) In a recording in the School of Scottish Studies, made by Hamish Henderson in 1954, Jeannie sings the chorus as given above except for the ending :– " . . . a solid man". In this recording she sings only the second half of v. 1, as follows :–

> When we're out walking, the people's talking,
> "There goes Bolerrol, he's a solid man."

In her disc *Jeannie's Merry Muse* (EMI 7EG 8534), made five years later in 1959, the chorus and the second half of v.1 are similar, except that "dacent" has now become "decent", but she has added as the first half of verse 1:

> As I strolled out on a summer's evening,
> Down by the waters of the pleasant Bann.

It transpires that Hamish Henderson himself had thought up these two lines and suggested them to Jeannie, to complete the four lines which are needed to fit the tune. He chose the river Bann (one of the chief rivers in Northern Ireland, which features in many songs) partly because it rhymed with "man", and partly because it fitted in with his conviction that the fragment was descended from an Irish song, a nineteenth century music-hall ditty called "Muldoon the solid man."

Irish ancestry is also suggested by the word "dacent" in Jeannies's original version. Stanley Robertson, Jeannie's nephew, sings the fourth line of v. 1 as "There goes Bold Errol, he's an honest man", and the fourth line of the chorus as "For Bold Errol he is an honest man" – another pointer to Irish origin, since Errol is an Irish name.

And finally, "Muldoon the solid Man": neither the National Library of Scotland nor Trinity College Library, Dublin, could find any trace of it. However, in 1954 Hamish Henderson had recorded two travellers, both singing a single verse of this song, after being asked specifically for "Muldoon the solid Man": Nellie McGregor of Aberdeen, and Davie White. Both were rollicking drinking verses, with similar words though different tunes, and "I'll fill your can" in both clearly meant the offer of a drink, with no sexual meaning. But Davie's not only had the same tune as "I'll lay ye doon, love", he also ended the verse "And I'll go drunk like a solid man." The letters 'l' and 'r' are very easily confused (I always thought Jimmy sang "solid" until he wrote it for me), and some languages can't distinguish between them – hence "sorried", for there is no such word.

Jimmy Hutchison, who has been recorded by BBC records, wrote verses 2 and 3 of this version himself. He says Owen Hand and possibly Dominic Behan also wrote verses of their own.

Norman Stewart: *Band o' shearers*
Kinross 1973; rec. A.M.   SA 1973/113.

Bon-nie las-sie, will ye gang And shear wi' me the hale day lang? Love will cheer us as we gang To join yon band o' shea-rers.

(*Chorus*)
Bonnie lassie, will ye gang
And shear wi' me the hale day lang?
Love will cheer us as we gang
To join yon band o' shearers.

(1)   Until the weather it be hot
I'll cast ma waistcoat an' my coat;
I'll shear wi' you amang the lot
When we join yon band o' shearers.

(2)   Until the thistle it be strang,
Until it chaps your milk-white hand,
It's wi' ma heuch I'll cut it off
When we join yon band o' shearers.

(3)   Aye and if the weather it be fine
They'll say there's love twixt you and I,
But we'll shyly pass yin anither by
When we join you band o' shearers.

(4)   And when the shearin' it's a' duin
We'll hae some rantin', roarin' fun,
We'll hae the rantin', roarin' fun
An' forget the toils o' the shearin'.

Norman Stewart is of Lewis descent, on his father's side, and he can speak Gaelic although not fluently. Part of his childhood was spent in Tain and he was strongly influenced by Gaelic ornamental psalm-singing in the Free Church there: one of the precentors was from Skye. The Gaelic style of singing is again unmistakable.

A version of these words, with no tune, is in Ord's *Bothy Ballads*; the introduction describes it as a harvest song which "is one of the oldest and best of its kind" and "was known in every county of Scotland". It was heard frequently during the seventies.

Tricia Johnstone: *Huntingtower* (Appendix to Child 232, as *The Duke of Atholl*)
Kinross 1975; rec. A.P.   AM2.

Oh   when ye gang a-wa' Jamie, Faur a-cross the sea lad-die, Oh

when ye gang tae Ger - ma-nie What will ye bring tae me lad-die?

(1) Oh when ye gang awa Jamie,
     Faur across the sea laddie,
     Oh when ye gang tae Germanie
     What will ye bring tae me laddie?

(2) I'll bring ye a braw new goon Jeannie,
     I'll bring ye a braw new goon lassie,
     And it shall be o' silk an' gowd
     Wi' Valencienne(s) lace a' roon' lassie.

(3) Oh that's nae gift ava Jamie,
     That wadnae dae at a' laddie,
     There's no a goon in a' the toon
     I'd wear when you're awa' laddie.

(4) When I come back again Jeannie,
     When I come back again lassie,
     I'll bring wi' me a gallant gay
     Tae be yer ain guidman lassie.

(5) Be ma guidman yersel Jamie,
     Be ma guidman yersel laddie,
     And tak' me wi' you tae Germanie
     Wi' you at hame tae dwell laddie.

(6) That wadnae dae at a' Jeannie,
     That wadna dae at a' lassie,
     For I've a wife and bairnies three
     An' I'm no sure ye'd 'gree lassie.

(7) Ye should 'a tellt me that in time Jamie,
     (Ye) should 'a tellt me that lang syne laddie,
     For had I kent o' your fause hairt
     Ye'd ne'er have gotten mine Jamie.

(8) Yer e'en were like a spell lassie,
     Yer e'en were like a spell lassie,
     That ilka day bewitched me sae
     I couldna help masel' lassie.

(9)   Gae back tae yer wife an' hame Jamie,
       Gae back tae yer bairnies three laddie,
       And I will pray that nane may thole
       A broken hairt like me laddie.

(10)   Oh dry yer tearful e'e Jeannie,
       Ma story's a' a lee lassie,
       For I have neither wife nor weans
       An' I'll wed nane but thee lassie.

(11)   Think well for fear ye rue Jamie,
       Think well for fear ye rue laddie,
       For I have neither gowd nor land
       Tae be a match for you laddie.

(12)   Oh Blair an' Atholl's mine Jeanie,
       Little Dunkeld is mine lassie,
       Saint Johnston's Tower and Huntingtower
       And a' that's mine is thine lassie.

This is a powerful, gripping performance. Tricia Johnstone, from Glagow, has a strong voice which contains very little vibrato. In 8 out of the 12 verses here the second line repeats the words of the first line, and the singer soars up the octave leap with a dramatic deliberation which impressively heightens this emphasis.

Tricia learned this in childhood, from her father's singing: "I was brought up in a background of Irish and Scots songs . . . I'm most interested in (these) songs as I feel they are 'my' history and portray the feelings and events which relate to my background. I am grateful to the 'revivalists'. As I don't read music, hearing the singing, live, on tape or record brought many 'poems' to life for me . . . I like 'answer' songs. I can't be analytical about the songs as I find I respond to music and particularly songs emotionally . . . A theme which occurs again and again in folk-song, where the girl is in love, the man tests her love then reveals he is rich enough for both of them!"

In succeeding verses, the first half of bars 1–3 is often sung at twice the given speed. The song is in very free time with some pauses during or more often at the end of the line. The declamatory, free style does not result in loss of basic time structure: one feels this was originally four-beat, and the pauses at the end of each verse line fit the uncertain, tentative nature of much of the dialogue. It is sometimes sung by a man and woman taking alternative verses – Belle Stewart and Willie McKenzie have done this very effectively.

John Barrow: *O gin I were a baron's heir*
Kinross 1975; rec. A.P.   AM1.

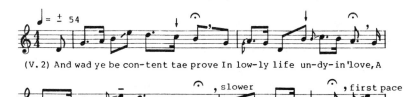

(V. 2) And wad ye be con-tent tae prove In low-ly life un-dy-in'love, A

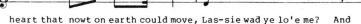

heart that nowt on ear th could move, Las-sie wad ye lo'e me?   And

ere   the lav'-rock wings the day Oh wad ye tae the for-est hie And

work wi' me right mer-ri-ly, Las-sie wad ye lo'e me?

(1)   Oh gin I were a baron's heir
       And could I braid wi' gems your hair
       And mak' ye braw as ye are fair,
       Lassie wad ye lo'e me?
       And gin I tak' ye tae yon toon
       And show ye braw sichts mony an ane
       And busk ye fine in silken goon,
       Lassie wad ye lo'e me?

(2)   And wad ye be content tae prove
       In lowly life undyin' love,
       A heart that nowt on earth could move,
       Lassie wad ye lo'e me?
       And ere the laverock wings the day
       Oh wad ye tae the forest hie
       And work wi' me right merrily,
       Lassie wad ye lo'e me?

(3)   And ere the moonlight glances o'er
       Oor wee bit bield and heathery moor,
       Will ye no greet that we're sae poor,
       Lassie wad ye lo'e me?
       For I hae nowt tae offer ye,
       Nae gowd frae mint, nae pearl frae sea,
       Nor dae I come o' high degree,
       Lassie but I lo'e ye!

John Barow's Tyneside origins show in his use of "nowt", twice, in preference to the more Scots term "nought" or "nocht", but he has lived in Edinburgh for the last fourteen years, including four years as a student, and says this period has been the most important as regards music. His deep voice and the unpretentious warmth of delivery of each song in his considerable repertoire are well-known to club members and festival goers. In common with many other singers represented here, he has devoted much time and hard work to the folk music movement, and at the time of writing he has been Director for the first four years of the highly successful Edinburgh Folk Festival.

John Barrow was initially attracted to the tune of this song, although he likes the words too. He sees it as a straight love song, and adds: "I have an impression of a bothy song, although verse 2 implies the man is a forester or wood-cutter . . . But I don't see the lass humping timber! Perhaps charcoal burning?" He learned the song from the text of Maver's *Collection of Genuine Scottish Melodies,* and first heard it sung by Tom Ward in the early seventies.

Vic Smith: *Johnnie lad*
Kinross 1973; rec. A.M.   SA 1973/112.

(V.2) When the sheep are in the fold and the cows are in the byre And a' the lads an' lassies sittin' round a roarin' fire,

There is me a like-ly las-sie, just as like that I was
Jin-kin' you ma John-nie lad-die, jin-kin' you ma John-nie

mad, Through the nooks an' bar - ley stooks jin - kin'
lad, Through the nooks an' bar - ley stooks jin - kin'

you, John - nie lad.
you, John - nie lad.

(1) Oh there is a handsome laddie, he lives down on yonder lea
And he's lookin' and he's jukin' and he's aye watchin' me;
Oh he's teasin' me an squeezin' me but his meanin's not sae bad,
If it's ever going to be tell me now Johnnie lad.

Tell me now me Johnnie laddie, tell me now me Johnnie lad,
If it's ever going to be tell me now Johnnie lad.

(2) When the sheep are in the fold and the cows are in the byre
And a' the lads an' lassies sittin' round a roarin' fire,
There is me a likely lassie, just as like that I was mad,
Through the nooks an' barley stooks jinkin' you, Johnnie lad.

Jinkin' you ma Johnnie laddie, jinkin' you ma Johnnie lad,
Through the nooks an' barley stooks jinkin' you, Johnnie lad.

(3) Oh Johnnie is blythe an' bonny, he's the pride o' a' yon lea,
And I love him best of ony though he's always teasin' me,
Oh he's teasin' me an' squeezin' me an ticklin' me like mad,
None comes near me that can cheer me like my own Johnnie lad.

Oh it's you ma Johnnie laddie, oh it's you ma Johnnie lad,
None comes near me that can cheer me like my own Johnnie lad.

(4) Oh Johnnie is not a gentleman nor yet is he a lord
But I would follow Johnnie lad although he were a card,
Oh Johnnie he is a bonny lad, he was once a lad o' mine
And I've never had a better lad though I've had twenty-nine.

Oh it's you ma Johnnie laddie and wi' you ma Johnnie lad,
I wad dance the buckles off ma shoes wi' you (ma) Johnnie lad.
Oh it's you ma Johnnie laddie and wi' you ma Johnnie lad,
I wad dance the buckles off ma shoes wi' you (ma) Johnnie lad.

This charming song, with its jig-like tune, is sung in a suitably lively, dance-like manner. Vic Smith comes from Edinburgh but has lived mostly in Sussex. He learned this from a student who in turn had discovered it in Aberdeen, in the library of Marischal College at the University. The upward leap of a ninth at the end of the first line suggests the possibility that the tune was more instrumental than vocal in origin, but the singer here takes the interval in his stride and with apparent ease.

A similar version appears in MacColl's *Personal Choice*, but the two halves of the tune there both finish on the tonic, i.e. the ending reserved in our version for the final cadence; the mid-cadence above, in effect on the "double tonic" (its dominant note) adds more drama and interest. Of the words, only the last verse shows any resemblance to Ord's version which is subtitled "A nursery Song". A more similar version to Vic Smith's words, with no tune, may be found in Ford.

Vic's first interest in folk song was stirred by his grandmother, from Aberdeenshire, who "sang a few songs and diddled"; but he has been totally involved in the Revival for the past twelve years or so. "I knew as soon as I had heard a couple of lines sung that I wanted to learn this song", he says. "The words seem to complement the tune perfectly. I love saying to people that I'm going to sing 'Johnnie lad' and seeing their faces fall as they expect the totally banal, up-tempo popular version, and then seeing their interest rise as they realise they've in fact got an interesting song to listen to! . . . The theme is 'uncertainty in love', which is surely universal."

Vic Smith has been recorded by Eron.

Sheila MacGregor: *My bold chailin donn*
Kinross 1972; rec. P.C.   SA 1972/188.

(V. 2) Oh ma - ny's the pro-mise he gives me When he comes e - ve - ry

Sun - day to me, And what can I do but be-lieve him When he whis-pers,"A chuis-le mo-chridh"? For his heart is so truth-ful and ten-der And his bright rol-ling eyes of dark brown, And I am sure e-ven a la-dy of splen-dour Would be charmed by my bold chai-lin donn.

(1) Oh my true love he dwells in the mountain
Like a war eagle fearless and free,
By the banks of a low-tuning fountain
That wanders through Wydan Lee;
For his heart and his soul have more honour
Than a king with his palace an' crown.
Like the blood of the race of O'Connor
Fills the veins of my bold chailin donn.

(2) Oh many's the promise he gives me
When he comes every Sunday to me,
And what can I do but believe him
When he whispers, "A chuisle mochridh"?
For his heart is so truthful and tender
And his bright rolling eyes of dark brown,
And I am sure even a lady of splendour
Would be charmed by my bold chailin donn.

(3) My father has riches in plenty
And suitors for me in his eye,
But oh come the time when I'm twenty
If I don't wish them all the good-bye!

> For I sigh for a night in the mountains
> Far away from the dust of the town,
> By the banks of the low-tuning fountains
> To the arms of my bold chailin donn.

Along with other members of the great singing family, the traveller Stewarts of Blairgowrie, Sheila MacGregor (daughter of Belle Stewart) has a superlatively flowing style with no breaks between the different gradations of her vocal range, with some sliding, fine phrasing and clear enunciation – a kind of traditional *bel canto* art. She had been actively involved in traditional singing since 1954. The Stewarts got this Irish song from a friend who lives near them: Flora Beaton, a native Gaelic speaker from Lewis. Yet the Gaelic words it contains are of Irish and not Scottish Gaelic origin. "Bold chailin donn" (pronounced "chollion down") was probably originally the Irish "buachaillin donn", which means brown-haired laddie and thus fits the context, whereas "chailin donn", means brownhaired maiden. "A chuisle mochridh" (pronounced "a cooshla mochree") means vein of my heart, a common poetic image for "beloved". Sheila MacGregor has been recorded by Tangent and by Topic.

See Appendix for "The echo mocks the corncake" and "Johnnie my man", two more songs in this group.

Group 2: REJECTED LOVE

Jean Redpath: *Barbara Allen* (Child 84)
Scott Ceilidh, Edinburgh 1971; rec. F.K.   SA 1971/192.

VV.5-7 end:

(1) I fell in love with a nice young girl,
     Her name was Barbary Allen;
     I fell in love with a nice young girl
     And her name was Barbary Allen.

(2) Till I fell sick and very ill,
     I sent for Barbary Allen;
     Till I fell sick and very ill,
     An' I sent for Barbary Allen.

(3) She pu'ed the curtains roon' my bed
     And said, "Young man ye're dyin'";
     She pu'ed the curtains roon' my bed
     And said, "Young man you are dyin'".

(4) "A kiss o' you wad dae me guid,
     A kiss o' you wad cure me".
     "But a kiss o' me ye ne'er shall hae
     Though your poor hairt were a-breakin'".

(5) "It's look ye up at my bed-heid
     And see what you'll find hangin':
     A silver watch an' a guinea-gold chain
     That hangs there for Barbary Allen,
     That hangs there for Barbary Allen".

(6) She hidnae gaen a mile or twa
     When she heard the death bells ringin',
     And every word they seemed to say,
     "Cruel-hairted Barbary Allen,
     Cruel-hairted Barbary Allen".

(7) "O mither dear do mak' my bed
     And mak' it saft an' narrow,
     For my true love has died for me
     And I'll die for him tomorrow,
     And I'll die for him tomorrow".

Although Child gives only 3 versions of the words of this very well-known ballad, Bronson gives no less than 200 tunes (not this one) as well as numerous sets of words. The gross disparity between the paucity of Child's harvest here and the plenitude of Bronson's underlines the danger of separating words from music.

Jean Redpath's ongoing tune is of form ABCD and thus contains no repetition except for the sequential nature of line 3 (bars 5 and 6). This makes the repeat of the fourth line in the last three verses more telling: starting on the lowest note in the tune, the leap upwards to the accented minor seventh strengthens the musical underlining of the repeated words.

It is interesting to note the increasing power and artistry of this brilliant singer over the years – in her 1977 televised series *Ballad Folk* (in which she introduced other singers, some of whom are featured here), in her discs, in her frequent live performances in Britain and the States, and in her recent work at Summer Schools as tutor and demonstrator in traditional song. Her true, clear voice, which has had no "training" apart from a few lessons on breathing, is of a kind which is acceptable to music-lovers of all kinds, and her style, which adapts to a wide and varied repertoire, is always unmistakably traditional.

Jean got this version from a tape of Jane Turriff's singing, recorded by Arthur Argo; Jane herself learned it in childhood, from her mother and grandmother. It has a second "legacy" verse which comes after v. 5 and is usually included by both Jean and Jane:

> It's look ye down at my bed-side
> And see what you'll find sittin':
> A basin full of my heart's tears
> That sits there for Barbary Allen.

Jean was attracted in the first place by this melody; she had been using the most commonly known, school-song-book tune until then. But she had a kind of gut reaction to the whole: "It's possibly a step down from the real heavy-weight ballads, the epic-tragic, stark spine-chillers. For every kind of hurt, and not only a hurt in your love-life, can be channelled into songs like this . . ."

Among the many discs of Jean Redpath's singing, an important American series should be mentioned: *The Songs of Robert Burns*. The original tunes are researched and arranged with instrumental and vocal accompaniment, by Serge Hovey (Philo 1037, 1048, 1071, 1072; further discs planned).

Caroline Carberry: *I once loved a lad*
Blairgowrie 1970; rec. P.C.   SA 1970/181.

(V.2) I saw my love tae the kirk go, Wi' bride an'bride mai-den they made a fine show; And I fol-lowed on wi' a hairt full o' woe, But noo he is wad tae a - no- ther.

(1) I once loved a lad, and I loved him sae weel
     I hated all others that spoke o' him ill,
     But noo he's rewarded me weel for my time
     For he's gaun tae be wad tae another.

(2) I saw my love tae the kirk go,
     Wi' bride an' bride-maiden they made a fine show;
     And I followed on wi' a hairt full o' woe,
     But noo he is wad tae another.

(3) I saw my love as he set doon tae dine,
     I stood at his elbow an' I poured oot the wine;
     An' I drank tae the laddie that should ha' been mine,
     For he's gaun tae be wad tae another.

(4) The men o' yon forest, they askit o' me,
     "How many strawberries grow in the saut sea?"
     I answered him back wi' a tear in my e'e,
     "How many ships sail in the forest?"

(5) Oh dig me a grave, an' dig it sae deep,
     An' cover it ower wi' flooers sae sweet
     That I may gaun in for tae tak' a lang sleep,
     An' maybe in time I'll forget him.

(6)   They dug me a grave, an' they dug it sae deep,
     An' covered it ower wi' flooers sae sweet;
     An' I'll lay doon for tae tak' a lang sleep
     An' I'm sure that in time I'll forget him.

This is sung in true elegiac vein, and in a strong voice used at times with a fittingly harsh edge to it. Caroline Carberry achieves no easy feat in employing a fluidity of time in her singing here without losing the time structure, especially at the slow tempo she has chosen. This song, now less often heard, can express a woman's or a man's feelings — "lad" becomes "lass", "he" is changed to "she", etc., (compare the version in Seeger and MacColl's influential collection *The Singing Island*, p. 31).

The flat seventh in bars 4 and 7 of the tune, followed by descending notes, seems to have a darkening effect. This may be comparable to the effect produced by flattening the third of the scale, which is to change a "brighter" major mode into a "darker" minor. (See also comment on blue notes, chapter 2.)

Riddles are an important element in popular story and song: correct answers are rewarded with a prize, but unsuccessful guesses with a penalty. The questions in v. 4 above bear some kinship to riddles, but no answers are offered — it is too late for the prize, and the penalty has already been exacted.

Duncan Williamson: *My laddie's bedside* or *The trees they are high* Lochgilphead 1976; rec. L.W.   SA 1976/65.

(V.2) Oh at my bed - side ma las - sie you'll no sit, At my bed-side ma las-sie you'll no sit, For I hae choosed a guide an' a far bet-ter fit, Be a - wa' las-sie, wha cares for ye?

(1)   Oh it's I am awa' tae ma laddie's bedside,
      I am awa' for tae be ma laddie's guide;
      I am awa' tae ma laddie's bedside
      Though his faither and mither be angry.

(2)   Oh at my bedside ma lassie you'll no sit,
      At my bedside ma lassie you'll no sit,
      For I hae choosed a guide an' a far better fit,
      Be awa' lassie, wha cares for ye?

(3)   Oh ye might have coorted one my love, ye might have coorted
      seven,
      You might have coorted eight, nine, ten or eleven;
      You could coort another one for tae mak' up the dozen,
      But be kind tae yer ain lass for a' that.

(4)   Oh come back ma bonny lassie, dinnae gang awa',
      Oh come back ma bonny lassie, dinnae gang awa',
      Oh come back ma bonny lassie, dinnae gang awa'
      I was only in the jest for tae try ye-O.

(5)   Oh if you were in the jest ma laddie, I was in nane,
      Oh lang lang ma bonny laddie may ye lie yer lane,
      Oh lang lang ma bonny laddie may ye lie yer lane
      And you'll weary lang before I come tae see ye again.

(6)   Oh the trees they are high ma love, the leaves they are green,
      The years are passing by ma love that you and I have seen;
      But the lang winter's nicht when ye have tae lie yer lane
      An' you'll weary lang before I come tae see ye again.

In this dialogue between a young couple, the man speaks at verses
2 and 4. Notice the difference between the reaction of the woman
here from that in "Huntingtower", to the man's lie or in this case
"jest" that he has another woman, which he uses as a test of her
love — "for tae try ye-O". Admittedly the words used by
Huntingtower's Jamie are less aggressive on the surface than those
in this song ("Be awa' lassie, wha cares for ye?") but the sudden
announcement of a wife and three children is one of extreme
violence. Our heroine in the present song is a woman of spirit who
takes a poor view of such a "test", even without the three bairns.

Duncan Williamson is of the travelling folk, until recently one of
the few who still live in the old-style tent supported by bent
boughs. He carries on the traditional work of his people and
sometimes moves around during the summer half of the year, with
his American wife and two young children.

Duncan sings with intensity and passion, but his style is more lyrical than dramatic. In his strong, resonant voice is heard a restrained and lovely vibrato, especially in his sustained notes. Tune and words are well delineated, with clear enunciation, persuasive phrasing and occasional sliding.

Duncan is quite sure that "the travellers have the only true version of this song". He first heard it from his father's sister, at Tarbert, Argyll, about 1942. Apart from his wife, Linda, I have not as yet heard anyone else sing it. He very often sings the last verse three times: as the opening verse, then again after verse 3 (at this point it will often end, "Be awa' laddie, wha cares for ye?"), and once more at the close. In verse 2, line 3, "a far better fit" means "more suitable". "He had chosen someone he thought was far superior to his own girl-friend in his mind," says Duncan. "But in case he was making a mistake and choosing the wrong one, he told his girl-friend it was only a joke — to keep her from falling out with him. So if he made a mistake he had always his own girl to fall back on".

A kind of cross-fertilisation is found in folk song and an example may be found in v. 6 above. It bears some resemblance to v. 1 of "The trees they do grow high" (see below), but even more to the first verse of the same song in Reeves's *The Everlasting Circle*.

Allan Morris: *Willie's lyke-wake* (*Amang the blue flooers and the yellow*) (Child 25)
Kinross 1973; rec. A.M.   SA 1973/111.

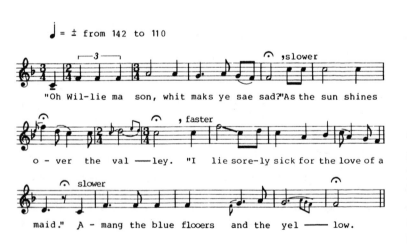

(1) "Oh Willie ma son, whit maks ye sae sad?"
    As the sun shines over the valley.
    "I lie sorely sick for the love of a maid."
    Amang the blue flooers and the yellow.

(The internal refrain is added in the same way to each verse)

(2) "Oh is she an heiress or lady fine,
    That she winna tak' nae pity on thee?"

(3) "Though a' yer kin were aboot yon bower,
    Ye shall no be a maiden one single hour.

(4) For a maid ye cam' here wi'oot a convoy,
    But ye shall return wi' a horse and a boy.

(5) Ye cam' here a maiden sae meek and sae mild,
    But ye shall gae hame a wedded wife wi' a child."

Allan Morris introduced this song in a not-too-serious vein: ". . . the story is roughly that a fellow's so much in love that he's lyin' on his death-bed . . . *gaspin'* . . . and his mother, who's got great pity for him, naturally, goes out and . . . *seizes* the young lady . . . brings her back . . . and nine months later she's able to go back home . . . wi' a baby". This explanation was necessary, since his version of the words is incomplete: it is Bronson's no. 2, with substantially the same tune converted here into triple time. Allan has since adopted one of the fuller versions, which tells the story of a trick to induce the girl to come alone to Willie's house: spurred on by their mother, his brothers bribe the bellman to play his "dead lyke-wake". Stricken with pity the girl, thinking he is dead, goes alone to his house; she is conducted to the "corpse" who proves he is very much alive when they're left together and who by varying methods persuades her to marry him. "The device of a lover's feigning death as a means of winning a shy mistress enjoys a considerable popularity in European ballads", (Child).

"I regard the song as a lesson in singlemindedness", says Allan; "i.e. you can always get what you want if you try hard enough, albeit using devious and dubious methods".

Alison McMorland: *The belt wi' colours three*
Kinross 1975; rec. A.P.   AM26.

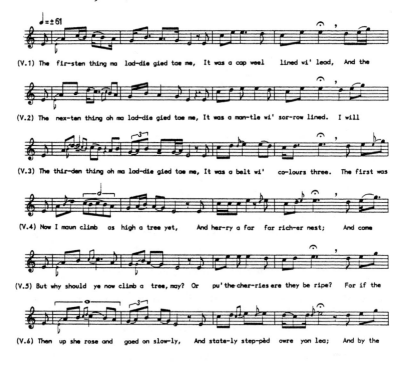

(V.1) The fir-sten thing ma lad-die gied tae me, It was a cap weel   lined wi' lead, And the

(V.2) The nex-ten thing oh ma lad-die gied tae me, It was a man-tle wi' sor-row lined. I will

(V.3) The thir-den thing oh ma lad-die gied tae me, It was a belt wi'   co-lours three. The first was

(V.4) Now I maun climb as high a tree yet,   And her-ry a far for rich-er nest;   And came

(V.5) But why should ye now climb a tree, may? Or   pu' the cher-ries ere they be ripe? For if the

(V.6) Then up she rose and   gaed on slow-ly, And state-ly step-pèd owre yon lea; And by the

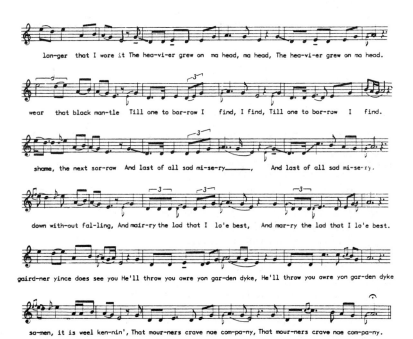

lon-ger that I wore it The hea-vi-er grew on ma head, ma head, The hea-vi-er grew on ma head.

wear that black man-tle Till one to bor-row I find, I find, Till one to bor-row I find.

shame, the next sor-row And last of all sad mi-se-ry_____, And last of all sad mi-se-ry.

down with-out fal-ling, And mair-ry the lad that I lo'e best, And mar-ry the lad that I lo'e best.

gaird-ner yince does see you He'll throw you owre yon gar-den dyke, He'll throw you owre yon gar-den dyke

sa-men, it is weel ken-nin', That mour-ners crave nae com-pa-ny, That mour-ners crave nae com-pa-ny.

Davie Stewart of Dundee: his tune of *The Dowie Dens of Yarrow*

(1)   The firsten thing ma laddie gied tae me,
      It was a cap weel lined wi' lead,
      And the langer that I wore it
      The heavier grew on ma head, ma head,
      The heavier grew on ma head.

(2)   The nexten thing oh ma laddie gied tae me,
      It was a mantle wi' sorrow lined.
      I will wear that black mantle
      Till one to borrow I find, I find,
      Till one to borrow I find.

(3)   The thirden thing oh ma laddie gied tae me,
      It was a belt wi' colours three.
      The first was shame, the next sorrow
      And last of all sad misery,
      And last of all sad misery.

(4)   Now I maun climb as high a tree yet,
      And herry a far far richer nest;
      And come down without falling,
      And mairry the lad that I lo'e best,
      And marry the lad that I lo'e best.

(5)   But why should ye now climb a tree, may?
      Or pu' the cherries ere they be ripe?
      For if the gairdner yince does see you
      He'll throw you owre yon garden dyke,
      He'll throw you owre yon garden dyke.

(6)   Then up she rose and gaed on slowly,
      And stately steppèd owre yon lea;
      And by the samen, it is weel kennin',
      That mourners crave nae company,
      That mourners crave nae company.

Alison MacMorland introduced this beautiful song to the folk
world, and so far seems to be the only person who sings it: it is the
title of one of her discs.[8] She adapted it from Christie's version in
Traditional Ballad Airs from the North of Scotland and has followed
his tune in the main, but she does not use the second strain, and
she ends the first strain differently. She said she was strongly
influenced throughout her shaping of the song by "the sweeping
feel" of old Davie Stewart's famous rendering of "The Dowie Dens
of Yarrow", in which he accompanies himself on melodion; his
tune for this, which closely resembles Alison's here, is given
underneath. Davie's performance of "The Dowie Dens" is truly

uninhibited, with an element of wild abandonment. It is included in the *Collection of Scots Songs* for undergraduate students of the School of Scottish Studies (see Chapter 3, note 49). These students tend either to love it or hate it, with no half measures — it's too strong meat for some. Alison says it's the one performance of a Scots song "which I can't hear without tears streaming down my face". Her style has also been influenced by Lucy Stewart of Fetterangus, whose "direct, minimal style" of singing greatly inspired her. It is perhaps a pity to alter Christie's version of the last two lines of verse 4 above: he has "And marry a lad I may lo'e best", which seems to make better sense. But this is debatable.

Alison's performance has "the sweeping feel" of Davie's plus her own very rich, spontaneous variation of the tune, but she eschews his wild abandonment (after all, "The Dowie Dens" is about the death of a best-beloved). She sings with a passionate restraint which matches the poetry and the dignity of the words.

Irene Riggs: *Hannah, loving Hannah*
Kinross 1977; rec. A.P.   AM10.

(1) I went to church last Sunday,
     My love she passed me by.
     I knew her heart was changing
     By the roving of her eye.

        By the roving of her eye,
        By the roving of her eye,
        I knew her heart was changing
        By the roving of her eye.

(2)   Oh Hannah, loving Hannah,
      Come give to me your hand.
      You said that if you married
      That I would be the man.

            That I would be the man,
            That I would be the man,
            You said that if you married
            That I would be the man.

(3)   My love she's pale and handsome,
      Her hands they're neat and small,
      And she is quite good-looking
      And that's the best of all.

            And that's the best of all,
            And that's the best of all,
            And she is quite good-looking
            And that's the best of all.

(4)   I'll go down to the water
      When everyone's asleep,
      And I'll think on my loving Hannah
      And then sit down and weep.

            And then sit down and weep,
            And then sit down and weep,
            I'll think on my loving Hannah
            And then sit down and weep.

(5)   (As v.1)

Irene Riggs comes from Kirkcaldy, and works in Fife. She picked up this song about eight years ago, "somewhere"; the source is forgotten, as so often in oral tradition. It is very popular in both clubs and festivals, in fact a man who frequents these described it as "one of the anthems of folk".

Sung here with simple artistry and in Irene's strong, clear voice, the tune is of form AA'BC — a form rich in dramatic possibilities. The first phrase or line is repeated but with a changed ending, and the following two different phrases, with some wide intervals, lead to an unexpected but fitting minor ending. Although a man's song it is sung here with total conviction by a woman – this practice has already been noted, for instance the reverse occurs in "Johnnie lad" above.

The same tune is used for the second half of each verse, which is a kind of refrain.

Irene says: "This is about a love affair gone wrong. Simply that. A rather sad man bemoaning his lost love. . . . I wonder if he really does something more serious than just 'go down to the river and weep'!"

Group 3: COMEDY AND MUSIC HALL

Sheila MacGregor: *When Micky comes home I get battered*
Scott Ceilidh, Edinburgh 1971; rec. F.K. SA 1971/191.

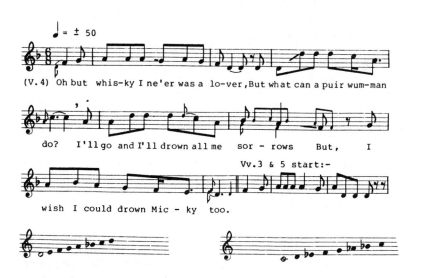

(V.4) Oh but whis-ky I ne'er was a lo-ver, But what can a puir wum-man

do? I'll go and I'll drown all me sor - rows But, I

Vv.3 & 5 start:-

wish I could drown Mic - ky too.

(1) Oh friends I have a sad story,
     A very sad story tae tell:
     I married a man for his money
     But he's worse that the devil himsel'.

(2) For when Micky comes home I get battered,
     He batters me all black and blue,
     And if I say a word I get scattered
     From the kitchen right ben to the room.

(3) So I'll go an' I'll get blue bleezin' blind drunk,
     Just to give Micky a warnin',
     And just for spite I will stay out all night
     And come rollin' home drunk in the mornin'.

(4) Oh but whisky I ne'er was a lover,
     But what can a puir wumman do?
     I'll go and I'll drown all me sorrows
     But, I wish I could drown Micky too.

(5) So I'll go an I'll get blue bleezin' blind drunk,
     Just to give Micky a warnin',
     And just for spite I will stay out all night
     And come rollin' home drunk in the mornin'.

Sheila MacGregor learned this song from her mother, Belle Stewart, who some thirty years ago heard an old ploughman sing it while tattie-lifting near Blairgowrie. His version started with v. 2 above . . . so Belle made up the first verse herself and inserted it, partly as an opening to the song and partly to provide a reason, a provocation, for the man battering his wife, viz. she'd married him for his money.

But in the repertoire of Alistair MacDonald, the T.V. folk-star, the song is simply about a battered wife, and it starts with the old ploughman's opening verse (v. 2 above). Even today the age-old practice of wife-beating persists, and "The recent laws helping battered women . . . do not apply here, [i.e. in Scotland] limited though they are for England and Wales".[9] I once heard a policeman say, when confronted with an injured wife (a total stranger, she had flung herself into my car to escape from her husband), "Of course we don't know what she did to annoy him". If comparable injuries had been inflicted in a fight between two men, the verdict would have been "grievous bodily harm" with no excuse of provocation. But sometimes the only way people can react to ugly facts is to joke about them, and "When Micky comes home" is obviously in this genre. Sheila gives it the full comic treatment and it is always received with gales of laughter.

Jean Redpath comments that this is the only Scots song she knows of in which a woman is shown to be drinking: ". . . and this fact certainly doesn't reflect the truth!"

Belle Stewart (joined by Sheila MacGregor in chorus): *Oh ma name is Betsy Bell*
Scott Ceilidh, Edinburgh 1971; rec. F.K. SA 1971/195.

Oh but o' lads I've had ma share, sure I've haen a score or

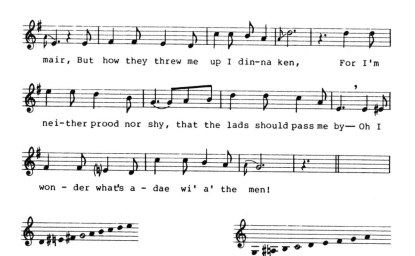

mair, But how they threw me up I din-na ken,   For I'm

nei-ther prood nor shy, that the lads should pass me by— Oh I

won - der what's a - dae wi' a' the men!

(1) Oh ma name is Betsy Bell, in the Overgate I dwell,
      Nae doot ye'll wonder what I'm daein' here,
      But if ye wait a wee, sure ma tale I'll tell tae thee,
      It's a tale nae doot ye'll think is very queer.

(2) Oh for I'm lookin' for a lad an' he may be guid or bad,
      I'm gaun tae tak' the first yin that I see;
      He may be young or auld, or greyheided, freends, or bald,
      It's onything that wears the breeks for me.

      (Chorus)
      Oh but o' lads I've had ma share, sure I've haen a score or mair
      But how they threw me up I dinna ken,
      For I'm neither prood nor shy, that the lads should pass me by –
      Oh I wonder what's a-dae wi' a' the men!

(3) Noo as I gaed oot last nicht, sure I met wi' Sandy Wricht,
      An' he hauled me in as I was passin' by;
      He asked me if I'd wed, so this is what I said,
      "Man, if you are quite agreable, so am I".

(4) So I was sae prood o' the chance, sure wi' joy it made me dance,
      The mairrage it was tae be right there an' then,
      But when I got ma marriage frock, ach he said it wis a' a joke,
      So I wonder what's a-dae wi' a' the men!

      (Chorus)

(5) Noo as I gaed oot yestreen, I could scarce believe ma e'en,
For I met auld Janet Cook wi' a lad,
And if it's true what a' folks say she'll be wed a month the day —
Man, the thocht's enough to drive a body mad.

(6) For I ken aul' Janet Cook and she drinks just like a duke,
Her age it runs aboot three score an' ten,
And as for husbands she's had three, [slower] and there's no a chance for me,
[usual speed] Oh I wonder what's a-dae wi' a' the men!

 (Chorus)

(7) [more slowly]
But if there's ony laddie here that wad like a little dear,
— A widower, or a bachelor, though he be —
If on mairrage he is bent then I'll gie him my consent
[coyly]It's no every day ye'll get a chance like me.

(8) For I can weave an' I can work, I can wash an' mend a sark,
I'm as thrifty as ony lass I ken,
But on the nail I'll hing, and I'll aye get leave tae sing,
I wonder what's a-dae wi' a' the men!

Belle picked these words up as a penny broadsheet in *The Poet's Box*, a little shop in the Overgate, Dundee, when she was about 12 years old. (This was during the first World War, which destroyed almost a whole generation of young men and left some two million women on the shelf.) To sing it to, she just picked a tune she knew which suited and fitted the words, both of verse and of chorus.

I asked Belle if she was sorry for the old maid; she replied that she knew many of that ilk today who had chosen not to marry and had plenty of boy-friends anyway. She agreed that Betsy Bell did not come into this category, and thought that behind the laughter with which people always received this song there was a good deal of sympathy and pity.

In v. 6, "she drinks just like a duke" does not mean what one might think (cf. the phrase "as drunk as a lord"). "A duke" here means "a duck", which is always drinking; it is the old Scottish pronunciation, the same as the word for the highest rung in the aristocratic ladder, and fits the internal rhyme nicely. Verses 7 and 8 become one composite verse: the first half of the tune is sung three times, so that the second half returns only for lines 3 and 4 of v. 8. This is a common device which serves to build up tension just before the end of a song.

"Betsy Bell" is a genuine antique of the Scottish music hall. It is rarely sung except by the Stewarts of Blair, and especially Belle herself — in fact Belle's personality is one of the chief clues to the popularity of this ditty. She is an extremely attractive person, she has a grown-up family and numerous grandchildren, and she puts the song over with a flirtatious, gently serio-comic kind of irony. With a different singer it could well turn into a slice of black humour.

Adam Young: *The three craws*
Kinross 1977; rec. A.P.   AM10.

(V.4) Oh but the third craw was gree-tin' for his Maw, Was gree-tin' for his Maw, gree-tin' for his Maw   The third craw was gree-tin' for his Maw, On a cold an' fros-ty mor-nin'.

(1) Oh an' three craws sat upon a wa', Sat upon a wa', sat upon a wa', Three craws sat upon a wa', On a cold and frosty mornin'.

(2) Oh the first craw he couldna flee at a', He couldna flee at a', he couldna flee at a',
The first craw he couldna flee at a', On a cold and frosty mornin'.

(3) And the second craw, he fell an' broke his jaw, (etc.)

(4) Oh but the third craw was greetin' for his Maw.

(5) Oh but the fourth craw, he wisna there at a'.

(6) Oh but the fifth craw flew awa' to Clatterha'.

(7)   Oh an' the sixth craw got a job in Hornieha'.

(pause)

(8)   Oh an' the seventh craw got drunk at Justinha'.

(pause)

(9)   Oh an' the eighth craw, they ca'ed him Heid-the-ba'.

(longer pause)

(10) Oh an' the ninth craw got stuck at tap i' (o') Law.

(still longer pause)

(11) Oh but the tenth craw — (pause) — got fed up an' walked awa'.

The first five verses are traditional. They were sung by the late Duncan MacRae, a brilliant and versatile actor with a fine flair for comedy, and were recorded by Robin Hall and Jimmy Macgregor in volume II of *Glasgow Street Songs* (Collector JES 5). The remaining verses are "just a make-up of my own", says Adam Young, who lives in Forfar.

The song evoked so much laughter, at this lunch-time ceilidh, that some of the words were drowned and I had to write to Adam. He kindly supplied notes as well as words. His allusions to local places, his gradually lengthening pauses and his straight-faced style of delivery, all combine to form a richly comic brew.

Many street songs and nursery rhymes have ancient pedigrees and sinister interpretations. In parts of Scotland crows are still regarded with fear, as omens of death; but no such (conscious) thought has occurred to Adam, who says, "I just seem to like the song as I always fancied Duncan's songs". As for his audience, any surviving element here of "cocking a snook" at death would surely tend to increase their enjoyment.

Adam Young's notes: Clatterhall was an old smiddy (smithy) between Forfar and Brechin; Horniehall is a farm up the glen, about 10 miles north of Forfar; Justinhaugh is a hotel 5 miles north of Forfar; the Law is a hill near Dundee.

See Appendix I for "He widna wint his gruel", also in this group.

Group 4: FEUDS AND WAR

Jean Bechofer: *The bonny hoose o' Airlie* (Child 199)
Kinross 1977; rec. A.P.   AM9.

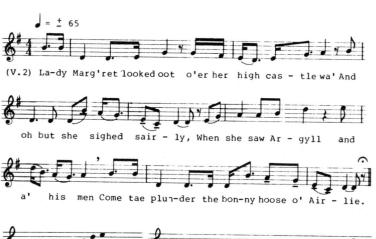

(V.2) La-dy Marg'ret looked oot o'er her high cas - tle wa' And
oh but she sighed sair - ly, When she saw Ar - gyll and
a' his men Come tae plun-der the bon-ny hoose o' Air - lie.

(1) It fell on a day, on a bonny simmer's day
     When the corn was ripe and yellow,
     That there fell oot a great dispute
     Between Argyll and Airlie.

(2) Lady Margaret looked oot o'er her high castle wa'
     And oh but she sighed sairly,
     When she saw Argyll and a' his men
     Come tae plunder the bonny hoose o' Airlie.

(3) "Come doon, come doon, Lady Margaret", he said,
     "Come doon and kiss me fairly,
     For gin the mornin's bricht daylicht
     I winna leave a stan'in' stane in Airlie."

(4) "I winna come doon, ye fause Argyll,
     And I winna kiss thee fairly.
     I wadna kiss the fause Argyll
     Though ye didna leave a stan'in' stane in Airlie."

(5) For if my lord was noo at hame,
As he's awa' wi' Chairlie,
There's no a Campbell oot o' Argyll
Dare to trod the bonny green o' Airlie.

(6) For I hae borne him seven bonny sons
And the eighth has never seen his daddy,
But had I borne as mony owre again
They wad a' be men for Chairlie."

(7) Argyll in a rage, he kin'led sic a blaze
That it rose tae the lift red and rarely,
And puir Lady Margaret and a' her weans
Were smothered in the black reek o' Airlie.

(8) "Draw yer dirks, draw yer dirks", cried the brave Lochiel;
"Unsheath yer swords", cried Chairlie,
"We'll kin'le sic a lowe roond yon fause Argyll
And we'll licht it wi' a spairk oot o' Airlie."

Jean Bechofer, who considers herself a revival singer, was born and brought up in Shetland. She has lived in England and in different parts of Scotland, and in Edinburgh for the past 15 years or so.

Jean got this song from a version in *Tocher* no. 21, 1976, which was recorded from Belle Stewart by Hamish Henderson in 1956. It appears in Bronson as no. 14. But Jean has made a number of changes in the words, and has adapted lines 1 and 4 of the tune (bars 3–4, and 7–8) in a way which improves the impact of the whole quite powerfully. She sings here with great intensity and deliberation, and her markedly dotted rhythms are reminiscent of a slow strathspey.

This story, horrific as it is, leaves out further details of savagery which are found in some versions. Since this recording was made, Jean has added a verse, obtained from Belle, concerning the ravishing of Lady Margaret by Argyll — "which she claimed she didn't sing to the School of Scottish Studies collector because it wouldn't be proper, members of the 'family' still being around". The sacking of Airlie, 1640, is brought forward to the time of Prince Charles Edward: this confusion as to dates is typical of accounts which were, at least to begin with, transmitted orally.[10]

Jean likes this song because "It tells a story involving patriotism, lust, fidelity and murder, without much embellishment but very vividly. . . . The tune, I was told by Belle, is a pipe-tune and is an early version of 'Loch Lomond'. The regular metre of the tune suits the stark nature of this ballad. . . . The theme is fidelity".

See Appendix I for *Willie Macintosh*, also in this group.

Group 5: SEXUAL VIOLENCE AND SEDUCTION

Dolina MacLennan: *The laird o' the Dainty doon-bye*
Heriot Watt University Students' Union, Edinburgh 1971; rec.
A.M. SA 1971/14.

(1) A lassie was milkin' her father's kye
When a gentleman on horseback he came ridin' by,
A gentleman on horseback he came ridin' by,
He was the laird o' the Dainty doon-bye.

(2) "Lassie oh lassie oh what wad ye gie
If I were tae lie ae nicht with ye?"
"Tae lie ae nicht that'll never never be
Suppose ye're laird o' the Dainty doon-bye."

(3) He took her by the middle sae sma'
And he drew her down where the grass grew long,
'Twas a long long time till he raised her up again
Saying "Ye're lady o' the Dainty doon-bye".

(4) It fell upon a day an' a bonny summer's day,
Tae face the lassie's father some money he'd to pay,
Tae face the lassie's father some money he'd to pay
Tae the laird o' the Dainty doon-bye.

(5)   "Oh good morning and how dae ye do,
      How's yer dochter Janeky noo,
      How's yer dochter Janeky noo
      Since I laid her in the Dainty doon-bye?"

(6)   "Oh my wee Janeky's no very weel,
      My wee Janeky cowks at her kail,
      My wee Janeky's lookin' unco pale
      Since ye laid her in the Dainty doon-bye."

(7)   He took her by the lily-white hand
      He showed her his rooms, they were twenty-one,
      He placed the key into her hand
      Sayin', "Ye're lady o' the Dainty doon-bye".

(8)   "Oh", says the auld man, "What will we dae?"
      "Oh", says the auld wife, "We'll dance till we dee,
      Oh", says the auld wife, "I think we'll dae that tae
      Since she's lady o' the Dainty doon-bye".

      [Note: the usual version of lines 2 and 3, v. 8, makes more sense:

      "Oh", says the auld wife, "I'll dance till I dee".
      "Oh", says the auld man, "I think I'll dae that tae. . . ."]

Janeky is a diminutive of Janet.

Dolina MacLennan is a native Gaelic speaker from Lewis who has
played an active and creative part in the Revival over the last
twenty years. She is chiefly known for her Gaelic songs but she also
sings the Scots: for example, this song which she learned from a
Ewan MacColl L.P. in the early '60s.

This recording was made at a ceilidh held in aid of funds for an
Edinburgh "People's Newspaper" entitled *Stampede*. After a film
which showed bad living conditions in Leith, a district of
Edinburgh, Dolina introduced the song as follows: "This next song
has a — moral of a kind to it — it should suit this occasion, The
Tenants' Association, because it proves that even very very far back
the tenants had to — sort of — kneel down to the laird. In this case
the parents of a young girl who was seduced by the laird — were
delighted — that their daughter had been seduced by the laird!"
Very shrewd remarks — and the singer gave an infectious chuckle
at the end of verse 7. Dolina sums up the theme of the song: "The
audacity of the aristocracy and the acceptance of the peasant", and
adds, "I'm aware that this attitude still exists".

This song appears to be very popular among both men and

women; it is at least two hundred years old. It's worth comparing this version with the one in Herd,[12] 1776, which has three main points of difference:

(1) The thyme motif is present (see "Sprig o' thyme", below) —
> This lassie being of a noble mind,
> She went to the garden to pu' a pickle thyme. . . .

(2) Although the version is longer, with 12 verses, the seduction statement is at once briefer and more inclusive — "He has made her to be at his command" — with no mention at this point of "Ye're lady o' . . ."

(3) The parents' reactions and comments are not included.

The story in the version given here is told in a kind of minimal short-hand. The sting is in the tail — "the parents . . . were delighted" — but were they pleased for their daughter's sake or for their own? Possibly for both. If for themselves only, they have in effect sold her; in either case they may even have in some way engineered the situation. On the other hand they could simply be making the best of a *fait accompli*, in which case the father's reply (verse 6) is a bold challenge, the suggestion being "You've got her into this, now get her out of it". (Imagine Mozart's Figaro, some twenty years after his marriage, scheming for his daughter with a son of Count Almaviva . . . a son who has not inherited his father's humane views regarding the *droit du seigneur* syndrome. Except that a German laird of that time would be less likely even to consider marrying the young woman.) The daughter's wishes are not considered at any time, and in view of her spirited refusal (verse 2) this is initially a story about rape. The laird makes a tentative declaration; he then delays his next visit, ostensibly till rent-collection day, but possibly also until enough time has elapsed to establish whether or not she is pregnant. Insofar as this hypothesis may be true, the story follows a pattern which was found until recently in parts of Scotland: for instance in Aberdeenshire, within living memory, pregnancy before marriage was considered advisable in some circles as a safeguard against possible infertility in either husband or wife. Two centuries ago arranged marriages were more common, while expectation of romantic love was comparatively rare. Janet's parents knew the struggle for existence of tenant-farmers and farm-workers, and might quite sincerely decide that a shot-gun marriage to the laird would by no means be a fate worse than death.

This song is obviously seen as embodying a hard and humorous realism; to the woman of today, surely, it is only tolerable if viewed in this light. It is usually sung at a lively tempo, as here.

Dolina MacLennan has been recorded by Topic and by Decca.

Walter Allan: *Eppie Morrie* (Child 223)
Blairgowrie 1970; rec. P.C.   SA 1970/180.

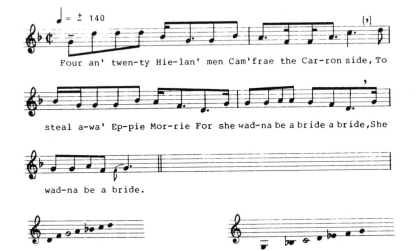

(1) Four an' twenty Hielan' men
     Cam' frae the Carron side,
     To steal awa' Eppie Morrie
     For she wadna be a bride a bride,
     She wadna be a bride.

(2) It's oot an cam' her mither then,
     It was a moonlicht nicht;
     She couldnae see her dochter
     For the waters shone sae bricht sae bricht,
     The waters shone sae bricht.

(3) "Haud awa' frae me, mither,
     Haud awa' frae me!
     There's no a' man in a' Strathdon
     Shall mairriet be wi' me wi' me,
     Shall mairriet be wi' me."

(4) They've taken Eppie Morrie then
     And a horse they've bound her on;
     And they hae rid to the minister's hoose
     As fast as horse could gang could gang,
     As fast as horse could gang.

(5) And Willie's ta'en his pistol oot
     And held it tae the minister's breist;
     "Oh marry me marry me minister,
     Or else I'll be yer priest yer priest
     Or else I'll be yer priest."

(6) "Hand awa' frae me Willie,
     Hand awa' frae me!
     I daurna vow tae marry you
     Except she's willin' as thee as thee,
     Except she's willin' as thee."

(7) "Hand awa' frae me guid sir,
     Hand awa' frae me!
     There's no a man in a' Strathdon
     Shall wedded be by me by me,
     Shall wedded be by me."

(8) They've taken Eppie Morrie then
     Sin' better couldnae be,
     And they hae rid owre Carron side
     As fast as horse could flee could flee,
     As fast as horse could flee.

(9) Then mass was sung and bells were rung
     And they're awa' tae bed,
     And Willie and Eppie Morrie then
     In ane bed they were laid were laid,
     In ane bed they were laid.

(10) He's ta'en the sark frae off his back
     And kicked awa' his shoon.
     He's thrawn awa' the chaumer key
     And naked he lay doon lay doon,
     And naked he lay doon.

(11) He's kissed her on the lily breist
     And held her shouthers twa
     But aye she grat and aye she spat
     And turnèd tae the wa' the wa',
     And turnèd tae the wa'.

(12) "Haud awa' frae me, Willie,
     Haud awa' frae me!
     Before I lose ma maidenheid
     I'll try ma strength wi' thee wi' thee,
     I'll try ma strength wi' thee."

(13) A' through the nicht they warstled then
Until the licht o' day,
And Willie grat and Willie swat
But he couldnae streitch her spey her spey,
He couldnae streitch her spey.

(14) Then early in the mornin'
Before the licht o' day,
In cam' the maid o' Scallater
Wi' a goon and shirt alane alane,
Wi' a goon and shirt alane.

(15) "Get up get up young woman
And drink the wine wi' me!"
"You micht hae ca'ed me maiden
For I'm sure as hale as thee as thee,
For I'm sure as hale as thee."

(16) "Weary fa' you Willie then
That ye couldnae prove a man;
You micht hae ta'en her maidenheid,
She wad hae hired your hand your hand,
She wad hae hired your hand."

(17) Then in it's cam' young Breidalbane,
A pistol on each side.
"Oh come awa' Eppie Morrie
And I'll mak' you ma bride ma bride,
And I'll mak' you ma bride."

(18) "Go get to me a horse Willie,
Get it like a man!
And send me back to ma mither
A maiden as I cam' I cam',
A maiden as I cam'."

(19) The sun shines owre the westlin' hills
By the lamplicht o' the moon;
"Oh saddle your horse young John Forsyth
And whistle and I'll come soon come soon,
And whistle and I'll come soon."

This ballad was made popular by Ewan MacColl. The words from Maidment's *North Countrie Garland* form the only version in Child — and (conflated, as here) in Bronson who gives MacColl's tune alone, "learned from his father", with the disc number. In 1824 Maidment wrote: "This ballad is probably much more than a century old, though the circumstances which have given rise to it were unfortunately too common to preclude the possibility of its being of a later date".

Norman Buchan has described the time he first heard MacColl sing it, as the late-night ceilidh in St. Columba's Church after the first Edinburgh People's Festival Ceilidh: he said Ewan leaned against a pillar — "I could almost take you to the particular pillar" — and belted out "Eppie Morrie", "and it came like a charging gallop".[13]

Walter Allan's version, very nearly the same as MacColl's,[14] is also taken at a "charging gallop" speed. It's a superb performance. He never falters, his diction is clear and he is as if possessed by the rhythmic drive of the music-and-story. Walter says that he identifies with Willie to some extent; he continues, "I like the story content of the song and the way it is made to fit the tune. The tune is also powerful and I think echoes the speed with which Wullie tries to gain his maid, then the hard struggle, and ultimate frustration. I think it is purely a story, perhaps based on true historical personalities although I don't find that quite important. Since Eppie Morrie at the end reveals her love for John Forsyth and not Wullie, perhaps there's also a moral in it!"

Alison McMorland: *Skippin' barfit through the heather.*
Kinross 1975; rec. A.P.   AM3.

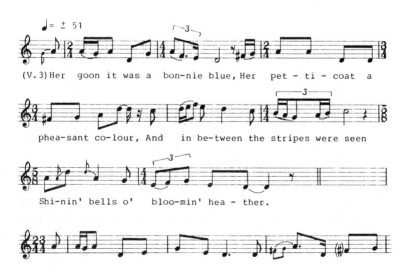

(V.3) Her goon it was a bon-nie blue, Her pet - ti - coat a

phea-sant co-lour, And in be-tween the stripes were seen

Shi-nin' bells o' bloo-min' hea - ther.

(1)   As I wis walkin' doon yon hill
      'Twas on a summer's evenin',
      There I saw a bonnie lass
      Skippin' barfit through yon heather.

(2)   Oh but she was neatly dressed,
      She needed neither hat nor feather.
      She was the queen among them a',
      Skippin' barfit through yon heather.

(3)   Her goon it was a bonny blue,
      Her petticoat a pheasant colour,
      And in between the stripes were seen
      Shinin' bells o' bloomin' heather.

(4)   "Oh lassie, lassie will ye come wi' me,
      Will ye come wi' me and leave your heather?
      Silks and satins ye shall hae
      If ye'll come wi' me and leave yon heather."

(5)   "Oh kind sir", she said, "Your offer's good,
      But weel I ken you'll deceive me:
      For gin I gie ma hairt awa'
      Better though I'd never seen ye."

This provides an interesting contrast to Jessie Murray's version
recorded nearly 25 years earlier (see Chapter 3 for this). Alison
McMorland's seems to have no regular time-structure, apart from
the metrical nature of the verbal text; while Jessie's is mainly duple
(with pauses at the end of the 2nd and 4th lines) which accords
better with the dance-like tune as she sings it. Particularly Jessie's
last line:

{ ♪♩. ♪♩ ♪ ♫ ♪ ♩ } — what could be "skippier"
{ Skip-pin' bar-fit through the heather }

than this simple rhythm? Alison's variations have something of the ingenious, colourful and decorative style of her "Belt wi' colours three", and she sings with much feeling again; but her more fluid time and her ornamentation seem rather less suitable here when compared with the "source" singer's version.

"Skippin' barfit" is included in this group because the man's intent is obvious: the girl jalouses this at once, and the last verse sums up her attitude, and his. It is also included as an example, albeit a moderate one, of the trend in singing style over the last quarter-century: one sometimes feels that ornamentation and freedom of time structure have developed almost to good stylistic limits, and it would be a pity if the dance-like nature of tunes such as this should be lost.

See Appendix I for "The banks o' red roses", also in this group.

Group 6: THE PREGNANT WOMAN IN TROUBLE

Gordeanna MacCulloch: *The cruel mother* (Child 20)
Kinross 1971, rec. P.C.   SA 1971/243.

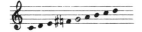 

(1)   There was a lady in the North,
          Hie the rose and the linsie O,
      And she's fa'en in love wi' her faither's clerk,
          Doon by the green wuid sidie-O.

[The internal refrain is added in the same way to each verse]

(2)   She's leaned her back against a tree,
      And there the saut tears blint her e'e.

(3)   She's leaned her back against a thorn,
      And there twa bonny boys has she borne.

(4)   She's ta'en oot her little pen-knife,
      And she's twined thae twa bonny boys o' their lives.

(5)   She's buried them 'neath a marble stane,
      Thinking to gyang a maiden hame.

(6)   She's looked owre her faither's wa',
      And she spied thae twa bonny boys playin' at the ba'.

(7)   "Oh bonny bairns gin ye were mine,
      I'd dress ye in the silk sae fine."

(8)   "Oh cruel mither, when we were thine,
      We didna see aucht o' the silk sae fine."

(9)   "Oh bonny bairns come tell tae me,
      What kind o' a death I'll hae tae dee."

(10) "Seeven years a fish in the flood,
      And seeven lang years a bird in the wood.

(11) Seeven years a tongue tae the warnin' bell,
      And seeven lang years in the cave o' hell.

(12) "Welcome, welcome, fish in the flood,
      Welcome, welcome, bird in the wood.

(13) Welcome, tongue tae the warnin' bell,
      But God keep me frae the flames o' hell."

["Hie" is pronounced "high"]

Vic Smith's tune
Kinross 1973; rec. A.M.   SA 1973/112.

A former pupil of Norman Buchan's at Rutherglen Academy, Gordeanna MacCulloch is a member of the Clutha, a Glasgow group one of whose thumb-prints of style is solo or unison singing, with harmonic content coming only from the instruments.

Gordeanna has become one of the finest of Scottish singers today. She uses her strong voice here with a fluid drive which conveys the dramatic compulsiveness of the story. She got the words from Norman Buchan at her school folkclub. They are very similar to the *Last Leaves* version, with four verses omitted; Greig and Keith state, "The numerous versions of this ballad are almost all Scottish". The implied tritone ending to the third line of the verse-tune (F sharp to C) leads with poignant effect to the inflected, now flattened seventh at the word "Doon".

The tune is that used by Ewan MacColl for his version of this ballad: he learned and possibly adapted it from the singing of his aunt, Maggie Henry Logan. MacColl also uses this tune, in a recording in the School of Scottish Studies, for his singing of the ballad "True Thomas": it is not the main tune of this song but is used only in the complete verses of the Queen of Elfland's words.

In verse 7, transcribed above, the mother's words including the first refrain "Hie the rose and the linsie-o" are sung as a cry of limitless yearning and regret; in contrast, the end-refrain "Doon by the green wuid sidie-O" is hushed, impersonal, age-weary . . . a "refraining" from comment because words are inadequate. Gordeanna herself describes this second refrain as "eerie . . . it seems to take you back to the scene of the crime". She has always liked the big ballads: "This one appeals to me mainly because of the words I think, because it is a situation which any young female can get into today although not all take such drastic measures as a solution. I think also the female getting her 'just deserts' appeals to me. I'm not sure that there is a message in ballads as I believe they were used as a method of carrying news from one community to the next. If there is any message it must be a warning to young females to beware of the same fate". Gordeanna has been recorded by Argo, by Topic and by Claddagh.

All the fuller versions in Child end with the Hell motif, and several include the "Welcome, welcome": the mother does not merely accept expiation, she *wants* it (cf. the murderer in Dostoievski's *Crime and Punishment*) — provided it ends at last.

Vic Smith's version, the tune of which is added above as a contrast, has rather appropriate words for the first of the two internal refrain lines: "All alone and alonie-O".

Jim Craig: *'Twas in the month of January*
Blairgowrie 1970; rec. P.C.   SA 1970/179.

(1)   'Twas in the month of January, the fields were white with snow,
As over hills and valleys a-roving I did go.
I met a fair and a pretty young maid with a salt tear in her eye,
She had a baby in her arms and bitterly she cried.

(2)   Oh cruel was my father to bar the door on me,
And cruel was my mother this dreadful shame to see,
And cruel was my own true love, he changed his mind for gold,
And cruel was the winter's wynd, it filled my heart with cold.

(3)   Now the taller that the palm-tree grows then the sweeter is the bark
And the fairer that a young man speaks then the falser is his heart,
He will kiss you and embrace you till he thinks he has you won,
Then he'll go away and leave you, and for some other one.

(4)   So come all you fair and pretty young maids and warning take by me
And don't ever try to build your nest on the top of any high tree,
For the leaves they will all wither and the branches will decay,
And the beauty of a false young love must soon fade away.

Jim Craig of Dundee got this from the Irishman Paddy Tunney, around 1963; the thrice-repeated note at the end of lines 1 and 4 is one characteristic of Irish tunes. Jim has been singing since he was two years old, and his mother taught him many songs: again, the categories "revival singer" and "source singer" are far from mutually exclusive, but Jim considers himself revival.

He sings this Irish song in very free time, with a kind of abandonment. As he says, "You've got to be able to let your back hair down to sing this kind of song". Further comments from Jim Craig: "Isn't it terrible the way people treat each other? This song is a classic example of unthinking cruelty. . . . It's a sad cry from a young woman who has been badly let down. The message: be kind to people".

The change of ending in verse line 3 of the tune, which is otherwise identical with line 2, is very effective and leads nicely back to the repetition of the first phrase. Also most telling emotionally is the upward leap of a minor seventh at the second bars of lines 2 and 3.

Owen Costello: *Bogie's bonny Belle*
Kinross 1973; rec. A.M.   SA 1973/111.

(V.5) Doon be the banks o'Cair-nie There we en-ded mo-ny's a day, And when

Bo-gie wis-na wat-chin' It was there we'd sport an' play.

(1) Ae Whitsunday in Huntly toon
     'Twas there I did agree
     Wi' Bogie o' Cairnie
     For six months tae fee.

(2) For tae drive his twa best horses,
     'Twas a job that I could do,
     Oh tae drive his twa best horses
     At ma harrow an' ma ploo.

(3) Noo Bogie had a dochter
     Her name was Isabel,
     And oh but she was bonny
     And she knew I lo'ed her weel.

(4) When she gaed oot walkin'
     She chose me for her guide
     Tae watch the trooties lowpin'
     By Bogie's waterside.

(5) Doon be the banks o' Cairnie
     There we ended mony's a day,
     And when Bogie wisna watchin'
     It was there we'd sport an' play.

(6) Doon be the banks o' Cairnie
     Where we watched the fishes glide,
     It was there I had my will o' her
     By Bogie's burnside.

(7) And the first three months being scarcely owre
     This lassie lost her bloom,
     And the reid fell fae her rosy cheeks
     And her eyes began tae swoon.

(8) And when six months were nearly owre
     Her waist began tae swell,
     And when her mother speired at her
     Oh the truth she had tae tell.

(9)   And when nine lang months were past an' gane
       She brocht forth tae me a son,
       And I was quickly sent for
       Tae see what could be done.

(10)   I said that I wad mairry her
       But oh no that wouldna dae;
       "For ye're nae match for ma bonny Belle
       And she's nae match for ye."

(11)   An' noo she's mairried til a tinkler chiel
       Wha bides in Huntly toon,
       He mends pots an pans an' ladles,
       An' he scoors the country roon'.

(12)   And maybe she's gotten a better match,
       Auld Bogie canna tell,
       But it's me that stole the maidenheid
       Fae his bonny Isabel.

The popularity of this bothy song may be due partly to the weel-gaun, up and down swing of its tune, but the words form at least an equal attraction. Owen Costello of Cumbernauld, originally from Glasgow, conflated his version from many others he'd heard, as well as from records and books. He says, "I like this song because it's political in the widest sense: it's untypical of bothy songs, most of which express grumbles against individual employers but that's about all. The song is a very bitter comment on the conditions and attitudes of farm life. Although the complaint here is underscored, this brings out the bitterness all the more".

Boasts about maidenhead-stealing can be supremely boring, but in this particular situation the last verse is a biting comeback, a piece of one-up-manship and nose-thumbing. "I had my will o' her" (v.6) is a well-worn cliché in Scots folk-song; its implications are various.

It's interesting that the "tinkler chiel", or tinker, whom Belle marries seems to have been more of a social catch than a farm worker would be: the song may thus have a fairly ancient ancestry, for it's a long time since the travelling tinsmiths lost their former status as skilled craftsmen. But in verse 11 the speaker suggests that the life of a tinker's wife is hard: "he scoors the country roon' " probably refers to moving camp. In other words, "she's got someone worse than me" — another piece of one-up-manship with which the rejected suitor comforts his bruised ego.

Cy Laurie: *Corachree*
Kinross 1971; rec. J.P. SA 1971/242.

(V. 2) Noo half-wey up the a-ve-nue they baith set doon tae rest. He
put his airms a-roon' her sayin', "Ma dear, I love ye best A
mai-den ye hae sit-ten doon, a maid ye're aye tae me But a
maid-en ye'll ne'er walk a-gain the grass o' Co-ra-chree".

(1) It was on a summer's evenin' I gaed oot tae tak' the air
  When comin' in be Tarlin toon I spied a lonely pair.
  The youth was tall and handsome and the maid fair tae see
  An' I kent their destination wasnae faur frae Corachree.

(2) Noo halfwey up the avenue they baith set doon tae rest.
He put his airms aroon' her sayin', "Ma dear, I love ye best,
A maiden ye hae sitten doon, a maid ye're aye tae me
But a maiden ye'll ne'er walk again the grass o' Corachree".

(3) "O Sandy lad ye'll ne'er deny this deed ye hae dene
My apron-strings are broken, Lord ma hairt flees wi' the win',
Ma maidenheid has ta'en a fricht, it's fairly flown awa'
An' the session clerk'll get tae ken this deed ye hae dene".

(4) "Cheer up ma bonny lassie ye neednae care a fig,
There's mony's a bonny lassie gaes daily on the rig.
There's mony's a bonny lassie aye an' juist as guid as thee
But a maiden ye'll ne'er walk again the grass o' Corachree".

(5) Well he comes doon in the evenin' as often as he can,
He comes doon in the evenin' juist tae see his lonely Anne.
They tak' their lane o' auld lang syne faur naebody can see
But ye'll easy fin' oot a' their beds aroon' be Corachree.

This song, although perhaps less popular than a few years ago, is still heard quite frequently, especially at competitions and in pubs. Its origin has not been traced or any printed version found, but the fear of the session-clerk takes us back at least 160 years or so. It carries with it a breath of country air and a suggestion of clandestine, chiefly out-doors love-making.

"My apron-strings are broken" is one of the recognised traditional ways of announcing pregnancy; it is received here with apparent insouciance (v. 4, line 1). This seems a sad little song, with an ending enigmatic, unfinished. It is sung chiefly by men.

Although Cy Laurie's time is free he achieves a firm base of time-structure, unlike some interpretations where the tune seems to wander rather aimlessly. He sings with a warm melancholy.

Janet Weatherstone: *The Magdalen Green*
Kinross 1977; rec. A.P. AM9.

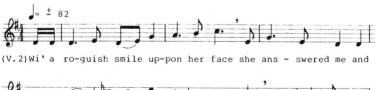

(V.2)Wi' a ro-guish smile up-pon her face she ans - swered me and

said, "Young man I would a - walk wi'you,but you know I am a -

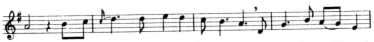

- fraid, For the paths they are so slip-pe-ry, the nicht be cauld an'

keen, And it would not do for me tae fa' doon by the Mag-d'len Green".

(1) "Noo here am I a sailor lad just newly hame frae sea,
My ship it lies at anchor in the harbour o' Dundee,
And your face it is the fairest that I hae ever seen,
Oh fair maid wad ye walk wi' me doon by the Magdalen★ Green?"

(2) Wi' a roguish smile upon her face she answered me and said,
"Young man I would a-walk wi' you, but you know I am afraid,
For the paths they are so slippery, the nicht be cauld an' keen,
And it would not do for me tae fa' doon by the Magdalen Green".

(3) Wi' kind words and promises alang wi' me she went,
We wandered here, we wandered there, mid love and pleasure
brent,
Day after day we met and roved amid yon pleasant scene,
And I fear that maid fell more than once doon by the Magdalen
Green.

(4) Well soon the time for partin' came, my ship had hoisted sail,
Nae longer could I see yon lass tae tell a pleasant tale,
So I bid fareweel tae her thon day, whaur I hae happy been,
And she was left to weep alone doon by the Magdalen Green.

(5) One night as I lay in my bed when my weary watch was done
I dreamt I was the father o' a darlin' little son;
Aye and in the dream his mither tae richt plainly could I see
And she was weeping bitterly doon by the Magdalen Green.

(6) So when my ship puts in again in the harbour o' Dundee
I'll search that town all up and down until my girl I see,
And I'll ask her tae forgi'e me for the rascal I hae been,
And I will make it up tae her doon by the Magdalen Green.

★ Pronounced "Maudlen"

(7) So come a' ye jolly sailor lads, a warnin' tak be me,
       Never slight that poor lass for a' her poverty;
       For tae lichtlie love and sail away, 'tis neither strecht nor clean,
       Aye 'n' never dae as I once did doon by the Magdalen Green.

The Weatherstons of Barnton, Edinburgh, have recently come to the fore as another singing family, with Mrs. Weatherston the immediate source of many songs which Jock and Janet sing. Jock is well known for his racy and authentic renderings of such rollicking Aberdeenshire tongue-twisters as "McGinty's meal and ale when the pig gaed on the spree", and "MacFarlane o' the Sprotts o' Birnieboosie" (both in Greig's *Folk-Song of the North-East*), as well as for his more serious songs.

Janet got her version of "The Magdalen Green" from her mother: it was her favourite, and is now Janet's. The words are almost the same as those obtained from *The Poet's Box*. "Brent" (v. 3, line 2) is given because it is sung here as transmitted, but since it has no meaning which fits the context it is possible that the words were originally "on love and pleasure bent".

With her powerful voice, which has great sustaining powers, her clear enunciation, and hardly any vibrato or ornamentation, Janet sings her straightforward version to a very steady beat. But there's much tight-lipped feeling too.

Group 7: FAMILY PRESSURE REGARDING MARRIAGE

Jane Turriff: *Andrew Lammie* (Child 233)
Fetterangus 1974; rec. H.H. and P.C.   SA 1974/150.

At Mill o' Tif-ty lived a man In the neigh-bour-hood o'
Fy-vie, And he had a love-ly daugh-ter fair, Her name was bon-ny
An - nie.

(1) At Mill o' Tifty lived a man
     In the neighbourhood o' Fyvie,
     And he had a lovely daughter fair,
     Her name was bonny Annie.

(2) Lord Fyvie had a trumpeter
     An' his name was Andra Lammie,
     And he had the art to gain the heart
     O' bonny Tifty's Annie.

(3) Her mother called her to the door,
     "Come here tae me, my Annie.
     Did e'er you see a prettier man
     Than the trumpeter o' Fyvie?"

(4) Oh nothing she said but sighin' sore,
     Alas for bonny Annie!
     But she durst not own that her heart was won
     By the trumpeter o' Fyvie.

(5) Oh the first time me an' my love did meet
     It was in the woods o' Fyvie,
     And he ca'ed me "Mistress" — I said, "No,
     I am Tifty's bonny Annie."

(6) With apples sweet he did me treat,
     And kisses soft an' many,
     And he had the art to gain the heart
     Of bonny Tifty's Annie.

(7) Oh loves comes in at my bedside,
     And love lies down beyond me:
     And love so oppressed my tender breast,
     Oh but love will waste my body.

(8) "Oh lovey I must go to Edinburgh toon
     And for a whilie I must leave ye".
     "Oh but I'll be dead or you come back,
     Oh bonny Andra Lammie".

(9) "I will buy you a bridal goon,
     And dearie it will be bonny".
     "Oh but I'll be dead or you come back,
     Oh ma bonny Andra Lammie".

(10) "I will buy tae you a bridal shoon
     And oh but they will be bonny".
     "Oh but I'll be dead or you come back,
     Oh ma bonny Andra Lammie".

(11) Oh love comes in at my bedside,
     And love lies down beyond me:
     And love so oppressed my tender breast,
     Oh but love will waste my body.

(12) Oh but lay me doon tae rest awhile
     And turn my face tae Fyvie,
     That I may see before I dee
     Oh ma bonny Andra Lammie.

(13) Oh it's up and doon in Tifty's glen,
     Whaur the burn lies clear and bonny;
     Whaur oft-times I have run tae thee,
     Oh my bonny Andra Lammie.

(14) Oh love it dwines and love it twines,
     And love decays ma body:
     And love so oppressed my tender breast,
     Oh but love will waste my body.

(15) Oh Andra hame fae Edinburgh toon
     Wi' muckle grief and sorrow,
     And he sounded his horn right loud and clear
     In the low lands o' Fyvie.

(16) Oh Fyvie's lands are broad an' wide
     And Fyvie's lands are bonny,
     Whaur oft-times I have gone tae meet
     My bonny Tifty's Annie.

This is a lengthy ballad. Jane Turriff, formerly of Fetterangus but now living in Mintlaw, has 52 verses, but for reasons of time she usually cuts it to about a third of this length. *She assumes that her audience knows the story*. The verses cut include those describing the physical brutality; says Jane, "I don't like to sing that verses". Her tune is similar to Jeannie Robertson's, but it is closer still to Davie Stewart's for "The dowie dens", given above under "The belt wi' colours three". Davie was Jane's uncle and a constant visitor to her home. (Detailed notes on the music of "Andrew Lammie", with Jane's harmonium accompaniment compared with Davie Stewart's melodeon accompaniment to "The dowie dens", may be found in *The Muckle Sangs* booklet.[15]) Jane is of the travelling people. Crippled since her childhood, she was nearly always in the house and so learned many songs, including this one, from her mother's, her grannie's and her uncle's singing. Of folk song generally she says ". . . it's *real*, and something that gets ye going".[16]

The rest of the ballad story: Annie's family strongly disapprove of the trumpeter as a suitor — musicians are of low status — and her father accuses him of having bewitched her by "wicked art". While Andra is in Edinburgh, Annie's family turn on her: her father, her mother, and — most violent of all — her brother. At first Annie shows some spirit:

> But if ye strike me I'll cry out,
> And gentlemen will hear me;
> Lord Fyvie will be riding by,
> And he'll come in and see me.

The laird does hear her cries, and comes in to intercede for her; but to no avail. When he leaves, the violence is in fact intensified, probably because Annie has dared to invoke outside help (this pattern is repeated to this day, if a battered woman reports her ill-treatment). Eventually the brother breaks her back, and Annie dies. Andra says later, "My love has died for me today, I'll die for her tomorrow".

This dreadful story is based on historical fact. In his notes on this ballad in the *Muckle Songs* booklet Hamish Henderson relates how Arthur Argo convoyed the two recorders to the actual ruined mill, in Aberdeenshire, and saw "Annie's flat gravestone in Fyvie kirkyard — dated 1673, and surmounted by a nineteenth century monumental stone on which are carved the leaves of two intertwining trees"; also to Fyvie Castle nearby, with the stone figure of the trumpeter on one of the turrets.

Child remarks, ". . . the gentleness and fidelity of Annie under the brutal behaviour of her family are genuinely pathetic, and justify the remarkable popularity which the ballad has enjoyed in the north of Scotland". One's first reaction might be that "pathetic" is the word in more senses than one: the slang meaning appears applicable to Annie's passivity. But on second thoughts, what more could she have done? She tries three times to warn Andra of the fate in store for her during his absence, but he ignores this warning.

Professor Trevelyan in his *History of England* writes: "Wife-beating was a recognised right of man, and was practised without shame by high as well as low. . . . Similarly, the daughter who refused to marry the gentleman of her parents' choice was liable to be locked up, beaten and flung about the room, without any shock being inflicted on public opinion. Marriage was not an affair of personal affection, but of family avarice . . ."[17]. The historian is speaking here of the year 1500, but these practices continued for many long years and died hard. (And violent treatment of women by members of the family still continues, in Scotland and elsewhere.[18]) The "remarkable popularity" of the ballad may have had something to do with an atavistic clinging to outworn mores. Women were supposed to be gentle and passive — "under the bludgeonings of chance" their heads should be bloody *and bowed*. Also this continuing popularity could well imply a touch of the sadism-masochism vicious circle; many people enjoy the depiction of violence.

Yet violence cannot be ignored, and it is of course an ingredient in many of the finest ballads. "Andrew Lammie" has an epic quality, with some powerfully evocative language. Above all it is a true love-story . . . a story which ends on a note of apocalyptic doom, with a hint of the Pauline "last trump":

> And he sounded his horn both loud and clear
> In the low lands o' Fyvie.

Jane Turriff's complete version ends on this repeated note:

> He hied him to the head of the house,
> To the house-top o' Fyvie;
> He blew his trumpet loud and shrill,
> 'Twas heard at Mill o' Tifty.

Heather Heywood: *What can a young lassie dae wi' an auld man?* Kinross 1975; rec. A.P.   AM2.

Whit can a young las-sie, oh whit can a young las-sie, Whit

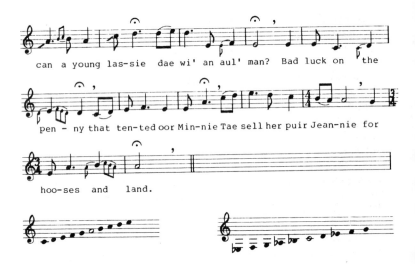

can a young las-sie dae wi' an aul' man? Bad luck on the pen - ny that ten-ted oor Min-nie Tae sell her puir Jean-nie for hoo-ses and land.

(1) Whit can a young lassie, oh whit can a young lassie,
     Whit can a young lassie dae wi' an aul' man?
     Bad luck on the penny that tented oor Minnie
     Tae sell her puir Jeannie for hooses and land.

(2) He hums and he hankers, he frets and he cankers,
     I never cuid please him, dae a' that I can.
     For he's peevish and jealous o' a' the young fellas
     Oh weary's me life wi' me crazy aul' man.

(3) Ma auld Auntie Kitty, on me she taks pity,
     I'll dae ma endeavour tae follow her plan;
     For I'll cross him, I'll crack him, until I hairt-brak him
     And wi' his aul' brass I will buy a new pan.

(4) For he's aye-ways complainin' frae mornin' till evenin',
     He hoasts and he hirples the weary day lang,
     He's dowie an' dosin' and his blood is gey frozen,
     Oh I rue on the day I met wi' ma aul' man.

(5) Whit can a young lassie, oh whit can a young lassie,
     Whit can a young lassie dae wi' an aul' man?
     Bad luck on the penny that tented oor Minnie
     Tae sell her puir Jeannie for hooses and land.

The villain of this piece is the mother, who has married her daughter to an old man for the sake of his money. The pauses shown in the transcription are not as frequent in subsequent verses.

This opening, and concluding, verse conveys a dull, dragging hopelessness, an incapacity for looking forward, with frequent stops as if for bitter reflection. Yet "for a' that" a youthful vitality surges through especially in the other verses, in Heather Heywood's clear, resonant voice and her thoughtful shaping of the melody.

The words are substantially those of Burns (see Kinsley,[19] though the order of verses is changed); but, as with Allan Morris's "Parcel o' rogues" below, these words are even more Scots than are Burns's, thus showing signs of oral tradition at work.

Heather's changing of the original, lilting jig-tune to this slower, more pensive tempo is entirely convincing and far more suitable. She learned this song from the singing of Janice Clark, and also that of Jane Turriff.

"The theme is the old saying, 'It's better to marry for love and not for money' ", says Heather. "It's obvious that all the man's money can't make up for the fact that he's far too old for the girl. . . . This song is usually a favourite of our local Folk Club," (i.e. Kilmarnock). She has been recorded by Springthyme and by Ayrshire Folk Club.

Jane Turriff: *The dowie dens of Yarrow* (Child 214)
Kinross 1977; rec. A.P.   AM9.

$\downarrow$ = ± 68

(V.8) "Gae hame, gae hame, ma bri-ther John, Whit's a' the dule an'

sor-row? Gae hame an' tell my la-dy dear That I sleep sound in

Yar - row".   or: Yar - - row".

(1) As he's gaen tae his lady gang
     As he had done before-O,
     Sayin', "Madam I maun keep a tryst
     On the dowie dens o' Yarrow".

(2) "Oh bide at hame, my lord", she said,
     "Oh bide at hame, my marrow,
     For my three brothers will slay thee
     On the dowie dens o' Yarrow".

(3) Oh she kissed his cheeks and she kissed his hair,
     As she had done before-O,
     Gied him a brand down by his side
     And he's awa' tae Yarrow.

(4) So he's gaed up yon Tenniesbank,
     And I wyte he gaed wi' sorrow,
     For there he met nine armed men
     On the dowie dens o' Yarrow.

(5) "Oh come ye here tae hawk or hound,
     Or drink the wine sae clear-O,
     Or come ye here tae pairt yer land
     On the dowie dens o' Yarrow?"

(6) "I come not here tae hawk or hound,
     Nor drink the wine sae clear-O,
     Nor come I here to pairt my land
     But I'll fight wi' you in Yarrow."

(7) So four he's hurt, and five he's slain
     On the bloody dens o' Yarrow,
     Till a cowardly man came him behind
     And he's pierced his body through-O.

(8) "Gae hame, gae hame, ma brither John,
     Whit's a the dule an' sorrow?
     Gae hame an' tell my lady dear
     That I sleep sound in Yarrow."

(9) So he's gaed up yon high, high hill
     As he had done before-O,
     And there he spied his sister dear
     She was comin' fast tae Yarrow.

(10) "Oh I dreamed a dreary dream yestreen,
     God keep us a' fae sorrow;
     I dreamed I pulled the birks sae green
     On yon dowie dens o' Yarrow."

(11) "Oh sister I will read yer dream
   And oh it has come sorrow,
   For yer true love he is dead and gone —
   He's killed, he's killed in Yarrow."

Jane Turriff says, "When I sing my old songs my mind and
memories go far back, and I always think I hear my mother
singing. . . ." Her clear voice with its soaring high notes has an
arresting edge to it. It's difficult to describe the impact her singing
makes, in particular her production of the first syllable of
"Yarrow", which ends each verse but one and gives one of the
most unforgettable and hard-to-analyse sounds heard in Scottish
traditional song. There is a kind of break in her voice here — one
might almost say heart-break, so poignant is its effect. In verse 8
above, the words "tell" and "my" are also given something of this
treatment, without any further ornamentation.

   There is a strong suggestion here that the *coup de grâce* (v. 7) was
delivered by a brother of the lady — this is supported by many
versions in Bronson but by fewer in Child. And "my brother
John", v. 8, sometimes appears as "my good-brother", meaning
brother-in-law. Jane's words are nearest to those of Scott (Child E),
but her last two verses are in Herd (Child O) — and her final line is
the best of all in any version.

   Tenniesbank is on the Tinnis Burn, near Newcastleton.

Group 8: POLITICAL, SOCIAL COMMENT AND WORK

Alan Morris: *Sic a parcel o' rogues in a nation*
Kinross 1973; rec. P.C.   SA 1973/109.

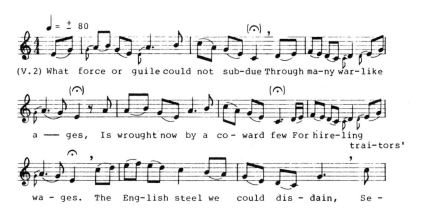

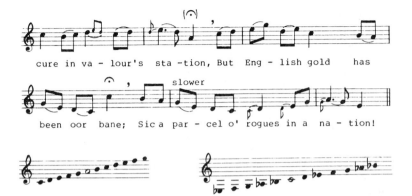

cure in va - lour's sta - tion, But Eng - lish gold has

been oor bane; Sic a par - cel o' rogues in a na - tion!

(1) Fareweel tae a' oor Scottish fame,
     Fareweel oor ancient glory;
     Fareweel even tae the Scottish name
     Sae famed in martial story.
     Noo Sark rins owre the Solway sands
     And Tweed rins tae the ocean,
     Tae mark whaur England's province stands;
     Sic a parcel o' rogues in a nation!

(2) What force or guile could not subdue
     Through many warlike ages,
     Is wrought now by a coward few
     For hireling traitors' wages.
     The English steel we could disdain,
     Secure in valour's station,
     But English gold has been oor bane;
     Sic a parcel o' rogues in a nation!

(3) Oh would or I had seen the day
     That treason thus could sell us,
     My auld grey heid had lain in clay
     Wi' Bruce an' loyal Wallace!
     But pith an' power till my last hour,
     I'll mak' this declaration:
     We're bought and sold for English gold.
     Sic a parcel o' rogues in a nation!

This version follows Burns's, including the tune, almost exactly,
although the words are even more Scots ("oor" for "our", "sic" for
"such", etc.). In the tune, pairs of quavers are often unequal in
length, but none are dotted as in Kinsley. Thomas Crawford
suggests that the original may have been one of the Jacobite songs

which Burns altered or touched up, although as always "it is extremely difficult . . . to say where tradition leaves off, and Burns . . . begins".[20] Allan Morris introduces the song by making in effect this last point, and adds, "I regard it as the first 'folk song' I ever learned. It's a protest against the Anglo-Scottish union of 1707 . . . and still remains to my mind one of the finest national songs we have". (See Francis Collinson[21] on the distinction between national and traditional songs.)

The noble, wide-ranging tune, with its constant shifts from minor to major and back again, fits the corresponding changes of mood in the words which express alternating feelings of melancholy and of pride. Burns had an uncanny gift for matching words and music.

Allan first heard this sung in the mid or late sixties, probably by the Corries or the Dubliners. A member of the S.N.P. since 1959, when he was 17, he comments: "The theme is the betrayal of Scottish nationhood in 1707 . . . such betrayal still proceeding today, with tacit agreement of some sections of the Scottish populace".

Hamish Imlach: *If it wasnae for the Union*
Heriot Watt University Students' Union, Edinburgh 1971; rec. A.M.   SA 1971/15.

(Ch.)   Too-ra loo-ra loo-ra loo, I'll tell ye some-thin' aw-fa true Ye

would-nae hae yer tel-ly the noo If it was-nae for the U-nion.

Note: each verse ends:—

(*Chorus*)
Toora loora loora loo,
I'll tell ye somethin' awfa true
Ye wouldnae hae yer telly the noo
If it wasnae for the Union.

(1) Noo I had a boss in Aiberdeen,
The nicest fella that ever was seen,
But he must 'a' thought me hell of a green
Before I joined the Union.

(2) And I had a boss named Allardyce,
He was really hell of a nice,
Except for the way he loaded the dice
Before I joined the Union.

(3) A pal o' mine has bought a car,
A second-haunded Jaguar —
He wouldn't 'a' travelled half as far
If it wasn't for his Union.

(4) The bosses they were daein' fine,
Wee weans workin' doon the mine —
They'd have them on the assembly line
If it wasn't for the Union.

(5) So men and women, all agree
It's time to rise up off yer knee
And raise the banner of unity —
Forward with the Union!

This is one of the many songs written by Matt McGinn of Glasgow.
For some he composed his own tunes, e.g. "A Miner's Lullaby";
others, as here, he wrote to existing tunes. The following is part of
Hamish Imlach's introduction to it . . . spoken, while he strummed
his guitar as background:— ". . . Matt's song . . . I've sung it
every night for eighteen months . . . it's a song written in the days
when Trade Union leaders were . . . sort of . . . working for the
people who paid them, not messing about getting on television . . .
—When the T.U.C. motto was still 'Non illegitimi carborundum'
. . . 'Don't let the bastards grind you down' . . .," — with other
topical and humorous cracks. After the first chorus he says (still
with guitar strumming), "It's my favourite song of Matt's. For any
tourists here, that's 'Toora loora loora loo, you wouldn't have your
television sets at present, if it wasn't for the Trade Unions'". Then
into verse 1.

The tune is the same as Jeannie Robertson uses for

"Killicrankie" in her disc *Jeannie's Merry Muse*[22], except that Jeannie ends every verse on the tonic as in the chorus above so that verse and chorus have exactly the same tune. Matt has greatly improved on this by making the verse end on a dominant cadence, as shown.

Hamish Imlach, a popular soloist, was born in Calcutta of Scottish parents; after eight years in India and five years in Australia, he came to Glasgow, and was at Hyndland School with Archie Fisher. He remembers Norman Buchan visiting the school with his Reivers group. An honorary member of the Indian Students' Club in Motherwell since 1961, Hamish studied engineering but has been a professional singer for some twenty years. "Matt wrote this song about 1964", he says. "The press were vilifying the Unions . . . both Matt and I adapted the words from time to time . . . it's an Irish tune, often sung to words which end, 'Come and join the British army'. People get ideas from the media, and it's good if they can get them in an entertaining way. . . . I still do anti-Polaris songs . . . 'You canny spend a dollar when you're deid' is still topical because the subs are still in the loch."

Hamish puts over this song with a kind of cool verve, never over-using his powerful voice. It is still popular in the more politically minded west, Matt's old home territory. Protest songs in general appear to be on the decline at present.

Hamish Imlach has been recorded by Transatlantic and by Autogram.

Ray Fisher: *The Fairfield Apprentice*
Kinross 1973; rec. P.C.   SA 1973/109.

I was born in the sha-dow of a Fair - field crane, And the blast of a freigh-ter horn Was the ve-ry first sound that reached my ears On the mor-ning I was born.   I

lay and lis-tened to the ship-yard noise Co-ming

out of the big un-known, And was sung to sleep by the

mo-ther tongue That was to be my own.

(1) I was born in the shadow of a Fairfield crane,
And the blast of a freighter horn
Was the very first sound that reached my ears
On the morning I was born.
I lay and listened to the shipyard noise
Coming out of the big unknown,
And was sung to sleep by the mother tongue
That was to be my own.

(2) And when I was barely one year old
I heard a siren scream
As that city watched in the blacked out night
A wandering search light beam.
And then one day I awoke and rose
To my father's day of peace,
And I knew the battle to stay alive
Was never going to cease.

(3) For I sat and listened tae my father tell
Of the Clyde that he once knew
Where you either sweated for a measly wage
Or joined in the parish queue.
Where life grew harder day by day
Along the riverside:
Oh it's oft I've heard my mother say
It was tears that made the Clyde.

(4) When I've sat in the school fae nine to four,
And I've dreamed of the world outside
Where the riveters and the platers watch
Their ships slip tae the Clyde.

And I'm serving my time behind ship-yaird gates
And sometimes mourn my lot
But if ever the bad old times return
I will fight as my father fought.

(5) For I was born in the shadow of a Fairfield crane,
And the blast of a freighter horn
Was the very first sound that reached my ears
On the morning I was born.

Still in the West of Scotland — with two of the best-known members of the singing Fisher family of Glasgow. The words and tune of this song were written by Archie Fisher and Bobby Campbell respectively.

Ray Fisher accompanies herself here on guitar and achieves some interesting shifts of rhythm by pausing vocally on certain notes, thus lagging temporarily behind the stricter rhythm of her instrumental backing. She has a strong voice of impressive quality, with an abrasive edge to it where needed. Her spoken introduction on this recording refers to the shipbuilding industry and she says, "Imagine I'm a seventeen-year-old apprentice . . . that's not so difficult because of my first name . . . all my life . . . I once won a Sunday School prize, a book called 'The Wonder Book for Boys'! . . . it started very early". She has had a powerful influence on the folk scene, and continues to be active and to help other less experienced singers.

This song was first heard in a series of six radio programmes called *Landmarks* (subtitle, *From the cradle to the grave*), 1964–65. Like the *Radio Ballads* series described in chapter 3, these were devised and presented by Charles Parker in conjunction with Ewan MacColl. "The Fairfield apprentice" song was in the second programme of the series, entitled *School*. Ray says, "It pinpointed the hardships on Clydeside in the 'bad old days' — parish queues and all — people's utter dependence on the Clyde's industries".

Ray Fisher has been recorded by Topic and by Leader.

Belle Stewart: *The berryfields o' Blair*
Kinross 1972; rec. P.C.   SA 1972/188. (Farewell ceilidh)

(V.3) Noo there's traiv-'lers fae the Wes - tern Isles,   fae

Ar-ran, Mull an' Skye, Fae Har-ris, Le-wis an'Kyles o'Bute they

come their luck tae try; Fae In-ver-ness and Ai-ber-deen, fae

Stor-no-way and Wick, A' flock tae Blair at the ber-ry-time the

straws an' rasps tae pick.

(1) Oh when berry-time comes roond each year, Blair's population swellin',
     There's every kind o' picker there an' every kind o' dwellin'.
     There's tents an' huts an' caravans, there's bothies and their bivvies,
     And shelters made wi' tattie-bags an' dug-oots made wi' divvies.

(2) Noo there's corner-boys frae Glesgie, kettle-boilers fae Lochee,
     An' miners fae the pits o' Fife, mill-workers fae Dundee,
     An' fisher-folk fae Peterheid an' tramps fae everywhere
     A' lookin' for a livin' aff the berryfields o' Blair.

(3) Noo there's traivellers fae the Western Isles, fae Arran, Mull an' Skye,
     Fae Harris, Lewis an' Kyles o' Bute they come their luck tae try;
     Fae Inversness and Aiberdeen, fae Stornoway and Wick,
     A' flock tae Blair at the berry-time the straws and rasps tae pick.

(4) Noo there's some who earn a pound or twa, some cannae earn their keep,
     And some wad pick fae morn tae nicht, an' some wad raither sleep.
     But there's some wha has tae pick or stairve, and some wha dinnae care,
     And there's some wha bless, an' some wha curse, the berryfields o' Blair.

(5) Noo there's faimilies pickin' for one purse an' some wha pick alane,
     And there's men wha share an share alike wi' wives that's no their
                                                                      ain.
     There's gladness and there's sadness tae, there's happy hairts an'
                                                                     sair,
     For there's comedy an' tragedy played on the fields o' Blair.

(6) But afore I put my pen awa' it's this I wad like to say,
     Ye'll traivel far before you'll meet a kinder lot than they,
     For I've mixed wi' them in field an' pub, and while I've breath to
                                                                    spare
     I'll bless the hand that led me tae the berryfields o' Blair.

Belle Stewart wrote these masterly words herself. As Geordie
McIntyre points out in his sleeve-notes for her latest disc,[23] "this
composition of Belle's, written in 1930 and set to 'The Queer
Folk o' the Shaws' or 'Pair o' Nicky Tams' tune, had entered the
anonymous stream of oral tradition before the authoress was
known". Her voice is somewhat lighter than that of her daughters
Sheila and Cathy but is perhaps even more persuasive and flexible.
In the first half of verse-lines 1 and 4 the tune here shows the
"double tonic", a characteristic of many Scots tunes.

One of the chief means of livelihood of the travellers was and still
is seasonal farm-work, but people of many other different origins
converge on the fertile fruit-growing land around Blairgowrie when
the berries are ready for picking. The crop, mainly raspberries, has
been gathered every year since around the end of last century. Belle
describes here the rich variety of the scene.

Songs, story-telling and instrumental music-making often arose
spontaneously after the day's work, in many a field or pub or
around the camp-fires, and the scene came to be described as "the
first unofficial folk festival in Scotland". When in 1966 the first
Traditional Music and Song festival was held in this little town, it
was in a sense simply a more organised version, with wider participation, of what had already been going on for many years. (In 1971
the locale of this festival was changed to Kinross.)

Belle's compound of charm, friendliness and complete natural-
ness gives her instant audience appeal: she has them eating out of
her hand before you can say 'The berryfields of Blair'.

Three other songs about work should be mentioned here: "The
wark o' the weavers" (AM1, Adam Young, Kinross 1975); "Jute-
mill song" (AM6, Bobby Dunbar, Kinross 1976) by Mary
Brooksbank, a worker in the Dundee mills, which includes these
memorable lines,

Oh dear me, the world's ill divided,
Them that works the hardest are the least provided;
and "The Blantyre explosion" (SA 1973/111, Owen Costello,
Kinross 1973) about a mining disaster. Versions of these, in the
order given, are in *101 Scottish Songs, The Singing Island* and *A
Collection of Scots Songs* (see chapter 3, note 49).

Group 9: SEXUAL SYMBOLISM

Bobby Dunbar: *Sprig o' thyme*
Kinross 1976; rec. A.P.   AM 6.

(1)   Aince I hed a sprig o' thyme,
      I thocht it never wad gae duin,
      But along there cam' a bonny sailor lad
      And he stole awa' ma sprig o' thyme.

          (*Chorus*)
          (For) time is sic a precious thing,
          Time brings a' things tae yer mind,
          And time wi' its labours along wi' a' its joys
          Oh time brings a' things tae an end.

(2)   The sailor gied tae me a rose,
      He said it never wad decay,
      He gied it tae me tae mind me o' the day
      He stole awa' ma sprig o' thyme.

(3)   Come a' ye maidens young and fair
      That are juist noo bloomin' in yer prime,
      Oh I wad like to see ye keep yer gairdens clean
      And let nae man steal awa' yer thyme.

This is perhaps one of the finest of all songs heard in the seventies. The words are reminiscent of those in Schubert's "Heidenröslein" — yet they say more, especially the chorus.

James Reeves in his chapter on "The Lingua Franca' " in *The Everlasting Circle* deals with the relation between specific flowers and human qualities. He defines thyme as virginity (though clearly it means far more than this in the above song), the rose as wanton passion, etc.

It's difficult to know whether to write "thyme" or "time" at several places where either would make sense, for there is a very subtle overlap between the two words. Anna Knight gave another fine rendering of the song at Kinross in 1975, with several felicitous phrases. A possible conflation of these two versions is the following:

Line 1 of chorus: Time it is a precious thing . . .
(Can be preceded by "Oh" or "For")
V.1 as above.
V.2, lines 3 and 4:   He gied it tae me tae mind me o' yon time,
                      'Twas then I heard ma mither say:
V.3:   Come a' ye maidens young and fair,
       A' ye that are bloomin' in yer prime:
       Now you be aware and keep yer gairdens fair
       And let nae man steal awa' yer thyme.

The time values in the tune are adapted as usual to fit the words, e.g. "sprig o' " and "never" (vv.1 and 2) are sung to the Scots snap rhythm. The song is not one of the most popular but is still well known and is heard fairly regularly. It is related to the English song "The seeds of love" (Reeves).

Bobby Dunbar sings it with a lyrical yet down-to-earth simplicity. His own guitar accompaniment adds a welcome dimension, for this tune's harmonic implications seem to clamour for some concrete expression. When set down in cold print this tune doesn't "look" so good: bars 3–4 in particular seem distressingly banal, with a kind of insipid sentimentality. Yet both the singers listened to made the song as a whole sound good, their performance caused the tune as it were to rise above itself. This shows the limitations of all transcription, descriptive or prescriptive. It also underlines the folly of judging either words or tune of a song in isolation one from the other. I have already referred to the transforming effect of music on words, and the same is true in reverse: good words can have a magical influence on the tune they are sung to.

A postal officer, Bobby has lived in Elgin all his life apart from army service during World War II. He heard this from an Englishman, at a ceilidh in Torridon, and remembered that his mother used to sing it. He is a song-writer as well as singer.

Arthur Watson: *She was a rum one*
Blairgowrie 1970; rec. P.C.   SA 1970/180.

(1) As I gaed oot on a fair muin nicht
 On a fair muin nicht in winter,
 It was there I spied a pretty fair maid,

　　　(Chorus)
　　　(An') she was a rum one, falla-diddle i-do-ay,
　　　But a bonny one, falla-diddle i-doh.

(2) It's she's walked up an' she's walked doon
 An' I've walked close beside her,
 An' I askit tae her ae reason why
 That she cuidna step nae wider.

(3) "Go 'way, go 'way, ye foolish young man
    An' stop yer idle talkin',
    For it ill becomes young men", she said,
    "Tae pick up young weemen walkin'."

(4) "But I'm a doctor tae ma trade
    An ma freends they cry me rare-O,
    An' gin ye tell me faur yer trouble lies
    I'll fix it neat an' fair-O."

(5) "Oh ma trouble lies in atween ma thighs
    And it's there it is abidin',
    An' it kittles me baith nicht an' day
    An' it keeps me fae ma stridin'."

(6) Oh I laid her doon upon the bank
    An' I've provided the plaister;
    She's lowpt up tae her feet again
    And says, "I think ye've cured me, maister."

(7) She's gien tae me ma winter's meat
    Likewise ma winter's firin';
    Far better than that she's gien tae me,
    It was a stable for ma stallion.

Arthur Watson of Aberdeen sings this vigorously, with an infectious lilt. In v. 1, line 4 of the verse is missed out and so the tune goes straight from "fair maid" to the chorus, with a quaver on low D for "An' ". Now Peter Hall tells me that Jeannie Robertson sang her v. 1 in exactly this way, so that yet again she was the Revival source and many singers learned it from her. Old Davie Stewart also sang it. Arthur Watson thinks he learned it from Norman Kennedy, and adds that many people have asked him for the words — he still sings it. It could once have been a broadside, probably English (the travellers may have got it thus): the word "rum", in the sense used here, is more an English than a Scots word. But the song has clearly become transmuted into something unmistakably Scottish. The last two lines of verse 7 supply a telling imagery for male sexual needs. By comparison, instead of a corresponding imagery for female needs, verses 2 and 5 supply what might be described as a figure of speech — and male speech at that, if understood in physical terms. But in psychological terms this figure of speech does not apply only to female needs: man or woman, if starved of love, may be affected to the point where he/she "cuidna step nae wider".

Arthur, director of the Aberdeen Artists' Printmaking Workshop, comments: "I found the song totally irresistible, with amazing flow in both words and tune as if honed down with all irrelevant detail removed. The singer is, I think, deliberately understating the case of his conquest and, in the last triumphant verse, its permanence".

Arthur Watson has been recorded by Topic.

Sheila Douglas: *O Mither, Mither*
Kinross 1976; rec. A.P.   AM7.

(1)   Oh Mither, Mither, what can a lassie dae,
       If I'm coorted by a fiddler in the merry month o' May?
       He'll touch me wi' his bow and mak' my strings tae play,
       And I'm feart I may rue it in the mornin' O.

(2)   Oh lassie, lassie, ye'll need tae learn the tune
       O' a slow air in April tae dance a jig in June,
       And if ye pay attention tae the manage o' your goon
       Ye'll never hae tae rue it in the mornin' O.

(3)   Oh Mither, Mither, what can a lassie dae,
       If he plays his penny whistle in the merry month o' May?
       He has the finest fingers upon the stops tae play,
       And I'm feart I may rue it in the mornin' O.

(4) Oh lassie, lassie, ye'll need tae learn the air,
And then you will discover that tae dance a reel is rare,
Jist place your steps aright an' ye never need despair
Nor fear ye may rue it in the mornin' O.

(5) Oh Mither, Mither, what can a lassie dae,
If I'm coorted by a piper in the merry month of May?
He has a braw chanter and his bag is never dry,
And I'm feart I may rue it in the mornin' O.

(6) Oh lassie, lassie, when ye hear him play the ground,
You'll learn the variations that mak' the pibroch sound.
You'll forget aboot *ceol beag* when *ceol mor* comes around
And never fear tae rue it in the mornin' O.

(7) Oh Mither, Mither, what can a lassie dae,
(If) he plays his concertina in the merry month o' May?
Wi' his reeds sae strang and free, he'll squeeze tae mak' me play,
And I'm feart I may rue it in the mornin' O.

(8) Oh lassie, lassie, ye'll need tae learn the keys,
If they're correctly fingered it can put you at your ease,
For it's the very box o' tricks a bonny lass tae please,
Ye'll never hae tae rue it in the mornin' O.

(9) Oh Mither, Mither, your words are wise I ken,
And I will ever mind them in dealin' wi' the men,
And when they play their music I'll dance baith but an' ben,
And never fear I'll rue it in the mornin' O.

Sheila Douglas says of this witty song that it's not intended to convey any message but mainly to entertain: "I was more interested in the symbolism of each instrument". The imagery is graphic and humorous — verse 5 in particular never fails to raise a laugh. Sheila also composed the attractive, dance-like tune, (see note 11 and note 8).

Group 10: NIGHT-VISITING

Davey Stewart: *I must away, love*
Kinross 1975; rec. A.P.   AM4.

(V.2) I step-ped up   tae ma true love's win-dow, And kneeled doon

gent - ly u-pon the stone. I whis-pered through her bed -room

win-dae, "Ma dar-lin' dear dae ye lie a - lone?"

(1) I must away, love, I can no longer tarry,
The morning's tempest I hae tae cross.
I will be guided without a stumble
Intae the airms I love the best.

(2) I stepped up tae ma true love's window,
And kneeled doon gently upon the stone.
I whispered through her bedroom windae,
"Ma darlin' dear dae ye lie alone?"

(3) She raised her heid frae aff the doon-soft pillow;
She's thrown her airms aroond her breist,
Sayin' "Wha is that at ma bedroom windae,
Disturbin' me frae ma lang night's rest?"

(4) I says, "Oh ma own love, it is thy own true lover;
I pray you rise, love, an' let me in,
For I have come on a lang night's journey
And I am weet, love, untae ma skin."

(5) She's raised her up wi' the greatest of pleisure,
She's raised her up and she's let me in;
We baith shook hands and embraced each ither,
Until the mornin' we laid as yin.

(6) Noo the cocks were crawin' an' the birds were whistlin',
The burns they ran frae up in the brae.
"Remember lass, I'm a ploo-boy laddie
And the fairmer I must obey.

(7) Oh I must gang my love, to leave you
Tae climb the hills, they're high above;
But I will climb wi' the greatest pleisure
Since I've been in the airms o' my ain true love."

The night-visiting custom is found in many countries, and the ambient mores are varied. Ewan MacColl wrote, of the Scots and English tradition, "The night-visit was essentially a consummation of love sanctioned by the girl's parents on the night before the wedding";[24] but Davey Stewart says this song is about "Joyful fornication". Many songs exist on night-visiting, and with different shades of meaning. Sometimes bits of one song cross over to another — for instance, the song above has almost the same words as "I'm a rover" (p. 96 of *The Scottish Folksinger*) which came from Aberdour. So has the next song, "Here's a health to all true lovers", though its first verse is again different; and the first verse of "I'm a rover" does not appear in the other two songs here. But the tunes of these three bear no relationship to each other.

Davey Stewart, a social worker in Fife, sings this with robust lyricism. He learned it at some time in the mid-sixties, when he was involved in running the folk club in St. Andrews. With John Watt and The Beggar's Mantle Ceilidh Band he has been recorded by Springthyme.

Belle Stewart: *Here's a health to all true lovers*
Blairgowrie 1970; rec. P.C.   SA 1970/181.

(V.2) Let the night be dark as the ve-ry dun-geon, Let not a star shine from the bowl, Still I will be gui-ded, oh safe-ly gui-ded, In-to the arms of my own true love.

(1) Here's a health to all true lovers
And here's to mine wherever she may be.
This very night I will go and see her
Although she is many a long mile from me.

(2) Let the night be dark as the very dungeon,
     Let not a star shine from the bowl,
     Still I will be guided, oh safely guided,
     Into the arms of my own true love.

The rest of the words, verses 3–7, are very similar to vv. 2–6 of the previous song and so are omitted here: both words and tune are close to the version in *The Singing Island*.

This is Belle Stewart in her most seductive vein: her flexible voice glides and slides its way till one feels, if female, one would definitely open that door, and, if male, would consider the long walk and getting drenched to the skin (a good line, that) well worth while. The tune, with its swooping intervals, is in what would appear to be a favourite mode for the Stewarts: a minor inversion of the pentatonic scale. The form is ABCA[1].

The melody is sung so smoothly, with such roundness and such understatement of accentuation, that the transcription poses a problem in rhythm. The time is certainly triple, but the bar-lines could all be placed one beat later, and the accents would then come on the words *dark*, *dun*(-geon), *star*, *bowl*, *gui*(-ded), *arms* and *love*.

Cilla Fisher, with Artie Tresize: *The laird o' Udny's wa's.* (*This ae nicht*)
Kinross 1976; rec. A.P.   AM7.

(V.3)   When he got in he wes sae gled He pu'ed the bun-net frae

aff o' his head, He kissed her on the cheek sae red And the

auld wife heard the din. Ah but weel she li - kit that

ae nicht That ae, ae, ae nicht, And weel she li -kit that

ae   nicht She   let her lad-die   in.

(1) Noo I'm the laird o' Udny's Wa's
    And I've come here withoot guid cause,
    And I've had mair than thirty fa's
    Comin oot owre the hill.
        Ah but let me in this ae nicht,
        This ae, ae, ae nicht,
        Aye let me in this ae nicht
        And I'll be back nae mair.

(2) We'll oil the door when it gets weet
    And it'll neither chirp nor cheep,
    No it'll neither chirp nor cheep
    And I'll gae slippin' in.
        Ah but let me in this ae nicht,
        This ae, ae, ae nicht,
        Aye let me in this ae nicht
        And I'll be back nae mair.

(3) When he got in he wes sae gled
    He pu'ed the bunnet frae aff o' his head,
    He kissed her on the cheek sae red
    And the auld wife heard the din.
        Ah but weel she likit that ae nicht
        That ae, ae, ae nicht,
        And weel she likit that ae nicht
        She let her laddie in.

(4) For when he got in he wes sae gled
    He knockit the bottom boards oot o' the bed,
    He stole the lassie's maidenhead
    And the auld wife heard the din.
        Ah but weel she likit that ae nicht
        That ae, ae, ae nicht,
        And weel she likit that ae nicht
        She let her laddie in.

Cilla Fisher and Artie Tresize have become increasingly popular,
and not only in Scotland. Cilla sings here in a relaxed, matter-of-
fact way, with Artie's effective guitar backing, and everyone joins
in the refrains.

A member of the famous Fisher singing family of Glasgow, Cilla has been a professional singer for the last six years. She learned this song from Jimmy Hutchinson around 1973, when he lived in Kirkcaldy — she draws most of her material from source when possible. She likes both words and tune of this song, and adds, "Seducation (sic) is timeless — so if it happened in a cottage or a block of flats it's the same. The theme is a story of an everyday happening (if you're lucky)".

Both words and tune of this song are almost identical with Jeannie Robertson's "The laird o' Windy Wa's" on her E.P. disc. (see notes to "I'll lay ye doon, love") and on Prestige International no. 13006. There is also a close resemblance in the words, though less in the tune, to "As I cam' ower the Muir o' Ord" in the *Bothy Ballads* disc (*Scottish Tradition* series). The "Muir of Ord" version has one appearance of the "O she likit that ae nicht" theme, as in the second half of vv. 3 and 4 above, but the ending is changed to "For O she rued that ae nicht". In the bothy version the use of the first person singular continues to the end, and the final effect is one of male boastfulness at success achieved against the woman's will. A whiff of this remains in the otherwise more equalitarian version given above. In the *Bothy Ballads* booklet Hamish Henderson suggests that the song belongs to a group which "tend towards broad comedy (or even, as in Jeannie's version, towards what looks like conscious burlesque)". If this is true then it appears to be an exclusively male comedy; certainly Cilla Fisher does not see her version as burlesque.

Morag MacLeod comments on the differences between Scots and Gaelic songs in this genre:

> Overt references to sexual success from the male point of view, boasting, almost, about stealing the girl's maidenhead and so on, hardly occur in Gaelic song. The majority of songs about sexual encounters are from the girl's point of view. Most of the bawdy songs in Scots probably originated in the bothy, and in such an exclusively male environment it would be natural for men to compensate for the lack of female company by talking and joking about women, boasting about their own sexual prowess and composing songs which were not meant for female ears.
>
> Gaelic males did not suffer the same deprivations. At the same time, in many accounts of waulkings it is said that men were not allowed to be present, and among the waulking songs you get "Young Alasdair son of MacNicol, /I wish I could bear a son to you/Five or six or seven/ . . ." The theme of women's songs relating to sexual encounters is more often regret: "My laugh of last year/Has made my step heavier" and "I had an apron of smooth silk/Prettily embroidered/And had I been so modest as to lie alone/I would not be heavy and pregnant under my apron."

There are references to night-visiting from both viewpoints. There is no indication that the intimacies involved were reserved for the night before the wedding, but regular visits by the same suitor led to expectation of marriage. Disappointment in this expectation would lead to complaint, for example: "That's how I passed the winter/Always longing for my sweetheart's love. . . Many a night throughout the season/Did I get up to the bench/My advice to other girls/Is to lie reasonably in their beds," (that is, not to bother with such a man!)

Songs by men about night-visits that give details, are usually humorous and self-deprecating. The element of forcing unwanted attentions on the girl does not show itself. Two friends decide to visit a girl in a shieling. When the bard approaches her she turns him down at first, but then she says, "All right, then, put off your clothes/I'll let you lie beside me/For fear you may satirise me/And not for love of your charms." There is an equality here that is missing, I think, in the Scots songs on this subject. This is not to say, of course, that Gaelic men did not take advantage of girls. But they did not make songs about it.[25]

Cilla Fisher has been recorded by Topic, Autogram, Trailer/ Leader, Kettle, and the BBC.

Group 11: ELEGIAC

Lizzie Higgins: *The college boy*
Aberdeen 1970; rec. A.M.   SA 1970/20.

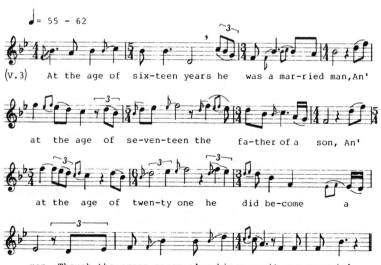

(v.3) At the age of six-teen years he was a mar-ried man, An' at the age of se-ven-teen the fa-ther of a son, An' at the age of twen-ty one he did be-come a man, Though the green grass o'er his grave it was grow-in'.

(1)   Oh father, dear father, pray what is this ye've done?
      You have wed me to a college boy, a boy that's far too young,
      For he is only sixteen years and I am twenty-one;
      He's ma bonny, bonny boy, and he's growin'.

(2)   As we were going through College wyn' some boys were playing ball
      When there I saw my own true love, the fairest of them all,
      When there I saw my own true love, the fairest of them all;
      He's ma bonny, bonny boy, and he's growin'.

(3)   At the age of sixteen years he was a married man,
      An' at the age of seventeen the father of a son,
      An' at the age of twenty-one he did become a man,
      Though the green grass o'er his grave it was growin'.

(4)   I will buy my love some flannel an' I'll make my love's shroud,
      With every stitch I put in it the tears will flow down.
      With every stitch I put in it the tears will flow down
      For cruel fate put an end to his growin'.

In the passage from his *History of England* quoted above (in the notes for "Andrew Lammie") Trevelyan continues: ". . . Betrothal often took place when one or both of the parties was in the cradle, and marriage when they were scarcely out of the nurses' charge".

This is Lizzie Higgins's own version, both words and tune, of "The College Boy", sung here with all the impressive dignity and restraint at her command. She underlines the point that, after this arranged marriage took place, the girl "fell very much in love with her young husband". Other versions are known as "The trees they do grow high" (see next song here), "Still growing", "Lang a-growing", "Lady Mary Ann" and "Young Craigston". Interesting notes on the last-named can be found in *The Singing Island*.

Lizzie Higgins uses ornamentation as an important means to expressiveness. Now a tendency towards increased ornamentation has been a feature of revival singing in recent years. The original impetus towards this probably came from Ireland, but as Peter Hall points out in his notes on Lizzie's last record, *Up an' awa' wi' the Laverock*, the suggestion made by Hamish Henderson that Lizzie's ornamented singing-style "almost recalls the *sean-nos* of the West of Ireland"[26] is mistaken, for, says Hall, "her style is distinctly Scots". He quotes Samuel Bayard's description of Irish ornamentation as "almost impeding the onward course of the melody", and as "wavering and unemphatic", and rightly comments, "This could never be a description of Lizzie's style".

Lizzie was of course strongly influenced by her famous mother Jeannie Robertson, but she was also influenced by her father Donald Higgins, a fine player of the Highland bagpipes and no mean singer himself. There has been much debate concerning Lizzie's claim that her father taught her to imitate the ornaments of pipe-music. To reproduce these ornaments vocally is literally a physical impossibility, and Lizzie has certainly been influenced by the general trend towards increased decoration. Nevertheless there's an unmistakable sound of the pipes in her singing — including, in some ways as yet not fully analysed, her ornamentation. More laboratory analysis needs to be done on this. But, ". . . it is possible that her comparative lack of dynamic variation and her freedom from vibrato may be attributable to the strong influence of pipe-music, since one of the chief characteristics of this music is its unwavering uniformity of volume".[27]

If you have never heard Lizzie Higgins sing, you have an unforgettable and unique musical experience yet to come. Her voice combines a husky tone, a kind of gutsy-ness, with a bell-like quality and very true pitch. Her large repertoire varies from the big ballads, or muckle sangs, to lighter songs such as the entrancing little "Tammy Toddles" which she sings to a strathspey-type tune.

Maggie Pycroft: *The trees they do grow high*
Kinross 1975; rec. A.P.   AM2.

(V. 4) Now at the age of sixteen he was a mar-ried man, An'
at the age of se-ven-teen the fa-ther to a son, An'
at the age of eigh-teen the grass grew o-ver him, Cruel
death soon put an end to his gro-win'. Gro-win', gro-win', cruel
death soon put an end to his gro-win'.

(1)   The trees they do grow high, the leaves they do grow green,
      An' many the cold winter night my love and I have seen.
      On a cold winter night my love, you an' I alone have been,
      My bonnie laddie's young but he's growin'.
        Growin', growin', my bonnie laddie's young but he's growin'.

(2)   "Oh father, dear father, you've done to me much wrong
      For to go an' get me married to one who is so young,
      For he is only sixteen years an' I am twenty-one,
      My bonny laddie's young but he's growin'."
        Growin', growin', my bonnie laddie's young but he's growin'.

(3)   "Oh dochter, oh dochter, I'll tell you what I'll do,
      I'll send your love to college for another year or two,
      An' all around his college cap we'll tie a ribbon blue
      Just to let the ladies know that he's married."
        Married, married, to let the ladies know that he's married.

(4) Now at the age of sixteen he was a married man,
An' at the age of seventeen the father to a son,
An' at the age of eighteen the grass grew over him,
Cruel death soon put an end to his growin'.
    Growin', growin', cruel death soon put an end to his growin'.

(5) For now my love is dead and in his grave doth lie,
The green grass grows over him so very very fine;
I'll sit here an' mourn his death until the day I die
An' I'll watch all o'er his child while he's growin'.
    Growin', growin', I'll watch all o'er his child while he's growin'.

This is another Scottish version of the same song. It is akin to
Ord's "My bonnie laddie's lang, lang o' growing", but the ages of
the couple have been advanced from the childish twelve and
thirteen, three verses are omitted and a very effective last verse
added. Maggie Pycroft, from Fife, thinks she learned it from an
L.P. of Martin Carthy around '72–'73, but is not sure. She
particularly liked the sentiments in this one, and the tune, which is
indeed fine, with its soaring refrain. She takes it at a flowing but
not excessive rate, and like Lizzie's her expressiveness is tightly-
reined.

Annie Bell: *Rare Willie drooned in Yarrow* (Child 215)
Kinross 1975; rec. A.P.   AM2.

Down in yon gar-den sweet and gay Where bon-ny grows the
li-ly, I heard a mai-den sing-in' say, "My wish is wi' sweet
Wil-lie, My wish is wi' sweet Wil-lie".

(1)   Down in yon garden sweet and gay
      Where bonny grows the lily,
      I heard a maiden singin' say,
      "My wish is wi' sweet Willie,
      My wish is wi' sweet Willie".

(2)   For Willie's fair and Willie's rare
      And Willie's wondrous bonny,
      And Willie's hecht tae mairry me
      Gin e'er he mairries ony,
      Gin e'er he mairries ony.

(3)   But Willie's gaen whom I thocht on
      And does not hear me weepin',
      O spare a tear frae true love's e'e(n)
      When other maids are sleepin',
      When other maids are sleepin'.

(4)   Oh gentle wind that bloweth south
      From where my love repaireth,
      Carry a kiss from his sweet mouth
      And tell me how he fareth,
      And tell me how he fareth.

(5)   And tell sweet Willie tae come doon
      And hear the mavis singin',
      Tae see the birds on ilka bush
      And leaves aroond them hingin',
      And leaves aroond them hingin'.

(6)   She socht him east, she socht him west,
      She socht him braid and narrow;
      Syne in the cleavin' o' a craig
      She fund him droon'd in Yarrow,
      She fund him droon'd in Yarrow.

John Barrow: *Rare Willie drooned in Yarrow* (Child 215)
Kinross 1973; rec. A.M.   SA 1973/112.

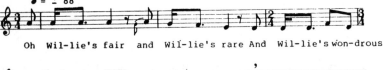

Oh Wil-lie's fair and Wil-lie's rare And Wil-lie's won-drous

bon-ny, And Wil-lie hecht tae mar-ry me Gin e'er he mar-ried

o - ny.

(1) Oh Willie's fair and Willie's rare
And Willie's wondrous bonny,
And Willie hecht tae marry me
Gin e'er he married ony.

(2) Yestreen I made ma bed fu' braid,
The nicht I'll mak' it narra,
An' a' the live-long winter's night
I lie twined of me marra.

(3) O come ye by yon water-side,
Pulled you the rose or lily?
Oh come ye by yon meadow green
Or saw ye ma sweet Willie?

(4) Oh she sought him east an' she sought him west,
She sought him braid and narra;
Syne in the cliftin' o' a crag
She found him drowned in Yarrow.

Annie Bell of Blairgowrie was born and brought up in Fife, and she has also lived in the Borders and in Angus. She is well-known at Kinross Festival as a champion whistler, diddler and melodeon player, has adjudicated for these classes and been a guest artiste. In recent years Annie has added singing to her accomplishments: she prefers "good Scots songs with good lyrics", and finds some of the longer traditional songs "repetitive and boring...too much dwelling on the theme of death". She is active in local affairs and entertainments, taking part regularly in Highland Night concerts, O.A.P. clubs, Burns Nights, etc.

The mixture of styles in Annie's version is most striking in her verse 4, which in contrast to the rest contains no Scots words or pronunciations. She got it from a book in her local library. Various collections, such as Greig's *Folk Song of the North East*, Palgrave's *Golden Treasury,* and Robert Chambers' *Scottish Ballads* include six similar verses. The beautiful tune (no. 5 in Bronson) was learned orally from other singers — compare Jean Redpath's tune, chapter 3. Annie Bell sings flowingly, in moderately free time and with some variation in dynamics, and her clear, true voice is pitched in a high register.

The words of John Barrow's version are Child A, with a few Tyneside pronunciations: he got it from *A Book of Scottish Verse*, ed. Mackie, OUP reprint, 1960. Its brevity was an attraction to him at that time. Not knowing of any tune for this Border ballad when he first found it, he made his own up...and a very good tune it is, suitable to the elegiac words. It is sung quietly and with warmth.

John regards this as "a fairly straight love song ending in tragedy", but to Annie Bell it is "a song of unrequited love where the heroine gives love which is not returned, and because of this fact, rather than let her down or marry her, he decides to take his life". Compare these two views with Jean Redpath's, of tragedy-through-accident (chapter 3), and it is clear that a singer may put his or her own interpretation into a song, with the aid of imagination and personal memory or fantasy.

Group 12: EXILE AND EMIGRATION

Willie Scott: *Jamie Raeburn*
Blairgowrie 1970; rec. P.C.   SA 1970/179.

(V.4) Fare-weel my a-ged mo-ther, I'm vexed for what I've done, I
hope none will a-cause to you the race that I have run; I
hope God will pro-tect you when I am far a-wa', Far
frae the bon-ny hills an' dales o' Ca-le-do-ni-a.

(1)   My name is Jamie Raeburn, in Glasgow I was born.
      My place of habitation I now maun leave wi scorn,
      My place of habitation I now maun gang awa'
      Far frae the bonny hills an' dales o' Caledonia.

(2)   It was early one morning just by the break o' day.
      I overheard the turnkey, which unto us did say,
      "Arise ye helpless convicts, arise ye yin and a',
      This is the day that we maun stray frae Caledonia".

(3)   We all arose, pit on oor clothes, oor hairts were filled wi' grief,
      And a' oor freends stood roond the coach, to grant us nae relief,
      And a' oor freends stood roond the coach to see us gang awa',
      Tae see us leave the hills an' dales o' Caledonia.

(4)   Fareweel my agèd mother, I'm vexed for what I've done,
      I hope none will a-cause to you the race that I have run;
      I hope God will protect you when I am far awa',
      Far frae the bonny hills an' dales o' Caledonia.

(5)   Fareweel my agèd faither, he is the best o' men,
      Likewise my sweetheart, young Catherine was her name.
      Nae mair I'll walk by Clyde's clear stream or by the Broomielaw,
      Farewell my freends, ye hills an' dales, o' Caledonia.

(6)   But oh perchance we'll meet again, I hope 'twill be above
      Where hallelujahs will be sung to him wha rules in love.
      Nae earthly judge shall judge us there, but him wha rules us a'.
      Fareweel my freends, ye hills an' dales, o' Caledonia.

It is not so long ago that comparatively trivial offences such as poaching could be punished by transportation for life to a convict settlement, e.g. Van Diemen's Land (see *Personal Choice* for a song with this title). "Jamie Raeburn", which describes the convicts' farewells in harrowing detail, is sung here by a veteran and much-travelled singer, a retired shepherd now in his eighties: Willie Scott of Hawick, known as the Border Shepherd. He is a source rather than a revival singer, in that he has absorbed his large repertoire of songs from his earliest years on, but he has been closely involved in revival events, and at festivals he has been an invited guest or adjudicator. He uses his rather light tenor voice with great musical charm and his enunciation is clear but unforced, with the added bonus of a fine Border accent. Willie says, "My mother used to sing 'Jimmy Raeburn' when I was a wee boy, and my brother Tom gave me the words before I left school". He has a special feeling for this "great song", and comments, "A shepherd has to be responsible for his sheep, and if not is just not wanted. Long ago sheep stealers were hanged. . . . As far as I have been told, he [Jamie Raeburn] stole a hen — that was what he was transported for — and his girlfriend said he was not near the place as they had a date that night".

Another equally affecting song which Willie often sings, this time about a party of emigrants leaving for America, has a chorus line "Hame fareweel, freends fareweel". This is "Callieburn", which Willie re-created from the original "Machrihanish" as sung by Alec MacShannon of Kintyre.

"Jamie Raeburn" has been recorded by Willie Scott in *Border Ballads* (Topic 12T 183).

Group 13: WANDERERS' SONGS

Charlie Murray: *Tramps an' hawkers*
Blairgowrie 1970; rec. P.C.   SA 1970/184.

Note: in 5 of the middle verses,
bars 1 and 13 become:

(1) Come a' ye tramps an' hawker lads, ye gaitherers o' bla',
That tramps the country roond an' roon', come listen ane an' a';
I'll tell to you a rovin' tale o' sichts that I hae seen
Far up intae the snowy north an' sooth by Gretna Green.

(2) I have seen the high Ben Nevis 'way towerin' tae the muin,
I have been by Crieff and Callander an' roond by bonnie Doon,
An' by the Nethy's silvery sands and places ill tae ken
Far up intae the snowy north lies Urquhart's fairy glen.

(3) Noo I aften laugh untae masel' when trudgin' on the road,
A bag o' bla' upon ma back, my face as broon's a toad,
Wi' lumps o' cake an' tattie scones, wi' cheese an' braxy ham,
Wi' little thocht whae far I've come an' less where I am gaun.

(4) Noo I've dene ma share o' huntin' wi' the gagers on the Clyde.
I've helped in Buckie trawlers hawl the herrin' owre the side.
I've helped tae build the mighty bridge that spans the hazy Forth,
An' wi' mony an Angus fairmer I hae ploo'ed the banks o' Esk.

(5) Noo I'm happy in the summer time beneath the bright blue sky,
Little kennin' in the mornin' where at nicht I'll hae tae lie,
In barn or byre, or anywhere, dossin' oot amang the hay,
An' if the weather suits me right I'm happy every day.

(6) Noo Loch Katrine an' Loch Lomond, they've a' been seen by me,
The Dee, the Don, the Deveron hurries tae the sea.
Dunrobin Castle, by the way, I very near forgot,
And aye the rickle o' cairn marks the hoose o' John o' Groats.

(7) Noo I'm often doon by Gallowa' and roon' aboot Stranraer,
My business taks me anywhere, sure I've wandered near and far;
I've got the rovin' notion there's nothing what I loss
In a' ma days, ma daily fare, an' what'll pey my doss.

(8) But I think I'll go to Paddy's land, I'm makin' up ma min',
For Scotland's fairly altered noo, I canna raise the win'.
But I will trust in providence, if providence proves true,
Then I will sing of Erin's isle when I come back to you.

This song breathes the very essence of the nomadic life — but the speaker is an itinerant worker, not a layabout: a loner describing the different jobs he's done and the places he's visited. Unlike

Woody Guthrie's migrant workers, forced to travel in search of work, our man has chosen his way of life and enjoys it — "Noo I aften laugh untae masel' when trudgin' on the road...wi' little thocht whae faur I've come an' less where I am gaun". And he's "got the roving notion" that he's missing nothing whatsoever.

This was one of Jimmy MacBeath's favourite songs. Charlie Murray of Forfar, a weel-kent figure on the East and North-East scene, has a really beautiful voice with a relaxed, vigorous, springing quality. He got this song from Jimmy MacBeath at Banff feeing market, around 1934–5 when Jimmy was in his hey-day as an itinerant singer. The fourth verse is less well-known, and Charlie says he "concocted" the last line himself. He has been recorded by Tangent, Springthyme, and BBC records.

Charlie Murray has always worked as a cattle-man, in Banff, Ross-shire (Black Isle) and now Forfar district. He learned a few songs from his parents, and others from street singers and from old 78 records. Of "Tramps and Hawkers" he says, "In Jimmy MacBeath's case I think he let the establishment know that despite hardships and harassment by police to street singers, he made a living by what he liked doing. Farm work in the thirties was rough, for little reward, and I think if I had not had family responsibilities in early life, I would have liked to have done the same as Jimmy".

Ray Fisher: *The moving on song*
Heriot-Watt University Students' Union, Edinburgh 1971; rec. A.M.   SA 1971/13.

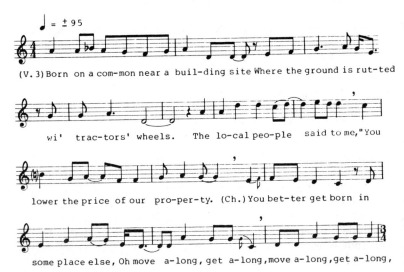

(V. 3) Born on a common near a building site Where the ground is rutted wi' tractors' wheels. The local people said to me, "You lower the price of our property. (Ch.) You better get born in some place else, Oh move along, get along, move along, get along,

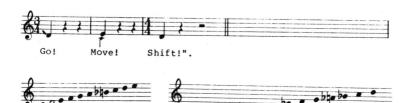

Go! Move! Shift!".

(1) Born in the middle o' the afternoon
In a horse-drawn wagon on the old A5;
The big twelve-wheeler shook my bed.
"You can't stop here," the policeman said —

> (*Chorus*)
> "You better get born in some place else,
> Oh move along, get along, move along, get along,
> Go! Move! Shift!"

(2) Born at the tattie-lifting time,
In an auld bell-tent near a tattie-field.
The fairmer says, "The work's a' done,
It's time that you were movin' on."

(3) Born on a common near a building site
Where the ground is rutted wi' tractors' wheels.
The local people said to me,
"You lower the price of our property."

(4) Born at the back of a blackthorn hedge
When the white hoar frost lay on the ground.
No eastern kings came bearing gifts,
Instead, the order came tae shift.

(5) Wagon, tent or trailer-born
Last week, last year, or in far-off days,
Born here or a thousand miles away
There's always men near-by who'll say —

This was written and composed by Ewan MacColl for one of his *Radio Ballad* documentaries. On the tape Ray Fisher, who accompanies herself again on guitar, introduces the song: she talks about the Radio Ballads and continues: "This one, *The Travellers*, was about tinkers and travellers all over Britain, who have been regarded as social misfits, people who wouldn't conform . . . the attitude to them has been 'We don't want you'. Here, the woman is about to give birth in a covered wagon by the side of the road . . . a police car arrives, the family are told to move on . . . so the child is born . . . on the road".

Remarks earlier on Ray's style apply equally here: her "Go! Move! Shift!" is quietly electrifying, and her occasional vocal rubato is even more free. There are few Scots words here for as Ray suggests, the song was written about the whole of Britain. The last two verses widen the horizons even further and it becomes a song about the whole world. "This song has a lasting message", says Ray, "— always minority groups will be seen as a threat".

Group 14: THE SUPERNATURAL

Lizzie Higgins: *Willie's fatal visit* (Child 255)
Aberdeen 1973; rec. S.S. SA 1973/174.

(V.3) "Oft hae ye tra - velled this road, Wul-lie, Yer bon - nie new love tae see. Nae mair ye'll travel this road, (w)-Wul - lie, For this nicht a-venged I'll be".

(1) Wullie's gane owre yon high high hills
     An' doon yon dowie dens,
     It is there he met a grievious ghost
     That wid fear ten thousand men.

(2) "Oft hae ye travelled this road, Wullie,
     Oft hae ye travelled in sin,
     Ne'er thocht ye o' my poor soul
     When yer sinful life did end.

(3) Oft hae ye travelled this road, Wullie,
     Yer bonny new love tae see.
     Nae mair ye'll travel this road, Wullie,
     For this nicht avenged I'll be."

(4) She has ta'en her perjured love
     And she's rived him frae gair tae gair,
     An' on ilkae side o' Mary's stile
     Of him she's hung a share.

(5) Yer father an' mither baith made moan
     Yer new love muckle mair,
     Yer father an' mither baith made moan
     An' yer new love rived her hair.

No-one else can make your flesh creep quite as Lizzie Higgins does in this spine-chilling ballad. She got it from her mother and has honed it down to its stark essentials. Jeannie Robertson's, both words and tune, is the second of Bronson's two versions. Child has only one, a longer story of which the above is in effect v. 13 to the last verse, 18; it contains no overt suggestion that the ghost is that of Willie's former, jilted love, though the implication is possible if you read between the lines. Child's version (from Peter Buchan's *Ballads of the North of Scotland*) has these two lines:

> Wan and weary was the ghost
> Upon sweet Willie did smile.

Jeannie replaces this second line with "On him that grimly smiled"; this is in her v. 2 (which Lizzie here omits), just before the revenant reproaches Willie and then tears him to pieces. Her version has two important additions (v. 3 above) which confirm the jilted-love hypothesis: "Your bonny love" becomes "Your bonny new love", and the last line introduces the revenge declaration. Child's final comment, "Stanzas 15–17", (in effect verses 2–4 above) "...are too good for the setting: nothing so spirited, word or deed, could have been looked for from a ghost wan, weary and smiling", indicates that he had not considered this hypothesis, for he would surely have remembered that jealousy is cruel as the grave.

Jimmy Hutchinson also sings this ballad, and his comments suggest a further twist to this grisly tale: "...it would lose a lot of its weight if the ghost was not that of Willie's jilted girl-friend seeking her revenge. It does not say in the song how she came to be dead but I would think that Willie himself bumped her off so that he could take up with his new love. That would make it a double revenge and twice as sweet maybe? Or she might have died of a broken heart as they did in those days, but I think myself that Willie dunnit".

Lizzie herself adds the final, Hardy-esque touch: '...the sweetheart he murdered was going to have a baby, but I'm very glad to say she avenged her murder by killing him, just as he had killed her without any compassion at all".

Lizzie Higgins sings this on *Ballad Folk* (BBC REC 293).

Group 15: PHILOSOPHICAL

Adam Young: *If ye only wait a wee*
Kinross 1977; rec. A.P.   AM10.

Oh I heard a mi-ther sin-gin' tae her wee slee-py wean, And oft-times frae the hill-side cam' a soft an' sweet re-frain; But of all the sangs that touch the hairt an' haunt us till we dee, It was "Din-na get doon-hair-ted, lad-die, learn tae wait a wee".

(1) Oh I heard a mither singin' tae her wee sleepy wean,
     And oft-time frae the hillside cam' a soft an' sweet refrain;
     But of all the sangs that touch the hairt an' haunt us till we dee,
     It was "Dinna get doonhairted, laddie, learn tae wait a wee."

(2) Noo ye dinna get doonhairted though the plains be clad wi' snaw,
     For the sun will still be shinin' and the gentle breeze will blaw;
     Though ye dinna see the mavis or the larks abuin the lea,
     They will set the echoes ringin' if ye only wait a wee.

(3) Noo ye canna sail life's oceans 'neath a sky o' simmer blue,
     For there's oft-times stormy seasons that we all maun westle
                                                           through;
     But there's aye a silver linin' tae the darkest cloud we see
     And yer boat will reach the harbour if ye only wait a wee.

A powerful impact is created by this, at first sight, artless song.
This due partly to the way it's put over: Adam Young is
"unashamed of soul", yet he eschews any hint of sentimentality.
He says, "This song has a general and sincere meaning of truth in
it". One feels a whole life-time of experience is being poured out,
for he is not a young man and indeed the slightly laboured quality
of his voice has perhaps a greater effect here than a young fresh
voice could achieve. But it's not only the singer's personality and
style that makes this performance moving, the song itself contains
the essence of good popular art. The tune has vitality of shape and
of form, and the words with their graphic imagery — the iron grip
of winter, the desperate situation of a storm at sea — illumine the
theme and say more than many sermons or philosophical treatises.
The opening verse suggests a kind of universal mother singing to
all of earth's children. Adam learned this song when he was at
school, and it was recorded on an old 78 record by the late Neil
MacLean.

Footnotes to Chapter IV

1. Stevenson, *Poems*. Chatto and Windus, London, 1914, pp. 171–2.
2. *The Concise Oxford Dictionary*. Fifth edition, 1970.
3. *Bothy Ballads*, no. 1 in *Scottish Tradition* series of discs from the archives of the
    School of Scottish Studies. (Tangent TNGM 109).
4. The term "transcription" is used in the sense of writing down what has been
    sung. Prescriptive notation sets down the music to be played or sung, as com-
    posed usually by one person, with instructions concerning tempo, dynamics
    and interpretation; although these three will vary considerably in performance,
    according to the performer's concept of the music, the actual notes and the
    time structure cannot be departed from. This notation is used for art music

(but see comments on p. 00 concerning ornamentation in certain periods of music history). Descriptive notation sets down, with varying degrees of detail, the music which has actually *been* produced at one single performance. Descriptive transcriptions have been made of art music performances, but comparatively rarely.

5. The fourth and last volume contains some more detailed transcriptions.
6. *Scottish Studies* 14 (1970), 35–58, 155–88, and 16 (1972), 139–59. Also examples by Percy Grainger, a pioneer in this field, in the *Journal of the Folk Song Society* 3 (1908–9), 147–242.
7. Grainger, far ahead of his time, introduced the concept of "one single loosely knit modal folk-song scale" (p. 158). For material on the modes and folk song, see Maud Karpeles, *An Introduction to English Folk Song*, pp. 31–38, which gives further references; and Bertrand H. Bronson, *The Traditional Tunes of the Child Ballads*, 1. xxviii and 2. xi–xiii. For a wider consideration of music analysis see Marcia Herndon, "Analysis: the Herding of Sacred Cows?", *Ethnomusicology* 18 (1974), 219–63.
8. *The Belt wi' Colours Three*, Alison McMorland (Tangent TGS 125). Sheila Douglas's song *Oh Mither, Mither* is included in this disc.
9. Eveline Hunter, *Scottish Woman's Place*, p. 12.
10. See also Edward J. Cowan's note on this in *The People's Past*, pp. 48–51.
11. The rhythmic figures ♩♪♩ and ♪♩♪ are sometimes interchanged here with ♫ and ♫.; this applies also in the tunes on pp. 166, 176 and 178.
12. David Herd, *Ancient and Modern Scots Songs*, 2.232.
13. Norman Buchan: interview, 20/8/77, Edinburgh.
14. In *Personal Choice* and *The Singing Island*.
15. *The Muckle Sangs* booklet, *revised edition*, accompanying no. 5 of the Scottish Tradition series (Tangent TNGM 119/D). The discs contain the same performance of "Andrew Lammie" by Jane Turriff.
16. Jame Turriff: interview, 8/11/76, Fetterangus.
17. Quoted by Virginia Woolf in *A Room of One's Own*, p. 36.
18. Eveline Hunter, *Scottish Woman's Place*, p. 103.
19. James Kinsley, *Burns: Poems and Songs*, p. 480.
20. Thomas Crawford, *Burns: A Study of the Poems and Songs*, p. 239.
21. Francis Collinson, *The Traditional and National Music of Scotland*, Introduction, pp. 1–3.
22. *Jeannie's Merry Muse* (EMI 7EG 8534).
23. *Queen Among the Heather*, Belle Stewart (Topic 12TS 307).
24. *The Singing Island*, p. 14.
25. For further reading on women's love songs in Gaelic, see articles by Alan Bruford in *Folk Review*, June and July 1978.
26. *Muckle Sangs* booklet (see note 15).
27. Ailie Munro, "Lizzie Higgins, and the Oral Transmission of Ten Child Ballads", *Scottish Studies* 14 (1970), 155–88. This article provides a detailed comparison of Jeannie's and Lizzie's styles and also contains biographical material on the latter. See also Munro's review of Lizzie's disc, *Up an' awa' wi' the Laverock*, in *Traditional Music* no. 6 (1977), and Peter Hall's notes on this disc (Topic 12TS 260) and on *The Back of Bennachie* disc (Topic 12T 180). For further and more detailed consideration, see Stephanie Smith, "A study of Lizzie Higgins as a transitional figure in the development of oral tradition in the Northeast of Scotland", University of Edinburgh M. Litt. thesis, 1975.

V   The Folk Revival in Gaelic Song

By Morag MacLeod

If all the music in the world was cut off, the music of the Western Isles would serve the whole world!

Nan Mackinnon, Vatersay. [1]

It may have become tedious to quibble at the use of the term "folk" with reference to a certain category of song, and to quote the clichéd expression of the American who said "All music's folk music: leastways I never heard of no horse making it," but when prestigious writers like Hugh MacDiarmid equate "folk" with "peasant" (Chapter 3, page 44) some attempt must be made to set the record straight. Not that one is making a qualitative assessment of any class of society, but that one must try to present the facts as they stand. I will generally use the term "traditional" instead of "folk". With Gaelic song it is even more important to make the distinction than it is in Scots or English, and in order to explain why, I shall start by relating, as briefly as possible, something of the history and social background of the various categories of song that exist.

As far as culture was concerned, Gaelic society was very much male-dominated. Musicians and bards were professional people attached to the courts of the chiefs. These artists, whose offices were hereditary, had to undergo a rigid training and the trained bards used very elaborate metrical systems to make poems about events pertaining to the clan. On important occasions these poems were recited to the accompaniment of the harp. Harpers could also compose songs. Social stratification was in terms of closeness in kinship to the chief. Younger sons of younger sons were lower in the scale, but still very much part of any social occasion within the clan.

The trained bards composed in a literary language and in a

variety of syllabic metres — i.e. in metres based on the number of syllables per line — a form that scholars believe may have originated from early Christian Latin hymns. Untrained bards came to use different kinds of metre with measured stresses rather than syllables. Harpers too were known to compose poetry and, judging by surviving examples, this was also of a type which employed regularly spaced stresses. The verses tended (within the poem) to be of the same length, usually of four, eight or sixteen lines. Another type of verse, usually known as "strophic", consisted of a varying number of lines containing x stresses, and a final line of $x+1$ stresses.

(1) My greatest concern
     In all that I hear
     Of the people I mention,
     A handsome Captain
     Of the family of Murdoch
     Who gave me the pocket money.

(2) The largest coin,
     Great in value,
     Great in profit,
     From your comely hand;
     And the intrepid men
     Who hunted in the high mountains.

(3)   Happily would I
      Travel to your homestead,
      Wine and feasting,
      Pipes sounding,
      Wax candles
      And witty sociable young men.

(4)   Versatile youths
      Hardy and vigorous,
      Who could fold sails
      On a squally day,
      They would not be weaklings
      Sailing in to Stornoway.

(5)   Greatly would I like to have
      Seaworthy ships
      Shod with iron
      And ropes steadying them,
      And splendid young men
      Who were skilful at sailing.

(6)   To go to your homestead,
      With its fire-arms,
      Your hunting on the mountains,
      Your slender deer-hounds,
      And your men
      Busy roasting wild fowl.[2]

Most types of Gaelic song may be traced back to those three. Musically, syllabic verse seems to have been chanted. Strophic verse seems to have been set to very distinctive melodies, as the form of the poetry itself is distinctive. Melodies attached to the *amhran* type — the type most commonly used by harpers — have an international flavour.[3]

Even before the break-up of the clan system in the eighteenth century, the professional bards and musicians who had depended on the native aristocracy for their livelihood had already, due to social changes, become reduced to the status of the ordinary people. But there are still people alive who can trace their ancestry back to members of this privileged professional caste of artists and musicians.

While the earlier system still flourished, the trained bards, in common with their counterparts in Ireland, composed in an archaistic and specialised form of Gaelic, whereas the untrained bards and harpers tended to use the vernacular of their day. It was all what could be termed "heroic" poetry even if the subjects were not invariably serious, especially in the harpers' compositions. Women were not expected to compose such songs and there are legends regarding some of those who did being buried face downwards. Women of high rank who composed conventional men's verse were tolerated, but regarded as almost immoral. It must, however, have been mainly women — not always aristocratic — who composed choral songs which were sung by a soloist for the verses and others would join in the chorus. Of such were the work songs, adapted for various purposes such as waulking (i.e. shrinking home-woven cloth), rowing or reaping, which have come down in oral tradition to the present day.

In the course of the eighteenth century — though there are significant earlier examples — it became common for other poets, not connected with the clan chief in a professional way, to compose poems which described and praised nature, and eulogies and elegies for their chiefs and others. From that time the composition of syllabic verse virtually ceased except for a specific type of 8-line verse which may appear even to this day, and is sung to variants of the same melody. (It probably survives because of this. The composers are certainly not consciously following any but the most basic rules of verse composition.)

Strophic verse is seldom heard sung now except in a form with three lines only.

But a large number of songs extant in oral tradition can be dated to the seventeenth century and earlier. An example of syllabic verse is the Ossianic ballad, sometimes referred to as Fenian ballad. Ossian, the legendary poet of Scottish and Irish tradition, was reputed to have been the last survivor of the Fianna, or Fenians, whose exploits he was believed to have celebrated in song. These ballads — probably medieval in origin — are in syllabic metre and were sung in Gaelic-speaking areas until quite recently. There are ballads from other cycles of Celtic hero-tales as well. The oldest written sources for these heroic ballads are manuscripts of the medieval period. And there lies a crucial factor in any discussion of folk-songs in Gaelic. A great many Gaelic songs in fact — and not only those very early examples — owe at least some part of their transmission down to modern times, to written sources of one type or another. The largest corpus which came from mainly oral tradition, with regard to verbal text, belongs to the work-song category, and there are a few others of the *amhran* type still extant, which may not have been written down until relatively recently.

For the melodies of songs, however, as distinct from the verbal text, we have to rely almost entirely on oral tradition. Most poems were expected to be sung, but most written sources for the melodies are negligible. Some are arranged for instrumental performances, some are written in rhythm and stress-patterns that suit the English translation only. All in all, the reader has almost to know the tune already before he can use the written source, and only a few scholars take the trouble to learn the melodies in that way. And yet even to the present day melodies can be found for songs that were previously thought to exist only in verbal form.

While verbal texts may have come from written sources originally, they have often been learned through oral transmission. This is natural, as tunes and words would be learned together, although non-singers may sometimes recite songs. You therefore have a situation where large amounts of sophisticated poetry are committed to memory by people of all classes and educational levels — as if dustmen, engineers, school-teachers, labourers, nurses and doctors could recite chunks of *Marmion*, *Paradise Lost* or *Morte d'Arthur*. It is only fair to say, however, that there were individuals and families who had a better oral tradition than others.[4]

Where could one hear those songs? One must avoid the danger of presenting an idyllic picture of an entirely musical existence on the croft, but there is no doubt that music — oral or instrumental — played a very important role in people's lives. In more recent times and up until the early fifties, the céilidh-house was a feature of rural and island life. Any house would have potential for a céilidh — topical discussions, story-telling, singing, reciting poetry — as long as the household was hospitable, but there were some that were more popular than others. Such houses would probably be the venue for tellers of tales, with or without melodies attached, and syllabic and strophic songs would be sung there, along with songs in lighter vein and recent local compositions of all kinds. Another locale for songs in general was weddings and all the gatherings connected with them. Songs with refrains and a good beat were especially popular at weddings, when the company would stand in a circle holding hands and stamping their feet, endangering the floor boards. It was very important to know a few songs of this kind if you had a reputation as a singer, and I myself have heard of singers hearing a song of twenty verses or more once, on the day before a wedding, and singing it faultlessly at the wedding. Women sang at the shielings, the temporary dwellings where they lived in the summer months while looking after the cattle. Finally, there were songs for accompanying work and other activities. People sang to themselves while carding, spinning, weaving, for which any variety of rhythms could be adapted. They sang in stricter rhythm when rocking a baby, or playing with him, and when milking cows.

On suitable occasions they sang communally, reaping, rowing, hauling in fishing nets, waulking tweed i.e. beating it against a board, wet and soaped, in order to wash it and shrink it.[5] Occasionally they sang for dancing.

The culture changed when the social organisation changed and everything that I have mentioned above was subject to this. The introduction of hydro-electric power has probably had the most long-reaching effect on the social organisation, combined with improvements in the financial status of people in rural areas. Beautiful light-coloured carpets, which became practical because they could be kept clean by electric vacuum cleaners, are discouraging to courteous visitors who are afraid they might dirty them. With electricity came facilities for television reception, and soon every household had a set. This not only caused people to stay at home instead of going to visit friends, but it discouraged them from visiting because, when they did so the television set was often not even switched off in the house they were visiting. The céilidh-house gradually became a very rare commodity.

Holding wedding receptions in houses created a lot of work for the families concerned and it became fashionable after a time for them to be left in the capable hands of hotel proprietors. Although weddings in hotels remained a source of opportunity for potential singers, they ceased to be so to the same extent as previously.

These changes came gradually, but were much accelerated by the two world wars for various reasons, partly because, having served in the armed forces, young people got the taste for a different kind of life. Educational opportunities were improved and alternatives to crofting began to be considered. As there were no opportunities for learning a profession and few for learning a skilled trade within the Gaelic-speaking areas, the tendency was to move south and the population that was left consequently became an aging one. The emigrants learned new ways, new songs, new stories. They also sent money home, they bought furniture and soft furnishings and generally helped to improve the standard of living in the home they'd left behind. Hence, in some part, the carpets, the electric sweepers, the television sets. At the same time the mills took over the finishing process for any tweed that was made: engines were well established by then, replacing sails and oars. Gradually, inhabitants of rural areas took to the machine and to an easier life. New ideas about the upbringing of children, smaller families and therefore less help for a busy mother (older girls in large families played a crucial part in the upbringing of their infant siblings) must have put a stop to the singing of lullabies. But above all, the improvement in communications caused the Gael, who had for so long and for divers reasons thought that he was no good, to imitate what he saw his mainland compatriots doing, having learned this through his own travels, through tales brought home by relatives or through radio and television. As part of this improvement in his status, he tended to dismiss Gaelic as a viable language, and many despised everything connected with it. Schools in general encouraged this attitude.

But changes had been taking place long before the two wars. Round about the beginning of the century the movement, partly encouraged by Queen Victoria's example, which made it fashionable to travel in the Highlands, had some influence on the islands as well. Writers of travel books and artists "discovered" the Hebrides and, in their wake, collectors of songs and other traditions descended on the islands. They thought that the old ways were changing so much that the indigenous songs would disappear. The changes were not taking place as rapidly as was to be the case later, but the collectors, most of them from outwith the Gaelic cultural area, thought that rescuing the songs was a matter of great urgency. The most famous of them was Marjory Kennedy-Fraser, from Edinburgh, and her work with the "Songs of the Hebrides" was one of the first attempts at reviving an interest in Gaelic songs. Mrs. Kennedy-Fraser used a phonograph to record the songs and she and her sister performed them, suitably accompanied and doctored according to urban Victorian tastes. In their chapter on "Art Versions of Waulking Songs" in *Hebridean Folksongs* (Vol 1), John Lorne Campbell and Francis Collinson give two significant quotations referring to Mrs. Kennedy-Fraser. First, George Malcolm Thomson in *A Short History of Scotland* (1929) writes of Mrs. Kennedy-Fraser's discovery "of an exquisite folk-poetry and folk-music among the Gaelic-speaking fisherfolk of Eriskay and other Hebridean islands: it is one of the most romantic and fortunate accidents in modern history that this small and lively world yielded up its treasure before it passed away." Rait and Pryde in *Scotland* (1934) wrote of the Kennedy-Fraser collection *Songs of the Hebrides*: "Not only is it clear that the essentials of the originals are generally preserved and that the alterations and additions are improvements; it is even doubtful if in many cases, anything would have survived without the interested labours of these collectors." It was generally thought that Mrs. Kennedy-Fraser had saved Hebridean song from oblivion, whereas the truth is that there is not one of the songs in her collection which cannot be recorded in its original form to this day, from people who may or may not have heard of her. Not only the tunes — especially the rhythms, tempi and placings of stress — were changed but the words were "improved" by her collaborator, the Rev. Kenneth Macleod. As Ailie Munro points out in Chapter 1, a moral outlook was present at the beginning of the century which resulted in a bowdlerisation of many "down-to-earth" verbal texts. The language of the songs — English or Gaelic — seems to us now ridiculously flowery. Shielings were traditionally occupied by unmarried young girls and were, inevitably, often visited at night by young men whose intentions were probably not honourable. A song composed by a would-be Casanova tells in terms of amusing self-mockery of one such visit where, unfortunately, the girl's mother was present, and she woke up and nearly caught the visitor *in flagrante delicto* so to speak. In the tradition the song is known as "I spent last night in a shieling"; in *Songs of the Hebrides* "An Island Shieling Song". Musically, the tempo and rhythm are changed so that it becomes suitably sentimental for its new text — "I spent last night in the shieling / with cattle dripping milk of lulling / the night's dew dripping kindness / on the maidens in the shieling" — (my translation). Other verbal texts were changed without even the amount of justification assumed here, merely to corroborate the "noble savage" idea that was so trendy at that time.

Societies founded by exile Gaels in Glasgow, Govan, Edinburgh, London put on ceilidhs (so called) and grand concerts. The piano began to be used as an accompanying instrument. Choirs were formed using vocal harmony, which was completely new to Gaelic song. It became fashionable for singers to have their voices trained. *An Comunn Gaidhealach* (probably best translated "the Gaelic Speakers' Association") was formed in 1891 and held its first festival of Gaelic song and literature in Oban in 1892. This became an annual, competitive, event known as the National Mod. Unfortunately, since few or no Gaels were musically literate, the music for these competitions was written by outsiders, and the performances were judged by outsiders. It takes a long, long time to learn about a different musical tradition. Those people thought — we are all British, after all — that it was easy. Scales and rhythms were adapted to the well-tempered easily-assimilated Western-European norm. They probably decided that deviations from these were just native errors. A wit from the Island of Lewis writing in the *Stornoway Gazette* in the 1950s, protests none too subtly: 'To win at the Mod, ye singers, leave the natural airs at home, then go to some professor of the musical arts who will train you in Eyetalian airs and the taafetiffies and the doramifasosos till such a time as you can hold a note from Queen Street [a railway station in Glasgow] to Mallaig [one of the railway terminals for the Western isles]. Don't sing like a ——— [various Gaelic phrases used here] granny with a child because that is too natural, too much like a boorish black-bird or a tone-lazy lark. And if you know any good-old songs, bury them, for of such is not the kingdom of medals. Never mind the Gaelic. It can be bought in phrases, unrationed." (George Morison, *One Man's Lewis*.)

Until the late fifties the small Gaelic Department of the BBC in Glasgow encouraged the Mod style of singing Gaelic, with auditions for solo recitals and performances by approved Gaelic choirs. To quote George Morrison again, "We heartily congratulate the Laxdale choir on their success at the Mod . . . the folk must live, as Laxdale does, in an area civilised enough to know that there are choirs and there was Gaelic. The two stages on either side are to know (a) that there are no such things as choirs, but plenty Gaelic, or (b) that there are plenty choirs but no Gaelic." (Originally published 1948).

Meantime, there were several individuals showing concern about the state of Gaelic singing and of Gaelic culture generally. In the late 1850s Frances Tolmie, a Gaelic speaker from Skye, wrote down the songs she heard from women she visited who were knitting stockings for different Highland regiments. Some of her collection was later published by the Folk-Song Society in their journal.[6] She probably did not have conservation in mind, however, although the result of her work should have fulfilled a conservationist's desires. The Folklore Institute of Scotland began to collect and record unpublished Gaelic songs in 1947. The Linguistic Survey of Scotland, operating from Edinburth University, was collecting Gaelic traditional material as well, before the School of Scottish Studies was itself established in 1951. The Irish Folklore commission extended its interests to Scotland in 1946 when Calum I. Maclean, employed by them, collected in the Highlands and islands. Of course, the tradition wasn't dying as people like Mrs Kennedy-Fraser would have had us think, but it was in great danger of becoming so diluted that rescue of its most indigenous elements was seen to be urgent. John Lorne Campbell of Canna and his wife, Margaret Fay Shaw, did a lot of collecting in their own island, but especially in South Uist and Barra.[7] Alan Lomax came from the States in 1950, commissioned by the Library of Congress and, with the help of Calum I. Maclean and Hamish Henderson, collected Gaelic songs in the Highlands and Hebrides, publishing some of them later on disc under the Columbia label.[8]

There were occasional broadcasts of traditional singers such as Alasdair Fraser, a schoolteacher from Wester Ross working in Conon Bridge, and Flora MacNeil and Calum Johnston, both from Barra. In 1955, Joan MacKenzie, a young teacher from Lewis, whose style of singing was definitely verging on the traditional, won the Comunn Gàidhealach's premier award, the Mod Gold Medal. Things were changing. The general folk-song revival in Britain was having an effect on Gaelic audiences too. The School of Scottish Studies started in a modest way in 1951 to create an archive of all kinds of oral tradition, Scots and Gaelic. It was fashionable for a time in Edinburgh to hold concerts featuring traditional Gaelic singers, and the organisers were fortunate to have, on the spot, such superb artists as Flora MacNeil and Calum Johnston, Kitty and Marietta Macleod — sisters from Lewis — and a few others. One of the series of events that focussed these singers was the People's Festival Ceilidhs described by Ailie Munro in Chapter 3. The reaction to the concerts was mixed. There is always a certain amount of snobbery attached to such gatherings, especially in a culture-conscious city such as Edinburgh.

Flora MacNeil is probably the best known of the pioneers of traditional unaccompanied singing. When she first started to sing in public in Edinburgh and Glasgow, collectors such as Alan Lomax, Norman Buchan and Ewan MacColl took an interest in her songs, and people like Sorley Maclean, his brother Calum and Calum Johnston of Barra were there to boost her own interest, but otherwise she was habitually asked to sing something "not *too* traditional". In Barra, a few were heard to say, "Flora only sings those unattractive old songs" — *Cha bhi Fleòrag a' seinn ach na seann òrain ghrànda sin,* — and at ceilidhs in Barra itself only the popular songs of the day were sung. Flora refused to compromise, and gradually attitudes changed.

When Fred MacAulay was appointed producer of Gaelic programmes for the BBC in Glasgow, having spent some time collecting traditional material for the Linguistic Survey of Scotland and the School of Scottish Studies, he may well have been following his own inclinations when he introduced less of the Western-European-Art-Music brand of singing to his public. Or he may have been catering for the taste of a minority that was possibly beginning to increase. There is no doubt, at any rate, that the BBC had the greatest influence on the Gaelic public, and "ordinary" people who had never left their island and rural homes saw the possibility of having their own repertoires featured on radio. Nothing could be better for the prestige of traditional song. This, in turn, has influenced An Comunn Gàidhealach, which has been trying in recent years to put more emphasis on the traditional way of singing, and to choose prescribed songs that are more attuned to the indigenous culture. The public is hard to convert, however, and it will be a long time before the adult competition of traditional songs will have as much prestige as the Gold Medal final where the emphasis is on musical prowess of a conventional kind.

Gaelic was not a part of the interest in folk-groups that came about in the mid-fifties. A group in Edinburgh called The Night Hawks invited Dolina MacLennan, a Gaelic singer from Lewis, to join them around that time and that was more or less the extent of Gaelic involvement in the "folk" world then. Folk-song societies heard too little of Gaelic singing of the authentic traditional type for its members to be able to judge it with any degree of discrimination. Certain singers, whose intonation was in fact suspect from any point of view, were regarded as good because of a misinterpretation of the subtleties of Gaelic melodic intonation. As is the case with other traditional genres, Gaelic melodies are not always based on either the major or minor scale, and their intonation sounds strange, therefore, to anyone reared on these. For that reason, there were those who showed that they were initiated by their "enjoyment" of what they thought was the genuine article when the singer was unable to hit the right notes.

Gaelic singers didn't really get into the folk scene until An Comunn Gàidhealach introduced a folk-group contest at the annual Mod. This brought to the fore groups such as Na h-Oganaich, Na Sgoilearan, Na Siaraich, Sound of Mull, etc. They all had their day. What constitutes a folk group? More than one performer, musical instruments, harmony and traditional songs — a mixture of old and new — fairly strong voices, youth, and preferably good looks. It was difficult to get all those ingredients together. Members of groups tended to be university students, or have recently left school. They tended not to have settled into permanent employment of any kind. Whether the group met in the cities or in island or country districts, there would always be one or two members who were in the area only temporarily. The tendency was, not to continue in the manner of the Seekers as New Seekers or New New Seekers, with numerous changes of personnel, but for the groups to disintegrate. One or two groups, like The Lochies and Sound of Mull have lasted well, and the others can still be heard on disc and are very popular on radio request programmes. Folk-groups contributed substantially to the revival of Gaelic traditional songs, since they were always looking for something new to add to their repertoire, and because of the years between, when only a limited variety of Gaelic song was heard by the general public, the most unusual "new" songs were the old ones. A group which had a very high potential in this direction was Am Bradan Breac (The Speckled Salmon) which formed in Edinburgh in the early seventies as a kind of concert party. There were fourteen of them, pipers, fiddlers, dancers, a clarsach player and singers. They sang, danced and played solo and in groups. They could therefore cope with such a variety of material as no ordinary folk-group could do. For example, they performed waulking songs in a more convincing way than could most groups of three of four members especially as those who played the instruments could sing as well. Am Bradan Breac lasted for only a year or two. The difficulties of keeping a normal-sized folk-group together were multiplied about three-fold in this ensemble! But new groups emerge all the time.

One musical phenomenon that has not needed much of a revival is the distinctive method of singing metrical psalms that is used in Gaelic-speaking congregations of the Presbyterian church. The method has survived from Reformation times and was in fact initiated by English Puritans in order to overcome the difficulty of congregational singing when people could not read, or there were not enough copies of written texts to go round. The practice was for someone to read a line of the verse before the congregation sang it. Gradually the spoken line must have developed into a chant, but this practice of precenting was given up a long time ago by the majority of congregations except Gaelic-speaking ones. It was very rarely that an English- or Scots-speaking congregation could be heard using it in this century. The Gaels have held on to it stubbornly and have made it their own, using it in church and in family-worship, although the ballad metre of the psalms is unknown otherwise in Gaelic, and although no more than one or two of the tunes were composed by Gaelic speakers.

The spoken line is chanted; melody notes have been changed, instinctively no doubt, to conform more closely with the melodic intervals that were familiar in the Gaelic tradition; and the melodic line is ornamented, the degree of ornamentation varying from place to place. (The Lewis style, for example, is more elaborately ornamental than that of other areas.) As well as all this, the line is sung very slowly, the same grace-notes do not always come together and the near-discordant polyphony which sometimes ensues creates a tension, so that the sound is very strange and puzzling to the uninitiated. Even among the uninitiated, however, Gaelic psalm-singing is often commented on as being strikingly beautiful. Singing with precenting in this way was never in danger of going under in the way that other Gaelic traditional music was, but it is interesting to speculate on what might have happened if the revival had not taken place. In the late forties, for example, the BBC was using a small choir for all the Gaelic religious broadcasts from the studio. The choir would sing each note as written, with few if any grace-notes, even when precenting was used. Sometimes it was not used, and the psalms were sung in the English way. From the sixties onwards, however, recordings of congregational singing have been used for almost all Presbyterian Gaelic religious services on radio. In recent years, interest has been stimulated through the production of cassettes, especially by Lewis Recordings Ltd., Stornoway. One of the Scottish Tradition series by Tangent is called *Gaelic Psalms from Lewis*, and it is accompanied by an explanatory booklet. While the language lives, the tradition is likely to remain fairly strong.

The situation in Gaelic music now is as strange as is the situation of the language. In the places where the language should be strongest, young people prefer to speak English. Children generally speak Gaelic until they go to school but after a very short time they speak more English than Gaelic and some forget their first language completely. Even parents who abhor this state of affairs can do little to counteract it. The taste among young Gaels is for Pop songs and the majority would rather listen to Radio Clyde than to Radio Highland. Country-and-Western music is very popular, and groups will sing in Gaelic using Country-and-Western tunes. It is probably true to say that some of the greatest interest in the Gaelic language is shown by learners nowadays. This also seems to be true of folk-groups. One of the first to win the folk-group competition at the Mod was based in Inverness and the lead singer was a learner. The most popular singing group (Gaelic folk/pop/rock? It's hard to say,) at the moment, Run-rig, irritates an older age-group that finds the words of their songs unintelligible. Again, their lead singer is not a native Gaelic speaker. Billy Ross, formerly of Ossian, a folk-group that has become well-known in Britain and on the Continent, sings Gaelic songs with a Glasgow accent. There are several singers, as solo performers or in groups, who have a predilection for Gaelic songs, and the Boys of the Lough (members from Shetland, Ireland and Tyneside) have had Gaelic singers such as Flora MacNeil, Finlay MacNeill (no relation) and Bessie MacLennan as guests on their concert tours.

There are young native Gaelic speakers who sing traditional Gaelic songs in the traditional manner or in all sorts of manner, but few of them know, or care about the words. Now while the sounds of the words lend beauty to a song, especially the richer vowel sounds, one likes to get the meaning of the words as well. Singers under thirty, as a general rule, seldom appreciate the nuances of the older poetry. Nevertheless, there is still an interest in indigenous material. A Historical Society in Ness, Lewis, has published three cassettes with local singers singing local songs in the traditional manner. The age-range of the performers is a wide one, and the subject matter varies from the comic to the sentimental to the tragic. Although the subject matter is also esoteric to some extent, the cassettes are being bought extensively outside their area of origin. Cassettes of religious songs and psalms in Gaelic have also been published recently and so have cassettes of young soloists singing songs old and new unaccompanied. Request programmes on radio feature a few of those singers, side by side with Gaelic "Country-and-Western", Gaelic "Music Hall" and Gaelic "Pop" performers. (By "Music Hall' I mean the popular, rhythmic, musical wallpaper types of song such as are often chosen by dance bands for Gaelic waltzes, and by singers for medleys.) In some ways the "revival" for Gaelic traditional songs is happening now. The words may not get their rightful place by way of pronunciation or stress pattern, but that can be learned and a new generation may arise who will be sufficiently interested to learn — the "proper" words, one is tempted to say — words that make sense in the song, at least.

Footnotes to Chapter V

1. Nan Mackinnon recorded four hundred songs and a thousand proverbs for the School of Scottish Studies. This was said to her — probably in Gaelic — by the late Donald Macpherson from Barra, who was the first person to record her on tape.
2. From *A Collection of Scottish Gaelic Songs*, p. 10 (see Chapter 3, note 49); recorded from Calum Johnston, Barra, by Calum MacLean in 1953, SA 1953/ 12. In Scottish Tradition Cassette Series (Tangent TGMMC 504).
3. For further information see William J. Watson, *Bardachd Ghaidhlig: Gaelic Poetry 1550–1900*.
4. See *Tocher* 13, 18, 20, 22, 24, 27 etc.
5. See booklet accompanying the disc *Waulking Songs from Barra* (Tangent TNGM 111).
6. *Journal of the Folk-Song Society*, 4, no. 16 (1911), 143–276; see also Ethel Bassin, *The Old Songs of Skye; Frances Tolmie and her Circle*.
7. Margaret Fay Shaw, *Folksongs and Folklore of South Uist*.
8. Vol. 6 (Scotland) of the *World Library of Folk and Primitive Music* (Columbia SL 209), 1953, Library of Congress.

VI   The Travelling People

It's a proud thing to be a traveller

Jane Turriff Stewart[1]

Substitute the word "tinker" for "traveller", and we have a statement which will surprise many yet which sums up the most important point to be made here.

The origins of tinkers and gypsies must be largely a matter for conjecture, but both were ancient nomadic castes of metalworkers and other craftsmen. The tinkers were indigenous to the British Isles; in Scotland the word derives from the old verb tink, meaning to mend or solder — which is partly onomatopoeic in that is suggests one of the sounds made when working with metal — and the Scots name is tinkler. The gypsies on the other hand came from all parts of Europe, moving into England in the fifteenth and sixteenth centuries and thence northward throughout Britain, and they themselves encouraged the idea of a possibly more distant country of origin: India, or North Africa . . . hence the name, from "egyptian". It has been said that in Scotland, "the two races fused and united in the sixteenth century because of the similar mode of life".[2] Some intermingling certainly occurred, and over the next four hundred years other subsidiary elements were added to the mixture: the dispossessed, resulting from disasters such Culloden[3] and the Highland clearances; Irish Romanies and tinkers; and deserters, with other "broken men". Nevertheless the two groups remained distinct, and the tinkers had existed for at least hundreds of years before the arrival of the gypsies.[4] In mediaeval Gaelic society, skilled craftsmen, particularly metalworkers, shared in the (graded) privileges which that society accorded other men of arts.

Today although many attend the annual fairs — for example at

---

1.   See footnotes page 229.

Aikie Brae[5], near Old Deer in Aberdeenshire — most gypsies are to be found in Central and Southern Scotland; and in the Borders and Galloway especially, considerable fusion took place between the two fraternities. It is the tinkers north of this with whom we are concerned here, but the name has acquired derogatory connotations and so is understandably disliked by the majority. They are now generally referred to as travellers, or the travelling folk, and this covers a range of social groups. The name may be accepted in a sense at least partly historical, rather than literal, thus resolving any contradictions arising from the settlement in houses of a considerable number. Many of those now settled, for part or all of the year, retain their traveller identity and culture.[6]

What is this culture? Basically it consists of the varied elements in the whole traditional Scottish culture — songs, instrumental music, stories and customs — but stamped with the hall-mark of the travellers' strongly individualistic style and content, forged by their hard yet rich life-style. They were isolated both socially, as outcasts from the accepted norm of society, and geographically, as regards camping sites. They were thus thrown back on their own resources for social intercourse and entertainment. Yet during their travels they would pick up tunes and songs from different parts of the country, from other travellers but also from non-travellers whom they met at work: for example, ploughmen and cottars — ploughmen often whistled at their work, and songs would be heard during "mid-yokin'" breaks. Isolation and travel thus led to a paradoxical combination of cultural inbreeding plus diversity, two factors which helped to build up a distinctive brand of tradition. Belief in fairies, elves and other supernatural beings is widespread, and appears in the story included below.[7]

It is in the tale *par excellence* that one finds the travellers' imprint: it is a more malleable form than the song, it is not bound up with a tune and so it provides more immediate opportunity for textual recreation, thus permitting infiltration of idiosyncratic touches and of symbolic material which supports and interprets their life experience. Factual and historical material also appears — for instance there are many Burker stories, based on the notorious murders committed in order to sell bodies for dissection. For obvious reasons travellers were unusually vulnerable to this hazard, but in their stories they have built it up into outsize proportions.

Duncan Williamson spoke of the close connection between songs and stories[8] revealed by his researches among his own people. "At a fire-side ceilidh and song cairry-on . . . I would say, 'I'll tell ye a story' . . . an' then, some old woman or some old man wad say,

'Laddie . . . that's no a story at a' — that's a sang!'" His father would tell stories, ". . . he maintained they were stories, but some parts — he'd sing them".[9] This may provide a link with the Gaelic tradition. We are concerned with Scots travellers here, but many of these still have a smattering of Gaelic and are possibly only a generation or two removed from Gaelic-speaking forebears. Although the verbal text of travellers' songs, especially the ballads, is often rather fragmentary, it is perfectly comprehensible to listeners who already know the stories.

A quality possessed to a marked degree by travellers, especially the women, is what Betsy Whyte of Montrose describes at "the gift of perception".[10] She herself can "read" a person's hand with uncanny accuracy and sensitivity, indicating his or her past experiences, struggles or personality difficulties, but she refuses to attempt any foretelling of the future.

Travellers' singing styles vary according to the singer's personality and mood,[11] but one quality almost always appears: they are impassioned, intense, often imparting a sense of hard-won victory and sometimes of grandeur.[12] This is not the same as singing loudly, although volume is always an element in expressiveness. But it has much to do with the ability to show feelings, and with the deep emotion aroused by many songs. "How would ye like to see one woman, or one man, sittin' singin', and ten or twelve women sittin' cryin' over the same song? Not because she was a good singer, but because of the song. . . . Men cry too, but not at a song. . . . A man that can't cry is not a man at all. I saw ma faither cryin' like a child, millions of times".[13] The tears may be for someone, now dead, who used to sing that song — as Betsy Whyte said, "It lets people know that he was important to them. In a way he's not dead as long as his songs are still alive". MacColl and Seeger comment on the singing style: "There is an almost heroic quality in the singing of travellers, a desire to declaim, to demand attention, an assertion of oneself as a singer".[14]

The heroism, the hard-won victory, are those of survivors from a centuries-old persecution and prejudice which still exists to this day. "Until the end of the sixteenth century gypsies and tinkers, with one or two notable exceptions such as Johnny Faw who was granted protection by James V, received nothing but punishment from the law". In fact, the death penalty could be inflicted on anyone merely rumoured to be an "egyptian".[15] Musicians and actors also suffered severe harassment in Reformation and post-Reformation Scotland;[16] gypsies and tinkers were often known to be good singers, pipers and fiddlers, so they were doubly penalised. Progress and understanding came at a snail's pace. During the nineteenth century legal measures restricting the use of traditional camping grounds, such as the verges of the old drovers' roads, were stepped up. Even in 1918 the Departmental Committee on Tinkers in Scotland referred to travellers as "representing a different stage of human development",[17] and in Government reports of the 1980s one finds accounts of continuing ill-treatment by the settled population.

To this settled community the travellers' chief faults are, first, they do not have a fixed home, and second, they have no regular job with an employer. Yet travellers take pride in these facts which they see as belonging to the essential nature of their existence. In practice they are not wholly consistent about the first, since there is movement in and out of houses for part or all of the year, and many travellers have become permanently settled though they may take an extended working "holiday" in the summer. Settlement of this kind has varied causes: to begin with there are both seasonal and economic factors, then age, infirmity and increasingly the difficulties of finding stopping-places in order to follow the traditional life. Yet the housed travellers do not consider themselves any the less "travellers". The two groups have an essentially symbiotic relationship. For the mobile traveller the settled families represent contact points, telephones for passing family news or for possible work contacts, while for the housed traveller those still on the road represent links with continued tradition.

The historical/sociological reasons for the emergence of itinerant peoples lie outside the scope of this chapter, but the travellers undoubtedly filled a social need. The lawmakers who lived in towns did not appreciate this fact. The farmers and the rural lairds, however, were generally glad of the travellers' seasonal help, manual skills and buying and selling, and as a result they usually allowed them to camp and often turned a blind eye to the odd spot of poaching. "With the travellers going round houses", says Danny Stewart of Mintlaw, "they brought a lot of news with them . . . the country people were glad to see them, and it saved them visits to shops . . . Our history is part of Scotland, and Scotland should be proud of it, as we are proud of Scotland." His wife Jane, the singer: "My grandfather *made* tin jugs, milk pails, plates . . . and he did soldering and other jobs." And centuries of nomadic living, in turn, bred within the travellers a need for this life — many of those now settled still feel caged in houses.

The great requirement is for places to camp, in tents or caravans, at a realistic rent and in suitable locations. All the reports I have studied[18] stress this and the fact that without such places, whether on sites or in fields, everything suffers: work opportunities, the children's schooling and the health of all. There has been a positive and constructive approach by central government since 1971, with substantial grants offered to local authorities to provide proper stopping-places. But again and again resolutions are deferred, local councils drag their feet and "respectable" householders carry out delaying tactics (some of these have been disturbingly violent). One of the travellers' defensive measures over the centuries has been the development of their own language, cant; in Scotland there exists both Scots-English cant and Gaelic cant.

The second "fault" of the travellers is that they have no regular job. The Puritan work-ethic is seen here — there must be something wrong with a man who doesn't work his seven or eight hours a day, five days a week. But travellers think it's normal and sensible to work only when you need to . . . seasonal work, anything that needs to be done, their own traditional occupations and skills . . . and to have more time for chat, for ceilidhing, for the really important things in life. This attitude deserves serious consideration even though it may appear somewhat romantic, and even though another interpretation is that they work at anything that comes up, often very hard, in order to survive the lean winter season. The traveller women — who have always earned money outside the home as well as doing all the work within it — still hawk goods, collect rags or clothes and do seasonal work. Much seasonal agriculture work is in fact carried out by the whole family, men, women and children. Sheila MacGregor: "The country hantle have routine, we never do . . . Travellers can always turn their hand to something — they'll never be stuck" (this came during a discussion on unemployment).

The versatility of travellers is an outstanding characteristic, but many of their trades are not compatible with house dwelling, particularly in modern urban housing. There is no accommodation for the used-car trade which has replaced the traditional horse-trading, and scrap-metal activities are not popular with either neighbours or planners. Neighbours also object if houses and gardens are littered with material pertaining to basket-making, second-hand clothes and household gear, pearl-fishing and other occupations adopted. Conservationists now appreciate the value of the trade in second-hand goods of all kinds: many useful artefacts are thus distributed which people need and which would otherwise be thrown on to unsightly and wasteful rubbish dumps. It is recognised that through their scrap dealing travellers often provide the first link in the recycling chain for scarce and valuable metals.

One of their most important contributions to society this century is that of having fought in two wars, ". . . and it rankles with them that though their names are carved on nearly every monument in Scotland, they are still not recompensed with citizenship."[19] It is clear that in practice travellers are still not accorded some of the rights which the settled community take for granted. Full citizenship includes minority rights — in this case the provision of campsites for those who do not wish to live in houses. Even the "inalienable" right to vote may elude them, for if you have no fixed address then your name may be missed out of the voters' register.

Duncan Williamson, originally from Argyllshire, has lived for most of his life in a traditional bent-boughs tent,[20] also known as a gelly. It is made from saplings — preferably hazel, rowan or birch — which are pushed into the ground, bent over and bound together. This structure is then covered with various waterproof materials firmly tied down. Duncan's tents are more spacious than any caravan and are always warmed by a closed fire, with circular chimney going up through the roof. He spoke of the satisfactions of the travelling life: "Ye wake up in the morning an' ye hear the birds singin' . . . ye've no worries, no one tells ye what to do . . . you have nothing but you have everything. It's so peaceful . . . you come and go as you like . . . no need to keep up with the boss". (Pause) "Ye don't *need* these things. . . ."[21]

As the oldest girl of a large family, Jane Turriff was sometimes left to look after her brothers and sisters when their parents went on the road. But she looked forward eagerly to the school holidays. "Seven weeks holidays . . . ma father an' mother travelled, an' . . . we *all* went. Ma mam an' dad was really happy though when they were away travellin', an' so was I. And I loved the horse — ma father had a good horse, an' he'd a lovely big caravan . . . Travellin' all day . . . the sun shinin', an' yir face was brown . . . yir hankie on yir head . . . an' the bairns was all lovely an' brown. An' the horse was just takin' its time . . . goin', ye know? — we never ran the horse, we'd *all day* — was nae hurry tae go anywhere, we jist travelled all day . . . (In the evenings) if it was fine weather, we'd have the fire outside, an' then they started cookin' . . . my mother did the cookin', when we were out . . . Oh me, we spent lovely times. An' then, we would've been on the road all day, and we'd mebbe come til a cross-roads . . . an' ye'd see mebbe another caravan comin', approachin', ye know? . . . I was so happy, I said, 'I wonder who it could be, I wonder who it could be' . . . an' here was . . . ma auntie, or ma grandma, or some o' them. . . . That's the life I loved. . . . We loved singin', you should hear the old people singin' in those days, it was great. . . . Some o' them wad jist sit an' play on the chanter . . . an' some o' them mebbe playin' a tin whistle. Ma granda used to play the tin whistle . . . an' Davie, ye ken m' uncle Davie? . . . I think he learned it aff o' him, because that was his father. . . . An' then ye'd have heard them singin' . . . they were aye singin', there wisnae much music in those days, so they were aye playin' their own kin' o' music . . . an' singin' round the camp-fire", (at Old Meldrum, Danny Stewart reported, the country hantle would come and listen) "an' even on the road, singin', ye know. An' then when we stopped at a place . . . where we was goin' to stay all night, the girls wad all get together, an' mebbe go away fir milk, tae a farm, ye know, an' I was . . . though I was lame, I wad go wi' them . . . I just hopped along on ma crutches" . . .(laughed" . . . I was young, an' I was swack! — though I had the crutches, I could go . . . I walked wi' them, an' enjoyed masel' wi' them, and . . . aye this singin' was in ma heid . . . an' then ma friends would say to me, 'You've a bonny voice, you can fair sing!' . . . an' they wad a' get singin', thegither . . . an' we'd come home again and . . . what happy we was! We loved animals, an' we always had a dog . . . a haund-dog, an' they used tae catch rabbits for wer supper . . . an' mebbe a big pot o' potatoes, an' . . . this stovies, in a great big iron pot . . . with onions . . . oh gosh, whit a great feed it was'. . . . I didna like hoosin' up, because ye dinna meet in wi' lots o' friends when ye're hoosed up. . . ."[22]

It would, of course, be wrong to give too idealistic a picture of traveller life. Persecution has devious effects, and injustices which already exist in a country or community tend to appear in harsher form amongst persecuted groups within that community. Misery and deprivation have led to excessive drinking, leading in turn to fighting and exacerbated feuds between family groups. There seems no doubt that traveller men beat their wives to an uncommon extent, and also that the double standard[23] of sexual morality for men and for women was almost universally imposed. These two points were made by all the travellers I spoke to, only one of whom excused the violence,[24] and they are supported by written testimony.[25] (The travellers also said that the women are no longer prepared to put up with this treatment[26] which has meant that they were in effect victims twice over). Black as are these two entries on the debit side, they do not figure among the usual complaints made against travellers by the settled community — doubtless because many of the latter still do not consider these to be really serious misdemeanours. It is possible that a vicious circle may be at work here. Exaggerated reports spread by settled people may have affected traveller men so that they come to regard this type of violence as a necessary characteristic of traveller manhood. There is very little divorce, although this is partly due to the fact that until recently women have had no redress against ill-treatment. The children are cared for with kindness and with exceptional lenience.

The two main causes of prejudice — itineracy, and the spasmodic work-pattern — have already been discussed. The other grumbles — travellers are dirty, they don't send their children to school,[27] they leave litter about,[28] they bring down the value of neighbourhood property — are either simply untrue, coals-in-the-bath-type accusations, or else they form part of the similar vicious circle initiated by an uncomprehending, uncaring society, and especially that part which seeks a scapegoat for its own unfulfilled needs. Andrew Douglas[29] has pinpointed the worst of this carping attitude as coming from the "poor white trash" of the settled population, and discerns an element of jealousy in it and possible fear of the unconforming: these people are different, they make us feel our lives are mediocre, some of them are famous and yet they've had less education than we have.

This brings us back to the special gifts of the travelling people. For various reasons indicated they are now the chief custodians of traditional culture, they form the richest seam in Lloyd's "submerged world". Yet the vast majority of Scots are still ignorant of the wealth of art and of wisdom on their very doorsteps, carried by the despised and unfairly treated "tinkers". Once again the stone which the builders refused is become the head stone of the corner. Evidence has been shown of the invaluable contribution made by travellers to the folk music revival over the past thirty years, chiefly at festivals but also at the clubs. This contribution could and should be extended to the wider community, by the media. Danny Stewart: "It's time now that the rest of Scotland should be shown what they're missing".

The BBC's television programme on "The Stewarts of Blairgowrie"[30] showed what can be done, but it also showed very clearly that this is the proverbial tip of the iceberg. A documentary film, "The Summer Walkers," made by Timothy Neat and Hamish Henderson in 1977, gives a graphic account of the travellers' situation and culture.[31] And the TV episode of January 7, 1981, showing the recent eviction of travelling people from a Glasgow site, helped to publicise the continuing injustice of that situation and called forth a strong letter from Lord Birsay, former chairman of the Secretary of State's Advisory Committee on traavellers. He described the eviction as "the abysmal nadir of human concern, and an affront to common humanity".[32] On all fronts, a vast amount of education and publicity is needed.[33]

Valuable written accounts of this culture in Scotland — songs, tales and memorabilia, including songs recently composed by travellers[34] — may be found in many issues of *Tocher* magazine; these are still available. Important articles have also appeared by Timothy Neat and — from inside the situation — by Linda Williamson.[35]

There has been no revival *per se* amongst the travellers themselves. Stanley Robertson: ". . . a folk revival was only taking place with the country people because they [i.e. the travellers] already kept alive and perpetuated these songs and stories . . . They were at first unaware of the important role they were to play in the folk revival".[36] Duncan Williamson reiterates this point: "We have no need to revive something that has really been there among us all these years". Duncan also declared that "a large majority" of travellers "like to keep the sacred things that were passed to them . . . they are a bit ashamed tae exploit their forbears' culture to the public", and says there are some songs which will never be passed on to non-travellers.[37] (Cf. the Navaho Indians' belief that "songs are a form of wealth").[38] On the other hand, Sheila MacGregor believes that "our language and culture are not secret — or sacred — any longer".

Looking now at the other side of the coin, what effect has the revival movement had on the traveller community? Although a comparatively small number have been closely involved, the results are more far-reaching than might have been expected: the internal grape-vine, always important among travellers, has spread awareness of their possible status as tradition-bearers and as purveyors of age-old truths. "The travellers were a race of people who kept very much to themselves and were a close community", says Stanley Robertson. "There was always a kind of stigma attached. . . . Suddenly they found themselves being sought after by scholars and teachers who were looking to them as a source of information. It made them feel very important and brought them into a new dimension of social intercourse. Even though their houses were clean, they would extra clean their homes if they knew the folk song collectors were coming up. They would say to each other, 'Bean rannie hantle binging up tae the cain, so stall yer wheezing an' sallaching'.[39] Sheila MacGregor: "The revival has taken songs to a wider audience, and taken travellers to places . . . the songs and the travellers are accepted more. . . . It works both ways, the travellers appreciate their own culture, and the settled community do too". Betsy Whyte states that the first reaction to collectors was often, "'They must be awful hard up for songs if they come to the travelling people'. but now they realise the value of what they have to give". Festivals and clubs give great pleasure: "they meet people there, too, not just the country hantle they met on farms". Betsy, whose maiden name was Townsley, visited some Edinburgh schools in March 1980[40]. She talked to the children, told them about her book, *The Yellow on the Broom*, told them stories and sang some songs. The teacher of one class later brought to Betsy a little girl whose name was also Townsley: the child said she had been ashamed before, but now felt proud to be a traveller. So the first effect has been an increased confidence and pride of identity.

The post-1945 years brought many world-wide changes. In Britain the welfare state came into being, and in general a more caring, a broader, more democratic and less class-ridden outlook spread. The folk revival was part and parcel of this new outlook. Can it have been entirely a coincidence that research for the first report of the Scottish Development Department on travellers was initiated in 1969, when the revival was firmly under way and had turned to Scottish material for its staple fare?[41] The Stewarts of Blairgowrie, and Jeannie Robertson of Aberdeen, had been discovered in the middle fifties. Stanley Robertson again, in the same letter: "The folk revival did many things for the benefit of the travellers. It gave them a better public image, and people began to understand that travellers were not the filthy, ignorant creatures they were so often made out to be . . . they realised that travellers were quite intelligent and had much to offer. The schools began to take a better interest in their children and many long-lasting animosities were being banished. With folks like Jeannie Robertson and Belle Stewart making good names in public circles it set the ball rolling for the improvement of conditions for travellers, especially those who were still living on the road. Many groups and organisations started to help travellers get better deals, and travellers themselves responded by mixing more with the country people. During the fifties many travellers inter-married with country people. On the whole the folk revival did the travelling people a vast amount of good.

On the other hand it caused a tremendous amount of jealousy among the travelling people themselves. There were bitter arguments about the songs that were collected because certain families claimed sole rights to certain songs". (Belle Stewart also spoke of this.) "Some people were being made a fuss of while others were being neglected. It caused family squabbles. It made some people very big-headed. . . . Sometimes it caused an intellectual snobbery. With some folks thinking that others were lesser than they were, a situation arose where travellers were calling each other names. Even up to date many families still bear grudges with each other. The folk revival also brought a new awareness of witchcraft, dope, vice and moral slackness. Traveller people would not participate in certain things but with the influence of the people socially, the revival brought many new hazards.

The folk revival opened up the eyes of the travelling people to new dimensions of exploration and exploitation".

Sheila Macgregor felt less strongly on one point: "There was some jealousy among travellers at the beginning, but we've got over it now". And as Belle Stewart said in another context, "There's no need to go to the travellers to find that". The green-eyed monster appears in all human situations. Willie MacPhee: "In a local pub recently, a local man said, "I've seen you before — were you on the TV with the Stewarts of Blair? Bet you made a packet".[42] Sheila: "That's envy, rather than jealousy". Commenting on the exceptional degree of integration of the Stewarts in Blairgowrie, Sheila Douglas says this is partly due to their becoming well-known through the folk revival.

There is wide recognition among travellers of the pioneering part which Dr. Hamish Henderson played in collecting their songs and stories. Bryce and Betsy Whyte: "Hamish started things . . . it took courage on his part". Courage indeed, for he took time to fraternise, to win confidence and trust, to sleep rough in tents. In the early fifties, to be on such friendly, equal terms with social outcasts was hardly the way to win friends and influence people of the Establishment, academic or otherwise. (In the early years of this century, Aberdeenshire collectors Greig and Duncan would seem to have collected little from travellers).[43] The successful collector must first establish a rapport with his or her informant, and this is especially important with travellers, whose history has bred into them a wariness and a suspicion of the outside world. Dr. Henderson has always had, to a superlative degree, this gift of getting alongside people from different backgrounds, of helping them to relax, to be as natural as possible and to give him the real stuff of their inherited lore.

Duncan Williamson spoke for several others interviewed when he expressed doubts about the possibility of travellers singing in a natural style for archive recordings, i.e. "for ever after". "Travellers is a very funny people . . . when someone makes a tape-recordin', they try to be, not theirselves, but . . . to be super, and try and sing like they were expected to sing . . . something *to please you* . . . they think that you want this . . . so they're not giving you the actual thing the way it should be. . . . If you were to say, '. . . nobody's going to listen to this', and 'this is just for fun, let's have . . . just a wee sing-song' . . . then the *next* time you come, the next time, well, they'll appreciate that more than you'll ever know".[44] These comments came from Duncan's own experience, as a traveller who was also a collector and recorder. "I made 174 tapes", he said. "An' I played them back to these travelling people, and *they loved it* . . . people come to visit me, even to get theirselves recorded, because I was the only one that possessed a recorder in those days". The Stewarts of Blairgowrie all agreed with the "this is not for the archives" approach, for at least the first recording. Jane Turriff and Danny Stewart said people were afraid of making mistakes, they had nerves when they were recording for the archives, they were not enjoying themselves or giving of their best, and they would be more natural if they were to get back to the "camp scene", with the collectors just watching on the outskirts, and listening, perhaps eventually recording. Bryce Whyte: "Travellers are used to way-out people coming, for their own gains" — Betsy: "or their own amusement" — and they would take a rise out of such collectors. To be "fly" is judged important: their natural astuteness is connected with "the gift of preception" already referred to.

The feeling for words is another gift. Here is Lizzie Higgins talking: "To me, the Scottish balladry, the Scottish folk pipe singin', is the word: magic. Proper, sheer, naked magic. . . . It lay dormant. . . . I hope there's millions will understand and find, in it, what is *there*. It's about human beings, their loves, their liberty or their broken hearts, the death, the grief, the sorrow, the . . . cups o' happiness flowin' over — they had everything in life, and they've left this in their songs and balladry — they've left everything there. An' if a person sings it with feeling, inside the inner *them* . . . they can *feel* this . . . they dinna need to tak' LSD to get the feeling, they can get it through singin' . . . the same beautiful, transcending heights, away among the mysterious gods. . . . And it's a very very good thing for a man or a woman's soul, to sing. . . . *Everyone* can join in, and sing it . . . and get this sheer magical feeling. Ye see, long ago, your great poets . . . your master painters, your Leonardo da Vincis and a' them . . . and your great composers of olden days, they *all* felt this *magic* thing, which their painting and their music brought. Well I find the same, as a woman today of forty-seven, 1976, in Aberdeen, I find the same thing . . . an' any man or woman, or teenager or child, can find this, it's most beautiful. . . . It's like evolution . . . and it's not evil, and it won't hurt nor man, woman or child in any way. It's a great inner beauty . . . it's good, it heals the mind an' it heals the soul, an' there's happiness in them as well as everything else, all human emotions are there . . . in these ballads and songs".[45]

Travellers are not only articulate, they can express themselves with a natural poetry and dignity, in spite of — or because of? —

their general lack of formal education. They are in a real sense the aristocrats[46] of the road. Like Jock Stewart they are folk "you don't meet every day", who will treat you with courtesy and sensitiveness. As always, categories tend to overlap, and rigid, hard-and-fast statements will blur important differentials within a group. Travellers are not to be confused with tramps or beggars, and their origin is different from that of the American hobos, but there are some factors common to all social groups found "on the road". The hobo's main objective is to find work — Allsop describes him as "the unemployed spoil cast aside by a bold and ruthless *laissez faire* system",[47] and he rejects the comfortably vague theory that the hobo is driven by "wanderlust".[48] Judging from the numerous statements by these men which Allsop records, it would seem that the primary need — the search for work — can sometimes engender a secondary need amounting almost to an addiction, in spite of the hardship and persecution involved, for being on the move. In any case, that primary need involved travel, and for the poor man surrounded by the vast distances of the United States this became the call not so much of the road as of the railroad. Above all, the freight-train was the magnet which over the years drew countless thousands with the hope of free travel, and around which a whole genre of poetry and song has centred. (And as we have seen, by a curious process of cross-fertilisation, songs from American work-fronts, with the freight-train as the central motif, became during the fifties the basic material for the British phenomenon of skiffle). The hate-love felt by the disparaged migratory worker for his hard life-style may be set against the ambivalent attitude shown to him by the rest of society: "the wraith of the adventurer with a bedroll hitting the cinder trail to elsewhere remains the *doppelganger* of the American who lives a steady and relatively anchored life".[49] This parallels closely the situation of Scottish travellers who have been described as the "alter-ego of the settled population".[50]

There is another American connection which was emphasized by all those I spoke to, and that is the travellers' strong predilection for cowboy stories, cowboy films and Country and Western music. The reasons are not far to seek: cowboys are not settled; they travel and work with horses; they live rough and sleep out of doors; they have their tea in cans, and they sing round an open fire. And the American expansion: ". . . they were all travellers, they set off across the West in their covered wagons, and they fought disease and they fought hardships of all descriptions just the same as the travellers had fought, *tae survive*. And they built their settlements and they built their houses and they built their towns. Probably if the travellers'd had a chance to do this in this country they'd have done the same thing. But travellers here had no land to do it with, because all the land was already owned before the traveller came on the roads . . ."[51] Historically doubtful as this may be, it shows the yearning and the contradictions in the traveller syndrome, and I queried the travelling versus settling-down paradox here. "If the travellers had land, *some* of them would have settled down — that doesnae mean to say they wouldnae have *moved* after . . . they want to own their piece o' land so they can go and come back, tae have some place to come back tae". (The Whytes also said they liked a base to return to.)[52] There were many travellers among the emigrants to the New World — "and there's not one traveller family in Scotland at the present day who hasn't got connections. . . . (A young traveller woman), she says to me, 'There's nothing going to stop me', she says, 'it disnae maitter if it costs me a fortune, I'm going to Edinburgh just to listen to Boxcar Willie. I *must* get', she says, 'I'll leave the kids, leave ma husband, leave everything, just to get there to listen to Boxcar Willie', in Edinburgh, at the Festival".

Danny Stewart: "When I was a boy, the farm workers, travelling people, sang cowboy songs — Bing Crosbie was number one favourite. . . . In Old Meldrum, there were 30 or 40 traveller families . . . all daft on cowboy series. . . . There are few horses now, yet travellers still like Country and Western songs and cowboy stories". His wife Jane knows a number of such songs, and is fond of yodelling (and good at it), "but I'm more into old Scottish songs now, and I prefer them". Belle Stewart said her husband Alec loved C. and W. songs, had learned them especially during their visit to the States and used to play them on his "goose".[53] Stanley Robertson remembers hearing his father sing these songs — also Jeannie Robertson, who liked trying to yodel.[54]

Duncan Williamson regards his stories and songs as constituting a more valuable legacy than anything material: "We're giving our children something that will last them for the rest of their entire life".[55] He has a huge repertoire. Dr. Alan Bruford has written: "When you consider that until 1950 less than 30 international folktale types (Märchen) in Scots or Scottish English were known to scholars, and Duncan alone certainly knows at least a hundred types and can tell many more stories of the same kind unknown to the Arne-Thompson catalogue, you may realise what a debt Scotland's culture owes to the travelling people and to this one exceptional traveller".[56]

Here is one of Duncan's stories:[57]

THE ELF AND THE BASKET-MAKER

Old John, an' his old wife, was an old travelling' basket-maker that travelled the west coast of Scotland, many's an' many's the years . . . an', he made baskets all over, ye know? . . . made baskets for everybody, an' mendit baskets, he was very good at his trade. And him an' his old wife . . . was on the road an' they had a wee donkey an' cart, ye know, for carryin' their stuff from place to place. So, one night, he says tae his auld wife, he said, "Mary", he said, "I think", he said, "we'll gae doon", he says, "tae this wee campin' place that I know", he said. "An' ", he said, "I remember", he said, "I used tae cut some nice willows for ma baskets", he says, "an' I cut them last year; an' this year", he said, "I think", he said, "they'll be growin' aboot the nice size noo for cuttin'", he said, "an' I'll stey there for a couple o' days an' make some baskets", he says, "an' there's plenty hooses aboot for ye 'ae dae yir hawkin'" – see? "Fine, John", she says, "that'll dae fine".

So they came tae this wee campin' place an' they pit up their camp, an' . . . they had their tea an' it wis . . . a nice evenin' so he says, "Mary", he said, "I think I'll go away up", he says, "an' cut some o' these wands". "Well", she says, "I'll take ma basket an' I'll go away up an' . . . hawk some o' these hooses roon' aboot". See? So she hawked places, an' peens an' thread an' things, she's through the hooses.

Auld John gets his knife, it . . . there was a bit, part of a . . . table knife, cut through the centre, he used for makin' his baskets, ye know? — he hadnae got a good knife. An' away he goes. An' he walks up through this wood, to where . . . he used tae cut his sticks, he'd cut them every year. That's the wild willows. An' he landed back, up this wee path, through the wood . . . back tae this wee place where he'd cut these sticks every year. An' as usual, oh they were growin' nice, growin' straight up, ye see. "Upon my soul", he says, "they really did grow", he says, "seein' I cut them last year". He said, "They're really good stuff". So he's cuttin' away an' he's leavin' them down, an' cuttin' away, leavin' them doon in wee bunches, when this voice says, "Well, John . . . ye're busy".

"God bless me", he said. "what was't I heard — is there somebody speakin'?" Th' old man looked around . . . not a soul to be seen. "Aye, John", he says, ':there's nice . . . condition this year for ye". An' he looked roon' again an' he couldnae see nothing. The auld man rubs his ears, he says tae his self, "Am I hearin' things", he said, "or whit is it?" So he started to cut some more. "Aye, John", he said. "They're nice stuff", he said, "ye've got this time". An' he looks roon' where the voice cam' fae — an' there, sittin' on a wee . . . a wee block o' a tree, was a wee elf . . . a wee elf aboot . . . six inches. The auld man rubs his e'es. "God bless me", he said. "Are you real, or are ye no real?" "Aye", he said, "John, I'm as real as what you are". "Well, upon my soul", said the old man, he says, "I never seen anything like you", he said, "*what* are ye?"

He said, "I'm an elf". "Ah, an *elf*", [scornfully] says the auld man, "there nae such thing as elves". "Well", he said, "seein's believin'", he said. "But", he says, "am I seein' things", he said, "are you really an elf?" "Aye", he says, "John", he said, "I'm an elf". "But", he says, "what dae ye want frae me?" he said. "Well John", he says, "we keen aboot you", he said. "We ken", he says, "that you've been comin' here cuttin' . . . these woods, these sticks", he says, "for years. And", he said, "I come . . . for you", he says, "to dae a job for me". "God bless me", says the auld man, he says. "Dae a job . . . I couldnae dae n' job for you", he said. "Aye", he said, "John", he says, "you can dae a job for me", he said. He said, "I come fae Elfland", he said. And he said, "We ken aboot you", he says, "for . . . numbers o' years", he said, "an' we want you to dae a job for us". "God bless me", says the old man, he said. "I heard ma faither", he said, "an' ma grandfaither tellin' stories aboot elfs", he says, "but . . . I've never had the pleasure o' seein' yin in ma life". "Well, John", he says, "ye're seein' yin noo".

"But", he says, "what could I", he says, "me an auld traiveller basket-maker", he says, "dae for an elf?" he said. He said, "You're supposed to hae magical powers an' everything", he said. He said, "Ye dinnae need the likes o' *me* tae dae things for ye". "Ah, but", he says, "John . . . whit we need you to dae for us, we cannae dae it". "*What* is it", he said, "ye want me tae dae?" He said, "We want ye . . . I want ye to mak' me a cradle".

"A cradle? . . . God bless me", he said. "*I* cannae mak' ye a cradle", he said. "Aye", he said, "John, you can mak' the cradle", he said. "But", he said, "what dae ye want wi' a cradle?" He said, "I want the cradle", he said, "for tae haud a baby". "Whit kind o' baby?" he said. He said, "An elfin baby" — "Oh no", says old John. "No, no", he said. "I cannae dae it for ye". "Oh aye, John", he says. "You can dae it". He says, "Look, are you a full grown elf?" He said, "Aye, I'm a full grown elf". He said, "What size are ye?" He says, "Ye're no much bigger than that . . . six inches. What size", he said, "is a . . . baby elf?" " Oh", says the elf . . . "no very big". "Well", he said, "hoo dae ye expect me", he said, "an old traiveller", he says, "to get stuff like that", he said . . . "as thick as that", he says, "to mak' a cradle tae haud a baby elf?" He said, "It's out o' the question". "Ah, but John," he says, "you can dae it". Old John, he says, "I doot", he says, "I couldnae dae it for ye", he said. He said, "I cannae even believe", he said, "that ye're . . . that such a thing", he said, "I must be dreamin'" — He says, "Ye're no dreamin'", he said. "Well", he says, "there nothing I can dae for ye." "Ah, but", he says, "th'are. . . ."

So auld John gaithered up his wee puckle o' wan's . . . the elf jumped on the tap o' the wan's, sat under his oxter . . . ye ken hoo ye carry somethin' under yir airm. "Where are you gaun?" says auld John. He says, "I'm gaun hame wi' ye". He says, "Ye cannae come back wi' me", he said, "I . . . I've got a . . . ma camp" — "I ken ye've got a camp", he said, "an' yir auld wife Mary's away wi' a basket", he says, "callin' the hooses", he said, "and you're camped the same place as ye were last year. An'", he says, "ye cut these wan's last year".

The old man left the wan's doon. "Well", he says, "one thing", he says, "we'll have tae get this squared before we go", he said. He said, "I'm goin' hame wi' you, John. And", he said, "you're gaunnae mak' me a basket". "Well", he says, "sit doon", he said, "an' tell me: how am I gaunnae dae it?" He says, "You're gaunnae dae it". "What dae ye want the basket for?" "Well", he says, "I'll tell ye. Noo", he says, "keep this tae yirsel".

He said, "In Elfland", he says, "we have got a new queen". He said, "This year the king has tooken a new queen, an' ", he says, "it's his second wife, an' ", he said, "she's gaunnae have a baby. And everybody", he said, "was welcome", he says, "tae the weddin' . . . o' the young queen gettin' mairried. But", he says, "they forgot aboot yin . . . wicked auld . . . elf . . . woman . . . they never gien her an invitation . . . an'", he said, "she pit a curse on the new-born baby, when it comes to the world, when it's born . . . that it'll never be right, unless it's rocked in a human cradle. An'", he says, "you're to mak' it".

"No me", he said, "I couldnae mak' a cradle for a wee baby infant" — he says, "John, you'll mak' it", he said. "I ken you can *dae* it. Are ye *willin'* tae dae it, if I help ye?" "Well, now", he says, "that's different", he said, "if you help me", he said, "that's different", he said. "Hoo're ye gaunnae help me?" "Never mind", he says, "John — pick up yir wands". John picked up the wan's, the elf jumped t' the top o' the wan's . . . pit them below his oxter. Back he goes to the camp.

The auld man's oot o' breath when he gets to the camp. The old woman's back. In these days the auld traivellers hardly used a kettle for makin' tea, they kept one o' these . . . a can, a tin can wi' a lid on it, ye ken, for makin' tea for the two auld folk.

He says, "Mary". She says, "What". He says, "Look what I got". She says, "Whit did ye get? Did ye find something?" "No", he says. "Look", he says, "what's sittin' on the top o' the wan's'". She says, "*What's* sittin' on the top o' the wan's?" She says, "I cannae see naethin'". He says, "Luik at the wee gadgie", — meanin' the wee man. She ways, "What wee man?" She says, "What's wrong wi' ye, were ye drinkin' or something?" "Aye, *drinkin'*", he says, "whaur wad I get a drink in the middle o' a waste wood?"

The old woman looks . . . and she sees the wee . . . "God bless ma soul an' body", she said, "what' that?" she said, "whaur did ye get that?" He says, "Hullo, Mary", he said, "I'm an elf". She says, "Ye're whit?" He says, "I'm an elf". "God bless me", she said, "I heard ma granny", she said, "an' ma great-granny speakin' aboot elfs", she says, "but you are the first elf that ever I seen in my life" — and the wee man cam' in. And the old woman was sittin' there, an' the old man was sittin' — and the elf sittin cross-legged wi' his legs foldit aside the fire, see?

She says, "Whit dae ye want fae us, for", she says, "we never done ye any hairm". "No", he says, the wee elf, "I ken", he says, "ye never done anything . . . that ye'd dae us nae hairm", . . . he said. "I only come", he says, "for John", he says, "to dae a wee job for me". "But God bless me", says the . . . auld woman, she says, "what could John", she says, "an auld tinker man", she says, "dae", she says, "for you — an elf", she said, "fae Elfland", she says, "(ye've) got all the magical powers: youse can get onything in the world". He says, "Aye, true", he said, "we're woodland elfs", he says, "we can dae a lot o' things, but", he says, "we cannae dae the thing that we needed done . . . but", he says, "John can dae it". . . . "*What* is it?" He said, "I want him to mak' me an elfin cradle . . . for an elfin baby". "Oh God bless me, maister", she says, "my aul' man couldnae mak' ye an elf's cradle", she said, "he can mak' *cradles*", she says, ". . . for a *big* wean". She says, "What size would the elfin wean be?" "Oh", he says, "aboot . . . three or four inches high". "Ah no", she says, "it's impossible". She said, "He couldnae get the stuff". "Well", John said, "I was tellin' him that", he said. "That I couldnae get nae stuff . . . thin enough for tae mak' a cradle fir a wee baby, elfin baby". "Aye", he says, "Mary . . . John can dae it". . . .

"Well", said the aul' man, he says, "if I'm gaunnae dae it I suppose I'll have to dae it". He says, "Gie him some tea". Noo, the wee elf was that wee . . . th' auld woman had tea in a can, so . . . she hadnae got a cup big enough for [to suit] the elf tae haud, so she took the lid o' the can and she holdit the lid like that tae him, and the wee elf held it in his two hands an' he . . . drunk up the tea. Eh? "Very good", he said. "That was good".

He says, "Mary. Are you willin'", he says, "tae help a wee babbie . . . get a cradle?" the elf said. "God bless me, wee maister", she said, "I'm willin' tae help", she says, "ony wee wean", she says, "God never gave me . . . th' blessin'", she said, "o' ony weans o' ma ain". She said, "I dinnae even hae a grand-wean or nothin'", she said, "and", she says, "I like wee weans", she said. "I was dae anything in the world tae help a wee babbie . . . even suppose it's a wee elf-babbie".

She said, "I want tae help — I'll dae onything in the world", she says, "tae help him". "Weel", he said, "wad ye let . . . auld John", he says, "have some o' yir hair?" She says, "He can have a' the hair he wants", she said. "He can get the lot", she said, "I'll give the lot, if it's ony guid gae him". This auld man, he says, "I cannae mak (a) cradle wi' human hair". "Ah, but", the elf says, "wi' my help ye can", he says", " — let me pull the hairs". The wee elf got up on th' auld woman's knee an' climbed up th' aul' woman's shouther . . . an' he pit his two hands tae yin o' th' aul' woman's hairs an' he gien it a pull . . . pull't a single hair oot . . . and he handit it tae auld John . . . an' aul' John pit his hand up an' catched it, and there was the beautifulst strip of fine, thin cane that John had ever saw in his life . . . thin as a human hair that ye could tie in roon' yir . . . finger in knots. "Well, upon my soul", says the auld woman, she says, "I never seen the likes o' that". "Nor me", says th' auld man, he says. He said, "I cuid dae anything wi' that", he said. . . . "I could do anything wi' that". "Well", says the wee elf, "you're gaunnae get plenty o' it", he said. An' he kept pullin', an' he kept pullin', an' he kept pullin', an' got . . . 'n' left it doon till he'd a bunch that size.

An' he pulled some more, an' he made it a wee bit thicker, for the ribs. "Noo", says the elf, "I'm goin' off", he says. "An'" he says, "I'll be back", he said, "when that cradle's ready". "Well upon my soul", says th' old man, he said. "I've never seen the like o' that", he said, "in all my days — noo", he says to her, he said, ". . . . if you ever mention a word o' this to ony other human being", he said, "I'll kill ye deid". He says, "Never you say a word to no human being'", he said. "John", she says, "I couldnae tell naebody", she says, "aboot that, because", she said, "naebody in the world'll ever believe us". "Well", he says, "a' the better", he said, "if naebody believes it", he says. "We don't want nobody (t') ken about it". He says, "That wee man'll be back", he said, "an' if it's no made", he said, "a jijimant'll follae us the rest o' oor days".

Meaning' bad luck.

So the old man got busy an' he sets . . . to work. an' he workit an' he workit an' he cut, an' he made the beautifullest cradle . . . it wasnae mair than three inches long, with a hood on it . . . an' he cut two nice pieces o' wood an' he pit lovely wee rockers on tae it. He says tae th' auld woman, he says, "Hae ye got ony bits o' . . . cloth aboot ye?" he said. She said, "The only thing that's in there, John", she said, "in ma basket is a roll o' red ribbon", . . . a bit broad ribbon . . . she was sellin', to the hooses. And the auld man took the ribbon an' he wove the ribbon inside it, an' made the beautifullest thing ye ever saw in yir life . . . fit fir any elfin wean.

"There", he said, an' he pit his finger to it on the floor an' it rocked back an' forrit like that — hood an' everything on it, — ken? — miniature, that size. He said, "That should please that wee man when he comes back". So th' auld man turned his back tae light his pipe, an' whit did th' auld woman dae? The auld traveller women used tae carry a big pocket roond their side at one time, ye ken . . . a big leather, a big pocket, that's (th') thing. She put her hand in her pocket, an' she took oot a wee silver thruppeny piece, and she dropped it into the cradle when th' old man wisnae lookin'. See? — this is to hansel a new-born baby, ye see — solid silver.

But early in the mornin' th' old man's up; th' auld woman had their wee cup o' tea in the mornin' but they're nae sooner up . . . in comes the elf. "Good morning, John", he said. "Oh good morning", says John . . . to the wee . . . to the wee elf. "Good morning, Mary", he said. "Ha-ha", he said, "I see ye got ma cradle finished. An'", he said, "it's a good yin it is". "Aye", says John, he said. "There it is", he said. "It's ready for ye". The wee elf put his finger tae it — "Oh", he said, "it's in first class order". He says, "John, you'll be repaid for this". An' he luiks again — The wee man was gone, cradle an' a'. See?

"Well, upon my soul", says . . . th' auld man, he says, "I never seen the like o' that". See? So, the old man an' woman, th' old man went aboot his wey, th' auld woman went away and she took two or three baskets th' auld man had made but she hadnae gone tae the first hoose till the woman bought the four o' them at once there — she wasnae minutes awa'. She come back. He said, "Ye're no back a'ready?" says the old man; "Aye", she said. "Yir four baskets is gone", she said, "an' I've an order for another two or three". "Well, upon my soul", he said. "I'll have tae try an' get them made". So they sat doon; the day passed by.

The next mornin' the old man got up, an' he took to break two or three sticks to start his fire, an' sittin' ootside at the top o' the stane was his wee cradle.

He says, "Woman". "What?" she said. He says, "Come 'ere".
He said, "Look — I tellt ye, I said I couldnae mak' a cradle for an
elf wean". She says, "What wey?" She said, "it was the best cradle
ye ever made in yir life", she says, "suppose it was wee", . . . she
said. He said, "Luik, sittin' oot there on the top o' the stane". He
said, "It's back". He said, "I tellt ye it was nae use".

Th' auld man goes an' he brings it in an' he luiks intae it and
then he luiks at the aul' woman. He said, "Mary". He said, "Whit
did you dae?" She said, "I never . . ." He says, "Whit did ye dae?"
She says, "I never done nothing" — he says, "What's that in the
cradle?" "Ah", she said, "a wee thrup'ny bit", she says, "I pit
intae't, for tae hansel the young wean". "Curse you, woman". he
said. He said, "You done it". He said, "You ken fine", he said,
"ye should never offer a elf silver, in no way", he said. She said,
"I didnae mean nae hairm". "Well", he said, "bad luck upon us
now", he said. "You done it", he said, "ye should never've put
that threepenny bit", he says, "into the cradle". He said, "It's a
good job", he said, "that I ken what tae dae . . . or", he said,
"we'd have bad luck the rest of our days". He said, "Look", he
said, "get me ma tools oot". The aul' man had a big box o' tools for
makin' his tin. "An'", he said, "You get aboot yir business", he
said. "An'", he said . . . an' he kin'led up his fire. She says,
"What're ye gaunnae dae?" "Never you mind", he said, "what I'm
gaunnae dae", he said, "I ken what I'm gaunnae dae", he said,
"you get aboot yir job", he says. "Only for you", he says, "I
wadnae need, to have to dae all this trouble. You pit me", he said,
"in this trouble, with you and", he said, "yir silly cairry-on", he
said, "wi yir hanselling new-born weans", he said, "that's an elfin
wean, no a traveller's wean ye're hansellin'".

The old man got his files oot, an' he kin'led the fire up red an' he
took the silver threepenny bit an' he put it in the fire an' he made it
red-hot till it was red. An' he took his tin cutters, and he sat and he
cut and he cut an' he cut it in thin strips. Th' old woman sitting
watching him. "What're ye daein'?" she said. "Never you mind",
he said, "what I'm daein'", he said, "it's your fault onyway", he
said, "that I wad need to dae this. You get aboot yir business", he
said. "Oh well', she said, "I'm no gaun any place today", she said,
"I'm bidin' hame". "Well", he says, "bide at hame but", he says,
"keep oot o' my road, don't come near me", he said, "it's your
fault".

He sat . . . and he soldered an' he hammered an' he hammered
an' he choppit an' he hammered an' he hammered an' he solder't
an' he hammered an' he polished an' he cleaned for a good strucken
hour.

He says, "Wumman. Have you any peens in yir basket?" She says, "Whit?" He says, "Peens". (*Pins*, y'know?) "Aye", she said, — y'know the auld traiveller women in the olden days that used to hawk the hooses, they kept wee bunches o' wee . . . yon wee brass pins, ye ken? he says, "Gimme yin o' the pins". She says, "Whit're ye gaunnae" — "Never you mind whit I'm gaunnae do wi't", he said, "it was yuir fault onywey. Gimme it. Never you mind what I'm gaunnae dae wi' it", he said, "I ken what I'm daein'. Curse upon you, he said, "you're the cause o't", he said, "ma wee cradle wasnae taken awa' wi' the . . . elves".

He polished an' he cleaned an' he soldered, an' the old woman's lookin' over his shoulder — "Dinna be luikin'", he said, "its your fault". An he held it up tae her, efter he's finished, he says, "Luik at that". An' there it was, Ailie . . . the bonniest silver butterfly ye ever saw, miniature butterfly, soldered on t' the pin. A solid silver butterfly, made from the thruppeny piece: legs, wings; as if it was just . . . made it annoled, soldered on to the pin. He took it, an' he pinned it in the side o' the wee cradle, an' he took the wee cradle in his hand, an' away he went.

She says, "Whaur are ye gaun?" — "Never you mind", he said, "where I'm gaun", he said, "it's your fault. No your business". "Will you be long till you're back?" — "I don't know when I'll be back", he said. "I don't know when I'll be back, but I'll be back sometime".

Away he goes, . . . back to the same bush where he met the elf. An' he takes the wee cradle an' he sits an' he has a good luik at it, his ain sel', — an' he felt sad, ye ken? An' he places it on the wee block where he had seen the elf, wi' the silver . . . butterfly pinned to the side o' the cradle.

Back he comes . . . over tae the front of his tent, an' he sits doon, an' . . . she says, "Whaur were ye?" "Never you mind where I was", he said, "nae business o' yours where I was", he said, "you done it", he says. She said, "I didnae mean any hairm". "Well", he says, "forget aboot it onyway", he said. He said, "I think I managed to right it . . . to right the wrong now", he said. "I'll tell ye the morn", he said. "I'll be better pleased tomorrow", he said, "when I . . . see what happened".

So the night passes by, an' the next mornin' th' old man got his breakfast an' away he goes . . . back to the block where he left the cradle, but when he arrives there the cradle's gone. [Spat.] He spat on his hands. [Rubbed hands.] He comes home, he's . . . dancin' an' singin' comin' home to the old woman . . . the old woman says, "What's adae wi' ye, are ye gaun mad?" "No", he says, "I'm no gaun mad", he said, "Mary", he said, "the cradle's away", he said, "it's been accepted". "What", she says, "John" — He says, "It's been accepted", he said. "Aye well", she said. An' he said, "It's no nae fault o' yours", he said, "— no wi' your help".

So . . . I'm going' through ma story . . . the cradle was gone an' he luiks up in the bush, where he was cuttin' the wands — the cradle was gone, an' there pinned to the bush, where he was cuttin' the wan's, was the most beautifullest pocket knife that ever he saw in his life. Solid, inlaid with silver an' mother o' pearls . . . stuck clasped to the tree where he'd cut the wan's, ye see?

Noo, in the olden days, to possess a good pocket knife . . . among basket-makers was just tae be out of this world, ye ken? Because they couldnae get a good knife, and if you had a good knife in these days they come fae all parts tae see it, an' everybody, when the basket makers met . . . together, to show off this knife was just like showin' off a Rolls Royce at the present day, ye know? An' when this old man saw this knife stickin' to the tree, he said, "Ah-h- it's for me", he said. Ye ken? He said, "Never in my days", he said, "have ever I saw a pocket knife like this", he said — it was juist out o' this world for him.

He took it, and he closed it an' he put in his pocket. It was silver an' ivory, inlaid wi' mother-o'-pearl, an' a four-inch steel blade, an' he went up an' he touched one o' the wee willows an' it just went . . . sailed through it, ye know? "God bless me", he said, "that was left for me", he said, "by the wee elf", he said, "in payment for ma cradle . . . for ma cradle".

Back he goes — pits it in his pocket, an' he's going skipping back the road. He couldnae wait tae get intae his tent an' tell his auld wife. "Well, John", she said, "what happened?" "Well", he says, "the cradle . . . ma cradle was accepted", he said, "the elfs have got it, an'", he said, "I hope it helps the wee babbie". "Well thank God", she says, "for that" — "an' it's nae help o' yours", he said, "mind it wasnae your help. But", he says, "look what I got in return for it, Mary". Th' auld woman looked. "God bless me", she said. "In all my days", she said, "John", she said, "that is a knife", she said, "that is a real knife", she said. "That's what ye call a pocket-knife", she said, "an' mony's the body that'll be wantin' that fae you" — "Ah but", he says, "it's mony's the body's no goin' to get it fae me".

"That", he said, "is a gift . . . an'", he said, "a gift it'll be . . . tae me for the rest o' ma days".

So . . . that knife done old John all his days, an' he became one o' the greatest basket-makers in the country, an' his fame o' makin' baskets spread far an' wide, an' every basket that was ever made wi' that knife was sold as quick as it was made. An' that knife passed doon, when old John died it passed tae his son,[58] and when his son died it passed to his grandson and so on right through the family, an' that knife could still be in circulation yet. Among the generation o' the travellin' basket-makers was the Burkes . . . an' the Burkes . . . was my ancestors, because they were Williamsons . . . because there were Burkes, . . . was Williamsons now . . . and Johnstons . . . among the travellin' people . . . and that knife could still be among some o' the family yet but naebody likes to talk aboot it. An' that's the last o' ma story.

Story-telling is the least widely known of all the aural folk-arts with which this book is concerned; even within the revival movement it has only recently been recognised and included, although scholars have over many years collected and studied a mass of fascinating material in the genre.[59] Generally speaking the Gaels have kept in closer touch with this ancient tradition, and spoken tales can be heard in Gaelic broadcast programmes from time to time; but some of the most remarkable socially functioning story-telling now goes on among Scots-speaking travellers. As with the other arts, story-telling is best heard — and seen — in the flesh. A good narrator can exert a near-hypnotic effect on a large roomful of people, so that nothing else seems to exist for the story's duration. Travellers again are among the leading spell-binders — Stanley Robertson is another noted virtuoso in this field.

The various aspects of traveller culture with which we are here concerned receive little mention in the official reports and academic theses referred to. But these reports were concerned primarily with social and community problems and with the search for practical solutions to these problems, and many theses are at least as circumscribed in their terms of reference; culture has thus been a side issue in all these studies. The value and interest of the traveller way of life, and their contribution in various fields, is only now — if belatedly — being recognised.

Not all travellers are inheritors of this music and story, but there may be many as yet undiscovered tradition-bearers amongst their number, as indicated by the high quality of much that has been garnered so far. Both the zeal of the collector, and the friendship and opportunity provided by the revival movement, are still necessary.[60] Amongst younger travellers — especially those who have married into the settled community, or at least moved into it — a process of acculturation is at work, and Betsy Whyte reports that some of them despise the "silly old songs and stories." As we have seen, this is very much what happened earlier in the wider, settled community.[61] Betsy Whyte also reports a related attitude among those who reject this material, a feeling that it was part of "the bad old days": "some travellers are afraid to appreciate the old culture because they were so held down in it."

On the other hand, a sizeable number of non-travellers have taken up the travelling way of life — the open air and the life-style in general have appealed particularly to those from large towns. There has always been some movement into as well as away from the travelling life, but there was a special appeal between the wars, with high unemployment and low social security. Adoptive travellers learned resourcefulness and versatility from those born to the life, along with many skills now dying out, and although some made poor travellers, others brought a fresh approach to the problems involved.

This chapter began with one of Jane Turriff Stewart's pithy comments and it must close with another: "We have kept up a' this culture.' Acknowledgement of this fact is one step towards repaying our debt to her people.

Footnotes to Chapter VI

1. Noted down at Mintlaw, Aberdeenshire, 30/11/80. Within a few days of this date, the author visited Betsy and Bryce Whyte at Montrose; Jane Turriff and Danny Stewart (recently married) at Mintlaw; and Belle Stewart, Sheila MacGregor and her son Ian, with their relatives Willie and Bella MacPhee, at Blairgowrie. These are all traveller folk who have been involved with the Revival, and their quoted comments were made during this field trip.
2. Hugh Gentleman and Susan Swift, *Scotland's Travelling People*, p. 9, quoting from L. Spence, "The Scottish Tinkler Gypsies", in *Scotland's Magazine* 51, no. 2 (1955). See also Frank Vallée, "The Tinkers of Scotland", typescript study in the School of Scottish Studies library, 1955, p. 4.
3. The travellers' claim that many Jacobites of noble birth joined them, before and after Culloden, is probably justified.
4. L. Spence, quoted by Gentleman and Swift, p. 9, and Duncan Campbell, *Reminiscences and Reflections of an Octogenarian Highlander*, p. 24.
5. Also at St. Boswells and at Musselburgh. Many English gypsies attend these fairs. And Stirlingshire, Perthshire, Angus and Fife all have substantial groups nearer to the gypsy mould.
6. See Hamish Henderson's article "The Tinkers" in *A Companion to Scottish Culture*, ed. David Daiches.
7. Several annual folk festivals now include competition classes in story-telling.
8. See Katherine M. Briggs, *A Dictionary of British Folk-tales*, part A. Many of these tales are the stories of Child ballads.
9. Duncan Williamson: recorded at camp, Lochgilphead site, with Linda Williamson, 26/9/80.
10. Many incidents are recounted which purport to illustrate this gift. For instance, Jeannie Robertson was once given hospitality in an Edinburgh flat: she knew nothing of its history but she soon became uneasy, said she didn't like the atmosphere and insisted on leaving. It transpired that a suicide had

taken place there some years before. (Travellers regard suicide as a very serious sin.)

11. For further comments, see notes (chapters 3 and 4, and Appendix) on the singing of Jeannie Robertson, Lizzie Higgins, Belle Stewart, Sheila MacGregor, Jane Turriff, Stanley and Anthony Robertson, "old" Davie Stewart, and Duncan Williamson. For recordings, see *The Muckle Sangs* discs; more than half the singers are of travelling stock.

12. Amongst those I have heard, the only exception to this is Betsy Whyte, and she does not think of herself as a singer. In fact, her more reserved and inward style can be meltingly persuasive.

13. Duncan Williamson: 26/9/80, Lochgilphead.

14. Ewan MacColl and Peggy Seeger, *Travellers' Songs from England and Scotland*, p. 21.

15. Gentleman and Swift, p. 10. This report includes further facts about anti-traveller legislation up to and including the twentieth century.

16. Henry G. Farmer, *A History of Music in Scotland*, part 2, chapter 2.

17. Gentleman and Swift, p. 10.

18. Gentleman and Swift; two reports by the Secretary of State's Advisory Committee, *Scotland's Travelling People*, 1971–74, and 1975–78; Planning Exchange Forum Report 14, *Scotland's Travelling People*, 186 Bath Street, Glasgow, 1978; circulars and letters from the Scottish Development Department and the Scottish Education Department, 1969–80.

19. Helen Fullerton, *The health and welfare of travelling families*, paper given at the 94th annual congress of the Royal Sanitary Association of Scotland, Inverness, 1969, p.35.

20. In December 1980 Duncan with his wife and two young children moved to a cottage in Fife.

21. Duncan Williamson: recorded at camp near Cupar, Fife, with Linda Williamson, 19/9/77.

22. Jane Turriff: recorded at Fetterangus, 8/11/76. Jane was severely crippled as a result of illness in childhood. Recommended reading: James Porter, "The Turriff Family of Fetterangus", *Folk Life* 16 (1978) 5–26.

23. Stanley Robertson quoted an old traveller saying (prefacing it with the remark, "It's horrible . . . very chauvinistic"): "'A man can always put on a collar and tie and look clean, but a woman canna take a needle and thread and sew herself up'. As if . . . sin's involved, but it doesn't matter for the man. The woman's left with the seed, and many times the issue". (Unless otherwise noted Stanley Robertson's comments in this chapter are from telephone conversations, late 1980 to early 1981.) Danny and Jane Turriff Stewart said, "It was an awful sin if a girl had a bairn", i.e. outside marriage.

24. This one (male) traveller said that if a man really loved a woman, and she upset him or hurt his feelings, then how could he *help* beating her up? Several others said that violence *used* to be considered as proof of love, and Betsy Whyte had often heard the comment, "He disnae think much o' her, he's never laid a hand on her since they were married". Danny Stewart said, "Any man who beats his wife, and says, 'I love you', must be crazy . . . Some women enjoy it, but it's wrong".

25. Gentleman and Swift, p. 59; F. Rehfisch, "The Tinkers of Perthshire and Aberdeenshire", unpublished study in the School of Scottish Studies library, 1958, pp. 102–3; and Betsy Whyte, *The Yellow on the Broom, the early days of a traveller woman*.

26. See also Gentleman and Swift, p. 59.

27. Traveller children are expected by law to put in 200 half-days attendance at school during the winter months. The possible total for the year is 400 half-days.

28. Probably some are untidy, but the travellers I spoke to maintained firmly that it is inexperienced and non-traveller campers, of various categories, who are the real offenders.

29. The trip referred to in Note 1 ended with a visit to Sheila and Andrew Douglas at Scone. Comments from them were noted at this time. Both are closely involved with travellers, especially in Perthshire, and Sheila Douglas is researching on the songs and stories of the Stewarts of Blair.

30. 24 September, 1980; presented by Ewan MacColl and Peggy Seeger. Sheila MacGregor commented, "The locals throw out the red carpet for us now . . . the recent [TV] film clinched what has been a very gradual process".

31. This film may be obtained for hire: apply Timothy Neat, Duncan of Jordanstone College of Art, Dundee.

32. *The Scotsman*, 13/1/81. (Ewan MacColl's "The Moving-on Song," given in Chapter 4, gives poignant expression to the horrors of eviction.)

33. See also *Scotland's Travelling People*, 1975–1978; paragraphs 6.34 and 6.35, pp. 20–21, recognise the pressing need for such education and publicity.

34. One of the most moving is Duncan Williamson's "The Hawker's Lament", p. 187 of *Tocher* no. 33; 3 out of the 6 verses also introduce the report by Gentleman and Swift. See also Belle Stewart's "The Berryfields of Blair" in Chapter 4.

35. Timothy Neat, "The Summer Walkers", in the second issue of *Seer*, Dundee Art College magazine, pp. 40–9; and Linda Williamson, "As I see it . . . From the Gelly", in the *Scots Magazine*, March 1980.

36. Letter from Stanley Robertson to the author, 18/11/80.

37. Duncan Williamson: recorded 26/9/80, Lochgilphead.

38. Gladys A. Reichard: *Navaho religion: a study of symbolism*, Pantheon Books, New York 1950. Quoted in *The Anthropology of Music*, p. 83, by Alan P. Merriam, who adds, "Music . . . is conceived as wealth in the form of intangible goods in many societies".

39. Traveller cant language, meaning: "Better class (or educated) folk (as distinct from 'scaldies' or 'flatties') coming up to the house, so mind your language" (or, "don't curse and swear").

40. These visits were organised by Edinburgh Folk Festival; see also Appendix II, p. 338.

41. Hugh Gentleman comments: "I'm afraid it was a *complete coincidence*. It arose out of earlier work in England and Wales and out of the 1968 Caravan Sites Act, Part II of which did not extend to Scotland." But Scotland is not the only part of the U.K. to have experienced a folk revival! A "complete" coincidence of this kind puts a strain on credibility . . . I prefer to leave the question for future researchers to answer.

42. Willie MacPhee, with his wife Bella, still travels extensively in the summer. He is a fine piper as well as a singer.

43. Hamish Henderson and Francis Collinson, "New Child Ballad variants from oral tradition", *Scottish Studies* 9 (1965), 1–33; in particular, see p.2.

44. Duncan Williamson: recorded 26/9/80, Lochgilphead.

45. Recorded in Aberdeen, 9/11/76.

46. To be called an aristocrat by a traveller is a real compliment.

47. Kenneth Allsop, *Hard Travellin', The Hobo and His History*, pp. 30–1.

48. Allsop, p. 164.

49. Allsop. p. 270.

50. Neat, p. 48.

51. All the quotations in this paragraph are from Duncan Williamson's recording of 26/9/80, Lochgilphead.

52. This is also reflected in the current policy which, with a proper network of

established sites, would allow travellers the freedom to move but to return to the same wintering spot if they wished.

53. "Goose": small practice pipe, with no drones.
54. For a transcription of Jeannie Robertson singing "The Hobo Song", see "Jeannie Robertson: the other songs," by Herschel Gower and James Porter, *Scottish Studies* 16, 1972, 158–9. In this recording Jeannie makes no concessions to transatlantic origins: she treats the song much the same as she does *Lord Randal* or any other tragic Scots ballad, and sings the "yodel" refrain without the slightest break in her voice. (Jane Turriff's yodelling, on the other hand, is the real Mackay).
55. Duncan Williamson: recorded 26/9/80, Lochgilphead.
56. *Tocher* no. 33, p. 150. This issue contains an outstanding special feature on Duncan Williamson, including other stories and songs he has recorded.
57. Duncan Williamson: recorded 19/9/77, Cupar. One problem in transcribing spoken tales is whether to insert all occurrences of "he says", "she said", etc., with which the dialogue is liberally sprinkled. To the listener, they act as slight pause marks, as a kind of oral punctuation; they are often spoken very rapidly, and they are not obtrusive. If they are removed from the written transcription the whole style is altered. Readers are asked to use their imagination, to try to hear the story as spoken.
58. Although this couple had no children of their own, Duncan pointed out that they would probably adopt and bring up an orphan, or a child from a large and poverty-stricken family, or more than one such child. This was a common practice among travellers, especially those who were childless, and they would regard such children as their own.
59. The School of Scottish Studies has an extensive Folk Tale Archive of recordings, chiefly in Gaelic. Those in Scots, though fewer in number, have greatly increased in recent years; they came firstly from travellers, and secondly from tradition-bearers in the Northern Isles.
60. At least three post-graduate students are working on aspects of traveller culture: Linda Williamson, who has herself become a traveller by marriage; Barbara McDermitt, also American; and Sheila Douglas of Scone.
61. This cycle of rejection followed by later revival is found in possibly every field of human endeavour — it is connected with fashion in the widest sense of the word.

Betsy Whyte
Photograph courtesy Barbara McDermitt

VII   Signposts

No matter what the reviver thinks of the present state of affairs, however, he must accept it as his given quantity and use it as the base that it inevitably is for whatever accretion it may accept. This base will in all probability be a conglomeration. . . . Indigestible? By no means. Oral tradition can digest anything, give it but enough time.

Charles Seeger[1]

To me, anything is acceptable. If it works, it will be absorbed: if not, rejected.

Dick Gaughan[2]

1.

At the outset of this book, a distinguished ethnomusicologist warned me against confusing traditional music, and especially song, with music of the Revival. Several years of investigating, however, have persuaded me that the dividing line between the two — if it ever existed — is disappearing. Tradition after all is not just something inherited from the past, it is the continuous development of a body of art or of general attitudes, etc. The Revival is the tradition of the present, but with one qualification: of the three factors named in the I.F.M.C. definition as shaping the folk music tradition — continuity, variation and selection — the third can be only partially effective in the present; selection exists, in plenty, but it has not yet been tested and changed by the passage of time. "Selection by the community" implies the possibility that different groups of people, at different periods of time, will make different selections. The influence of methods of transmission other than the oral must also be taken into account. Once a song, for instance, is in print it is less likely to go under, whether topical or not; it may be ignored by one generation and seized on by another. At the same time oral transmission will still continue. There are fashions in all the arts, dependent on the many-sided conditions of society, and this is a continuous, recurring phenomenon. The songs and articles contributed to *The Buchan Observer* by Gavin Greig in the early years of this century, and the interest aroused by them, might be considered as a kind of revival. We have seen, however, that the post-world-

---

1.   See footnotes page 252.

war-II revival shows some quite unique features.

Here is a contribution from Jack Foley, the Glasgow journalist, singer and songwriter whose version of the "Corncrake" song is discussed in Appendix I:

> I've been through all the phases — from 'anything goes, never heard a horse sing'[3] to 'if you can't stick it in your ear it's not a folk song'[4] — and I now believe the term 'folk song' is closer to the first set of quotes. The Louis Armstrong definition is of course simplistic, but I believe that what people sing — and most importantly *CREATE* by the fact of their singing — is 'folk song'. And I'm not too worried whether what they bring into creation started out as a pop song, a football chant or a bothy ballad, so long as it is *THEIR* song at the moment of performance. Yes, there are songs that were carried by travelling people, yes, there are songs that were sung by sailors, yes, there were songs hauled from village gathering to 'castle and ha" bearing a version of the news. But in the hands — and voices — of some so-called folk singers, these songs are as dead as the age they were born in. Let these people form their antiquarian musical societies — I'll probably join 'cause I like the material — but don't let them call it folk singing. That only comes from someone who can reincarnate the emotions contained in such material and for whom they still hold meaning.

After summarising the "general upheaval in society which expressed itself in many ways: clothes . . . politics . . . mass media . . . theatre . . . Bill Haley, Elvis Presley, Chris Barber, . . . and . . . the music of the revival", he continues:

> . . . as I see it, what happened was that folk song — centred on the 'folk song club' — was an easily-obtainable method of participating in the general freedom movement of the times. There were few other outlets for the majority of people. Nowadays, there's more available. . . .[5]

"A method of participating"? It's remarkable that the fifties, the time when developing technology made home listening more available to all, was also the time when people started going to clubs, to play a closer part in the live performance of this music. Lloyd's "function" definition comes to mind: after a review of developments in Europe and the U.S., he wrote, ". . . the test of a folk song may be neither in its origin, as was thought in the 19th century, nor in its evolution, as maintained by most 20th century folklorists, but in the positive function it fulfils in a society; e.g. it is still far closer bound to the material life of men than art music is, it is still capable of acting on the prime conditions of existence as in its ancient magical days. . . ."[6] Function . . . or process? The two words rub shoulders with each other, and Karl Dallas inclines towards the second: ". . . I have never been able to understand the difficulty . . . of establishing usable criteria as to what is folk and what is not, so long as one realises that the subject under discussion is a process rather than a thing".[7] The difficulty referred to is undoubtedly shared by most writers on the subject — this whole area has been a battle-ground and is still a mine-field. There is as yet no definition of folk music which will not be hedged about with qualifications. There are only approximations, asymptotes which continually approach the truth but never reach it.

2.

The question of class, both in the past and in the present, is important in any consideration of folk culture. Who were the folk who played this music and who sang these songs? In an investigation into the verbal content of ballads, Dr. David Buchan includes the second half of this question,[8] and although he is concerned solely with ballads, his answers shed much light on folk song in general. When the only available method of transmission was the oral, the folk were defined by nonliteracy and not by class, although there was some correlation between the two. Lairds who were nonliterate, and there were many, would participate in the oral ballad tradition. But after the advent of literacy, class became an important factor in demarcating the folk, and the ballads descended in the social scale, passing from the tenant-farmers to the ploughmen to the travellers. It is clear from what Morag MacLeod has said in Chapter 5 that this process did not occur to any comparable extent in the Gaelic sector of Scotland, but this has alas been an ever-shrinking minority and we are concerned here with the majority. The identification of folk music with the lower social classes was in fact a phenomenon of at least European dimensions. However, as Antonio Gramsci, the Italian revolutionary thinker, wrote: "That which distinguishes folksong in the framework of a nation and its culture is neither the artistic fact nor the historic origin; it is a separate and distinct way of perceiving life and the world, as opposed to that of 'official' society".[9] This profound statement implies some class alignment but goes beyond it, to the idea of the "man of independent mind"[10] who can fight back against the overwhelming tide of mass consumer culture. Yesterday's rebels may be tomorrow's "officials", but folk song continues to present the alternative, the nonconformist, the unofficial viewpoint which is perennially necessary for society's health. And it makes us at least potentially aware of the time dimension, the evolutionary perspective in human affairs.

With this insight in mind, it is less strange than might otherwise appear that the revival of this predominantly working class culture should have drawn its leaders from the middle class (and it was a movement which depended greatly on leadership). The majority of folk club members and attenders at festivals have also been middle class. Dick Gaughan spoke recently of "an unusual folk club" where the membership was almost totally working class, and where both men and women dress up for a night out at the club, in striking contrast to the jeans-and-sweater image adopted by most folk enthusiasts. John Watt stressed the middle class involvement,[11] and Norman Buchan agreed, with qualifications: "Most of my kids [at Rutherglen] had a working class background, they were becoming educated into the middle class". He mentioned the improvement in pop culture which was effected by the Revival, by jazz and by other American — especially Black — material: "The stuff that emerged from this was far removed from the schmalz and treacle of the earlier period. . . . It's part of what I think Hamish [Henderson] would call the kind of anti-fascist struggle of *strengthening* people by presenting them, giving them, and learning from them too . . . one thinks of the recreation of a popular culture by Ewan MacColl in his Radio Ballads documentary. . . . Anything that gives [people] confidence, morale, is important and therefore . . . cannot be shrugged aside as *only* middle class".[12] The revival was also a mainly urban phenomenon, especially in its early years. Although the Industrial Revolution had given birth to many songs about city and factory life, most of the older songs were of rural provenance. People search for what they need, for what they feel is missing; to the urban and middle class youth of the fifties and sixties, this need was for their cultural roots as well as for development, progress, change.

In Scotland, these roots were connected with a re-emerging sense of national identity. Take the obvious example of speech accents. Jean Redpath remarked that while a Scottish accent was a positive advantage in the States, back home it still had a social stigma attached to it.[13] From the latter part of the eighteenth century onward, the ambitious Scot tended to cultivate an upper-class English accent, and only comparatively recently has this begun to change — for instance, regional announcers in radio and television are now permitted to have regional accents. Peter Hall noted that he could not achieve the right accent for blues and other American songs, "and this turned me towards my own Scottish tradition".[14]

Although as we have seen the protest songs of the fifties and sixties tended to be couched in the Scots vernacular, there is a sense in which these songs had a broadening effect. "Essentially, the folk music revival is *international* in outlook. This is because of its protest function which, it feels, it must fulfil wherever protest has to be made about injustice in any part of the world".[15] How effective were these protest songs? Did they influence people's attitudes to any appreciable extent, thus helping towards the rectification of injustices protested against?

As regards the U.S.A. the latter question (in Chapter 2) was answered with an affirmative from Dunson in the mid-sixties. This is supported by the ethnomusicologist Merriam. Writing in the same period, after noting that where song texts are a reflection of culture they tend to be *post facto*, he continues: "But song texts may also be considered to lead the way. . . . This is seen in the United States of 1963 in which desegregation demands are often put into the form of song, as in Bob Dylan's 'Blowin' in the Wind'. John Greenway (1953) has traced 'American folksongs of protest' back as far as 1800. . . ."[16]

As regards Scotland, the more immediate effect of the anti-Polaris and other topical songs described in Chapter 3 was to heighten the sense of nationhood, and the anti-nuclear, peace-movement part of their message seems only to be growing now, or regerminating, from the seeds sown in the early sixties. The reaction against Reagan *et al* is an important new factor. Songs like "Ye canny spend a dollar when ye're deid" were right for their time but they now appear rather oversimplified, and hardly adequate for the resurgent CND movement. Not many new songs of "protest" (there must be a better word, e.g. "political") were heard here during the seventies. Sheila Douglas wrote one against the American war in Vietnam; and from Eric Bogle, an expatriate living in Australia, came two anti-war songs which have made a powerful impact: "The band played Waltzing Matilda", and "No man's land" ("Private William Mac-Bride"). Josh MacRae spoke nostalgically of the conviction and comradeship of twenty years ago: "It would be nice if things were clear-cut — it would be a lot easier — it's getting *hard* nowadays!" He quoted "Bob Dylan's Dream":

> How easy it was to tell wrong from right,
> It was all that easy to tell black from white.

But, he said, "It's a good time to have been around, to have seen the birth of something starting as a wee thing which snowballed to a great big thing. . . ."[17]

By the late sixties Dylan and most of the other American song-writers were producing songs in a more contemplative and introverted vein. By the seventies this trend was intensified, and many enthusiasms of "the turbulent sixties" gave place to cynicism. This was exacerbated by the increasing deviousness of politics in general, with Watergate a crowning manifestation, and by the general ebbing of social optimism and personal confidence since the end of the sixties. But many protest songs have appeared in other parts of the world: in Argentina, Spain, Chile, Portugal, and now in Poland. In the more sophisticated of these regimes, official, unofficial and even self-imposed censorship is so strong that song is often the only form of political expression — albeit in oblique, symbolic form — that people dare to take part in.

Perhaps the most clear-cut issue to be expressed in recent song from the U.S.A. is that of the women's movement, which has formed the impetus for a similar trend in British song-collecting and writing.

3.

The first book of women's songs to be published in Britain, *My Song Is My Own*,[18] contains in fact no American material. Similar collections, referred to in its introduction, had already appeared in the States after the women's movement started there in the late sixties. Only a third of the hundred songs in this book are less than fifty years old, and about a fifth, new or old, are from Scotland. But, with a few performances by Kathy Henderson (editor of the book), Frankie Armstrong and Sandra Kerr (assistants in its production), Alison McMorland, Peta Webb, and Peggy Seeger, the new songs have only just begun to penetrate the Scottish folk scene; and Alison McMorland, the only Scot in this list, has lived south of the Border for many years. Why then is the subject relevant to a consideration of the Scottish revival?

There are several reasons. Statements of women's protest and resistance are not found only in the relatively new songs, although in these the statements are more overt, more articulate, and with some completely new implications. Women's songs are "a huge but largely unrecognised culture"; they contain ". . . material that . . . links up the largely invisible tradition of women's resistance", because a song "doesn't even have to be explicitly militant to be a song of resistance".[19] This applies to many of the songs appearing in Chapter 4 and Appendix I of the present book: in "When Micky comes home", in "The bonnie hoose o' Airlie", and in the first two songs, plus "The banks o' red roses", of Part 5 (fear of physical violence, rape or death); in all five songs of Part 6 (fear of unwelcome pregnancy); and in all three songs of Part 7 (fear of family pressure regarding marriage). Although some of these songs may be by men, or may be sung by men, they concern hazards to which women are either uniquely or peculiarly vulnerable, and all of them — with the possible exception of "What can a young lassie", Part 7 — describe situations caused by male-to-female attitudes which range from the insouciant to the violent.

In addition to the five songs of Part 6, two others — "The laird o' the Dainty doon-bye" and "The banks o' red roses" — are also concerned with unwanted or unplanned pregnancies. It is no exaggeration to say that the advent of reliable contraceptive devices, in particular the pill, was to revolutionise the lives of women to whom they were available: contraception, representing women's control over their own conditions of existence, was in face the *sine qua non* of the present movement, it was the completely new factor which distinguished it from all such previous struggles. And this may be why, with a few notable exceptions (for instance "Eppie Morrie"), women in traditional songs so often appear rather passive, their resistance minimal.

But folk songs in general tend to reveal a passive attitude towards the ills of life, with little hint of an awareness which might lead to positive action let alone organised resistance. Even in categories where one might expect such awareness, they are chiefly songs of individual experience: songs of personal suffering, plaint or simply comment, (". . . . the direct protest song is rare outside the radical labour tradition that began to form with the nineteenth century").[20] Their creators were too immersed in events out of their control, too much victims of these events, to perceive the social forces at work. Our "songs heard in the seventies" announce reactions which are emotive rather than constructive: "I'll go and I'll get blue bleezin' blind drunk" (from "When Micky comes home"); "Draw yer dirks" ("The bonny hoose o' Airlie"); "I'll cross him, I'll crack him" ("What can a young lassie"); and in "Willie's fatal visit" the revenge is assigned to a supernatural being. Interpretations given by the singers also come into this personal, plaint or comment category: "Be kind to people" (Jim Craig, of "'Twas in the month"); "a warning to young females" (Gordeanna MacCulloch, of "The cruel mother"); "a very bitter comment . . . political *in the widest sense*" (my italics) (Owen Costello, of "Bogie's bonny Belle"). Only in "If it wasnae for the Union" and "The Fairfield apprentice" — both relatively new songs — do we find a more conceptual reaction: "Raise the banner of unity", and "I will fight as my father fought". We have seen that folk songs, at least since the advent of literacy, are predominantly working class in origin, i.e. from the most subordinate section of society, that "submerged world" referred to earlier.[21] Since women in turn form the subordinate half of that section, is it any wonder that their songs take on an even paler hue of passivity?

Kathy Henderson has something to say on this, and also on the fact that so many songs are about women getting a poor deal: "Sure, it's true in many songs, but more to the point is that these songs have been selected (by men?) to be sung, reprinted, collected, while other songs representing the female point of view have not been so selected; i.e. it's a reflection of male attitudes in the revival and research and collecting just as much if not far more than in the song-making/singing. Indeed my experience in doing the research for our book . . . has been that there's a hugely rich tradition of women's songs that have simply been ignored, suppressed or (this particularly) neutralised by being sung in contexts where their real meaning fails to get a hearing".[22] (This last remark may apply to those songs named above, from Chapter 4 and Appendix I.)

Geordie McIntyre has similar views but goes a step further. He thinks there are probably many "female" songs, songs expressing women's feelings, attitudes to sex etc. — including bawdy songs — which are not sung (because of the predominantly male leadership and the general ambience) but which are *there*, somewhere, and need to be collected by women researchers. Women informants would not easily give or volunteer these songs to male collectors, and many husbands would not allow male field-workers to collect from their wives. Collectors have tended to be male, or, if female, accompanied by a male. Geordie strongly suspects there's a kind of secret language which men would not understand: he instanced bottling parties in Glasgow (the female equivalent of stag parties) on the night before a wedding, where he has reason to think some of these "secret" songs are heard and specifically female jokes are cracked (see note 53 concerning McIntyre's disc). There are many songs, whether of male or female authorship, which need to be *sung* by females, such as "The brisk young lad",[23] where the girl gently mocks the man ("and there are harder songs") which he has only once heard . . . sung by Ewan MacColl! "Women have avoided singing these 'edgy' songs, by women about men, in male-orientated Scotland".[24]

Bawdy songs are rightly considered to be of especial importance in traditional culture, partly because they have been orally transmitted to a greater extent and are therefore less subject to the various influences of print. Gershon Legman has spoken of songs which are "wholesomely bawdy"; Burns's version of "John Anderson my jo" in his *Merry Muses* collection is a possible candidate for this. But even eliminating the nudge-nudge-wink-wink horrors, a fair number remain which may be "wholesome" in all-male company but in a mixed gathering will be found tasteless and unsingable, by men as well as women of any sensitivity. There are probably similar female songs which await discovery, perhaps containing biting comments on women's experiences with men, and these might also be embarrassing in mixed company. This remains to be seen.

Is the folk scene more male-orientated in Scotland than in other parts of the British Isles? — is it packed with MacHismoists? First, a comment from America on feminism and folklore in general: "Anything that reinforces or suggests sex role stereotypes is subject to attack. Literature has been scrutinised and criticised, but oral material, because of its seemingly more elusive qualities, has been much harder for feminists to combat".[25] Then, from London, Kathy Henderson writes of the revival songs, i.e. the new songs, ". . . remarkably few of these have been concerned with women's experience";[26] and Karl Dallas in his review of the song book comments ". . . this speaks volumes about how out of touch with currents in contemporay society the folk revival has become".[27] (In 1972 Dallas had written: "Pete Seeger has stopped singing male supremacist folksongs, which must have cut into his repertoire more than somewhat".[28]) Brian Pearson, who sings with Frankie Armstrong's group in London, thinks that in "sexual politics" the folk clubs are a long way behind, and people sympathetic to the women's movement are in a considerable minority there. There's a lot of male fantasizing, he says . . . in this area attitudes have remained around the 1960s level, i.e. are still very male-dominated.[29]

In Scotland this is even more true. Hayden Murphy, the Irish poet now living in Edinburgh, wrote after the 1981 Folk Festival: "I attack the all-male bastion the major concert stages . . . after 3 years, Flora MacNeil is the only female to have headed a major concert . . . many who had packed the concert given by Alison McMorland, Frankie Armstrong and Peta Webb returned for their workshop next day . . . I feel that this trio deserved a larger venue. . . ."[30] The Festival director, Dr. John Barrow, has an answer to this: "I have to think of hard economics, and there is not one female singer, or group of singers, who can fill the Usher Hall", (the largest hall in Edinburgh).[31] One wonders how he can be so certain. An adventurous spirit is surely needed here, to match the adventurous nature of Edinburgh audiences which Hayden Murphy has observed. Frankie Armstrong and her group are certainly not lacking in charisma or vocal charm. As regards women singers who stick to safer or more traditional material, one might hazard a guess that John Barrow's statement, if true now, may possibly be disproved by the time this appears in print. (Like the former colonies, people in a sense are never "ready" until they are given the chance.)

"The two-edged battle facing Scottish women" is how Carol Craig describes the situation: "Like all oppressed peoples, the predominant characteristic of the Scots is dependency . . . the conscious feeling of being Scots is often based on the fact we're not English. . . . There are many parallels to be drawn between women and Scottish people in terms of dependency and marginalisation from the dominant culture . . . women, like the Scots, are defined with reference to a dominant group. Self-deprecation is another characteristic women and Scots share. . . . Language provides a further example of similarities . . . for example . . . the use of 'man' to mean human being. . ." and ". . . the use of 'chairman'. . . It's only a word, they'll say, so why is it important? But Scots, too, are very aware of the importance of language . . . we wince when England is used to mean Britain. . . . Despite the insights Scots might gain from feminism there has been little contact between feminists and those interested in Scottish politics and culture. . . . Sexual domination is a good balm for men suffering from a national inferiority complex and so Scotsmen might have more of a psychological investment in perpetuating women's subordination than men whose national identity is secure. . . ."[32] Scotland seems to move slowly in this respect; years ago Naomi Mitchison wrote: "Any woman who has worked in any kind of field in Scotland after working in England (or indeed in many other countries, including India. . .) will be aware of this curious, deep anti-feminism which is still present even among those who would disown the Knoxian father. Perhaps too few Scottish women have worked in any fields other than in Scotland to be able to make the comparison, to detect the antipathy, to recognise their own subordination".[33]

We have noted that in the U.K. and the U.S. many song-writers have been looking away from the straight-line squibs; one reaction to macro-sociological and tortuous complexities is to turn to the micro-sociological, "small-is-beautiful", etc. (We can't really start singing Wobbly-type songs again. . . . *or can we?*) But the chief demands of the women's movement *do* embody a clear-cut issue, as clear-cut as the demands of the Civil Rights movement in the States during the sixties. It is difficult to see how anyone with pretensions to be a thinking, caring person could deny the justice of either of these causes, or allow any lunatic fringe to cloud the issues. Dealing with the upheavals of the sixties, an American historian has said this: "Far more fundamental than the revising of various sexual attitudes and prohibitions was the new vitality that came into the movement for women's liberation. . . . Out of this new perspective for considering male and female values emerged a line of enquiry and action whose implications were at least as profound as that which stemmed from the black revolution".[34] The women's songs have also the merit of emphasis on personal, intimate matters — love, marriage, child-raising — as well as on wider issues, and even the most militant, at least in *My Song is My Own*, are not crude, anti-men rubbish. Dick Gaughan, who declares "I'm a hundred per cent in support — you've had a dreadful deal by society", takes exception to the words in one of Leon Rosselson's songs (in *My Song is My Own*), "Don't get married, girls, for men are all the same". He feels this is an example of female sexism. What Dick misses here is the humour of the song, albeit slightly on the black side, and the fact that it is protesting against the *institution* of marriage as it was, and still is in large measure. (Perhaps the only really honest attitude for men to adopt today, and for women too, is to say, "I'm still full of this shit" — and then to take some mental purgatives.)

The personal, intimate element in women's songs points to a unique feature of the movement, not only in its present stage but in many past manifestations of it which have been ignored or buried by historians. The noble army of martyrs in other struggles . . . scientists or religious believers who would not recant when faced with rack or stake, trade union pioneers who stood firm come dungeons dark or gallows grim, or the blacks and their supporters who suffered in the Civil Rights movement . . . none of these had a close emotional and physical need for those they resisted. But "woman needs man, and man must have his mate", and the stalwarts of this particular struggle may suffer emotional traumas. Physical injuries too: the increase in the mugging, rape and killing of women is directly related to increased female independence. It is the insecure and frustrated men who feel threatened by this.

The old predication of "men and women are equal but different" was generally used to cover up the fact that women were not in fact treated as equal with men. Only when many more legal and psychological positions have been entrenched, only then can whatever it is that constitutes real femininity and real masculinity be revealed and only then can women be truly equal without any danger of injuring their essential nature.

In some form or other, from the acute to the less acute, from the conscious to the latent, the struggle to which the women's songs give voice is world-wide. (An extreme form of patriarchal exploitation survives in parts of Africa and the Moslem world, where millions of women are still subjected to female circumcision — see Report No. 47, Minority Rights Group, 1980. Whoever may perform this operation, or insist on it, its purpose is the ensuring of male domination; if you can't ever enjoy sex then you will never rove and probably never rebel). Whether a shout or a whisper, it's the voice of half the human race. Women's songs are at least incipient folk songs, and Lizzie Higgins' comments apply (chapter 6): "It's about human beings, their loves, their liberty or their broken hearts. . . . And it's a very good thing for a man or a woman's soul, to sing. . . . *Everyone* can join in. . . . It's like evolution. . . ."

Peace is the most urgent issue of today but it is not separate from that of the women's movement. For women are by nature life-givers, rarely death-dealers. None of the songs in *My Song Is My Own* deals directly with the nuclear threat; for this collection Kathy Henderson chose songs which work *as songs*, which polemic ditties do not often achieve. However, Frankie Armstrong has since written and recorded "Out of the Darkness",[35] an impressive song which subtly links the themes of women and peace. All the signs are that other good songs on this joint topic will soon be forthcoming.

4.

American inspiration, American impetus — signs of this appear again and again and have long been recognised in Scotland. An unusual fragment of song collected by Gavin Greig in Aberdeenshire is entitled "Vive la Republican", and has this for a chorus:

> Vive la the new convention
> Vive la Republican
> Vive la America
> For it was in you that it a' began.[36]

It was not only in Republicanism, which in this century especially has been a strong thread in Scottish thinking, that "it a' began" there. American influence on the English language itself (except in certain academic circles) has been towards creative directness, against formal stuffiness. Walt Whitman, one of the inspirations of the sixties youth movements, wrote prophetically:

> "Language is not an abstract construction of the learned, but is something arising out of the work, needs, ties, joys, affections, tastes, of long generations of humanity, and has its bases broad and low, close to the ground. Its final decisions are made by the masses, people nearest the concrete, having most to do with actual land and sea."[37]

Then the related matter of speech crops up again. One does get sick of American accents in singing but their omnipresence is significant. In most areas of demotic song in the English language, apart from traditional folk, transatlantic influence is shown in this clearest and most obvious way: in singing blues, all kinds of pop including rock, and C. and W., an American accent is *de rigeur*. (A recent exception is punk, in which determinedly regional accents are employed.)

If we summarise other American influences which have so far appeared in these essays, we find:

(1) Since early this century, influential topical and other songs appeared in the U.S.A., from the Wobblies, Woody Guthrie, the Almanacs, Pete Seeger and the Weavers, on to Dylan, Joan Baez *et al*. These paved the way towards revival of more traditional material.

(2) Black America was the birthplace of jazz, probably the most internationally accepted form of popular music.

(3) The majority of songs in the early folk revival in Scotland were American.

(4) Developing from (3) we have the birth of skiffle, a British phenomenon but based on American material, leading on to an awareness of indigenous traditional culture.

(5) The anti-Polaris songs, directed against American military bases in Scotland, with intentional irony made use of many American tunes.

(6) The immense popularity of C. & W. songs and related stories was noticeable in the early revival years. This still continues, in particular among the travellers, the chief custodians of Scottish traditional song and story.

(7) The first drive towards a resurgence of demands for women's rights came from the States. Women's songs are being collected (or unearthed), written, published and sung in Britain, and have begun to achieve recognition in Scotland.

It is good to note that the transatlantic connection, especially in recent years, has worked in the opposite direction. Witness the enormous popularity in the States of The Boys of the Lough, of Jean Redpath, of Ossian, and of many other singers, players and groups from Scotland. It is disappointing, however, to note that these musicians, with a few exceptions, are less well-known in their home country than in the rest of Europe as well as in America, and that "the best Scots performers are forced to become virtual exiles in order to survive".[38] A classic symptom of "national inferiority complex"[39] in a country is this inability to recognise its own native talent.

5.

What of the relationship between folk and art music during the post-war years?

Comparisons are odious ("odorous", quipped Dogberry). "I need the vitamins I get from folk song more than the vitamins I get from Covent Garden', says Sydney Carter;[40] the crowds who attend S.N.O. or Prom concerts get vitamins from orchestral art music; others again need a balanced diet. Josh MacRae told me in 1976, "It's getting impossible to write a mannered song, an art-song . . . no-one can sit down in cold blood and write an art-song, sung by a lady with clasped hands". But folk song has its own mannerisms — for instance, the hand-to-ear trick (note 4). The Mock-Mozart and Phoney Folklore take-offs of Peter Ustinov are equally telling.[41] If a certain magic is present then who cares what pigeon-hole the music may be slotted into, or whether a singer clasps his/her hands or waves them about or whatever? As the indigestion-prone Davey Warbeck said, "I never mind rich food, it's poor food that does one such an infinity of harm".[42]

There are signs that the separation of folk from art music in Scotland is lessening. A bridge-builder here is Ronald Stevenson: composer, pianist, writer and lecturer, he has sought to base many of his compositions on native folk idioms, both Scots and Gaelic. To start with, his concerts are generally less formal than the usual kind; he will talk about what he's going to play, and he is equally at home performing in London's Albert Hall or to friends and neighbours in the village of West Linton where he lives.

He has also used indigenous Scottish instruments. *Sounding Strings* is an album of arrangements for clarsach of folk song and dance tunes from the six Celtic countries (Scotland, Ireland, Isle of Man, Wales, Cornwall and Brittany).[43] In his *Young Scotland Suite* for youth orchestra, the first movement employs a quartet of bagpipes playing in canon, the second has two clarsachs with string orchestra, and the third and last movement combines pipes, *without drones*, with the two clarsachs.[44] He has also explored Scottish folk dance idioms in his *Scots Dance Toccata* for full orchestra.[45] Then there is his *Violin Concerto* of 1980, commissioned by Yehudi Menuhin; in the finale, the rhythms of strathspey, reel and jig have been conflated into one metre in 5/4 time, thus creating a completely new rhythm out of three traditional ones.

The developmental procedures of western art music contrast with the chiefly incremental procedures of folk rhythms and melodies. The combination of the two, when carried out with mastery, can lend an extra dimension to original folk material.

The second of the four works mentioned above is written for amateur music-making. Ten years ago André Previn and Antony Hopkins united in a plea for composers to "write for young people and not be too remote".[46] There are of course numerous orchestras, chamber music groups, choirs and clubs which cater for amateur players and singers of art music; there are also many professional folk singers/players/groups, but the Revival is undoubtedly based more closely on the amateur. "It's do-it-yourself music rather than a spectator sport", said the English folk singer and songwriter Peter Bellamy, much of whose work has centred round the poems of Rudyard Kipling. "I think it's of great importance even for a guy that doesn't sing that his mate does, because that is still personal involvement which isn't shared by . . . the man in the most expensive seat at the Albert Hall." Replying to a comment on folk music as "the last stronghold of amateurism", Bellamy continued: ". . . it's for this very reason that folk song will not pass the way other fashions pass in entertainment . . . it's with the amateur, in the amateur, that the strength of the revival lies".[47] And Yehudi Menuhin, fascinated by different musics of the world, from Bach to Indian ragas to Scots fiddle music: "The wonderful thing about all these Scottish violinists is that they exemplify what my father used to tell me about the ancient Jewish injunction to musicians — that you should play your music, but that you were actually a locksmith or a potter, or whatever".[48]

When Menuhin became interested in the Scots fiddle tradition he set himself to learn the necessary techniques from the master fiddler, Hector MacAndrew. Technique acquired for playing art music on certain instruments *can* be a good foundation on which to build folk technique, provided the player is willing to work at the different skills required.[49] This is in contrast to vocal art technique, which is much harder to adapt (see Appendix II). As compared with folk song, fiddle music (the violin becomes a fiddle when it plays folk) has for over 200 years had closer links with art music in Scotland.

A fascinating mixture of the professional and the amateur is a Glasgow group, The Whistlebinkies. Christened thus by Mick Broderick — founder-member, raconteur, singer and bodhran-player — the group now numbers seven. Other instruments are clarsach, Lowland pipes, two fiddles, flute, piccolo and Scottish side-drum.[50] Clarsach player Rhona MacKay, former principal harpist with the Scottish National Orchestra, also sings Gaelic songs. Arrangements and new compositions based on Scottish traditional material provide an interesting example of joint creation, with all members of the group contributing and discussing ideas. The Whistlebinkies provided incidental music for the recent Scottish production of *Macbeth*. Although his influence does not dominate the group, academy-trained flautist and composer Eddie McGuire, born 1948, is the only one to create in both folk and art genres. He writes short pieces in traditional style, reels and slow airs etc. — as does piper Rab Wallace — but in his main output he aims at integrating folk material into his own idiosyncratic art music compositions, using serial and chromatic as well as modal procedures. He also desires "to express in music the struggle for survival and revolution on both the emotional and social levels."[51] McGuire's commissioned works include *Martyr(s)* for viola(s), *Calgacus* for orchestra with bagpipes, and *Quest* for voice and ensemble.[52]

6.

The last decade has brought many fruitful developments in the folk music scene, among the most important of which has been the emergence of song-writers following in the steps of Hamish Henderson, Thurso Berwick (Morris Blythman) and Matt McGinn. Adam MacNaughton of Glasgow is among the most wide-ranging: some of his children's songs, notably the earlier "Skyscraper Wean",[53] were quickley absorbed into oral tradition. Eric Bogle, Norman Buchan, Sheila Douglas, Archie Fisher, Jack Foley, Dave Goulder, Andy Hunter, Ed Miller and John Watt appear elsewhere in these pages. Among many other songwriters are Rab Noakes and Matt Armour, from Fife; Lesley Hale, Nancy Nicholson and Ken Thomson of Edinburgh; and Ian Sinclair of Thurso. In a class by himself is the hugely entertaining Glaswegian Billy Connolly, folk-singer, songwriter and comedian, who often uses humour as a weapon in the battle of ideas. "Folk music is not a precious antique to be treasured; it is one of the tools with which we can hope to hammer out the shape of our future".[54] One of those tools is laughter — it literally shapes our future, since doctors tell us it's good for our health.

The recent folk-instrument explosion has been noted. Dr. Peter Shepheard has pointed out that increased public interest in the massed fiddle music of Reel and Strathspey Society gatherings may herald an interest in solo fiddle, just as the popularity of pipe-bands came before the increased interest in solo piping and pibroch.[55]

The most popular revival instrument has been the acoustic (i.e. non-electric) guitar. The advent of electric folk — hailed by Karl Dallas as bringing back the Dionysian element in contrast to the Apollonian[56] — has had far-reaching influences in folk-rock, but the expense involved tends to restrict its use in clubs. Scottish bands have included Five Hand Reel, the J.S.D. band and the Tannahill Weavers.

Dance is a vital part of traditional culture. The Royal Scottish Country Dance Association started some fifty years ago, and its work has expanded recently due to the great popularity of this activity. There are clubs all over the world, not only in Commonwealth countries but in France, Germany, Sweden, the U.S.A., Hong Kong and Japan. Scottish dancing — in spite of, or because of, the straight-backed posture and the neat foot-work involved — has more fire than some of its close neighbours.

The other organisation of similar vintage, but concerned with the broader arts in Scotland, is The Saltire Society. Established in 1936, long before the folk revival, its aim has been to stimulate revival in all spheres of Scots and Gaelic arts, literary, musical and visual.

While its musical interests lean more to "musick fyne", it is also concerned with the folk tradition and it has presented many fine recitals of music from the area overlapping the two genres, notably the songs of Robert Burns alongside his poems.

In 1970 a new kind of club, centred round "the poetry and music of Scotland's living tradition", appeared on the Edinburgh scene. Started by the late Dr. Stuart MacGregor, the Gaelic singer Dolina MacLennan and the Gaelic poet William Neill, The Heretics ran for ten years, with regular meetings which became more frequent during the Edinburgh Festival weeks. Both Scots and Gaelic traditional music were presented, vocal and instrumental, and the subtly different atmosphere, partly due to the poetry readings, attracted people not often seen at folk clubs. Hugh MacDiarmid, Robert Garioch, Norman MacCaig, Derrick Thomson, Billy Connolly, Hamish Henderson and Shetland fiddler Aly Bain, with Dolina MacLennan and other singers, all appeared during one Festival season — an interesting mixture, but it worked. No kind of art music was included. This might suggest that in Scotland today, although *belles-lettres* has many roots in the "living tradition", art music has few. This again would seem to be contradicted by the work of the Saltire Society.

Although Richard Demarco's main contribution has been in the visual arts, his Gallery, opened in 1966, has involved concern with education and this has led to ventures such as the Edinburgh Arts tours. Since 1972 he has conducted annual expeditions, with students of differing age-groups and nationalities, to "places specially honoured by our ancestors over the last 5,000 years", including sites of burial or of ritual, such as the Callanish standing-stones in Lewis. The journeys are supplemented by lectures and demonstrations in linked aspects of tradition including native music. Recent tours have extended to Celtic parts of the Continent.

Since the demise of *Chapbook* there had been no regular folk magazine. In 1973 this gap was filled by *Sandy Bell's Broadsheet* (editors until recently John Barrow, Ian Green and Ken Thomson) which has appeared every fortnight since and is read by subscribers all over Scotland and far beyond. Containing short articles, letters, and news on folk events of every kind, *SBB* has proved invaluable.

The School of Scottish Studies has greatly extended its work. In 1969 Professor John MacQueen became director, and 1971 saw a triple launching: the first undergraduate teaching course; the *Scottish Tradition* disc series, which later included cassettes; and the informal magazine *Tocher*. The more scholarly journal *Scottish Studies* had started in 1957. A second undergraduate course was added in 1977. The Archive now contains almost 5,000 hours of tape recordings, not counting those of the Place Names section or of the Linguistic Survey; there are also donations such as the John Levy collection of tapes, chiefly of Asian music. There is a Photographic archive, and a Tale archive. Most of these tales are in Gaelic, but more attention has recently been given to tales-recording in the Scots sector, which is linked with the increasing recognition of travellers as tradition-bearers. The work of editing *The Greig-Duncan Folk Song Collection* is continuing. In 1970 equipment for 16 mm. sound filming was acquired, and other laboratory facilities and techniques expanded to meet the needs of disc/cassette publication and of increasing numbers of post-graduate students; these include students of ethnomusicology (Scottish and international aspects), some of whome have made notable contributions in field-work and recording. Video-tape recording was started in 1978.

Three series of radio broadcasts over the last few years deserve special mention. Norman Buchan's six programmes of early 1978, entitled "For You, Johnnie Sangster", gave a masterly account of the Scottish folk revival, with songs and commentary. In 1980 and 1981 "Odyssey" dealt with episodes and periods in Scotland's oral history: in two series of ten and twelve programmes respectively, producer Billy Kay presented the voices of men and women who had heard, seen and felt the historical experience of the events examined. These very successful programmes included some songs.[57] The year 1981 also saw the start of "The Music Makars", an excellent weekly series in which Alastair Clark, of *The Scotsman*, presents talks and recordings on the multifarious aspects of folk music past and present, with news of current folk events.

A new grass-roots organisation with great potentiality is PERFORM — the PERformance of Folk and Other Related Music. This was set up at a London conference in February 1981 which was attended by delegates from all parts of the British Isles, and by some from across the Channel. Its aims are "to encourage the performance and furtherance of folk and other related musics, to bring it to a wider audience and to improve communication throughout the folk world". Pioneered by Dick Gaughan, the *raison d'être* for PERFORM was a general feeling that the Revival was "the best kept secret in Britain". "If we don't tell anyone we are here," says the leaflet, "we can't expect them to take any notice of us. We must make some noise. We must encourage the media to give more exposure to folk music". PERFORM now has area representations throughout Britain, Ireland and the rest of Europe.

In September 1981 a working party was set up by the Scottish Arts Council to investigate the state of native traditional and folk arts, particularly those relating to the performed and oral traditions.

The fourth Edinburgh Folk Festival, held during the last ten days of March 1982, saw it established as one of the premier events of its kind in Europe.

7.

The title of this final essay is optimistic. Signposts are of little interest to those who are stationary, either physically or mentally. Signposts are for the adventurous and the questing. Signposts are for travellers.

But choices are difficult, from among the profusion of avenues now being explored. Dick Gaughan supports free experimentation as the only road forward:

> Where the folk revival has got it wrong, for me anyway, is that it is trying to act as arbiter to which forces are acceptable and which are not. People who can't cope with artistic freedom draw up rules. . . . Many second generation kids of the revival are now playing in Punk bands. . . . I suggest that Punk, Ska and Reggae are all folk musics — I don't like them much but they *are* the spontaneous comments of the broad mass of humanity in Britain at the moment. What the revival should be doing is to preserve the old styles to act as an influence upon the younger creative musicians of today. . . . We must give folk music back to the folk . . . in an acceptable fashion and with humility, not as an evangelical crusade with the 'now listen, this is good for you' attitude of a lot of folkies today.[58]
>
> The folk revival should aim at the end of the folk revival, at the restoration of folk music back to national consciousness, with no need to have special folk music programmes. . . . I would love to be in a position where I was no longer branded a folk singer, but just a singer, singing traditional songs . . . not considered unusual. *Remove the label.*[59]

There may be differing views on the desirability or otherwise of labels; but a glance at any *Radio Times* shows that while programmes of Radio 3 are not labelled "Art Music", nor those of Radios 1 and 2 "Pop Music", yet programmes of folk and traditional music are almost invariably announced as such. As Scots in relation to the English . . . as women to men . . . so folk music is defined in terms of marginalisation from the dominant group or culture, in this case both art music and pop music. It's ironic, considering the universality of folk music origins . . . yet inevitable, considering Western history.

The cry of "remove the label" has a prophetic ring which is found in other recent thoughts on music. A. L. Lloyd saw the possible emergence of ". . . One Music that begins to embrace not only Western high art, popular and traditional musics, but also the musics of other continents and cultures. . . .",[60] and Ronald

Stevenson, ". . . I believe that the future will see — or rather, hear — musical multilingualism, analagous to the polyglot poetry which has already been written by Ezra Pound, Hugh MacDiarmid and others".[61]

Meanwhile, when is a revival not a revival? "The sooner we lose this word 'Revival' the better. It's long outlived its usefulness".[62] ". . . the revival is over. . . . It set folk song along a different course. But let's now stop concentrating on the signpost and get moving along the road".[63] Perhaps the very ability to move on is a measure of how effective this revival has been, and of how outdated the word may now be.

What we do need is a new word for this kind of music: something at once wider and more precise than "folk", less restricting than "traditional", a word for music which tells us what we already know and gives advance news of what may come. For

> . . . there's mair nor a roch wind blawin'
> Through the great glen o' the warld the day.[64]

Footnotes to Chapter VII

1. Charles Seeger, "Folk music in the schools of a highly industrialised society", *Journal of the International Folk Music Council* 5 (1953), 43.
2. Talk with the title "Revival: The Tradition of the Future" given by Dick Gaughan at the School of Scottish Studies, 25/3/81, as part of the Edinburgh Folk Festival. Quotations from Dick Gaughan throughout this chapter are from this talk unless otherwise noted.
3. See opening of Chapter 5.
4. A reference to the habit, adopted by many singers including Ewan MacColl, of cupping a hand round one ear during performance: this is said to help the singer hear the actual sound that he/she is producing.
5. Letter from Jack Foley in response to questions asked, May 1980.
6. A.L. Lloyd, "Folk Music", *Encyclopedia Britannica* (1969), 9.523.
7. *The Electric Muse* by Dave Laing and others, p. 94.
8. David Buchan, *The Ballad and the Folk*, Chapter 20.
9. Antonio Gramsci, *Opere*, Vol. 6 *Letteratura e Vita Nazionale* (1950), p. 220, as translated and quoted by Hamish Henderson in Edward J. Cowan, *The People's Past*, p. 14.
10. Robert Burns, "For a' that and a' that".
11. John Watt: interview, 25/10/76. Milnathort.
12. Norman Buchan: interview 20/8/77, Edinburgh.
13. Jean Redpath: interview 23/10/76, Leven.
14. Peter Hall: interview, 9/11/76, Aberdeen.
15. Virginia F. Plumbe, "The Modern Folk Song Revival" (undergraduate Sociology dissertation, University of Edinburgh, 1968), p. 72.
16. Alan P. Merriam, *The Anthropology of Music*, p. 207.

17. Josh MacRae: interview, 10/11/76, Strathmiglo. Later quotation in this chapter is also from this interview.

18. *My Song Is My Own: 100 Women's Songs*, collected by Kathy Henderson with Frankie Armstrong and Sandra Kerr (1979). A disc is also available.

19. Kathy Henderson, pp. 11–12.

20. A.L. Lloyd, *Folk Song in England*, p. 410.

21. See chapter 1, Note 18.

22. Letter from Kathy Henderson, summer 1980.

23. In Robert Ford's *Vagabond songs and ballads of Scotland*, p. 294, Ford refers to "the prevailing sarcasm of the song". The tune is a lively jig.

24. Geordie McIntyre's comments are from conversations, 1981.

25. Mary Ellen Brown Lewis, "The Feminists Have Done It", *Journal of American Folklore* 87 (1974), 85–7.

26. Kathy Henderson, p. 11.

27. *Acoustic Music*, May 1980, p. 46.

28. Karl Dallas, *The Cruel Wars*, p. 67.

29. Brian Pearson: conversation, August 1981.

30. *Sandy Bell's Broadsheet*, Vol. 8, issue 17, 20/4/81.

31. John Barrow: conversation, September 1981.

32. Article by Carol Craig under "Open House" section, *The Scotsman*, 8/9/80. Postscript: "Lament of the Working-Class Hero's Wife" (no. 39, *My Song is My Own*), to a traditional Scots tune, came from Edinburgh and Glasgow women's liberation groups, 1977.

33. Quoted by Gillian Shepherd in "Scottish Women Novelists", *Chapman* 27/28 (Vol. 6, nos. 3–4), p. 54.

34. Sydney E. Ahlstrom, *A Religious History of the American People*, p. 1084.

35. On the disc *Nuclear power, no thanks*, The Plane Label, Interaction impress.

36. Quoted, with notes, by Hamish Henderson in Edward J. Cowan, *The People's Past*, p. 10; see also Patrick Shuldham-Shaw and Emily B. Lyle, *The Greig-Duncan Folk Song Collection*, 1.351, 533.

37. Essay on "Slang in America" in the *Complete Prose Works* of Walt Whitman.

38. Alastair Clark, "Sounds Around", *The Scotsman* 28/11/81.

39. See note 32. See also a letter from James Cameron Stuart, *The Scotsman* 12/12/81; he supports Alastair Clark's statement, and contrasts the Breton peoples' "spectacular advancement in terms of their culture in recent times".

40. *Folk Review*, August 1973, p. 9.

41. *The Two Peters*, Sellers and Ustinov (EMI GEP 8853).

42. *The Pursuit of Love* by Nancy Mitford, 1945.

43. U.M.P. London, 1979.

44. MS., 1978; commissioned by Lothian Regional Council.

45. Novello 1968; premiered by the S.N.O. at the Glasgow Proms, 1974.

46. *Music Face to Face*, p. 128.

47. "Testament to Bellamy" by Andrew Means, *Melody Maker*, 4/12/71.

48. Interview by Chris Dunkley, *Radio Times*, 28/11/74.

49. Recommended: Alistair Hardie's *The Caledonian Companion*. This contains many tunes and is also a fiddle tutor. A companion disc is available.

50. Discs: *The Whistlebinkies* and *The Whistlebinkies 2* (Claddagh CC 22 and CC 33); the second was placed top of the chart, *Melody Maker*, 18/10/80.

51. Quoted by Richard McGregor in an article on Edward McGuire, *The Musical Times*, June 1979.

52. *The Times Educational Supplement for Scotland* recently published correspondence on McGuire's work. In a letter headed "Mating of Scottish folk and Western classical", Dr. David Johnson praises McGuire; he also explains

disarmingly why his own present position has become inconsistent with that of a decade ago, when he described such "mating" as "an unnatural liaison". T.E.S.S. 27/3/81. (See Johnson's valuable *Music and Society in Lowland Scotland in the Eighteenth Century*, p. 199; and Cedric Thorpe Davie, *Scotland's Music* (1980).) Other items in this T.E.S.S. controversy include: " 'Scotland's Music': in search of identity", by David Johnson, 13/2/81; letters from Ian Robertson, 6/3/81 and 10/4/81; and "Monarch of the Glen", by Ian Robertson, 7/8/81.

53. In *The Scottish Folksinger*. This song, sung by a boy from Barmulloch Primary School, can be heard on a fascinating disc *The Streets of Glasgow*; produced by Geordie McIntyre, it features The Clutha group with Flora MacNeill and others. It also features songs from women's "bottling parties" in Glasgow, referred to earlier. (Topic 12TS 226).

54. Gordon McCulloch; from a pamphlet produced by The Parkhouse Conventions group for Loughborough Festival 1972. Quoted by Andrew Means, *Melody Maker* 15/7/72.

55. Pete Shepheard: interview, 1/11/76, Balmalcolm, Fife. By that date discs of massed fiddle music were selling better than C. & W. in Scotland.

56. David Laing and others, *The Electric Muse*, p. 83–137.

57. The book *Odyssey* edited by Billy Kay was based on this series.

58. Letter from Dick Gaughan in response to questions asked, May 1980.

59. Dick Gaughan; see note 2.

60. *Folk Song in England*, p. 411.

61. *Western Music: an introduction*, p. 207.

62. Fred Woods, *Folk Revival: The rediscovery of a national music*, p. 128.

63. Letter from Jack Foley, May 1980.

64. From the song "Freedom Come-all-ye" by Hamish Henderson.

Ray Fisher
Photograph courtesy Karin Lea

Appendix I

As an extension of chapter 4, and as a comparative study, transcriptions of 4 versions of each of 5 songs are given below. Music transcriptions for each song are of those verses included by all four of the singers, numbered according to the order in which they are sung. Complete verbal texts are given separately, plus notes on each set of performances. Each song belongs to one of the groups outlined in Chapter 4, as follows:

He widna wint: *Group 3,* COMEDY AND MUSIC-HALL
Willie Macintosh: *Group 4,* FEUDS AND WAR
Banks o' red roses: *Group 5,* SEXUAL VIOLENCE AND
                                SEDUCTION

The echo mocks the
corncrake: *Group 1,* LOVE
Johnnie my man: *Group 1,* LOVE

He widna wint his gruel

cruel   Oh the ve-ry first nicht that he got wed   He

cru-el,oh, For the ve-ry first nicht that he got wad   He

cruel   For the ve-ry first night that he got wed   He

cru ------ el The ve-ry first nacht that he got wad   He

sat an' grat for gruel. He wid-na wint his gruel,   He

sat an' he grat 'for gruel. He win-na want his grüel,No he

sat an'he grat for gruel. He sat an'grat for gruel,Aye he

sat an' he grat for gruel. He wud-na want his gruel,Oh he

wid - na wint his gruel, Oh the ve-ry first night that he got wed He

win-na want his gruel, Oh the ve-ry first nicht that he got wad He

can - na wint his gruel, Noo the ve-ry first night that he got wed He

wud - na want his gruel, Oh the ve-ry first nacht that he got wed He

sat an' he grat for gruel. (V.2) "There's nae a pot in

sat an' he grat for gruel. "There's no a pot in

sat an' he grat for gruel. "Noo there's nae a pot in

sat an' he grat for gruel. "Oh there's nae a pot in

a' the hoose That I can mak'yer gruel";"Oh(ho ho)the washin'pot it-'ll

a' the hoose That I can mak'yer gruel"; "Oh   the wa-shin'pail it-'ll

a' the hoose For ye tae mak'yer gruel"; "Och   the wa-shin'pot it-'ll

a' the hoose That I can sup ma gruel"; "Ah   the wa-shin'pot it-'ll

dae wi' me For I maun hae ma gruel. For I maun hae ma gruel,   I

dae for me For I maun hae ma gruel". He win-na want his gruel,No he

dae wi' me For I maun hae ma gruel. For I maun hae ma gruel, Aye I

dae for you For I maun hae ma gruel. For I maun hae ma gruel Oh I

can-na wint ma gruel, Oh the·wa-shin'pot it-'ll   dae wi' me For

win-na want his gruel,"Oh the wa-shin'pail it'll   dae for me For

can-na want ma gruel, Och the wa-shin'pot it-'ll   dae wi' me For

can-na wint ma gruel, Oh the wa-shin'pot it- 'll   dae for you For

I maun hae ma   gruel."(V.3)"There's nae a spoon in a'the hoose That

I maun hae ma   gruel."   "There's no a spuin in a'the hoose That

I maun hae ma   gruel."   "But there's nae a spoon in a'the hoose For

I maun hae ma   gruel!""Oh(ho)there's nae a spuin in a'the hoose That

you can sup yer gruel"; "Oh the gair-den spade it-'ll dae wi' me For

ye can sup yer gruel"; "Oh the gair-den spade it-'ll dae for me For

ye tae sup yer gruel"; "Och the gair-den spade it-'ll dae wi' me For

ye can sup yer gruel"; "Ah the gair-den spade it-'ll dae for me For

I maun hae ma gruel. For I maun hae ma gruel, I can-na wint   ma

I maun hae ma gruel". He win-na want his gruel, No he win-na want his

I maun hae ma gruel. For I maun hae ma gruel, Aye I   can-na want   ma

I maun hae ma gruel. For I maun hae ma gruel, Oh I   can-na want   ma

gruel, Oh the gair-den spade it-'ll dae wi'me For I maun hae ma

gruel, "Oh the gair-den spade it-'ll dae for me For I maun hae ma

gruel, (S)o the gair-den spade it-'ll dae wi'me For I maun hae ma

gruel, Oh the gair-den spade it-'ll dae for me For I maun hae ma

gruel." (V.4) She gaed ben the hoose for cakes an'wine, And

gruel." She went ben the hoose for cakes an'wine, She

gruel." She gaed ben the hoose for cakes an' wine, She

gruel." Oh she came ben the hoose wi'the cakes an'wine, An'she

brocht them on a too'el; "Oh gy-a-wa' gy-a-wa'wi'yer fal-de-rals For

brought them on a towel; "Och gy-a-wa' gy-a-wa' wi'yer fal-de-ral For

[laughter]

brocht them on a too'el; "Ach gy-a-wa' gy-a-wa' wi'yer fal-de-rals For

brocht them on a too'el;   "Ah gy-a-wa' gy-a-wa'wi'yer fol-de-rols For

I maun hae ma gruel.   For I maun hae ma gruel, I can-na wint ma

I maun hae ma gruel." Oh he win-na want his gruel, No he win-na want his

I maun hae ma gruel.   For I maun hae ma gruel, Aye I can-na wint ma

I maun hae ma gruel.   For I maun hae ma gruel, Oh I can-na want ma

gruel, Oh gy-a - wa'gy-a-wa'wi'yer fal-de-rals For I maun hae ma

gruel,"Gae a - wa'gy-a-wa'wi'yer fal-de-ral For I maun hae ma

gru-el, Gy-a - wa'gy-a-wa'wi'yer fal-de-rals For I maun hae ma

gruel, Ah gy -a - wa'gy-a-wa'wi'yer fol-de-rols For I maun hae ma

gruel." (V.5) Come all young las - sies take my ad-vice And

gruel." So come a' ye las - sies where-ere ye be An'

gruel." You, come a' young las - sies tak' my ad-vice An'

gruel." Oh come all young las - sies take my ad-vice An'

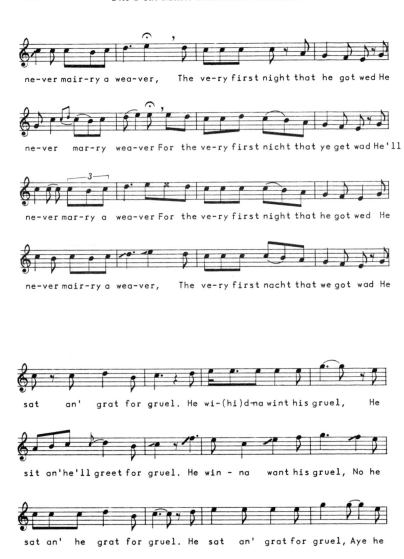

ne-ver mair-ry a wea-ver, The ve-ry first night that he got wed He

ne-ver mar-ry wea-ver For the ve-ry first nicht that ye get wad He'll

ne-ver mar-ry a wea-ver For the ve-ry first night that he got wed He

ne-ver mair-ry a wea-ver, The ve-ry first nacht that we got wad He

sat an' grat for gruel. He wi-(hi)d-na wint his gruel, He

sit an'he'll greet for gruel. He win - na want his gruel, No he

sat an' he grat for gruel. He sat an' grat for gruel, Aye he

sat an' he grat for gruel. He wud -na want his gruel Oh he

Note: Scales in this Appendix are given in their original keys only.

Jimmy MacBeath. SA 1960/109, Aberdeen 1960 Rec. H.H.

(1) There was a weaver o' the North
    An' oh but he was cruel
    Oh the very first nicht that he got wed
    He sat an' grat for gruel.
       He widna wint his gruel,
       He widna wint his gruel,
       Oh the very first night that he got wed
       He sat an' he grat for gruel.

(2) "There's nae a pot in a' the hoose
    That I can mak' your gruel";
    "Oh, the washin' pot it'll dae wi' me
    For I maun hae ma gruel.
       For I maun hae ma gruel,
       I canna wint ma gruel,
       Oh the washin' pot it'll dae wi' me
       For I maun hae ma gruel".

(3) "There's nae a spoon in a' the hoose
    That you can sup your gruel";
    "Oh the gairden spade it'll dae wi' me
    For I maun hae ma gruel.
       For I maun hae ma gruel,
       I canna wint ma gruel,
       Oh the gairden spade it'll dae wi' me
       For I maun hae ma gruel."

(4) She gaed ben the hoose for cakes an' wine,
   And brocht them on a too'el;
   "Oh gy-awa' gy-awa' wi' your falderals
   For I maun hae ma gruel.
       For I maun hae ma gruel,
       I canna wint ma gruel,
       Oh gy-awa', gy-awa' wi' your falderals
       For I maun hae ma gruel".

(5) Come all young lassies take my advice
   And never mairry a weaver,
   The very first night that he got wed
   He sat an' grat for gruel.
       He widna wint his gruel,
       He widna wint his gruel,
       Oh the very first nicht that he got wed
       He sat an' he grat for gruel.

Heather Heywood. AM2, Rec. A.P. Kinross 1977

(1) For there was a weaver in the North,
   An' oh but he was cruel, oh,
   For the very first nicht that he got wad
   He sat an' he grat for gruel.
   He winna want his gruel,
   No he winna want his gruel,
   Oh the very first nicht that he got wad
   He sat an' he grat for gruel.

(2) "There's no a pot in a' the hoose
   That I can mak' yer gruel;"
   "Oh the washin' pail it'll dae for me
   For I maun hae ma gruel".
   He winna want his gruel,
   No he winna want his gruel,
   "Oh the washin' pail it'll dae for me
   For I maun hae ma gruel".

(3) "There's no a spuin in a' the hoose
   That ye can sup yer gruel;"
   "Oh the gairden spade it'll dae for me
   For I maun hae ma gruel."
   He winna want his gruel,
   No he winna want his gruel,
   "Oh the gairden spade it'll dae for me
   For I maun hae ma gruel."

(4) She went ben the hoose for cakes an' wine,
   She brought them on a towel;
   "Och gy-awa' gy-awa' wi' yer falderal
   For I maun hae ma gruel."

Oh he winna want his gruel,
No he winna want his gruel,
"Gae awa' gy-awa' wi' yer falderal
For I maun hae ma gruel."

(5) So come a' ye lassies where'er ye be
An' never marry a weaver
For the very first nicht that ye get wad
He'll sit an' he'll greet for gruel.
He winna want his gruel,
No he winna want his gruel,
For the very first nicht that he gets wad
He'll sit an' he'll greet for gruel.

Willie Mackenzie. AM5, Rec. A.P. Keith 1976

(1) Noo there lived a weaver in the North
An' oh but he was cruel
For the very first night that he got wed
He sat an' he grat for gruel.
He sat an' grat for gruel,
Aye he canna wint his gruel,
Noo the very first night that he got wed
He sat an' he grat for gruel.

(2) "Noo there's nae a pot in a' the hoose
For ye tae mak' yer gruel;"
"Och the washin' pot it'll dae wi' me
For I maun hae ma gruel.
For I maun hae ma gruel,
Aye I canna want ma gruel,
Och the washin' pot it'll dae wi' me
For I maun hae ma gruel."

(3) "But there's nae a spoon in a' the hoose
For ye tae sup yer gruel;"
"Och the gairden spade it'll dae wi' me
For I maun hae ma gruel.
For I maun hae ma gruel,
Aye I canna want ma gruel,
(S)o the gairden spade it'll dae wi' me
For I maun hae ma gruel."

(4) She gaed ben the hoose for cakes an' wine,
She brocht them on a too'el;
"Ach gy-awa gy-awa wi' yer falderals
For I maun hae ma gruel.

For I maun hae ma gruel,
Aye I canna wint ma gruel,
Gy-awa' gy-awa' wi' yer falderals
For I maun hae ma gruel."

(5) You, come a' young lassies tak' my advice
An' never marry a weaver
For the very first night that he got wed
He sat an' he grat for gruel.
He sat an' grat for gruel,
Aye he canna wint his gruel,
Noo the very first night that he got wed
He sat an' he grat for gruel.

Tommy Truesdale. AM12, Rec. A.P. Kinross 1978

(1) Oh there was a weaver o' the North
And oh but he was cruel
The very first nacht that he got wad
He sat an' he grat for gruel.
He wudna want his gruel,
Oh he wudna want his gruel,
Oh the very first nacht that he got wed
He sat an' he grat for gruel.

(2) "Oh there's nae a pot in a' the hoose
That I can sup ma gruel;"
"Ah the washin pot it'll dae for you
For I maun hae ma gruel.
For I maun hae ma gruel
Oh I canna wint ma gruel,
Oh the washin pot it'll dae for you
For I maun hae ma gruel.

(3) "Oh (ho) there's nae a spuin in a' the hoose
That ye can sup yer gruel;"
"Ah the gairden spade it'll dae for me
For I maun hae ma gruel.
For I maun hae ma gruel,
Oh I canna want ma gruel,
Oh the gairden spade it'll dae for me
For I maun hae ma gruel."

(4) Oh she came ben the hoose wi' the cakes an' wine,
An' she brocht them on a too'el;
"Ah gy-awa' gy-awa' wi' yer folderols
For I maun hae ma gruel.
For I maun hae ma gruel,
Oh I canna want ma gruel,
Ah gy-awa' gy-awa' wi' yer folderols
For I maun hae ma gruel."

(5) Oh come all young lassies take my advice
   An' never mairry a weaver,
   The very first nacht that we got wad
   He sat an' he grat for gruel.
   He wudna want his gruel
   Oh he wudna want his gruel,
   Oh the very first nacht that he got wad
   He sat an' he grat for gruel.

This is a bothy song. It was collected by Hamish Henderson from several farm workers of pre-first-war vintage, including Jimmy MacBeath himself, who found the bothy life so harsh that he determined not to return to it after the war. Instead he became an itinerant singer, and a highly successful one. This was one of his favourite songs; the other three singers above all learned it from him — two of them directly, and Heather Heywood indirectly — and it is still very popular.

Jimmy MacBeath is the only singer represented in Chapter 4 and in this Appendix who is no longer alive. His performance of this song makes it quite clear that he appreciated the satire as well as the comedy of its theme. His rich, gravelly voice changes as he acts out the parts of bewildered, anxious-to-please bride and domineering, petulant husband, the latter's part rising to high G at the end of verses 1, 4 and 5 as if to underline the final word "gruel". In bar 11, the repeated plea "widna wint his gruel" or "canna wint ma gruel" is broken up by rests, these breaks suggesting an ironic pseudo-pathos; and a gleeful chuckle or slide accompanies some of the more bizarre remarks. It's not just a pretty song; the satire is savage enough even to hint that he's got cold feet about the whole business of consummation, and seizes every chance of postponing it. Not surprisingly, the only direct comment on all this is the word *cruel* (the perfect rhyme for gruel) — comedy often includes cruelty as an ingredient. Jimmy adopts a relatively slow tempo, leaving time for the performance details mentioned, and so blending serious satire with high comedy.

Heather Heywood, of Kilmarnock, says that at the time her recording was made she felt much sympathy for the woman here. This sympathy is shown in the slow pace she adopts — the slowest of these four versions — and in the *caveat* that issues from her use of the future tense: first, "he winna. . .", twice in each verse (with a rhythm which fits the word), and then in the last verse where she addresses her female listeners directly:. . .". . . the very first nicht that *ye* get wad *he'll* sit an' *he'll* greet for gruel" (my italics). In other words: "Watch out, or this will happen to you!" She prefers a curve of stepwise links in the melody, rather than a leap. This is exemplified in bars 7 and 15 of each verse, and also in bar 10 and the second half of bar 9. This last variant is also found in Tommy Truesdale's version. Heather adds this comment: "I think the man in the song shows his determination to have what he wants no matter how much he is tempted. (Typical stubborn man!)".

Willie Mackenzie, from Elgin, has the lightest approach. He sees this simply as "a nice wee catchy song", and goes no deeper. He adopts the fastest pace of these four, and gives more chuckles than Jimmy. He says the theme is "It's the belly that keeps up the back".

Tommy Truesdale from Girvan, now living in Glasgow, takes it at a relatively fast pace, second only to Willie's. His is a robust and fairly straightforward interpretation, but like Jimmy he combines comedy with irony. He comments: "'The way to a man's heart is through his stomach'. It could be a dig at the importance of gruel in the daily diet of most Scots at that time, and that a man would prefer his gruel before love. I know of some men who would prefer, not so much gruel, but other pleasures in life before their wives. . . ."

These three singers keep fairly closely to Jimmy MacBeath's tune-model, and melodic and rhythmic vaiations are slight. Singers sometimes make slight slips in words, but it's usually easy to spot these.

Willie Macintosh (The burning of Auchindoun) (Child 183)

met wi' Wil-lie Mac-in-tosh An hour be-fore the daw - nin'.

I spied Wil-lie Mac-in-tosh An hour be-fore the daw - nin'.

I spied Wil-lie Mac-in-tosh An hour a-fore the daw - nin'.

spied Wil-lie Mac-in-tosh An hour be-fore the daw - nin'.

(V.2)"Turn a-gain, turn a-gain, Turn a-gain I beg ye,

"Turn a-gain, turn a-gain, Turn a-gain I bid ye,

"Turn a-gain, turn a-gain, Turn a-gain I bid ye,

"Turn a-gain, turn a-gain Turn a-gain I bid ye, If

If ye burn Au-chin-doun Hunt-ly he will heid ye."

If ye burn Au-chin-doun Hunt-ly he will heid ye."

If ye burn Au-chin-doun Hunt-ly he will heid ye."

ye burn Au-chin-doun For Hunt-ly he will heid ye."

(V.3)"Heid me or hang me, It will ni - ver grieve me:

Slower

"Heid me or hang me, That will ne - ver fear me:

"Heid me or hang me, That will ne - ver fear me:

"Heid me or hang me, Hunt-ly he'll nae fear me: For

I'll burn Au-chin-doun Al-though the life'ud leave me." (V.4) As

Usual speed

I will burn Au-chin-doun Though the life leaves me." And as

I will burn Au-chin-doun Though the life will leave me." As

I'll burn Au- chin-doun Though a' the breath shall leave me." As

I gaed doun by Fid-dich-side on a May mor - nin',

I gaed in by Fid-dich-side on a May mor - nin',

I came in by Au-chin-doun on a May mor - nin',

I gaed in be Fid-dich-side on a May mor - nin',

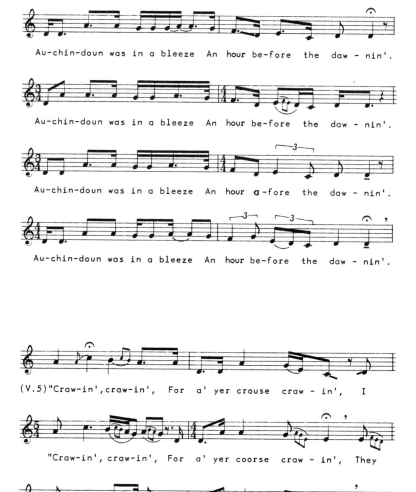

Au-chin-doun was in a bleeze An hour be-fore the daw - nin'.

Au-chin-doun was in a bleeze An hour be-fore the daw - nin'.

Au-chin-doun was in a bleeze An hour a -fore the daw - nin'.

Au-chin-doun was in a bleeze An hour be-fore the daw - nin'.

(V.5)"Craw-in',craw-in', For a' yer crouse craw - in', I

"Craw-in', craw-in', For a' yer coorse craw - in', They

"Craw-in', craw-in', For a' yer crouse craw - in', Ye've

"Craw-in', craw-in', A' yer grouse are craw-in', I've

brunt yer crops an' tint yer wings An hour be-fore the daw-nin'."

burnt yer crops an' tint yer wings An hour be-fore the daw-nin'."

brunt yer crops an' tint yer wings An hour a-fore the daw-nin'."

burnt yer crops an'I've tint yer wine An hour be-fore the daw-nin'."

Madeleine Taylor. SA 1971/243, Rec. P.C. Kinross 1971

(1) As I gaed doon by Fiddichside
On a May mornin',
I met wi' Willie Macintosh
An 'oor before the dawnin'.★

★The word "hour" is spelt here as it is pronounced by the four singers.

(2) "Turn again, turn again,
Turn again I beg ye,
If ye burn Auchindoun
Huntly he will heid ye."

(3) "Heid me or hang me,
It will niver grieve me:
I'll burn Auchindoun
Although the life 'ud leave me."

(4) As I gaed doon by Fiddichside
On a May mornin',
Auchindoun was in a bleeze
An 'oor before the dawnin'.

(5) "Crawin', crawin',
For a' yer crouse crawin',
I brunt yer crops an' tint yer wings
An 'oor before the dawnin'."

Dick Gaughan. SA 1971/192, Rec. F.K. Edinburgh 1971

(1) As I came in by Fiddichside
On a May mornin'
I spied Willie Macintosh
An 'oor before the dawnin'.

(2) "Turn again, turn again,
Turn again I bid ye,
If ye burn Auchindoun
Huntly he will heid ye."

(3) "Heid me or hang me,
That will never fear me:
I will burn Auchindoun
Though the life leaves me."

(4) And as I gaed in by Fiddichside
On a May mornin',
Auchindoun was in a bleeze
An 'oor before the dawnin'.

(5) "Crawin, crawin
For a' yer coorse crawin',
They burnt yer crops an' tint yer wings
An' 'oor before the dawnin' ".

Allan Morris. SA 1973/109, Rec. P.C. Kinross 1973

(1) As I came in by Fiddichside
On a May morning',
I spied Willie Macintosh
An 'oor afore the dawnin'.

(2) "Turn again, turn again,
    Turn again I bid ye,
    If ye burn Auchindoun
    Huntly he will heid ye."

(3) "Heid me or hang me,
    That will never fear me:
    I will burn Auchindoun
    Though the life will leave me."

(4) As I came in by Auchindoun
    On a May mornin',
    Auchindoun was in a bleeze
    An 'oor afore the dawnin'.

(5) "Crawin', crawin',
    For a' yer crouse crawin',
    Ye've brunt yer crops an' tint yer wings
    An 'oor afore the dawnin'."

Anthony Robertson. SA 1977/4, Rec. K.C. Aberdeen 1977

(1) As I gaed in be Fiddichside
    On a May mornin',
    I spied Willie Macintosh
    An 'oor before the dawnin'.
(2) "Turn again, turn again
    Turn again I bid ye,
    If ye burn Auchindoun
    For Huntly he will heid ye."

(3) "Heid me or hang me,
    Huntley he'll nae fear me:
    For I'll burn Auchindoun
    Though a' the breath shall leave me."

(4) As I gaed in be Fiddichside
    On a May mornin',
    Auchindoun was in a bleeze
    An' 'oor before the dawnin'.

(5) "Crawin' crawin',
    A' yer grouse are crawin',
    I've burnt yer crops an' I've tint yer wine
    An 'oor before the dawnin'."

This ballad is based on a historical incident, but two different characters with the title-name are confounded in it. The possible incidents are dated 1592 and 1550. The terrain is Banffshire, near Dufftown. Bronson gives only the above tune, recorded by Ewan MacColl who learned it from his father. Once again MacColl is the

Revival source — Anthony Robertson got his version from his own traveller family. The words are very similar to Child B, but the last verse has been changed now to a final taunt, addressed presumably by Willie Macintosh to Huntly's clan, in the continuing feud which was started by the murder of the "Bonny Earl of Murray". The meaning of this taunt is not obscured by the slight variations in the words above: only Allan Morris has MacColl's "Ye('ve) brunt yer crops", (meaning "you've brought this on yourself"), two have "I('ve) brunt/burnt. . ." and Dick Gaughan has "They burnt. . ."

Maddy Taylor's is the most dramatic and extrovert statement. She sings with contained urgency, in a loudish voice with an edge to it ("a good song for exercising the lungs!" she says), and she keeps the potentially fierce strathspey rhythm. A touch of *parlando* style, in the last syllable of the second line, verses 1, 2, 4 and 5, heightens the drama. She draws out the first line of verses 1 and 4, "As I gaed doon by Fiddichside", into two bars instead of one, thus giving it a more declamatory air, as if introducing both parts of the story. Anthony Robertson does the same. Maddy, who was raised in Perthshire, has been a professional singer and guitarist for some years. She learned this song from the singing of Mike Whelans, and notes that several words have become altered (compared with the MacColl version). She describes the song as ". . . a wee story, a narrative, it speaks for itself", and takes it at a pace considerably faster than the other three.

Dick Gaughan's interpretation is also highly dramatic, but in a more personal way . . . as if he is re-living the events as Willie Macintosh himself, risking his life yet hell-bent on revents. By postponing the first appearance of the note G, in bar 1, to the first syllable of "Fiddichside", he is able to end this line on the dominant note, A: an "open" ending, which affects the beginning of the next line also. The strathspey rhythm is again pronounced. This singer is a master of fleeting, delicate ornamentation — which goes well with the slight but fast vibrato in his voice — and is capable of a beautiful *sostenuto*. The tempo is slower, more reflective, and the timing flexible. Dick is of mixed Highland and Irish blood, and has lived most of his life in Leith, just north of Edinburgh. He can't remember where or when he learned this song, and he describes its theme as "evidence of a particular phase of barbarity in the evolution of human society".

Allan Morris's rhythms are less dotted than the first two singers', but the drama comes over in his strong, positive voice and in the sense of more objective involvement which he projects . . . as the story-teller this time, the observer. His emotion, if not recollected in tranquillity, is at least tempered by distance. The tempo is the same as the last singer's. Allan learned this from Ewan MacColl's singing, on disc or tape, in the late sixties or early seventies. He likes it because of the terse words, because it has something to say about Banffshire four centuries ago, and because "its vengeful mood allows you to 'cut loose' ". Asked what he felt was the theme, he replied, "Using words alone, I would say, a 'revenge' theme".

Anthony Robertson of Aberdeen learned this when he was about ten, from the singing of his father (Stanley Robertson) and grandfather. He has never heard anyone else sing it. As always in oral transmission, changes in words are unlikely to occur unless they make sense, even if the sense is changed, and the two words in v. 5 here, which differ from the other three versions, are: "A' yer *grouse* are crawin'", and ". . . I've tint yer *wine*. . .", but they are at least as likely to be the words of a version older than the other three. (Stanley thinks that "tint" means "destroyed", or "blighted", as used at the end of his version of "Davie Faa", Child 200). Anthony takes this at the slowest tempo, his voice is rounder, and he makes the ballad sound almost lyrical. In the first bar of verses 2, 3 and 5, the note B is avoided; the tune goes up to high D, and then leaps rapidly from C down to G, the Scots snap here coming most effectively on the word "turn".

Although there are some differences in words and tune amongst these four versions, they are not extensive and there are no fundamental differences in interpretation.

The banks o' red roses

doon,   And   he's taen oot his chai - r(ə)m box   tae

tune, An' in the mid-dle o' the   tune

tune, In the   mid-dle o' the   tune   his

doon,   And   he took oot his   fid - dle   for tae

play his love a   tune. In the mid-dle o'the tune   she

she stood up an cried, "Oh   John-ny dear, oh John-ny dear,

l'ove sat doon an' cried, In the mid-dle o'the tune his.......his

play his love a   tune. In the mid-dle o'the tune   oh   she

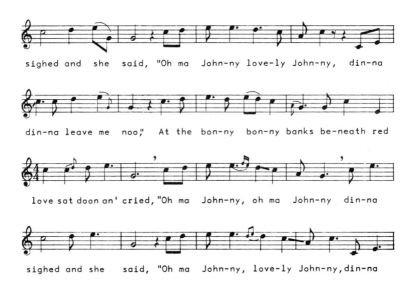

sighed and she said, "Oh ma John-ny love-ly John-ny, din-na

din-na leave me noo," At the bon-ny bon-ny banks be-neath red

love sat doon an' cried, "Oh ma John-ny, oh ma John-ny din-na

sighed and she said, "Oh ma John-ny, love-ly John-ny, din-na

leave me." (V.2)   When I was a wee thing and ea-sy led a -

ro - ses. (V.1)   When I was a wee thing I heard ma mo-ther

leave me." (V.2)Oh when I wis a young thing I heard ma mam-my

leave me." (V.1)   When I was a wee thing an' easy led as-tray

stray A - fore I wad work I wad rai - ther sport and

say, A - fore I wad work I wad rai - ther sport an'

say, 'At be - fore I wad work I wad rai - ther sport an'

—— Be - fore I would work I would ra - ther sport and

play, Aye a - fore I wad work I'd rai-ther sport and

play, A - fore an'I wad work I wad ra -ther sport an'

play, Oh be - fore I wad work I wad ra-ther sport an'

play, Be - fore I would work I would ra-ther sport and

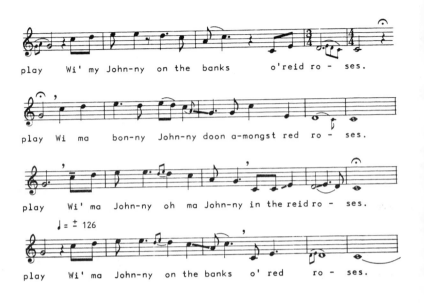

play   Wi' my John-ny on the banks   o'reid ro - ses.

play Wi ma   bon-ny John-ny doon a-mongst red ro - ses.

play Wi' ma John-ny oh ma John-ny in the reid ro - ses.

♩ = ± 126

play   Wi' ma John-ny on the banks   o' red   ro - ses.

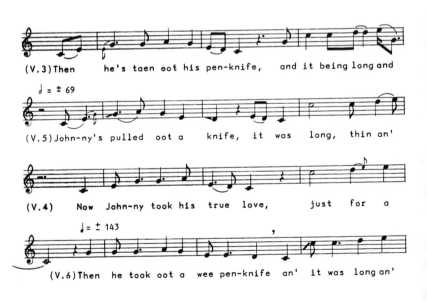

(V.3) Then   he's taen oot his pen-knife, and it being long and

♩ = ± 69

(V.5) John-ny's pulled oot a   knife, it was   long, thin an'

(V.4)   Now John-ny took his true love,   just for a

♩ = ± 143

(V.6) Then he took oot a wee pen-knife an' it was long an'

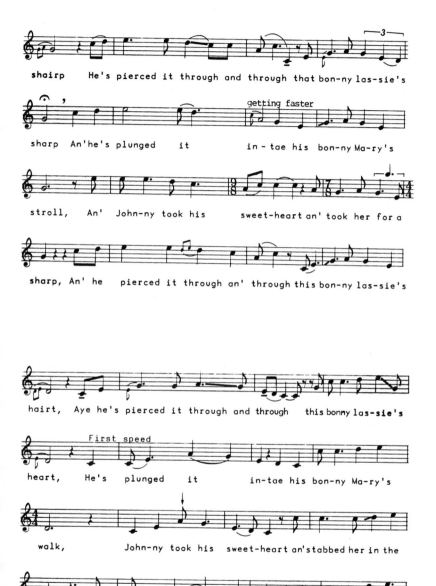

shairp He's pierced it through and through that bon-ny las-sie's

sharp An'he's plunged it in - tae his bon-ny Ma-ry's

stroll, An' John-ny took his sweet-heart an' took her for a

sharp, An' he pierced it through an' through this bon-ny las-sie's

hairt, Aye he's pierced it through and through this bonny las-sie's

heart, He's plunged it in-tae his bon-ny Ma-ry's

walk, John-ny took his sweet-heart an'stabbed her in the

heart, He pierced it through an' through this bon-ny las-sie's

hairt And he's left her ly-in' there a-mang reid ro - ses.

heart An' he left her ly-ing low be-neath red ro - ses.

heart An' he's left her ly-in' there 'neath reid ro - ses.

heart An' he left her ly-in' low 'mong red ro - ses.

Sheila Douglas. SA 1971/243, Rec. P.C. Kinross 1971

(1) On the banks o' reid roses my love and I sat doon,
And he's taen oot his chairm-box tae play his love a tune.
In the middle o' the tune she sighed and she said,
"Oh ma Johnny lovely Johnny, dinna leave me."

(2) When I was a wee thing and easy led led astray
Afore I wad work I wad raither sport and play,
Aye afore I wad work I'd raither sport and play
Wi' my Johnny on the banks o' reid roses.

(3) Then he's taen oot his penknife, and it bein' long and shairp
He's pierced it through and through that bonny lassie's hairt,
Aye he's pierced it through and through this bonny lassie's hairt
And he's left her lyin' there amang reid roses.

(4) As verse 1.

Stanley Robertson. AM2, Rec. A.P. Kinross 1975

(1) When I was a wee thing I heard ma mother say,
Afore I wad work I wad raither sport an' play,
Afore an' I wad work I wad rather sport an' play
Wi' my bonny Johnny doon amongst red roses.

(2) Johnny pulled oot his tune-box tae play his love a tune,
An' in the middle o' the tune she stood up an' cried,
"Oh Johnny dear, oh Johnny dear, dinna leave me noo",
At the bonny bonny banks beneath red roses.

(3) Johnny's took her tae his hoose an' he treated her to tea
Sayin', "Arise my bonny Mary an' come awa' wi' me,
Arise my bonny Mary an' come awa' wi' me
Tae the bonny bonny banks beneath red roses".

(4) Johnny's gaed owre the high road, diggin' wi' a spade,
Johnny's gaed owre the high road, diggin' at a grave,
Johnny's gaed owre the high road, diggin' wi' a spade,
And the bonny bonny banks beneath red roses.

(5) Johnny's pulled oot a knife, it was long, thin an' sharp
An' he's plunged it intae his bonny Mary's heart,
He's plunged it intae his bonny Mary's heart
An' he left her lying low beneath red roses.

(6) Come a' ye bonny lassies, a warnin' tak' o' me,
For it's never let a young man in yer company,
For it's never let a young man in yer company,
Wi' ma bonny Johnny doon amongst red roses.

Jane Turriff. AM12, Rec. A.P. Keith 1978

(1) Oh Johnny took oot his churn-box tae play his love a tune,
In the middle o' the tune his love sat doon an' cried,
In the middle o' the tune his . . . love sat doon an' cried,
"Oh ma Johnny, oh ma Johnny dinna leave me".

(2) Oh when I wis a young thing I heard ma mammy say,
'At before I wad work I wad raither sport an' play,
Oh before I wad work I wad rather sport an' play
Wi' ma Johnny oh ma Johnny in the reid roses.

(3) As verse 1.

(4) Now Johnny took his true love, just for a stroll,
    An' Johnny took his sweetheart an' took her for a walk,
    Johnny took his sweetheart an' stabbed her in the heart
    An' he's left her lying' there 'neath reid roses.

(5) Now Johnny took the high road, howkin' wi' a spade,
    An' Johnny took the high road, howkin' at a grave,
    Johnny took the high road, howkin' wi' a spade,
    An' he's left her lyin' there beneath reid roses.

Peter Shepheard. AM12, Rec. A.P. Keith 1978

(1) When I was a wee thing an' easy led astray
    Before I would work I would rather sport and play,
    Before I would work I would rather sport and play
    Wi' ma Johnnyy on the banks o' red roses.

(2) On the banks o' red roses his love and he sat doon
    And he took oot his fiddle for tae play his love a tune.
    In the middle o' the tune oh she sighed and she said,
    "Oh ma Johnny, lovely Johnny, dinna leave me".

(3) Noo they walked and they talked till they cam' untae a cave
    Where all night long her Johnnie had been digging at her grave,
    Where all night long her Johnnie had been digging at her grave
    By the bonny bonny banks o' red roses.

(4) "Oh Johnny, lovely Johnny, oh that grave is not for me";
    "Oh yes, my lovely Jeannie, that your bridal bed shall be,
    Oh yes, my lovely Jeannie, that your bridal bed shall be
    By the bonny bonny banks o' red roses".

(5) As verse 2.

(6) Then he took oot a wee penknife an' it was long an' sharp,
    An' he pierced it through an' through this bonny lassie's heart,
    He pierced it through an' through this bonny lassie's heart
    An' he left her lyin' low 'mong red roses.

(7) Noo as he was comin' homeward his heart was filled with fear,
    For every face he met he thocht it was his dear,
    For every face he met he thocht it was his dear
    Lyin' cold upon her bed 'mong red roses.

(8) As verse 2.

Of the five examples chosen this song shows the greatest differences within the four versions, differences in the words, in the details and the interpretation of the story, and in the musical interpretation. The versions of the tune itself show but slight variation. All start with the same two verses, but in differing order. In the music transcription all the related verses are aligned, including the murder verse, and only the three which correspond to those in the first version are shown. (The same procedure is followed in *Johnnie my man*.)

Where the theme of the girl murdered by her boy-friend appears in Western folk song, it is generally understood that she is pregnant, even when this is not explicitly stated.

Sheila Douglas regards this as a story which ends in tragedy, and she shapes the song accordingly. She sings very slowly, with a sad lyricism and with deep feeling, and one feels the seeds of tragedy are there from the very beginning. "It is the love that is doomed", she says, and there is no anger or harshness in her singing. She finds sexual symbolism in the second line of v. 1, and so does Peter Shepheard. Except for the ending, the two halves of the melody are almost identical, and Sheila's rounded, soaring voice unites words and tune into an artistic whole. "I love the beautiful long-drawn phrases of the tune, and the way it rises to a climax and falls so expressively down at the end. The words have that dramatic intensity and economy of all great ballads. It seems to me to be about the way all-consuming sexual passion can wreck peoples' lives and bring about tragedy and death."

Stanley Robertson of Aberdeen, a nephew of Jeannie Robertson, treats the song very differently. His fuller version of the words, and Peter Shepheard's, makes it clear that the murder was calculated. This is the fastest account, sung at more than twice the speed of Sheila's. On the occasion of this performance, Stanley's introductory remarks included the following: ". . . a song my mither used to sing — I've heard it sung a lot in the folk scene — it's usually sung slow — I've heard Heather Heywood sing it awfa bonny . . . but I'll have to sing it the wey't I kenned it frae my mither, which is mair — a serious song, but it had — a pleasant *wey* to think o' the serious . . . and ye *do* think o' the seriousness o' the song because of the pleasantness o' the tune. . . 'The banks o' the red roses' . . . for me it's something pleasant." He has since described it as ". . . a horror ballad — if sung slow, it's too much; the tune is euphemistic and puts it over in a digestible way." He is very hard on the woman: "In the song the girl admits she is loose — 'Before I wad work I wad raither sport an' play wi' ma Johnny. . .' She obviously becomes pregnant and the young man feels trapped. He could cope with fatherhood but not with her constant nagging." The only reason he gave in support of the "constant nagging" charge was that she had interrupted her lover in the middle of the tune he was playing her, having always taken the "tune-box" line literally. As for the "sporting and playing" he evidently regards this as all the woman's fault, and he says "wee thing" can refer to an adult. Once when he sang this, ". . . a lady started to cry. I thought she was moved with the song but on investigating further I found out that she had a daughter murdered in the same fashion. Many travellers used this song to teach their daughters the dangers and perils in breaking their moral standards, and that the aftermath could bring much suffering and heartbreak." (It seems it was not used as a warning to sons.) His aunt Maggie Stewart also sang this: "It was one of those songs that always seemed to crop up at travellers' parties and gatherings". His cousin Lizzie Higgins also sings it, but slowly.

The chief difference in Stanley's version of the tune, also found in Jane Turriff's, is in bars 6 and 14 of each verse: with two exceptions, none of their verses have the octave leap downwards, from C to C. Since Jane and Stanley are both of traveller stock, such resemblances are not surprising. Verbal similarities also appear, including the opening verse (v. 2 of Stanley's) where the girl "stood up/sat doon an' cried" (instead of "sighed an' . . . said"), and the triple reference of each to "the high road". A third resemblance is to some kind of "box" for playing the tune, and the fact that Jane also takes this literally. At first she thought "churn-box" referred to part of the butter-churning equipment, but then she realised this could not produce a "tune" and said the reference might be to a melodion, often called simply "the box". In this performance Jane accompanies herself on guitar, strumming the tonic chord gently throughout the song so that it sounds rather like a pedal-point, or a drone. She lends variety to the verse-ending by rising to high C, or falling to middle C, in alternate verses. The song was learned in childhood, from her mother's singing. Although Jane does not take it as slowly as Sheila, her account is also in her own way unmistakably tragic — the cutting edge in her voice seems to be emphasized — and she is very definite that this should be sung "in a sad way, it should feel like the real thing". She finds the reason for the murder hard to understand: "It's a funny song — I can't make much of it — but it's very tragic . . . I sing very sad when it is a true sad song".

Dr. Peter Shepheard learned his version from Jane's uncle, old Davie Stewart, "and conflated it with other versions". He has heard it sung at many different speeds, from very slow (old Davie) to even faster than his own ("a local Fife singer"). His highly individual conflation is sung to his own lilting, dance-like accordion accompaniment, the whole effect being not only relaxed but almost jolly, and *with gusto*. The tempo is second only to Stanley's here. (But Stanley, although he described the tune as "pleasant", and chooses a fast pace, does not sound relaxed or jolly; his fast-driven version has a certain grimness, probably directed against the girl for causing the man to undergo the terrible experience of murdering her!) Peter sings most of his songs fast. He is also convinced that the speed and the scale of a melody are unrelated to tragedy, and he is certainly right about the scale or mode. I am not so sure about the speed. (One classic example in art-music is Orpheus' famous lament for Euridice, "Che faro senza Euridice. . ." in Act III of Gluck's opera *Orfeo ed Euridice*, set in the "cheerful" key of C major. If sung in a happy manner — which would *include* a faster tempo — it could easily become a song of joyful release: "She is lost and gone for ever"! as one translation has it.) A tragic song may be sung fast because it was learned in childhood and hence "gabbled" through without thinking of the meaning. It has been suggested that a fast tempo may either indicate stoicism, or else come into the "laughing that he may not weep" category. Certainly "The banks o' red roses" is frequently sung in Peter Shepheard's way by men, but I have never heard, or heard of, a woman singing it thus.

One interpretation of this song is that the girl is not really murdered at all but only lying back exhausted after vigorous lovemaking, the knife and the stabbing "through and through" being another piece of erotic imagery; and there are versions where this is clearly indicated, including some from Ireland. This under-lines the fact that the same words are used in each of these four versions to announce the start of lovemaking and to announce the start of killing, viz. "he's taen oot" (Sheila), "Johnny('s) pulled oot" (Stanley) and "he took (oot)" (Jane and Peter). Going a step further, the connection between murder, and sexual love which is doomed and hopeless, has been made before, perhaps especially in fiction (e.g. Tolstoy's Vronsky and Anna Karenina, after the first con-summation of their love: "He felt what a murderer must feel, when he sees the body he has robbed of life".)

I was particularly interested to find that Stanley Robertson and Jane Turriff, the two travellers, should ignore the sexual implica-tions in verse 1 (of music transcription) and wondered at first if this was common in traveller versions generally. But the evidence does not support this. In a recording made by Linda Williamson in 1978, Sissy Johnston and Bella Townsley both sang the words "tunin' box" in the line referred to. Betsy Whyte of Montrose, who is related to both these women, is quite definite that they would understand this sexually rather than literally. Betsy's childhood was spent in the real travelling life; she often heard the song and says that "You could see everyone understood this meaning". She thought the symbolic words were probably used partly to avoid being explicit in front of the children, who were with the grown-ups all the time. She also says she heard it sung, "He took oot his grinding-box to play his love a tune": "grinder" is a name for the penis.

Peter Shepheard comments: "A beautiful tune that is apparently unique to this song. When I started singing it, the much less interesting Irish version was well known in the revival. . . . On the other hand the Scottish form was widely known by traditional singers, always with variants of the same tune and words. And it had never been published — an excellent survival in oral tradition". The song is widespread, and Dolina MacLennan suggests that in Skye the literal meaning is generally understood.

We may conclude that this is probably a very old song, and that the symbolic meaning (in v. 1 of the transcription) was suppressed and frowned on at certain times and in certain places.

Postscript:

(1) Bella Townsley's 3 verses start with these words:–

Oh when I was a wee thing ma Mammy used to say,
She would rather see me deid an' buried in the clay
Than to see me get married to any runaway,
An' [on?] the bonny sweet banks o' the roses.

The second verse is identical except that "Daddy" is substituted for "Mammy", and "he" for "she". Betsy Whyte thinks "runaway" means a deserter, a coward, a man who has run away from battle. The third verse corresponds to our v. 1.

(2) Stanley Robertson offers an interesting theory about roses, and refers to his versions of 4 other songs:–

"Some travellers considered this song as being unlucky because it contained the word 'roses'. Roses many times are associated with superstitution and ill luck. For example: "The butcher boy" ("For the murder of sweet Maryanne, fa lies now whar the roses bloom"); "The bonnie bunch o' roses" ("For trying tae catch the bonnie bunch o' roses"); "Tamlin" ("She hadnae pu'd a red red rose, a rose but barely three, When up an' spake a wee wee man at Lady Janet's knee"); "Matty Grove" ("And oot o' her grave grew a rose, and oo o' his grew a briar"). In each case a woman was pregnant.

Maryanne was murdered by the butcher boy.

The girl is singing and lamenting for Bonaparte. [The bunch o' roses refers to the British army, the red coats].

Lady Janet is looking for the father of her child (Tamlin).

Lord Darnel's wife was pregnant by Matty Grove, her former sweetheart, and they were both murdered by Lord Darnel.

There are many examples. . . . This of course was one of my mother's theories."

Stanley Robertson has been recorded by Springtime and by Landmark.

The echo mocks the corncrake.

The lass that I lo'e best of all she's

Oh the las-sie I lo'ed first o' all she was

Noo the lass that I lo'ed first of all was

Oh the lass that I lo'ed best of a' was

hand-some young and fair, Wi'her I've spent some bon-ny nichts doon

hand-some young and fair, Wi'her I spent some mer-ry nichts a -

hand-some young an' fair, Wi'her I spent some mer-ry nights on

hand-some young and fair, Wi'her I spent some mer-ry nichts up-

-mang the whin-ny knowes. (V.2)We loved each o-ther dear-ly, dis-

-mang the whin-ny knowes. We hae lo'ed each i-ther dear-ly, dis-

-mang the whin-ny knowes. We loved each o-ther dear-ly,and dis-

-mang the whin-ny knowes. We loved each o-ther dear-ly,and dis-

-putes we sel-dom had, As cons-tant as the pen-du-lum our

-putes we sel-dom had, As con-stant as the pen-du-lum her

-putes we sel-dom had, As cons-tant as the pen-du-lum her

-putes we sel-dom had, As cons-tant as the pen-du-lum her

hearts beat al-ways glad, And we searched for love and found it where

heart beat al-ways glad,   We socht for joy an' found it where

hairt beat al-ways glad,   We sought for joy an' we found it whaur

heart beat al-ways glad,   We socht for love an found it where

yon wee bur-nie rows And the   e-cho mocks the corn-crake a-

yon wee bur-nie rows, Aye and the e-cho mocks the corn-crake a-

yon wee bur-nie rows Whaur the   e-cho mocks the corn-crake   a-

yon wee bur-nie rows An' the   e-cho mocks the corn-crake a-

-mang the whin-ny knowes.(V.3)Oh ye plea-sure maids and ci-ty dames come

-mang the whin-ny knowes. Ye mai-dens fair an'pleasure's dames drive

-mang the whin-ny knowes. Ye mai-dens fair aye an'plei-sure dames drive

-mang the whin-ny knowes. Ye la-dies a' and plea-sure dames drive

tae the banks o' Doon, Ye'll dear-ly pey yer ev-'ry cent tae a

tae the banks o' Doon, Ye'll dear-ly pay for ev-'ry scent tae a

tae the banks o' Doon,An ye'll dear-ly pey for ev-'ry scent tae the

tae the banks o' Doon, Ye'll dear-ly pey wi' ev-'ry cent tae the

bar-ber for per-fume, (Mm)But ru-ral joy is free tae a' where

bar-ber's for per-fume, But ru-ral joys they're free tae a' where

bar-ber's for per-fume,Aye(bu)t the ru-ral joys they're free tae a'whaur the

bar-ber for per-fume, But ru-ral joy is free tae a' where the

yon wee bur-nie rows And the e-cho mocks the corn-crake a-

scen-ted clo-ver grows,Aye and the e-cho mocks the corn-crake a-

scen-ted clo-ver grows Whaur the e-cho mocks the corn-crake a-

scen-ted clo-ver grows An' the e-cho mocks the corn-crake a-

-mang the whin-ny knowes. (V.4)But noo the sum-mer it is passed and the

-mang the whin-ny knowes.   Well the corn-crake she's noo a-wa' an'the

-mang the whin-ny knowes.

-mang the whin-ny knowes.   Noo the corn-crake is noo a-wa',   the

burn is tae the brim,   The whin-ny knowes are capped wi'snaw an' it

burn is tae the brim,   The whin-ny knowes they're clad wi'snaw that

burn is tae the brim,   The whin-ny knowes are clad wi' snaw   that

taps the high-est yin;   But soon cauld win-ter will be past and the

taps the high-est whin;   But when cauld win-ter it's a-wa', aye an'

tops the high-est rim;   But when the win-ter it is past   and the

sum-mer come a-gain And we'll wel-come back the corn-crake a-

sum-mer claes the skies We'll wel-come back the corn-crake, the

sum-mer comes a-gain   We'll wel-come back the corn-crake, the

-mang the whin-ny knowes.

bird o' ru-ral charm.

bird of ru-ral joy.

Ed Miller. AM9, Rec. A.P. Kinross 1977

(1) The lass that I lo'e best of all she's handsome young and fair,
Wi' her I've spent some bonny nichts doon by the banks o' Ayr.
And wi' her I've spent some bonny nichts where yon wee burnie rows
And the echo mocks the corncrake amang the whinny knowes.

(2) We loved each other dearly, disputes we seldom had,
As constant as the pendulum our hearts beat always glad,
And we searched for love and found it where yon wee burnie rows
And the echo mocks the corncrake amang the whinny knowes.

(3) Oh ye pleasure maids and city dames come tae the banks o' Doon,
Ye'll dearly pey yer every cent tae a barber for perfume,
But rural joy is free tae a' where yon wee burnie rows,
And the echo mocks the corncrake amang the whinny knowes.

(4) But noo the summer it is passed and the burn is tae the brim,
The whinny knowes are capped wi snaw an' it taps the highest yin;
But soon cauld winter will be past and the summer come again
And we'll welcome back the corncrake amang the whinny knowes.

Norman Stewart. SA 1971/195, Rec. F.K. Edinburgh 1971

(1) Oh the lassie I lo'ed first o' all she was handsome young and fair,
Wi' her I spent some merry nichts along the banks o' Ayr.
Wi' her I spent some merry nichts where yon wee burnie rows
Aye an' the echo mocks the corncrake amang the whinny knowes.

(2) We hae lo'ed each ither dearly, disputes we seldom had,
As constant as the pendulum her heart beat always glad,
We socht for joy an' found it where yon wee burnie rows,
Aye and the echo mocks the corncrake amang the whinny knowes.

(3) Ye maidens fair an' pleasure's dames drive tae the banks o' Doon,
Ye'll dearly pay for every scent tae a barber's for perfume,
But rural joys they're 'free tae a' where scented clover grows,
Aye and the echo mocks the corncrake amang the whinny knowes.

(4) Well the corncrake she's noo awa' an' the burns tae the brim,
The whinny knowes they're clad wi snaw that taps the highest whin;
But when cauld winter it's awa', aye an' summer claes the skies
We'll welcome back the corncrake, the bird o' rural charm.

Jack Foley. AM1, Rec. A.P. Kinross 1975

(1) Noo the lass that I lo'ed first of all was handsome young an' fair,
Wi' her I spent some merry nights on the banks o' Ayr.
Wi' her I spent some merry nights whaur yon wee burnie rows
Whaur the echo mocks the corncrake amang the whinny knowes.

(2) We loved each other dearly and disputes we seldom had,
As constant as the pendulum her hairt beat always glad,

We sought for joy an' we found it whaur yon wee burnie rows
Whaur the echo mocks the corncrake amang the whinny knowes.

(3) Ye maidens fair aye an' pleisure dames drive tae the banks o' Doon,
An' ye'll dearly pey for every scent tae the barber's for perfume,
Aye but the rural joys they're free tae a' whaur the scented clover grows
Whaur the echo mocks the corncrake amang the whinny knowes.

Sheila Douglas. SA 1978/80, Rec. I.P. Edinburgh 1978

(1) Oh the lass that I lo'ed best of a' was handsome young and fair,
Wi' her I spent some merry nichts upon the banks o' Ayr.
Wi' her I spent some merry nichts where yon wee burnie rows
An' the echo mocks the corncrake amang the whinny knowes.

(2) We loved each other dearly and disputes we seldom had,
As constant as the pendulum her heart beat always glad.
We socht for love an' found it where yon wee burnie rows
An' the echo mocks the corncrake amang the whinny knowes.

(3) Ye ladies a' and pleasure dames drive tae the banks o' Doon,
Ye'll dearly pey wi' every cent tae the barber for perfume,
Bur rural joy is free tae a' where the scented clover grows
An' the echo mocks the corncrake amang the whinny knowes.

(4) Noo the corncrake is noo awa', the burn is tae the brim,
The whinny knowes are clad wi' snaw that tops the highest rim;
But when the winter it is past and the summer comes again
We'll welcome back the corncrake, the bird of rural joy.

Before Robert Ford published his *Vagabond Songs and Ballads of Scotland* in 1904, a selection had already appeared in the columns of *The People's Journal* — "with the result", Ford noted in his Preface, "that I obtained fresh and interesting particulars about some and additional verses to others". Having stated earlier in the Preface, that in addition to noting down these songs whenever he had the opportunity of hearing them, he had also obtained some songs "through correspondence" and some "from obscure publications", his conclusions seems somewhat naïve: "What was most surprising and gratifying . . . as a result of the 'sifting' of the pieces through the columns of that paper, was to discover that in all parts of the country, despite the fact of their enjoying an *almost exclusively oral existence*, the versions in use, north, east, south and west, were nearly always identical", (my italics). A decade later an exactly identical version of the words of Ford's "Corncrake" song appeared in one of the articles which Gavin Greig contributed to the *Buchan Observer* from 1907 to 1911, (and which were later collected and reprinted in *Folk-Song of the North-East*). Bearing this in mind, a glance at the variations in words of the four versions shown above, at least two of which were learned orally, leads rather to the conclusion that Ford's "almost exclusively oral existence" for the songs is an overstatement.

Ford comments on the "Corncrake" song: "It is quite evidently a modern effusion, and the author may be living. I have met with it in various cheap song-sheets, but nowhere with any name attached. Presumably an Ayrshire ditty, it has yet been sung over the wider area of Scotland". He supplies an air, which only slightly resembles the four closely-related tunes here given, but in any case this might be suspect, for in the Preface Ford bestows grateful thanks on the musical experts, not only "for the supply of tunes" but "no less for their painstaking and capable revision [sic] of many of the melodies"! *Folk-Song of the North-East* gives no melodies, but Greig remarks, of the *Corncrake* words, "This is a pleasant lilt and fairly popular. It is not, however, a true folk-song, but belongs to the class of what may be called 'composed' songs, in the construction of which a certain amount of literary skill and device is exhibited".

Two points about the Ford-Greig words deserve mention: verse 2, line 2 is, "As constant as the pendulum her heart-beat always gaed." And verse 3, line 2 supports the first and the fourth versions above: "You'll pay dearly pay your every cent to barbers for perfume."

Ed Miller learned the song orally from Jimmy Hutchison's singing (and it was a combination of the tune and the treatment of it by Jimmy which he liked: "The same song sung by other singers would probably not have made any impression on me".) An Edinburgh man, of Border family background, Ed has been a student and post-graduate student of Folklore at Austin University, Texas, during most of the seventies. When someone said, during a discussion at Kinross, that it should be "scent" and not "cent" in v.3, he assumed that the line should have run, "Ye'll dearly pey for every scent tae the barber for perfume" — as in two of the versions above. But such a line is clumsy and tautological. "Every cent", which Sheila Douglas also sings, makes more sense and has been endorsed by Ford and Greig. The word for the smallest unit in American currency has been absorbed into common English usage for many years now. But this is another indication that the song is not traditional in origin and is of comparatively recent vintage, unlikely to be earlier than 19th century. The next line, continuing the subject of perfume, should probably end "where the scented clover grows", as in the other three versions.

Singers will often sing a certain song, says Ed, "because their mother did, or their grandfather did and it's therefore part of their personal or family identity, just like accent or other forms of expressive behaviour, the songs become recognisable links with the past which become clichés or verbal landmarks they can cling to. In my case, I didn't learn songs from my family so that my 'family' in terms of learning songs comprises the older and longer established singers of the revival community, and by singing songs like this one, I suppose I was expressing my 'membership' of that community, because the song itself certainly doesn't express anything personal for me in itself, like I can do via "Freedom come all ye", "Generations of change", "Edinburgh toon" and other more recent songs. . . ." Nevertheless he did choose to sing this song, at the Men's Traditional Singing class at Kinross in 1977 — there were no "set" songs — so it's hardly likely that it expressed *nothing* personal for him at that time. There are many other songs through which he could have expressed his "membership of the revival community". He is a very accomplished singer, with a large and varied repertoire, (and I must admit I have heard him sing other songs which moved me more than this did.) His ornamentation is very skilfully put over and he makes use of considerable changes in dynamics.

An outstanding element in this performance is the singer's strong feeling for the rhythmic pulse. He never allows the time structure to falter, but combines a very steady, slow beat with a soaring, floating melodic line. He is the only one of the four singers to introduce B as an integral note in the scale (second last note in the sixth bar of each verse) and not simply as a grace-note. The word "rows", the last word of the third line in the first three verses, does not stop on C as in the other versions but descends a minor third to A, as if in preparation for the first note of the next line. But in the last verse, on the second syllable of "again", he omits this descent and for the first time stops on the C. This change has the effect of slightly arresting the time and of highlighting the approaching end, with the thought that the corncrake will return next year in the continuing cycle of nature, and of human love, which the song celebrates.

Norman Stewart also decorates the melody lavishly. The first line is taken a little more slowly than the rest, and makes an impressive start, with a pause halfway through. One of the most distinctive factors in this interpretation is the pause which marks the close of every line. When combined with the delicate ornamentation, this has a kind of meditative effect, as if time were standing still in nature as well. The timing generally is fairly free throughout, and calls to mind the wilful, brooding *rubato* of pibroch music.

Jack Foley noted his version from his grandmother's singing, her recollection of it being touched off by hearing the beginning of this song-track on *The Stewarts of Blair* record (Topic 12T 138). She learned it while she was a teenage girl in Central Scotland, towards the end of last century. She did not have a fourth verse. Jack likes the song because it is (1) evocative of the countryside (he is a keen walker and climber), (2) anti-materialistic, (3) reasonably local, and lastly (4) because it has a good tune. He is attracted in the first place to the tune of a song: "if the tune is good enough, and I don't like the words, I'll try and write better ones". A journalist by profession, his songs are "mostly climbing songs", and although not as yet published they have begun to enter oral tradition. (The connection between the folk song movement and walking or climbing was stronger in its earlier years). Jack also finds links between the words of this song and his own experience: "(1) boyhood wandering in the countryside, (2) idealistic teenage 'puppy-love', (3) boredom with the shallow rat-race mentality of today's society. (Unfortunately, like most climbers and campers, I hate corncrakes — they never give you a minute's peace!)"

As often happens, the tune of his first verse is not quite typical. The octave leap down, at "of all", appears in bar 1, as it does in all other versions, but by bar 7 the lesser leap of a major sixth, from A down to C, has appeared instead, and is repeated in bars 1 and 7 of the other two verses. By contrast, the lift of the tune from D to high D in bars 3 and 5 of each verse is accomplished more quickly, and more dramatically, with only a short bridging-stop on the A, as compared with the other three versions which take longer to reach the high D and proceed by smaller and more frequent steps. This is, too, the only version which is predominantly in simple time rather than in compound. But the most striking characteristic of this rendering is the utter conviction which comes through. All four have some of this but Jack's wins by at least a length — and I felt this at first hearing, before discovering any of his special associations with the song. It is true that Jack Foley always sings in this impassioned way, with swirling decorations and a kind of controlled abandonment, and this may be because he subscribes to "the now unfashionable theory that a song only comes into existence at the time it is sung, by me or someone else", and you can hear — and see — that he is actually re-creating every time he sings. I doubt if this kind of performance would be possible unless the song expressed something personal for the singer, and this singer's comments make it clear that he only chooses songs which do this.

Sheila Douglas recorded her version at the School of Scottish Studies, and the tape includes her comments: ". . . the reason I like it so much is because my father's from Ayrshire and I have childhood memories of hearing the corncrake in the fields around Dalry — so it really conjures that up for me". Her singing here is markedly different from the other three represented above. It is simpler, very sparingly ornamented, and the warm, rich voice and liquid phrasing supply the expressiveness. The first accented note of lines 1 and 4 of each verse is always A (Ed Miller does this only at the beginning of the song) in contrast to the other versions where it is high D, and she is the only one to use F as an integral part of the scale (bars 3 and 5 of each verse) and not as a grace-note. Sheila and Ed both have "love" in v. 2, line 3, while the other two have "joy", as in the Ford-Greig words. Sheila first heard Norman Stewart sing this song, and later Sheila MacGregor from whom she got the words.

Jimmy MacBeath used to sing this (see chapbook, vol. 3 no. 2). According to Sheila Douglas the song is very closely linked with Davie MacQueen, the Border singer accidently killed in the late sixties, from whose singing Norman Stewart learned it.

In these four versions there are no extensive differences in the words and in the basic shape of the tune, but the actual performances vary considerably. These variations are due to the differing personalities and vocal styles of the singers and to their conception of the whole song — the words, the music, the meaning and the associations.

Johnnie my man.

(V. 1)"John-nie my man, dae ye no think o' ri-sin',The nicht it's weel

"John-nie my man, will ye no think o' ri-sin',The night is weel

"John-nie my man, dae ye no think on ri-sin',The day it is

"Oh John-nie ma man, dae ye no think o' ri-sin', For the fire is gaen

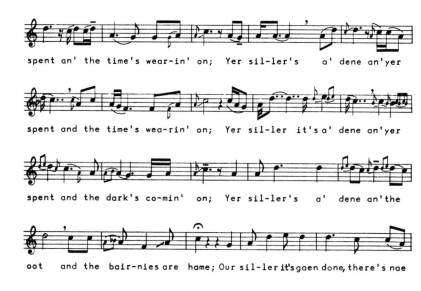

spent an' the time's wear-in' on; Yer sil-ler's a' dene an'yer

spent and the time's wea-rin' on; Yer sil-ler it's a' dene an'yer

spent and the dark's co-min' on; Yer sil-ler's   a' dene an'the

oot   and the bair-nies are hame; Our sil-ler it's gaen done, there's nae

stowp's toom be-fore you, A-rise up my John-nie an' come a - wa'

stowp's toom be-fore you, A-rise up   my Johnnie an' come a - wa'

stowp's toom be-fore ye, Rise up my man John-nie and come a - wa'

meal in the bar-rel,   Oh rise up   my Johnnie an' come a - wa'

hame". (V. 2) "Oh wha   is that I   hear spea-kin' sae kind-ly, For I

hame."   "Oh wha's that I hear fa   is spea-kin' sae kind-ly, Fine I

hame."   "Whae is   that I hear   spea-kin' sae kind-ly,   I

hame"."Who is that there at the door there her voice sounds sae kind-ly, It

ken it's   the voice o' my ain wi-fie Jean; Syne **come by me**

ken weel **the voice** o' my ain wi-fie Jean; Come **sit doon, ma**

ken be   the voice it's ma ain wi-fie Jean;   Come **be   ma**

sounds like the voice o' my wee wi-fie Jean; Oh haud ye   a -

dea - rie   an' sit doon be - side me, There is   room   in this

dea - rie, come sit doon be - side me, There is room in this

dea - rie   and sit doon be - side me, There is room in this

- while,   my   bon - ny wee las-sie For you   ken I've been

taiv-ren for   mair   than ene". (V.3)"John-nie my   man,   oor

tai -vern for   mair than jest ene". "John-nie my man,   oor

tai -vern for   mair for-bye me". "John-nie my man,   your

drin-kin' o' whis-kyan'wine"She said,"Johnnie ma lad-die,that's what I've

bairns is a' gree-tin', Nae meal in the bar - rel tae

bair-nies are a' gree-tin', Nae meal in the bar - rel tae

bairns are a' gree-tin', Nae meal in the bar - rel tae

come for tae tell you, You're sit-tin' there drin-kin' o'

fill their wee wames; While sit-tin' here drin - kin' ye

fill their wee wame(s); While ye sit here drin - king you

fill their wee wames; While ye sit here a-drin - kin' ye

whis-ky an' wine; The fire is gaen oot an' the

leave me la - men - tin', A - rise up my John - nie an'

leave me la - men - tin', A - rise up my John-nie and

leave me la - men - tin', Rise up my man John-nie and

bair-nies are hun - gry, Oh rise up my John-nie an'

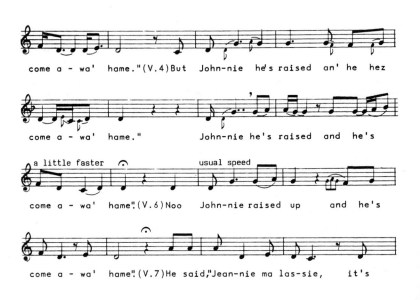

come a - wa' home."(V.4)But John-nie he's raised an' he hez

come a - wa' home."   John-nie he's raised and he's

a little faster   usual speed
come a - wa' home".(V.6)Noo John-nie raised up   and he's

come a - wa' home".(V.7)He said,"Jean-nie ma las-sie,   it's

got the door o -pen, Say-in', "Cursed be the taiv - ren that's

pushed the door o - pen, Cry-ing, "Cursed be the tai - vern that's

flung the door o - pen, "My curse on the tai - vern that

tak' you ma hand, dear, Oh gie me yer bon - nie wee

e'er let me in; An' cursed be the whis-ky that maks me sae

e'er let me in; And cursed be the whis-ky that maks me sae

first took me in; My curse on the whis-ky that mak'd me aye

hand in mine, An' I'll give up drin-kin', oh Jean-nie ma

thir-sty, Fare - weel tae ye whisky for I'll a - wa' hame".

thir-sty, Fare - weel tae ye whis-ky for I'm a - wa' hame".

thir-sty," Say-in', "Far'thee weel whis-ky for I'm a - wa' hame".

las-sie, And   I'll   go   hame to that faim'-ly o' mine".

Lizzie Higgins. SA 1973/174, Rec. S.S. Aberdeen 1973

(1) "Johnnie my man, dae ye no think o' risin',
   The nicht it's weel spent an' the time's wearin' on;
   Yer siller's a' dene an' yer stowp's toom before you,
   Arise up my Johnnie an' come awa' hame."

(2) "Oh wha is that I hear speakin' see kindly,
   For I ken it's the voice o' my ain wifie Jean;
   Syne come by me dearie an' sit doon beside me,
   There is room in this taivren for mair than ene."

(3) "Johnnie my man, oor bairns is a' greetin',
   Nae meal in the barrel tae fill their wee wames;
   While sittin' here drinkin' ye leave me lamentin',
   Arise up my Johnnie an' come awa' hame."

(4) But Johnnie he's raised an' he hez got the door open,
   Sayin', "Cursed be the taivren that's e'er let me in;
   An' cursed be the whisky that maks me sae thirsty,
   Fareweel tae ye whisky for I'll awa' hame."

Stanley Robertson. SA 1973/112, Rec. A.M. Kinross 1973

(1) "Johnnie my man, will ye no think o' risin',
   The night is weel spent and the time's wearin' on;
   Yer siller it's a' dene an' yer stowp's toom before you,
   Arise up my Johnnie an' come awa' hame".

(2) "Oh wha's that I hear fa is speakin' sae kindly,
   Fine I ken weel the voice o' my ain wifie Jean;
   Come sit doon, ma dearie, come sit doon beside me,
   There is room in this taivern for mair than jest ene".

(3) "Johnnie my man, oor bairnies are a' greetin',
   Nae meal in the barrel tae fill their wee wame(s);
   While ye sit here drinking you leave me lamentin',
   Arise up my Johnnie and come awa' hame".

(4) Johnnie he's raised and he's pushed the door open,
   Crying, "Cursed be the taivern that's e'er let me in;
   And cursed be the whisky that maks me sae thirsty,
   Fareweel tae ye whisky for I'm awa' hame".

Cy Lawrie. SA 1971/242, Rec. J.P. Kinross 1971

(1) "Johnnie my man, dae ye no think on risin',
   The day it is spent and the dark's comin' on;
   Yer siller's a' dene an' the stowp's toom before ye;
   Rise up my man Johnnie and come awa' hame."

(2) "Whae is that I hear speakin' sae kindly,
    I ken be the voice it's ma ain wifie Jean;
    Come be ma dearie and sit doon beside me,
    There is room in this taivern for mair forbye me."

(3) "Johnnie my man, your bairns are a' greetin',
    Nae meal in the barrel tae fill their wee wames;
    While ye sit here a-drinkin ye leave me lamentin',
    Rise up my man Johnny and come awa' hame".

(4) "Dae ye no remember on the first days we coorted,
    On a bed o' primroses we baith did sit doon
    A-pickin' the floo'ers in each ithers' company,
    We ne'er thocht it lang then nor thocht tae gae hame."

(5) "Aye weel I remember on the days that ye mention,
    But they are awa' and they'll ne'er come again.
    Just think on the present an' try tae amend it,
    Rise up my man Johnnie and come awa' hame".

(6) Noo Johnnie raised up and he's flung the door open,
    "My curse on the taivern that first took me in;
    My curse on the whisky that mak'd me aye thirsty,"
    Sayin', "Far' thee weel whisky for I'm awa' hame."

Duncan Williamson. SA 1976/29 Rec. L.W. Lochqilphead 1976

(1) "Oh Johnnie ma man, dae ye no think o' risin',
    For the fire is gaen oot an' the bairnies are hame;
    Our siller it's gaen done, there's nae meal in the barrel,
    Oh rise up my Johnnie an' come awa' hame".

(2) "Who is that there at the door there, her voice sounds sae kindly,
    It sounds like the voice o' my wee wifie Jean;
    Oh haud ye awhile, my bonny wee lassie,
    For you ken I've been drinkin' o' whisky an' wine."

(3) She said, "Johnnie ma laddie, that's what I've come for tae tell you,
    You're sittin' there drinkin' o' wisky an' wine;
    The fire is gaen oot an' the bairnies are hungry,
    Oh rise up my Johnnie an' come awa' hame".

(4) He said, "Jeannie ma lassie, come sit doon beside me
    There's plenty o' room in this tavern for two,
    For I've been a-drinkin', oh Jeannie ma lassie,
    But I've been a-thinkin', oh ma lassie o' you.

(5) Oh curse tae the whisky, it's what I've been drinkin',
    An' curse tae the whisky an' curse tae the wine,
    Oh curse tae the whisky, it's what I've been drinkin',
    For it's made me neglect that fine faim'ly o' mine".

(6) She said, "Johnnie, my laddie, it's one thing I'll tell you
You've been sittin' here drinkin' noo since nine,
The fire is gaen oot an' there's nae meal in the barrel
An' I'm gettin' worried aboot that faimly o' mine".

(7) He said, "Jeannie ma lassie, it's tak' you ma hand, dear,
Oh gie me yer bonny wee hand in mine,
An' I'll give up drinkin', oh Jeannie ma lassie,
And I'll go hame to that faim'ly o' mine".

Versions of these words are to be found in both Ford's and Ord's collections, and also in Greig's *Folk-Song in Buchan*. Ord supplies a tune which is fairly closely related to the four shown above but which differs in lines 2 and 4 of the verse (bars 5–8 and 13–16 above, and bars 3–4 and 7–8 in Ord). All three collectors give six verses corresponding to Cy Laurie's. Ford and Ord add on another three which describe in some detail Johnnie's resolution to "leave aff the drinking" — or "the auld deeds" (Ford) — and the happier home of the family thereafter. These three verses, cast in the explicitly moralising vein so popular in Victorian times, have since it appears been dropped. Ord's version is the first item under his heading of "Convivial Songs" — though anything less convivial it would be hard to imagine. Both Ford and Ord state that it was a favourite street song all over Scotland in the 1860's and seventies, or even earlier, and, Ford adds, "found ready sale always in penny-sheet form, chiefly among those who required most its pointed lesson". Greig's remarks in introducing his version of the words, and apropos the "temperance" lay he has referred to, are profoundly important: "It does not so much matter what has been the origin or genesis of these lyrics. The fact remains, significant and satisfactory, that they have been adopted by the folk-songist".

Lizzie Higgins learned "Johnnie my man" when she was a child, from the singing of her father Donald Higgins. She likes the song, "because of the tune first and then the words. The message . . . is to stop drinking and feed his children, and look after his wife, children and his home, and to stop them suffering uncalled-for hardship caused by his drinking. No connection with this song in my life as I never knew hunger or cold, my father always saw we were well fed, and well clothed". Lizzie always starts this song by pitching the opening three words a fifth higher than in the remaining three verses, and a very fine start it makes. Part of her distinctive style is her masterly treatment of grace-notes. There is very little variation in dynamics (which may be defined as change of tone, mainly in volume) and the contrast with the other three singers, particularly Stanley Robertson and Duncan Williamson, is striking. One of her variations in the tune, which although not written here as grace-notes produces the impression of decoration, is in bars 3 and 11 of verse 3. In all the other verses there is an uninterrupted downward leap of a fifth from A to D, and this is found also in the other singers' versions (although not in Duncan's bar 3 of verses 2 to 4, where he has a different tune for the opening line). But in verse 3, where the wife speaks of the children's sufferings and of her own, Lizzie fills in this downward leap with intermediate steps in the scale, in a somewhat wavering and less definite way. It may be fanciful to see in this an attempt to express the intensity of feeling at these points, but it is worth considering. Lizzie is extremely sensitive to the meanings in her verbal text, and her artistry in expressing these through the music is conscious (Another version of this song is on Lizzie Higgins's first record, *Princess of the Thistle* (Topic 12T185)).

Stanley Robertson got his version from his father William Robertson, and from his great-aunt Maggie Stewart, sister of Maria (Jeannie Robertson's mother). Here are his introductory remarks to this performance, recorded at Kinross in the Men's Singing (competition) class: "I'd like now to do more a lament type — a very, very old song that's been in the family . . . sometimes when I'm singing the song I get very emotional so if I greet dinnae take any notice, just listen to the words o' the song. It's cried "Johnny ma man", it tells the story of a man who drinks, and I suppose if any of yez have been brought up by a drunken father ye would understand . . . what the story is about". In a letter replying to questions (1980) he wrote: "I like this song because it is true to life. How many basically good men have ruined their homes because of whisky, and I know personally many 'Johnnies'. . . . When the realisaton comes to the drunkard of how much he has deprived his wife and children it leaves a feeling of deep remorse but to many a reconciliation and resolution. I love the haunting tune that sends shivers up my spine and I like its beautiful grace-noting. It is a song that lingers in the mind long after the singer has stopped. . . . Its message is for fathers to make their homes their castles and their wives queens. . . . It is against any other organisation that detracts from that home-loving spirit . . . and that peace and plenty abide in the homes that have love abundant. It advises against going to taverns. I am temperant and abhor alcohol taken in large quantities at any time. I have experience seeing my father drunk many times and I hated the scenes that took place. [Stanley also said that his father, like Johnnie, later gave up drinking.] Perhaps for this reason I preferred not to imbibe myself. . . . I belive it would be an old song because of the verse 'Nae meal in the barrel tae fill their wee wames', because long ago in Scotland folk used only meal and herring tae live on.

Although I only sing four verses I have heard more verses but I feel that they were added at a much later time. The tune of the longer version is different and the wording seems more modern, nearer music-hall period style. My version I believe is from an older version than the longer one commonly sung in the folk scene".

I have not found any other tune for this song, but a careful examination of the various sets of words lends support to Stanley's last point. In comparison with the succint 4-stanza version shown above, the two extra verses of "flowery" reminiscence lack punch (Cy Laurie's and Greig's verses 4 and 5, Ford's and Ord's verses 3 and 4), and don't accord with the urgent, minimal 4-verse dialogue which indeed says everything. As for the last 3 verses in Ford and Ord, they are embarrassingly *de trop* and sentimental to our taste in a "nearer music-hall period style". (Although one has to admit that the description of subsequent happier conditions does show Johnnie's good resolutions as actually put into practice.)

Stanley sings this even more slowly than Lizzie, and at less than half Cy Laurie's fastest pace. I remember well the performance recorded on this tape: it was one of the most grief-laden I have ever heard, and although Stanley himself didn't greet, a few furtive handkerchiefs appeared amongst the rest of us. He is the only singer here who regularly (at bars 2 and 10 of the verse) introduces the minor sixth, B flat, thus placing the melody in the Aeolian mode. The mid-cadence on C, bar 8, preceded by F and A in bar 7, feels like the dominant note of the relative major, F major. Duncan Williamson does almost the same at these two bars. (The other two also have a mid-cadence on C, but in the bar before they descend only to G and not F: the C therefore sounds more like the third of A, the dominant. The tonic is always a minor mode on D.) At the end of each verse, Stanley arrives at the low tonic note, D, at least a bar before the others, which in this particular instance seems to add to the sombre mood.

Cy Laurie thinks he heard Lizzie sing this, at Glasgow Folk Centre in the late sixties, at one of her first public appearances. He represents the man as recalling their courtship (v. 4), and the woman replying, whereas in the three printed sources mentioned the order of these speakers is reversed. Although this is taken at the fastest pace of the four it is not at all hurried. It is more relaxed and straightforward but it still has "the hairt-feeling", as Stanley would say.

Duncan Williamson's words are considerably different from the others, and all seven verses have the same hall-mark of style. V. 6 seems to repeat v. 3, although in somewhat different words. Duncan does something similar in "Ma laddie's bedside". His opening melody, with its rising fifth in contrast to the more common fourth, has settled by v. 2 into another which he adheres to for the rest of the song. This new 4-bar phrase (bars 1–4 of vv. 2 onwards) recalls most hauntingly the opening bars of that powerful and — at least in Scotland — rarely heard Irish song, "The bold Fenian men". Duncan first heard "Johnnie my man" sung by his father's sister, around 1942, at Tarbert in Argyll. He says, "I like this song because it was sung by a person I respected. . . . I like the theme of the song. A man who was a drunkard all the days of his life had made a promise to his wife and kept it — he is worthy of anybody's respect. It connects with everybody's life who respects that kind of man: those who would like to be like him, who have tried and perhaps failed". Duncan also says that this song among the travellers is "as old as the travellers", and that his auntie had said this (i.e. the story in the song) had actually happened to a traveller man and woman.

The words of these four versions contain more Scots words and pronunciations than any of those in the three printed collections, although Grieg has rather more than the other two.

Appendix II

Folk Music In Education

Music is my best friend. People alter and don't want you any more but music never lets you down.

A schoolgirl on TV[1]

Has the Revival had any influence on educational practice in Scotland? Are children and young people exposed during their school years to this kind of culture, the "common" culture of their own or other countries, as they are undoubtedly exposed to "high" culture?

In an attempt to answer these questions, and especially the second one, I sent questionnaires (a) to secondary schools — state, grant-aided and independent — and (b) to centres for tertiary education, during the period between June 1979 and March 1981. A quarter of the independent schools approached have an upper age limit of 14 years for pupils; the remaining three-quarters, plus all the grant-aided and almost all the state schools, cater for young people of up to 16 years or over. Primary schools have not been questioned, chiefly because children's songs and singing-games, while constituting an immensely important area for research, lie somewhat outside the scope of this book.[2] (Many of the songs, ballads and tales which have come to the force during the last thirty years are, however, suitable for inclusion in primary school work.) Special schools — for physically, mentally or psychologically handicapped chlidren — are not included, although many teachers in these schools have found the use of folk music to be beneficial.

SECONDARY EDUCATION
Questionnaires were addressed to the Head Teacher, and contained three questions:

---

1. See footnotes page 340.

(1) Does your school include folk music, vocal or instrumental, in any part of its curriculum, in e.g. English, History, Languages etc., as well as or apart from Music lessons?

(2) Does your school have a folk music club, in after-school hours or during a lunch-hour?

(3) If the answer to either of the above questions is "Yes", how valuable do you think this has been to the pupils and to the school generally? If "No", do you think it would be valuable if folk music *were* to be included in either or both of these ways?

The aim of the first two questions was to obtain information on the basis of which a general picture could be sketched, an initial outline rather than a detailed portrayal, (which could be filled in by possible future investigation.) The term "folk music" was left undefined, in the hope that teachers would particularise in their replies: a few did, but detailed comments appeared mainly in the answers to question 3 which concerned value judgements. It follows that, in question (1), the term "folk music" must cover a wide range of meanings, from for example the traditional, unaccompanied singing of a ballad, on disc or tape or very occasionally by a visiting folk singer, to the conventional version of one such as "Barbara Allen" (*Oxford Song Book*) sung by a whole class with piano accompaniment. In question (2) the field narrows, and "yes" replies are confined to voluntary participation by pupils outwith school lesson hours.

In the second table percentages, except for the totals, have been omitted because absolute values are small. (See table 1 for the relations expressed by these percentage figures, given in parenthesis). The fifth column of figures is also omitted, since the only school with a folk club did not include folk music in the curriculum.

In both tables, percentages are given correct to the nearest whole number, or the nearest even number when a half occurs.

For State schools, batches of questionnaires were sent to each Region's Director of Education, who then sent a copy to every school. The Shetland Islands and Renfrew were exceptional — see footnote below table 1 — and also the Borders region who received their Directors's form of the questionnaire. This contained questions 1 and 2, with request for details, but no question regarding value. No second attempt was made to elicit replies from schools which had received questionnaires but had not returned them: it was felt that failure to reply was itself noteworthy. There could be various reasons for such failure . . . for example, lack of interest in the subject? Overwork and exhaustion? Irritation at a superfluity of other questionnaires received?

The results are summarised in Tables 1 and 2.

TABLE 1 STATE SCHOOLS

Region	No. of schools	No. of replies (In parenthesis: % relative to no. of schools)	Folk music in curriculum (In parenthesis: % relative to no. of replies)	Folk Club	Both
1. Borders	9	7 (78)	7 (100)	3 (43)	3 (43)
2. Central	21	11 (52)	7 (64)	4 (36)	3 (33)
3. Dumfries & Galloway	18	14 (78)	11 (79)	4 (29)	3 (21)
4. Fife	21	5 (24)	3 (60)	2 (40)	1 (25)
5. Grampian	42	17 (40)	11 (65)	5 (29)	4 (24)
6. Highland	29	7 (24)	3 (43)	3 (43)	3 (43)
7. Lothian	47	14 (30)	9 (64)	6 (43)	4 (29)
8. Orkney Islands	7	2 (29)	1 (50)	0 (0)	0 (0)
9. Shetland Islands*	9	–	– (c. 50)	1 (11)	–
10. Strathclyde Divisions: –					
Argyll & Bute	9	6 (67)	2 (33)	1 (17)	0 (0)
Ayr	31	10 (32)	4 (40)	4 (40)	2 (20)
Dunbarton	25	5 (20)	2 (40)	3 (60)	1 (20)
Glasgow	57	29 (51)	17 (59)	5 (17)	5 (17)
Lanark	36	9 (25)	6 (67)	5 (56)	4 (44)
Renfrew*	32	–	– (c. 50)	– (c. 50)	–
Str'clyde totals (excluding Renf.)	158	59 (37)	31 (52)	18 (30)	12 (20)
11. Tayside	32	24 (75)	15 (62)	4 (17)	3 (12)
12. Western Isles	15	6 (40)	2 (33)	3 (50)	2 (33)
13. Anonymous replies	–	17 (–)	11 (65)	7 (41)	5 (29)
Totals (excluding Shetland & Renfrew	399	183 (46)	111 (61)	60 (33)	43 (24)

* For Shetland Islands Region, and for Renfrew Division of Strathclyde Region, in both cases the Music Adviser replied giving approximate percentages, based on enquiries which he made in lieu of sending out questionnaires; these approximations are given. Only one secondary school in Shetland, in Lerwick, has a folk club; due to travelling schedules, the more isolated schools have very few societies.

TABLE 2 GRANT-AIDED AND INDEPENDENT SCHOOLS

Region	No. of schools	No. of replies	Folk music in curriculum	Folk Clubs
1. Borders	1	1	1	
2. Central	2	2	2	
3. Dumfries & Galloway	7	3	1	1
4. Fife	2	2	2	
5. Grampian	9	2	1	
6. Highland	1	0		
7. Lothian	24	8	4	
[8. Orkney 9. Shetland]	no such schools			
10. Strathclyde	19	7	2	
11. Tayside	7	2	2	
[12. Western Isles]	– no such schools			
Totals	72	27 (38)	15 (56)	1 (4)

State schools: The response rate (second column of figures) varies considerably, but almost half of the schools which received questionnaires returned them. Of those that did, just under two-thirds include folk music in the curriculum, and a third have folk clubs.

Borders, and Dumfries and Galloway, show the highest response rate; they also have the highest proportion of schools with curricular folk music. The four lowest percentages for curricular activity come from the west: Western Isles (notwithstanding an enthusiastic letter from the Music Adviser — see below for an extract), and the three coastal divisions of Stathclyde: Argyll and Bute, Ayr and Dunbarton. The next lowest figure for folk music in the curriculum comes from Highland, the largest and the most sparsely populated region in Scotland. Only Western Isles and Dunbarton have a greater percentage of schools with folk clubs than with curricular folk music. The four divisions of Strathclyde containing numbers of schools ranging from 25 to 36 show relatively high proportions with folk clubs. The two remaining divisions in this region show the second lowest figure for clubs: Argyll and Bute probably for reasons similar to Shetland (see footnote to Table 1), and Glasgow possibly because it offers abundant alternative musical activity for young people — folk, pop or art music. Tayside also has a low proportion of folk clubs.

Grant-aided and Independent schools: The response rate is considerably lower than with State schools; the proportion with folk music in the curriculum is also lower, while folk clubs are almost non-existent. Only two regions gave sufficient replies for a comparison with State schools to be possible: in both these regions, Strathclyde and Lothian, state schools have a higher proportion of schools with folk music in either category.

The third question brought forth a spate of comments and reflections, some of which are quoted below. The words in parentheses indicate first the category to which the school in question belongs (G.A. = Grant Aided, Ind. = Independent; all others are State schools), and second the answers given by the school to questions 1 and 2 in that order. "Both" means two "yes"s; "neither", two "no"s. Comments have been placed under headings which show the aspect referred to; where more than one aspect is dealt with, that which seems the most important decides the heading. Additions in square brackets are my own.

General aspects of value

'I feel that folk music has an important part to play in education as folk items are "the abstracts and brief chronicles of the time". Parents are also interested and a most successful "folk night" was organised for the parents.' (Both)

'I feel it should be. . . .' (Neither)

'I would be interested in any material if available.'[3] (Both)

'We find there is a great ignorance nowadays even of the best folk songs, and we hope at least we are bringing them to the pupils' attention' (Both)

'Of course, since it is part of their culture.' (Yes, no)

'There is only small interest, but what there is, is increasing.' (Ind., yes, no)

17 schools returned a plain "No, no, yes" to the three questions, showing that, although these schools did not give any scope to folk music, it was felt that it would be a valuable activity.

Value as related to particular subjects: Music, English, History, Languages, etc.; also integration between subjects

'Use of folk music is of value — descriptions of social conditions, and in case of narrative songs, a form of presentation that pupils find enjoyable as well as interesting. Some music also creates a mood.' (Yes, no)

'I feel it is extremely valuable for pupils to be aware of the historical and social relevance of the folk tradition, particularly here in the North East where the tradition is so rich.' (Yes, no)

(1) 'Themes are essentially human. (2) May often be relevant to local history and places. (3) Traditional Scots folk songs can introduce elements of Scots vocabulary which pupils may not know. (4) It may gain from feelings of "nationalism" and/or "patriotism".' (Yes, no)

'Relating subjects taught . . . to real life experience is a constant aim . . . — hence the important role of including folk song . . . (Both)

'Co-relation with History, Geography, Scottish Crafts, and all aspects of Scottish life.' (Yes, no)

'Value for "Jacobite Patch". "Scotland in the days of Wallace and Bruce". Mining theme in O-grade.' (Yes, no)

'My aim is to intensify the depth of feeling for, and understanding of, our history.' (Ind., yes, no)

'Very valuable to English and Music depts. of the school, and has helped the school curriculum very much by making it more attractive.' (Both)

'Folk song culture — Related to the classics — Tchaikowski, "Cappriccio Italian" — Liszt — Brahms etc. . .' (Yes, no)

'The value of folk music is as great as that of composed music.' (Ind., yes, no)

'Sections of music syllabus extensively taught through folk music: e.g. Spread of culture through U. States; Spread of instruments Far East to West

Europe; Tonality in world music; Social purpose and development of Folksong types; Comparative studies in Western European and American melodies and words. Scottish fiddle music types; Music as the voice of Revolution, nineteenth and twentieth centuries; etc. etc.' (Both)

'Used in English as follows:
Thematic material, e.g. Adam McNaughton — "Where is the Glasgow", Jim McLean — "Farewell to Glasgow".
Unit Study: Street Songs, Playground Songs etc.
Background material to literature, e.g. songs from Civil Rights Movement to set context for a study of "To Kill a Mocking Bird".
Illustrative or stimulus material for writing, e.g. Matt McGinn's "The Dundee Ghost", Eric Bogle's "The Band Played Waltzing Matilda".
Provides variety — relates to other parts of culture which have been overlaid — a direct method of communicaton.' (From a Glasgow school; yes, no)

The national (not confined to Scotland) and local aspects; use of the Scots language

'A knowledge of the music of a variety of folk cultures is necessary for all pupils. . . . (Yes, no)

(From a Border school which holds an annual competitive festival, vocal and instrumental, concerned with music related to the local Common Riding.) 'No doubt that this will assist future generations to keep the "Common Riding" alive.' (No other replies)

'Yes. It gives a link with the living music of the people of Scotland and [is] therefore very enjoyable.' (Yes, no)
(This school has a Scottish Country Dance band, holds Scottish dances, and often stages all-Scottish evenings for parents' association, etc.)

(From Tiree) 'As far as the island culture is concerned, the revival and performance of traditional Gaelic airs with words has appealed to the children, who are taught Gaelic anyway.' (Yes, not as yet)

'Very valuable. Though small at the moment the club is expecting new members from the incoming pupils from Primary; then the work can be extended. A Gaelic choir is also to be formed in the new session.' (No, yes)

'The pupils have the opportunity to make music in a less formal atmosphere and to maintain the tradition of the local culture.' (Both)
(This comment is from a Stornoway school. The Region's Adviser of Music also wrote: ". . . the Western Isles Council policy on Bilingualism has led to a development in the art of folk singing which is probably unique to Scotland. Two full-time instructors are employed by the Council to teach and develop the traditional art of folk-singing and in addition there are piping instructors employed solely to visit and instruct in the art of piping".)

'Folk music, not necessarily restricted to Scotland, is an important component in formal and informal education, not only for its musical quality but to convey by another medium something of the culture of our own or another country.' (Both)

'. . . it is generally accessible music for the pupils and it ought to be an acknowledged part of their national identity.' (G.A., yes, no)

See also last quotation under *Difficulties.*

Enjoyment by pupils. This has been referred to in several of the above quotations, but some replies particularly stressed this aspect.

'. . . the enjoyment factor is large, and anything that provides enjoyment is of great value. It is important for this generation at least to attempt to play the music of their ancestors.' (Both)

'. . . may motivate pupils by appealing to an established interest. (Both)

'Very valuable indeed in creating communal activity of a creative kind. In conferring pleasure, it helps create a happy school environment.' (Both)

(Of folk club) 'It has been an invaluable source of enjoyment for both pupils and staff. Helping pupils to appreciate each other and work together for a common purpose.' (Both)

(Of annual Folk Music night) 'Very enjoyable — to staff, pupils and parents. Adds another dimension to school life.' (No, yes)

'It is much enjoyed by many pupils.' (G.A., yes, no)

Service to the community, and involvement of parents (referring mainly to Folk Clubs)

'Very valuable to both pupils and school. Club well known in community for entertaining old folk etc. Also used to help school fund raising events.' (No, yes)

(Has Scottish country dance band) 'Makes a valuable contribution to pupils' broad education. Very valuable to school — play in concerts, musical evenings, school Summer Fair. Community Service — entertaining at hospitals, eventide homes.' (No, yes)

'*Very.* The club entertains senior citizens, holds an annual concert, does a great deal of good work.' (Both)

Experience of performing . . . reference to Pop music . . . and reference to pupils not musically literate (i.e. the large majority)

'A high value is set on the activities of the Folk Club, it being felt that it affords what might be described as an outlet for natural, hopefully spontaneous singing, dancing etc. The "gimmicks" used in the reproduction of pop music make it impossible for the individual child to participate actively in "pop". . . . (Both)

'The main value arises from the fact that school children tend to reject folk music in favour of pop *but* the moment they become involved practically, i.e. playing guitar or tuned percussion etc., the world of Folk Music opens to them. I feel that the revival is largely due to massive involvement with guitars etc.' (Both)

'Very good medium for development of expression and self-confidence, particularly through public performance. Good method of forming links between school and community through [local] Festival.' (No, yes)

'Valuable in its ability to accommodate the talents of those who are not good music readers and its ability to reach those not involved in other musical activities in the school.' (Both)

'The ceilidh band makes a great contribution to the extra-curricular activities in the school. It is trained by the principal teacher of mathematics.' (Both)

'A very successful Folk Evening has been organised in two successive years in conjunction with the Parent Teacher Association.' (Both)

'Extremely valuable — lunchtime folk club over-subscribed.' (Both)

'Valuable as groups contribute to school concerts, church services, etc., as well as developing leisure interests for the pupils.' (G.A., no, yes)

Instrumental music (see also comment from Stornoway, p. 326, and several others above)

(From the Adviser in Music, Shetland) 'Traditional fiddle instruction [chiefly by Tom Anderson] is offered in a number of schools, and we have in the region of 70–80 children learning at present. They are taught initially in small groups and later individually, and they feature frequently in school and village hall concerts and on local radio.'

'In Music Department, Folk Song (vocal and instrumental) is studied. There is a strong feeling for traditional music in this area. We present certificate candidates in Bagpipes and Accordion.' (Yes, no)

'Would like personally to see much more folk music taught, e.g. — Tom Anderson type of Fiddle Instruction. There is nothing like this I understand in our region.' (Yes, no)

'At lunch times there are daily piping sessions.' (Both)

'Twice weekly there are Piping and Drumming classes and our small pipe band is an enthusiastic group.' (Ind., yes, no)

'. . . Pupils learn to recognise the different speeds, rhythms and general musical features of the March, Strathspey, Reel and Slow Air, and we listen to Ron Gonella's recording especially, in detail.
I myself play the bagpipes (having been Pipe-Major of . . . a very successful band which still exists along with many other independent school — and a growing number of state school — bands). . . . We spend time in

class discussing the pipes and investigating their construction, and social and historical significance.

A useful and enjoyable lesson is to demonstrate the wide-ranging styles of music with which the pipes have become involved. . . . (Ind., yes, no)

Doubts and reservations

'The "club" type activities have educative value only in the broadest definition of education.' (Both)

'I find there is not a general response to folk music (i.e. *trad* folk) but some to work songs etc. . . . (Yes, no)

'The philosophy of this Music Department . . . deals with the Training of Sensibility. Any introduction of separate music clubs is unnecessary and would put the school back in terms of methodology and credibility.' (Yes, no)

'It has some value but must never play a really prominent part. So much so-called folk music is bogus.' (Yes, no)

'Limited value but much more should be made of it.' (Yes, no)

'"Folk" suffers a little in my personal prejudiced judgement from too close an association with "pubs".' (Yes, no)

'At the moment we have other priorities higher than a folk music club. Nor has there been any noticeable demand for one. . . .' (Ind., yes, no)

Only 14 of the questionnaires returned show definitely negative answers to question 3 (and of these, 6 have folk music in the curriculum and 1 has a club). Two give a plain "No", and comments in the others range from the brief (Doubtful, Dubious, Of little value, Not particularly, etc.) to one longer reply:

'Minimal — the words may be significant to the social historian but the music is often puerile. Leisure Arts [i.e. courses given for classes V and VI] — means it was studied in isolation — classes enjoyed it passively, but it was not an important integral part of the short course'. (Both)

27 schools give no answer at all to the third question: of these, all but 5 return a double negative for the first two.

Difficulties, arising either from the present education system or from lack of suitable material or suitable staff.

'I do feel that the teaching of folk is beneficial to pupils, that they enjoy it, but that there is too little printed material available which is suitably laid out and well enough bound to be entirely suited to school use.' (Yes, no)

'The only teacher who might be concerned with this says he did intend to introduce Folk Music to the English Curriculum but found difficulty with material of the right kind for our pupils — this is a 4-year Secondary School.' (Neither)

'Yes — valuable — Difficult to get enough instruction. (This school has links with the local Fiddle and Accordion Club.)' (Yes, no)

'I am a lover of folk music. How can it flourish in schools when all music teachers are classically trained, SCE examinations give NO encouragement to English teachers (I can defend this in detail if you wish) and TV represents only crap or . . . kitsch.' (Yes, no)

'I consider it an essential part of general music appreciation that the children should hear different aspects of Scots folk music . . . and would like more information. . . .' (Ind., yes, no)

'I think it would be valuable if folk music were to be included in Music, English and History teaching. We have a tradition of folk music that is the admiration of the world. . . . Yet no recognition, or very little, is given to the fact that folk music is a distinct category that has its own technique and style. It is also an important part of our national identity which has been deliberately played down for political reasons since the eighteenth century. Our heritage of folk tales is also neglected. Our folk songs are very often valuable social history documents. . . . As oral literature they could play a big part in an aspect of English teaching that is often neglected, in our system that is so dominated by the written examination. Unfortunately, there are not many teachers who could themselves sing or play folk song or music, in their lessons. Even music teachers tend to be too classically trained for this. But there are good recordings . . . and if education authorities were to make use of the excellent traditional singers and musicians who exist in Scotland, either live or on cassettes, there would be plenty of material available for use in class. Training colleges could obtain the services of such artistes (e.g. Stirling University's employment of Jean Redpath) or know-ledgeable people to teach students something of the Scottish folk tradition. The TMSA of Scotland (president, Hamish Henderson) would also help in any way possible.' (Yes, no)

The last quotation above answers some of the difficulties already raised, but underlines others; it confines itself to Scottish material, and this should certainly come first according to a prominent trend in progressive educational theory: "start with the local and more familiar before proceeding to the distant and less familiar". Material is available,[4] but has obviously not been adequately publicised at Training Colleges, in-service courses for teachers, etc. — I shall return to this presently. But more material is needed, both in print and in recorded sound, produced and planned to suit the needs of young people in secondary schools.

The first entry under *Experience of Performing*, etc., pin-points one practical objection to the playing of pop music by young people at school, viz. expensive equipment. Other reservations, or objections, may be raised on this subject; but facts are chiels that winna ding, and there is no possible doubt that pop is the predominant musical influence on a large majority of school teenagers and so, if for no other reason (and there are other reasons), it demands serious attention.[5] The present enquiry is directed solely towards folk music, but folk and pop are related and there is a considerable area of overlap. Roy Carnegie, a teacher of Modern Studies in Glasgow, has produced two booklets of *Songs to Think About*, with each song presented under a Theme heading. He gives the words followed by notes and questions for discussion, and the songs are taken from discs (listed in the index) which cover the overlap area from folk to pop. These booklets are now used by many schools including some primary, and are proving successful and stimulating.

Perhaps the most encouraging development of all in this field was reported by Alex Stirling, Adviser in Modern Studies of Glasgow Division, in Strathclyde Region. He sent a sheet entitled *Folksong in the Classroom*, describing a series of 6 programmes devised by Jim Craig of the Islander Folk Group, which is offered to Glasgow schools. The programmes, each lasting $1\frac{1}{4}$–$1\frac{1}{2}$ hours, are headed: The World of Folk, an introduction; The World of Work; Crime and Punishment; Music of Protest; Love, Courtship and Marriage; and Rich Man, Poor Man. Mr. Stirling reports, "This has proved very popular indeed in schools and colleges". It is of prime importance that students and pupils should have the chance to hear the thing live, as well as recorded on disc or tape.

Over the last decade the BBC have made increasing use of Scottish traditional music in their school broadcasts, chiefly but not exclusively those designed for primary age-groups, in areas including Scottish History and Scottish Literature. Sometimes the music is used to lend atmosphere, as a link between scenes or as introductory or closing material; but sometimes it is treated more as a subject in its own right, and to illustrate and highlight topics in the manner suggested by many of the school questionnaire replies quoted above. Examples are: *Allan Ramsay and the Folk Tradition*; a series of 6 history programmes entitled *Victorian Scotland*; *Three Border Tales*, based on stories which appear in Child ballads, one of which was sung during the programme; *The Music of Scotland*, a series of four dealing with bagpipes, fiddle, clarsach and accordion in turn; and *Folk Sing*, part of the series of *Exploring Scotland*. Teacher's booklets provide excellent notes (though some of the music transcriptions are questionable). These programmes are produced in Scotland. Traditional music from different countries is heard in several London-directed series, including those under such headings as English and Drama, and Understanding a changing World, and some which are for Scotland only. Again the majority of these are for primary children, i.e. up to age 12.

There is no Scottish production of school programmes on music *per se*; all of these are directed from London. There are several sets of nationwide music broadcasts for primary schools, and some of these present traditional songs sung in an authentic style. But for secondary schools there is only one series: the reason given for this is that there are more specialist music teachers in secondary than in primary schools. The secondary series "Music Projects" consists of twenty weekly broadcasts of twenty minutes each, spread over two terms; for 1981–82 these include two on The Beatles, two on Jazz, one on Drums, and nothing on folk (though aspects of folk music may come up in future editions). This series is marked "Not Scotland" — so no music programmes whatsoever are received by Scottish secondary schools.

TERTIARY EDUCATION

Similar questionnaires were sent to Colleges of Education (for the training of teachers), Further Education Colleges (i.e. those marked on the Scottish Education Department's list as including music in the curriculum) and Universities. They were addressed to the Principal, or the Head of the Music Department.

Colleges of Education

Of the ten sent to, 9 replied. 6 include folk music as part of the curriculum and their replies to question (1) are as follows:

1. '(a) A student can opt to study "folk music" as a Personal Study in our 3-year Music Course. (b) Students, especially our "Specialists" are encouraged to include folk music in their curriculum planning' [number of Curriculum Paper given].
2. 'Yes. Mostly songs used as a means of linking musical activities with local industries (e.g. railways, textiles, etc.), traditions, history and geography. The simple form of some folk music lends itself to easy instrumental arrangement for class use — mainly with students following courses in Primary Education. Folk songs from many countries — arranged with guitar accompaniment — form the bulk of primary school song repertoire covered. Appropriate emphasis is given to Scottish songs, but other countries are also featured e.g. as a basis for guitar ensemble work — using pentatonic tunes in the early stages'.
3. '"Bothy Ballads" etc. are used with our music diploma course. An *awareness of the broadest musical scenes is encouraged*'.
4. 'Yes — Secondary Graduate Course'.
5. 'In the Holst/Vaughan Williams "tradition": decidedly, yes! In the sense of modern popular so-called folk songs, no!!!'

6. 'Yes! in all areas, vocal and instrumental.'

The other 3 replies to question (1) show that although folk music occurs in singing and instrumental work, and reference to it is made in courses, it is not present as a "particular topic", "separate unit" or "title".

None of the colleges have folk music clubs now, but more than half had until recently and two considered the drop in student numbers to be responsible for such closures.

With two modified exceptions, all the replies to the third question were affirmative. They are given in the same order as the answers to question (1) above, with "the other 3" coming last:

1. 'Folk music, especially Scots folk music, doesn't enjoy the place it used to have in Primary and Secondary schools. Therefore, it is important for us to hold on to our heritage in whatever ways we can'. [Surprisingly, this was from the rich folk song area of the North East.]

2. 'This is difficult to assess. It must be of benefit if it widens the horizons of students trained hitherto in a fairly narrow academic musical tradition'.

3. 'Widest means of musical expression and tastes should be part of the prospective teacher's background'.

4. 'It is valuable in [question] (1) especially with regard to music of the British Isles'.

5. 'Difficult to evaluate. If students leaving . . . know "Sumer is icumen in" — and they do! — then it has been of value, if they ensure that their pupils will also know it'.

6. 'We deem it to be absolutely essential to include material which reflects the heritage of our own — and other — countries'.

7. 'The study of folk music is beneficial in my opinion'.

8. 'Of value and relevance in Music teaching in schools'.

9. 'Such folk music as we do cover is very valuable to the work we do which concerns, almost entirely, work in primary schools. I would like to see more folk music in the primary school classroom and in out-of-school activities both primary and secondary, but I cannot think it would be helpful to separate this from music in other spheres. It seems to me that folk music, particularly Scottish folk music, should be intermingled with other kinds of music to the benefit of both'.

These answers show an overwhelming majority in favour of adding the "folk" to "music", and they make some important points: (2) '. . . of benefit if it widens the horizons. . . .'; (3) 'Widest means of musical expression. . . .'; and (9) '. . . folk music . . . should be intermingled with other kinds of music. . . .' It would be churlish not to acknowledge the efforts being made by some long-sighted educationists in this sphere. But as with all declarations, what is not said is as important as what is said, and there is one vital omission in these replies. Not one mentions a visiting folk singer, instrumentalist or group, nor is there any mention of whether the members of staff who teach or supervise these studies have ever attended a folk festival or club, have ever heard the music live rather than on disc or tape, or — even more important — have ever made themselves part of the social situations which are the natural ambience (source, revival or both) of this music. It will be said that these points were not raised in the three questions asked, and this is true, but there is a strong likelihood that they would have been raised in the answers had there been any basis for them in fact. *It did not occur* to the college staff who replied: this is what is significant.

Further Education Colleges

These include Colleges of Technology and of Commerce, and — under the heading "Central Institutions" — the Royal Scottish Academy of Music and Drama; this is the only Music Academy in Scotland and it produces many of the specialist music teachers. To start with this institution, whose reply came from a member of the Students' Representative Council:

> For third year students in the Diploma in Musical Education course, there are opportunities for arranging [sic] folk songs but no lectures on it, as such. There is no organised folk club, but I know that many of the students are interested in folk, and traditional music, and some get together to play. I think most of the staff, probably inevitably, are biased towards 'classical' music, and so the students are not encouraged perhaps as much as they could or should be. Music in Scotland really started with folk music (mouth music, ballads etc.) and I think it would be invaluable certainly to prospective music teachers to know more about our musical heritage. . . . If you could write to the College authorities, with a case for introducing Folk Music into the curriculum, . . . you would be pushing a worthwhile cause.

Of the 54 colleges written to, 28 replied and of these 5 have no music course. A mere 6 include folk music in the curriculum — several only minimally — and there are 2 folk clubs There are 17 affirmative replies to question 3, but clearly "syllabus requirements of external bodies", and "the nature of courses offered", are stumbling blocks to action; here are some further extracts from these replies, with answers to questions 1 and 2 in parentheses as before.

'The staff responsible for teaching English in co-operation with the librarian, have tried to collect selections of Scottish traditional songs for use in courses of Scottish Studies which are organised from time to time. Here the emphasis is on the words rather than on the tunes, though frequently recognised collections on record are used as teaching aids. Collections both disc and book forms are freely available to the students and are frequently borrowed.' (Yes, no)

'Folk music has a part in music. Some songs are easier to learn and remember and are more enjoyable than classical to some children. More books should be made available.' (No, yes)

'We have an Elective Course in Scottish Art and History and Scottish folk music is a modest component of this course. I know that this component has always been immensely enjoyed by the students. I feel that it would be nothing but an advantage, both to the academic curriculum and the social life of the college, if more folk music (vocal and instrumental) were to be used. I do not know whether your terms of reference intended to include dance, but I feel that dance, in the traditional sense, should be considered as an integral part of the folk enjoyment of music.' (No answers)

Universities

There are 8 universities in Scotland, 5 of which have Music Departments. 5 answers were received, including 4 from music departments; since the numbers were small I supplemented these replies by phone-calls and other enquiries. Edinburgh Music Department includes a single-term, introductory and voluntary course in ethnomusicology, so the opportunity exists for students to become interested in this subject; a further 3rd year optional course is planned. Stirling has proposals for a course on popular music in the twentieth century; Glasgow and Aberdeen refer to folk music only "as necessary in European history courses" or "as part of studies under other headings"; and at St. Andrews, "Folk music is not included in any part of our curriculum".

Of the 8 universities, 6 have folkclubs, and in 3 cases the Head of the Music Department was ignorant of the club's existence. 2 replies to the third question showed an unqualified affirmative and 2 a more conditional affirmative. The concept of ethnomusicology as a worthwhile study for university students is still in its infancy. Only at the School of Scottish Studies — a department in the Arts Faculty at Edinburgh, whose students need have no music qualifications — is folk music included as an integral part of the undergraduate course, although music questions in examinations are optional. University interdisciplinary attitudes tend to lag behind in music as compared with some other subjects. Post-graduate work is a different matter: the School is one of the main centres in the U.K., and there are links with the Music faculty.

For tertiary education my enquiries on folk music were directed firstly to centres where music is taught, but not all work of this kind goes on in music departments. For example, Stirling and Aberdeen Universities both include post-graduate work in folk life studies.

Courses open to the public are organised by Continuing Education departments and a notable example is Stirling University's, which since 1978 has run a Summer School lasting about 6 weeks. This covers traditional Scots and Gaelic singing, fiddle, accordion, clarsach, Highland piping, country dancing, and Scottish history and literature. Tutors include such distinguished exponents as Tom Anderson, Jean Redpath, Anne Lorne Gillies and piper Hugh MacCallum. Jean Redpath was singer-in-residence at Stirling University in the spring of 1980, and she undertook a series of informal talks and performances at Central Region schools which started at that time: these were jointly organised by the University's Department of Continuing Education and the Region's Education Department. A cassette tape of songs used in these visits to schools is available.[6] Jean Redpath is also honorary lecturer in Stirling Unversity's Department of English Studies, and sings in the first-ever recording of Burns's songs in their original unaccompanied form.[7]

It is clear from the foregoing pages, and especially from the numerous comments of teachers in secondary schools, that much interest and goodwill is felt towards the idea that children and young people in school should have the chance to hear, sing and play traditional music. But one gets the impression that there is also a good deal of ignorance among teachers as to *how* this music and song is to be presented, and that while some are aware of their ignorance others are not. This is not to suggest that there are no teachers who are knowledgeable on the subject, only that they are probably few in number. This is confirmed by the gap, already mentioned, in the replies from Colleges of Education. Similar gaps in replies from schools — and even from Further Education Colleges and universities — are rather less serious, for a simple reason. One would expect a closer study and a more faithful, realistic presentation in a teacher's training course, of any subject which that teacher is going to present to school pupils, otherwise how can he or she teach that subject with any pretensions to adequacy? *Quis custodiet ipsos custodes?*

This complaint looks to the future. Present teachers cannot go back to their training college days, but they can attend in-service courses; more of these could be arranged on this subject and these should involve the presence of in-the-flesh traditional singers and players. Interested teachers would also be well advised to make some acquaintance of the folk scene, preferably starting with a TMSA festival.

It has been suggested that traditional music has always had what might be called an underground or rebel element in it — an inherent part of material which was transmitted orally for hundreds of years — and that for this reason something in it would wither and die if it were presented in the relatively establishment and authoritarian atmosphere of school. (This refers mainly, but not entirely, to songs and especially their verbal content.) This might have been true of pre-war schools; but the empire-building approach has surely been dropped almost completely by today's teachers. A more valid objection, at least as regards the music class, is that some of the old lesson structures will have to go. Again this is in part backward looking, to the days when school music was synonymous with "class-singing", i.e. some thirty to forty children (sometimes many more) all singing together with piano accompaniment. But it is true that a fruitful approach to folk music will demand further changes of attitude in school music teachers.

"Traditional music, instrumental and vocal, is a system of music in its own right. It has its own rules, and by these it must be judged".[8] How far is this true? The writer here is of course talking about the music of Ireland, not of Africa or the Far East, and some of the criteria which we apply to our own art music may also be applied to our folk music. But there are important differences, the first and probably the most striking of which is the style of singing, and the vocal quality.

If you want to sing art-song, lieder or opera professionally then you must have your voice trained. This includes the whole process of re-forming diction, vowel sounds must be re-shaped to get rid of any hint of dialect, and graded voice and breathing exercises develop the voice into an instrument suited for this kind of singing. It's a lengthy process, but worth it for the end desired. If however you want to sing folk song, at any level of "proficiency", then this voice-training will not only be a waste of time but will leave you at a positive disadvantage (though some breathing lessons are helpful for any kind of singing). The trained singer who falls under the spell of traditional song will have to unlearn much of his or her acquired disciplines before being able to carry any kind of conviction in the singing of it, and it's doubtful if this reverse process can ever be fully carried through. (It is easier for the singer of traditional songs who wishes to train for art-song . . . he or she will have to change only relatively natural singing habits, not an artificially acquired style.) I'm talking of fully trained singers, those who have undergone a long and intensive training: for those who have had a few lessons, or even a year or so's training, the process is easier. But again this reversing process cannot be easily re-reversed: it's almost impossible for a singer to switch at will from folk song to lieder or vice versa. As with so many artistic matters, we are now in a highly subjective area, and no-one can reach a satisfactory decision without becoming *familiar* — not just listening to a few examples — with both styles of singing.

But I would hate the above strictures to put anyone off: if you want to sing folk, sing it . . . the folk ambience, the folk magic will surround you and influence you, and if you have love it will carry you through.

Teachers of music will come up against snags in the present examination system. Although bagpipes (coming into the "tradition-al art-music" category rather than that of "folk music") are now accepted as an instrument for these examinations, singing candidates are still expected to sing in a "formal" or "trained" way. Examiners want a demonstration of what is regarded as "musicianship", and because of their own restricted (in this respect) training it is easier for them to estimate the singing of a Schubert song than a folk song. In time, a broader approach will develop; again, *quis custodiet.* . . .

Fortunately, in the present context, not all school music teachers have had their voices trained . . . but what of those who have? How can they encourage folk song in school? If traditional music were properly presented during their training, in particular at the one music conservatoire in Scotland, then this question would be answered. But in the present status quo the following suggestions and comments may help:

(1) Invite folk singers and players to come and perform to the pupils and talk to them — funds are available and need not go exclusively towards the provision of orchestral instruments and other items now considered acceptable, valuable though these are. (Edinburgh Folk Festival has played a pioneering role here, from its beginnings in 1979: in 1981 visits to schools by no fewer than seven folk-artists took place throughout the week. Their songs, story-telling and informal talk about both have met with a lively response from the children. Visits have been mostly to primary schools. Dr. John Barrow, the Director, reports that secondary schools are "harder to get into", with curricular pressure and looming examina-tions especially in 4th and 5th years. He thinks however that there is more interest here than in England).

(2) Play discs and tapes of good singers, players and groups in this genre, with study and discussion. It need hardly be said that, as always, response will be in proportion to the teacher's own involve-ment in the subject.

(3) Cooperate with other departments in inter-disciplinary pro-jects, as suggested in many of the quotations from questionnaires.

(4) Let the girls and boys sing and play themselves — initial shyness can be overcome, especially if they start in groups — and you may be surprised at what you can learn from them, especially in local songs and tunes learned from their families and friends, and with a little encouragement they might even start collecting. Solo,

unaccompanied singing will probably arise in due course: this is the most "immediate", and in many ways the most idiosyncratic, form of traditional singing, and again it sounds better with untrained voices. Although I would be the last to undervalue music literacy,[9] the fact is that most singers in this field, and many players, learn the music aurally, from listening to other performers live or recorded. It's possible that some children might gain more from learning songs which they find moving, than from learning to read music. Learning this way also makes the ear more sensitive, and is good for musical memory. Many folk instruments, the fiddle excepted (and the violin is widely taught in schools now), are cheap and moreover do not demand long years of practice to attain a reasonable standard.

(5) There will be times when some of the pupils (the word "children" hardly seems suitable for those who have crossed the Rubicon of puberty) may not feel like singing or playing. Then let them listen. Listeners are an important ingredient, almost a *sine qua non* in all music-making situations, and young teenagers are prey to conflicting moods — more so than any other age-group either in school or outside.

(6) The elitist attitude so prevalent in music teaching (and specialist schools are appearing which cater for aspiring art-performers) can be combated through folk music: the idea that some pupils are musical and the rest are mere also-rans. Far too many leave school with the idea that they "can't sing", for example, and this persists as a life-long conviction. We all know adults who say they "can't sing" yet are to be heard carolling joyously in the bath, or around the house, when they think no-one is listening and when they don't feel they are "performing". We might even entertain the idea that singing is a basic human activity, like speaking. Besides, there is a certain affecting charm about singing which comes from an untrained voice, and this applies not only to folk song. Have you never enjoyed the singing of Frank Muir and Dennis Norden as much as, or occasionally even more than, that of professionals Ian Wallace and John Amis?[10] (Seriously.) And pupils who appear intrinsically musical may simply have been conditioned by their home backgrounds, where art-music is a familiar sound to which they have been accustomed to listen.

(7) Recent songs, by Matt MacGinn, Sandra Kerr, Eric Bogle, Sheila Douglas, Adam MacNaughton, Malvina Reynolds, Leon Rosselson and others, will complement more traditional songs: they will feed mind and spirit of young people, who need to hear the voice of their contemporaries as well as of their ancestors.

Little has been said about primary schools, but the importance of introducing folk music at an early age should be stressed again.

Fortunate children already know a stock of singing-games,[11] street songs, bairn-sangs, etc., and all children will enjoy and benefit from learning other folk material not in common circulation at present.

Most of the above suggestions are addressed to teachers of music, partly because this is my own subject, but partly too because music teachers have the greatest need. Their professional training has almost wholly neglected this kind of music, in fact all demotic music. And they bear an awesome responsibility. Music is a basic need in human beings, and it arouses in teenagers a nerve-tingling intensity of response which they may never again experience in future adult life.

The most recent report on *Music in Scottish Schools* has this to say, in the section "Music for Older Pupils":[12] "Although recent surveys have indicted music at this stage as the most boring school subject, the same surveys point to music as a highly popular out-of-school interest. Is there no point of contact?" And this, on "Education and Training of the Music Teacher": "The young teacher may come to his first school able to instruct pupils in the language and techniques of the present SCE examinations in music, but ill-equipped to deal with the majority of pupils who are only mildly interested in music of this kind and who will never take these examinations. *He is unlikely to have been introduced to music of the popular genre or to have been encouraged to play it, and he may have little interest in it* (my italics). . . . We recommend that a new scheme of training and assessment be devised which will give prospective music teachers much wider horizons and expose them to literary, aesthetic and educational studies which have relevance for music."

Amen to that.

Footnotes to Appendix II

1. Quoted by Sydney Carter in *Dance in the Dark*, p. 96.
2. Alison McMorland has specialised in this area. Her own collection of songs, games and rhymes for children, *The Funny Family*, contains some Scottish traditional material. A disc of the same title is issued by Transatlantic.
3. Recommended for introductory reading: *Folk Music in School*, ed. Robert Leach and Roy Palmer, covers primary as well as secondary school work. There are 12 contributions, mostly from teachers, on practical and theoretical aspects; it includes a chapter on "Resources" and one on "Singing style and accompaniment". See note 4 for Scottish material.
4. BOOKS: *101 Scottish Songs*, selected by Norman Buchan. (This small leatherette-bound volume is well suited for classroom use; at the time of writing it has been out of print for some years and is long overdue for reprinting.) *The Scottish Folksinger*, collected and edited by Norman Buchan and Peter Hall, (modern and traditional folksongs.) *Sing a Song of Scotland*, collected and edited by

Sheila Douglas (designed for upper primary and lower secondary school). DISCS AND CASSETTES: *Scottish Tradition* series (Tangent). See also p. 331.

5. *Pop Music in School*, ed. Graham Vulliamy and Ed Lee, supplies this careful attention. It is an apologia for school music to flourish now "as a many-headed plant", with pop as a strong off-shoot, and describes the experience of certain English schools which have incorporated it. There is a useful bibliography; an accompanying tape is also available.

6. *Young Folk with Jean Redpath*, issued by the Department of Continuing Education, Stirling University.

7. Cassette tape, from Scottish Records, Brig o' Turk, Callander: the culmination of research by the Robert Burns project, English Studies department. With notes by Dr. Donald Low. See also Chapter 4, p. 108.

8. Brendan Breathnach, *Folk Music and Dances of Ireland*, p. 92, quoted by Sandra Kerr in *Folk Music in School*, ed. Robert Leach and Roy Palmer, p. 137.

9. Zoltan Kodaly, the Hungarian composer and folk music collector, was an enthusiastic advocate for the teaching of music literacy to the young: he devised extensive series of graded vocal examples for sight-reading, based on Hungarian folk tunes.

10. On *My Music*, BBC, both TV and radio; chaired by Steve Race.

11. See Iona and Peter Opie, *The Lore and Language of Schoolchildren.*

12. *Music in Scottish Schools*, issued by the Scottish Education Department (1978), pp. 21 and 29.

Recordings

Record companies which produce folk music recordings are now in an increasing state of flux, with mergings, take-overs and deletions. Record shops can provide lists and will order records with the labels which they stock. Full lists of available discs and cassettes can be obtained from folk specialists, e.g. Peter Hamilton, 3 West Bank Quadrant, Glasgow, G12 8NT, and Ian D. Green, 3 Morven Street, Edinburgh 4. These firms, and some record shops, also have stocks of deleted records. Deleted recordings can sometimes be obtained from record lending libraries, and by advertising in *The Gramophone* or in regional Folk magazines.

The National Sound Archive, at the British Institute of Recorded Sound, 29 Exhibition Road, London SW7, has a public play-back service. This institution possesses a very wide international range of folk and other recordings, including many which are deleted and which are not available in shops or libraries.

Instalments of *A Select Discography of Scots Folk Song*, by Hamish Henderson, are published in *Tocher*, issues 25, 27, 28, 30, 32 and 35; copies may be obtained from the School of Scottish Studies, Edinburgh University, 27 George Square, Edinburgh, EH8 9LD. At the time of writing this series is continuing, with detailed comment on recordings from the early fifties on. A discography which includes instrumental music as well as folk song is contained in *The Observer's Book of Folk Song in Britain*, by Fred Woods.

Glossary

GENERAL NOTES

a', ca', ba'	all, call, ball
alang, amang	along, among
aroon', oot	around, out
aucht, socht	aught, sought
beggit, askit	begged, asked
doot, doon	doubt, down
guid, cuid	good, could
ither, brither	other, brother
mairry, faim'ly	marry, family

---

ablow	below, under
abuin (abin), abune	above
ae	one, or only
aff	off
afore	before
ahint	behind
ain	own
aince	once
alane	alone
ane	one
aneath	beneath, under
annoled (annealed?)	Duncan Williamson:– "As if it were moulded from the exact thing."
atween	between
aul', auld	old
ava	at all
awa'	away
awfa, awfu'	awful
baith	both
bauld	bold, courageous
barfit	barefoot
ben	inside, further in
bide	to stay, dwell
bield	shelter, protection
birks	birch trees
bivvies	(from bivouac) tents
bla'	meal, e.g. oats
bleezin'	blazing
brae	hill, hillside
brak	break
brand	a burning peat or glowing cinder; or, a sword.

braw	fine, splendid
braxy ham	the salted meat of a sheep that died from the disease "braxy"; or simply, very salt ham (quoted from *Chapbook* 3, (4))
breist	breast
brunt	burnt
bunnet	bonnet
callants	lads
canker	to fret, become peevish or ill-humoured
caul', cauld	cold
Ceòl-Beag [Gaelic]	the small music ⎤
Ceòl-Meanach [Gaelic]	the middle music ⎬ bagpipe music terms
Ceòl-Mór [Gaelic]	the great music ⎦
chaumer	chamber
chiel	a lad, a man
clipe, clype	to tell tales
coniach ⎤	used to describe the feeling expressed in a
conniach ⎦	performance, vocal or instrumental: an indefinable something which moves the listeners.
coorie	to stoop, bend, crouch
coort	court
couldna	couldn't
country hantle	see hantle
cowk	to retch or vomit
crawin'	crowing, exulting
cried	called
crouse	conceited, arrogant, proud
dae	do
dang	to knock, strike, push suddenly
daur	to dare
deid	dead
dene	done
dinna(e)	don't
divvies	(from divot) pieces of turf
doss	to throw (oneself) down, sit down heavily; to stay, sleep, for the night
dowie	sad, melancholy, dismal
duin (din), dune	done
dule	grief, misery, suffering
dwine	to pine, waste away
dyke	low wall or hedge
een	eyes
eence	once

fae	from
faur'd	favoured, (good or bad)-looking
fause	false
feart	feared, afraid
fee	wages; engagement; to hire as a servant
fit	foot
flatties [*cant*]	non-travellers
fly	knowing, shrewd
forbye	besides, in addition
foumart	usually ferret, weasel. (Stanley Robertson: "The travellers always understood it to mean a wolf".)
fower	four
frae	from
freends	friends
gae, gang	to go
gaen, gane; gaun	gone; going
gager	probably guager, i.e. customs official
gair	gore
gallus	devil-may-care, reckless
gear	possessions in general (including money)
gey	considerable, or very
gie	to give
gin	if
gled	glad
Glesgie, Glesca	Glasgow
goon	gown
gowd	gold
greet	to cry, weep. Past tense: grat
guid, gweed	good
gyang	see gang, gae
hadna(e)	hadn't
hae	to have
hairt	heart
hale	whole
hame	home
hanker	to loiter, linger, hang about expectantly
hantle [*cant*]	people. *Country hantle*: polite or friendly expression for non-travellers
haud	to hold
haud awa'	to keep away, keep out or off
hecht	promised, engaged
heelster-goudie	head over heels
heid; heid-the-ba'	head; a football expression
herry	to harry
hert	see hairt

heuch (heuk)	reaping hook, sickle
hidna	see hadna
hie	to hasten, proceed quickly
hing	to hang
hirple	to hobble, walk as with a limp
hoast	to cough
howk	to dig, delve the soil
hum	to chew, or to eat greedily
ilka	each, every
jalouse	to suspect
jijimant (jidgimant)	judgement
jink	to frolic, dance, or flirt
juist	just
jouk, juke	to dart about; or to evade by trickery
keel	red ochre, used especially for marking sheep
ken, kent	to know, knew
kittle	to whet, sharpen
lane	lone, alone
lee	lie
lift	the air, sky
loanin's	lanes, byways
lo'e	to love
lowe	to flame or blaze
lowp	to leap
lyke-wake	vigil over a corpse until burial
ma	my
mair	more
makar	a poet, a writer of verse
maun	must
Maw	Ma, mother
minnie	mother (diminutive)
mischanter	mischance
mither	mother
mony	many
mou	mouth
muckle	much, great, big
muin	moon
mun	see maun
nae	no
nane	none
nickum	scamp, rogue, mischievous boy

noo	now
nor	than
ony	any
outwith	outside of
ower, owre	over
oxter	arm-pit
pairt	part
pleisure	pleasure
ploo	plough
polis	police
puckle, pickle	a little, a few
puir	poor
redd	to free, rid
reive, rieve	to plunder, rob
rickle	a loose heap
rin	to run
rive	to tear asunder, rend
roch	rough
rowe	to impel forward, or push
saft	soft
sair	sore
samen	same
sark	shirt
saut	salt
scaldies [cant]	derogatory term for non-travellers
scoor (*scour*)	to rush, run about, search hither and thither
shouther	shoulder
sic	such
siller (*silver*)	money
simmer	summer
snaw	snow
sodger	soldier
speir	to ask, enquire
spoliat, or *spulyeit*	despoiled, stolen
sprog	a crop, usually rye or barley (Stanley Robertson)
spuin	spoon
stovies	a dish made with potatoes
stowp	drinking vessel
strecht	straight
streitch	to stretch
strucken	past tense of to strike; used to mean exact
swack	pliant, nimble
syne	since, or thereupon

tae	to
tattie	potato
tent	to tempt
thae	those
thon	that
thraw	to throw, or twist
til	to
tint, from tinte	injury, harm, damage
toom	empty
twa	two
twine	to separate, part, deprive
unco	unusual, strange; or remarkable, great
wad	would; or to wed
wadna(e)	wouldna, wouldn't
wame	belly
wan'	wand
warstle	to wrestle
wasna(e), wisna(e)	wasn't
wean	child
weel	well
weemen	women
weet	wet
westle	wrestle
wha	who
whaur	where
white heather	refers to TV series of the sixties — Scottish dancing and song — very smooth, respectable, middle-class, well dressed, etc.
wi'	with
wid	would
windae	window
winna	willna, won't
wis	was
wint	want
wuid	wood
wumman	woman
wyte	to know
wyn', wynd	a lane, narrow street
yin	one
yince	once
yowes	ewes

Bibliography

Ahlstrom, Sydney E., *A Religious History of the American People*. Yale University Press, New Haven, 1972.

Aitken, A.J., and McArthur, Tom, *The Languages of Scotland*. Chambers, Edinburgh, 1979.

Allsop, Kenneth, *Hard Travellin'*, *The Hobo and His History*. Penguin, Harmondsworth, 1972. First published 1967.

Baggelaar, Kristin and Milton, Donald, *The Folk Music Encyclopaedia*. Omnibus Press, London 1977. First published 1976.

Bassin, Ethel, *The Old Songs of Skye: Frances Tolmie and her Circle*. Routledge and Kegan Paul, London and Henley, 1977.

Benedict, Ruth, *Patterns of Culture*. Routledge and Kegan Paul, London, 1935.

Blacking, John, *Black Background*. Abelard-Schuman, New York and London, 1964.

———— *How Musical is Man?* Faber and Faber, London 1976. First published 1973.

Brand, Jack, *The National Movement in Scotland*. Routledge and Kegan Paul, London, 1978.

Brand, Oscar, *The Ballad Mongers*. Minerva Press, Toronto, 1967. First published 1962.

Breathnach, Brendan, *Folk Music and Dances of Ireland*. Talbot Press, Dublin, 1971.

Briggs, Katherine M., *A Dictionary of British Folk-tales*, Part A. 2 vols. Routledge and Kegan Paul, London, 1970.

Bronson, Bertrand H., *The Traditional Tunes of the Child Ballads*. 4 vols. Princeton University Press, Princeton, N. J., 1959–72.

Brown, Gordon, *The Red Paper on Scotland*. Edinburgh University Students' Publication Board, Edinburgh, 1975.

Buchan, David, *The Ballad and the Folk*. Routledge and Kegan Paul, London, 1972.

Buchan, Norman, *101 Scottish Songs*. Collins, Glasgow, 1962.

———— and Hall, Peter, *The Scottish Folksinger*. New edition. Collins, Glasgow and London, 1978. First published 1973.

Campbell, Duncan, *Reminiscences and Reflections of an Octogenarian Highlander*. Published by subscription, Inverness, 1910.

Campbell, Ian, *Kailyard: A New Assessment*. Ramsay Head Press, Edinburgh, 1981.

———— *Nineteenth Century Scottish Fiction*. Carcanet Press, Manchester, 1979.

Campbell, John Lorne and Collinson, Francis, *Hebridean Folksongs*. 3 vols. Clarendon Press, Oxford, 1969–81.

Carter, Sydney, *Dance in the Dark*. Fount Paperbacks, London, 1980.

Chambers, Robert, *The Scottish Ballads*. William Tait, Edinburgh, 1829.

Child, Francis James, *The English and Scottish Popular Ballads*. 5 vols. Dover Publications, New York, 1965. First published 1882–98.

Collins, Mal and others, *Big Red Songbook*. Pluto Press, London, 1977.

Collinson, Francis, *The Traditional and National Music of Scotland*. Routledge and Kegan Paul, London, 1966.

Cowan, Edward J., *The People's Past*. Edinburgh University Students' Publication Board, Edinburgh, 1980.

Craig, David, *Scottish Literature and the Scottish People*. Chatto and Windus, London, 1961.

Crawford, Thomas, *Burns: A Study of the Poems and Songs*. Oliver and Boyd, Edinburgh and London, 1960.

Daiches, David, *A Companion to Scottish Culture*. Edward Arnold, London, 1981.

Dallas, Karl, *The Cruel Wars*. Wolfe Publishing, London, 1972.

Davie, Cedric Thorpe, *Scotland's Music*. Blackwood, Edinburgh, 1980.

Denisoff, R. Serge and Peterson, Richard A., *The Sounds of Social Change*. Rand McNally, Chicago, 1972.

Ding Dong Dollar: Anti-Polaris Songs. Several editions. Glasgow Song Guild, Glasgow, 1961–2.

Donaldson, Gordon, *Scotland: The Shaping of a Nation*. David and Charles, Newton Abbott, 1974.

———— and Morpeth, Robert S., *A Dictionary of Scottish History*. John Donald, Edinburgh, 1977.

Douglas, Sheila, *Sing a Song of Scotland*. Thomas Nelson, Surrey, 1982.

Dubofsky, Melvyn, *We shall be all; a history of the Industrial Workers of the World*. Quadrangle Books, Chicago, 1969.

Dunson, Josh, *Freedom in the air*. International Publishers, New York, 1965.

Elliott, Kenneth and Rimmer, Frederick, *A History of Scottish Music*. BBC, London, 1973.

Emmerson, George S., *Rantin' Pipe and Tremblin' String*. Dent, London, 1971.

Farmer, Henry George, *A History of Music in Scotland*. Hinrichsen, London, 1947.

Finnegan, Ruth, *Oral Poetry*. Cambridge University Press, Cambridge, 1979. First published 1977.

———— *The Penguin Book of Oral Poetry*. Allen Lane, London, 1978.

Foner, Philip S., *The Case of Joe Hill*. Central Books, London, 1966. First edition, International Publishers, New York, 1965.

———— *History of the Labor Movement in the United States*, Vol. 4 *The Industrial Workers of the World, 1905–1917*. International Publishers, New York, 1965.

Ford, Robert, *Vagabond songs and ballads of Scotland*. Alexander Gardner, Paisley, 1904.

Gentleman, Hugh and Swift, Susan, *Scotland's Travelling People: Problems and Solutions*. H.M.S.O., Edinburgh, 1971.

Gramsci, Antonio, *Opere*. Vol. 6 *Letteratura e Vita Nazionale*. Einaudi, Turin, 1950.

Greenway, John, *American Folksongs of Protest*. University of Pennsylvania Press, Philadelphia, 1953.

Greig, Gavin, *Folk-Song of the North-East*. 2 vols. Peterhead, 1909–14. Reprinted in 1 vol. by Folklore Associates, Hatboro, Pennsylvania, 1963.

Grove. *The New Grove Dictionary of Music and Musicians*. Macmillan, London, 1980.

Guthrie, Woody, *Bound for Glory*. Pan Books, Picador edition, London, 1974. First published 1943.

Hardie, Alastair J., *The Caledonian Companion*. EMI Music Publishing, London, 1981.

Harker, Dave, *One for the Money: Politics and popular song*. Hutchinson, London, 1980.

Henderson, Hamish, *Ballads of World War II*. The Lili Marleen Club, Glasgow, [1947].

Henderson, Kathy and others, *My Song Is My Own, 100 Women's Songs*. Pluto Press, London, 1979.

Herd, David, *Ancient and Modern Scots Songs*. 2 vols. Edinburgh, 1776.

Hunter, Eveline, *Scottish Woman's Place*. Edinburgh University Students' Publication Board, Edinburgh, 1978.

Johnson, David, *Music and Society in Lowland Scotland in the Eighteenth Century*. Oxford University Press, London, 1972.

Karpeles, Maud, *Cecil Sharp: his life and work*. Routledge and Kegan Paul, London, 1967.

Kay, Billy, *Odyssey: Voices from Scotland's Recent Past*. Polygon, Edinburgh, 1980.

Keith, Alexander, *Last Leaves of the Traditional Ballads and Ballad Airs*. The Buchan Club, Aberdeen, 1925.

Kennedy-Fraser, Marjory and MacLeod, Kenneth, *Songs of the Hebrides*. 3 vols. Boosey, London, 1909–21.

Kinsley, James, *Burns: Poems and Songs*. One volume edition. Oxford University Press, London, 1971.

Kornbluh, Joyce L., *Rebel Voices: An I.W.W. Anthology*. University of Michigan Press, Ann Arbor, 1964.

Laing, Dave and others, *The Electric Muse: The Story of Folk into Rock*. Methuen paperback, London, 1975.

Lampell, Millard, *California to the New York Island*. Guthrie Children's Trust Fund, New York, [1960].

Laslett, Peter, *The World we have lost*. Methuen, London, 1971. First published 1965.

Law, T. S. and Berwick, Thurso, *Homage to John MacLean*. The John MacLean Society, Edinburgh, 1973.

Leach, Robert and Palmer, Roy, *Folk Music in School*. Cambridge University Press, Cambridge, 1978.

Legman, Gershon, *The Horn Book*, University Books, New York, 1966. First published 1964.

Lloyd, A. L., *Folk Song in England*. Panther Books, London, 1969. First published 1967.

Lomax, Alan, *The Folk Songs of North America*. Cassell, London, 1960.

Lyle, E. B., *Andrew Crawfurd's Collection of Ballads and Songs*, Vol. 1. Scottish Text Society, Edinburgh, 1975.

MacColl, Ewan, *Folk Songs and Ballads of Scotland*. Oak Publications, New York, 1965.

——— *Personal Choice*. Workers' Music Association, London, n.d.

——— *Scotland Sings*. Scottish Branch of the Workers' Music Association, 1953.

——— and Seeger, Peggy, *Travellers' Songs from England and Scotland*. Routledge and Kegan Paul, London, 1977.

MacDiarmid, Hugh, *Contemporary Scottish Studies*. Scottish Educational Journal, Edinburgh, 1976.

MacDougall, Ian, *Essays in Scottish Labour History*. John Donald, Edinburgh, 1978.

McGinn, Matt, *Once Again*. Plough Press, London, 1970.

——— *Scottish Songs of Today*. Harmony Music, London, 1964.

McLean, Jim, *25 Scottish Rebel Songs*. Socialist Review Publishing, London, 1968.

McMorland, Alison, *The Funny Family*. Ward Lock, London, 1975.

Maver, Robert, *A Collection of Genuine Scottish Melodies*. Maver, Glasgow, [c. 1866].

Merriam, Alan P., *The Anthropology of Music*. Northwestern University Press, [Evanston, Illinois], 1964.

Moffat, Alistair, *The Edinburgh Fringe*. Johnston and Bacon, London, 1976.

Morrison, George, *One Man's Lewis*. Stornoway Gazette, Stornoway, n.d.

Music in Scottish Schools. H.M.S.O., London, 1978.

New Edinburgh Review, Festival issue: *Folk song and the folk tradition*. August 1973.

Newton, Francis, *The Jazz Scene*. Penguin, Harmondsworth, 1961. First published 1959.

Opie, Iona and Opie, Peter, *The Lore and Language of Schoolchildren*. Oxford University Press, London, 1959.

Ord, John, *Bothy Songs and Ballads*. John Donald, Edinburgh, [1973?]. First published 1930.

Orwell, George, *Decline of the English Murder and other essays*. Penguin, Harmondsworth, 1968.

Partridge, Eric, *Dictionary of the Underworld*. Routledge and Kegan Paul, London, 1949.

Patriot Songs for Camp & Ceilidh. Bo'ness Rebels Literary Society, Bo'ness, West Lothian, n.d.

Pocket Song Book. Second edition. Workers' Music Association, London, 1949. First edition, 1948.

Previn, André and Hopkins, Antony, *Music Face to Face*. Hamish Hamilton, London, 1971.

Rebels Ceilidh Song Book, The, [no. 1] and no. 2. Bo'ness Rebels Literary Society, Bo'ness, West Lothian, [1951], 1965. Another edition, *Rebel Ceilidh Song Book '67*. Glasgow Song Guild, Glasgow, 1967.

Reeves, James, *The Everlasting Circle*. Heinemann, London, 1960.

——— *The Idiom of the People*. Heinemann, London, 1958.

Rehfisch, Farnham, *Gypsies, Tinkers and other Travellers*, Academic Press. London, 1975.

Sangs o' the Stane. Scottish National Secretariat, Glasgow [c. 1951].

Scotland's Travelling People, 1971–1974, and 1975–1978. Two reports by The Secretary of State's Advisory Committee. H.M.S.O., Edinburgh, 1974, 1978.

Seeger, Peggy and MacColl, Ewan, *The Singing Island: A collection of English and Scots Folksongs*. Belwin-Mills Music, London, 1960.

———— *Songs for the Sixties*. Workers' Music Association, London, 1961.

Seeger, Pete, *Woody Guthrie Folk Songs*. Ludlow Music, New York, 1958.

Sharp, Cecil J., *English Folk Song: Some Conclusions*. Third edition. Methuen, London, 1954. First published 1907.

Shaw, Margaret Fay, *Folksongs and Folklore of South Uist*. Routledge and Kegan Paul, London, 1955.

Shuldham-Shaw, Patrick and Lyle, Emily B., *The Greig-Duncan Folk Song Collection*, Vol. 1. Aberdeen University Press, Aberdeen, 1981.

Siniveer, Kaarel, *Folk Lexicon*, (in German). Rowohlt, Hamburg, 1981.

Songs of the workers to fan the flames of discontent. 34th editon. Industrial Workers of the World, Oldham, 1973. First published 1909.

Stavis, Barry, *The Man Who Never Died*. Dramatists Play Service, New York, 1954.

———— and Harmon, Frank, *The Songs of Joe Hill*. Oak Publications, New York, 1960.

Stearns, Marshall W., *The Story of Jazz*. Oxford University Press, London, 1977. First published 1956.

Stevenson, Ronald, *Western Music: an introduction*. Kahn and Averill, London, 1971.

Szabolcsi, Bence, *A History of Melody*. Corvina Press, Budapest, and Barrie and Rockliff, London, 1965.

Thompson, Fred and Murfin, Patrick, *The I.W.W.: Its First Fifty Years*. Industrial Workers of the World, Chicago, 1955.

Vansina, Jan, *Oral Tradition*. Penguin, Harmondsworth, 1973. First published in English 1965.

Vulliamy, Graham and Lee, Ed, *Pop Music in School*. New edition. Cambridge University Press, Cambridge, 1980. First published 1976.

Waters, Edgar and Murray-Smith, S., *Rebel Songs*. Australian Student Labor Federation, n.p., 1947.

Watson, William J., *Bardachd Ghaidhlig: Gaelic Poetry 1550–1900*. Third edition. An Comunn Gaidhealach, Inverness, 1959.

Whitman, Walt, *Complete Prose Works*. Appleton, New York, 1909.

Whyte, Betsy, *The Yellow on the Broom, the early days of a traveller woman*. Chambers, Edinburgh, 1979.

Woods, Fred, *Folk Revival: the rediscovery of a national music*. Blandford Press, Poole, Dorset, 1979.

———— *The Observer's Book of Folk Song in Britain*. Frederick Warne, London, 1980.

Woolf, Virginia, *A Room of One's Own*. Penguin, Harmondsworth, 1945. First published 1929.

Song Index

General Index